Postwar Stories

Postwar Stories

How Books Made Judaism American

RACHEL GORDAN

OXFORD
UNIVERSITY PRESS

Oxford University Press is a department of the University of Oxford.
It furthers the University's objective of excellence in research, scholarship,
and education by publishing worldwide. Oxford is a registered trade mark of
Oxford University Press in the UK and in certain other countries.

Published in the United States of America by Oxford University Press
198 Madison Avenue, New York, NY 10016, United States of America.

© Oxford University Press 2024

All rights reserved. No part of this publication may be reproduced, stored in a retrieval system, or transmitted, in any form or by any means, without the prior permission in writing of Oxford University Press, or as expressly permitted by law, by license or under terms agreed with the appropriate reprographics rights organization. Inquiries concerning reproduction outside the scope of the above should be sent to the Rights Department, Oxford University Press, at the address above.

You must not circulate this work in any other form and you must
impose this same condition on any acquirer

Library of Congress Cataloging-in-Publication Data
Names: Gordan, Rachel, author.
Title: Postwar stories : how books made Judaism American / Rachel Gordan.
Description: [New York] : Oxford University Press, [2024] |
Includes bibliographical references and index.
Identifiers: LCCN 2023051106 (print) | LCCN 2023051107 (ebook) |
ISBN 9780197694336 (paperback) | ISBN 9780197694329 (hardback) |
ISBN 9780197694343 (epub)
Subjects: LCSH: Antisemitism—United States—History—20th century. |
Antisemitism in literature. | Jews in literature. |
American literature—Jewish authors—History and criticism. |
Judaism—United States—History—20th century. | Jews—United States—Identity.
Classification: LCC DS146.U6 G67 2024 (print) | LCC DS146.U6 (ebook) |
DDC 808.8/03529924—dc23/eng/20231129
LC record available at https://lccn.loc.gov/2023051106
LC ebook record available at https://lccn.loc.gov/2023051107

DOI: 10.1093/9780197694367.001.0001

For my brothers,
Michael and Israel
And our parents,
Miriam and Dennis Gordan

Contents

Acknowledgments ix

Introduction: Popularizing Judaism 1

1 From Race to Religion and the Challenge of Antisemitism 26

2 The Roots of 1940s Anti-Antisemitism Fiction 48

3 When Women Made Anti-Antisemitism Fiction Popular 59

4 The Limits of Anti-Antisemitism Literature 81

5 How Basic Is *Basic Judaism*? 106

6 Philip Bernstein and the 1950s Religious Revival 129

7 *Life*'s "Old-Fashioned Jews" 147

8 "Why I Choose to Be a Jew" 176

Conclusion: After the Middlebrow Moment 198

Notes 205
References 259
Index 279

Acknowledgments

This book began as a dissertation in the Committee on the Study of Religion at Harvard. I am forever grateful to my advisors, Robert Orsi and Leigh Schmidt, and to my dissertation committee members, Jonathan Sarna, Ann Braude, and Ruth Wisse, who helped me think about Jews, religion, and literature—and figure out what exactly I had to say about these subjects. It made such a difference that they believed in me. I would also like to thank my teachers, mentors, and peers at Harvard: Eliza Barstow, Brandon Bayne, Wallace Best, Lauren Brandt, Heather Curtis, Curtis Evans, Linford Fisher, Marla Frederick, Sara Georgini, Rachel Greenblatt, Marie Griffith, David Hall, Liora Halperin, David Hempton, Michael D. Jackson, Hilary Kaell, Jon Levenson, Kevin Madigan, Noam Maggor, Max Mueller, Taylor Petrey, Kip Richardson, Jon Roberts, John Seitz, Sasha Senderovich, Katherine Shaner, John Stauffer, Adrian Weimer, Clinton Williams, and Jonathan Zittrain.

I was fortunate to be a postdoctoral fellow at two wonderful universities. In the religion department and the center for Jewish Studies at Northwestern, I found friendship and support among colleagues including Mira Balberg, Yakir Englander, Phyllis Lassner, Michelle Molina, Claire Sufrin, Sarah McFarland Taylor, Barry Wimpfheimer, and Laurie Zoloth. Robert Orsi and Christine Helmer made Northwestern and Evanston feel more like home. In Toronto, I am thankful to Doris Bergen, Ben Bryce, Sol Goldberg, Kenneth Green, Sara Horowitz, Jeff Kopstein, Peter Loewen, Andrea Most, Naomi Seidman, Anna Shternshis, and Christopher Stolarski. I was also lucky to have the Paula and Irving Frisch clan as my Toronto family.

I am so grateful to those who invited me to present research along the way, including Robert Abzug, Jeremy Dauber, Rachel B. Gross, Susannah Heschel, Aaron Hughes, Nora Rubel, Nancy Sinkoff, Helene Sinnreich, and Barbara Levin and Josh Gettinger.

This book benefited greatly from fellowships from the following organizations: the American Jewish Archives; the Berman Foundation Dissertation Fellowships; the Center for Jewish History; Charles Warren Center for Studies in American History; the Fordham-NYPL Research Fellowship in Jewish Studies; the Jordan Schnitzer First Book Publication Awards;

the Hadassah-Brandeis Institute; the University of Florida Humanities Scholarship Enhancement Fund; and the University of Florida Rothman Faculty Summer Fellowship at the University of Florida.

Staff at the following archives made my research possible: the American Jewish Archives, the Beinecke Rare Book & Manuscript Library, Boston University Howard Gotlieb Archival Research Center; the Center for Jewish History, the Columbia University Rare Book and Manuscript Library; the Harvard Library Judaica Division (thank you, Vardit Samuels!); and the University of Rochester Rare Books and Special Collection. I remain indebted to Harvard librarian Steve Gerald Kuehler for his librarian-detective work.

Several scholars generously read parts of this text at different stages and provided very helpful feedback. Much gratitude to Jenny Caplan, Jessica Cooperman, Jodi Eichler-Levine, Leah Garrett, Jeffrey Gurock, Lori Harrison-Kahan, Rachel Kranson, Laura Levitt, Laura Arnold Liebman, Shari Rabin, Emily Sigalow, Tisa Wenger, and Laura Yares. In addition to reading multiple drafts, my colleagues Deborah Dash Moore, Gayle Zachmann, and Josh Lambert went above and beyond through the guidance they offered me. A Jewish Studies writing group organized by Sarah Imhoff and Eli Sacks provided helpful structure. Friendships with Argo Caminis, Dana Frisch, Jay H. Geller, Dara Horn, Samira Mehta, and Cynthia Weiss that included conversations about all aspects of this project—and life in general—mean so very much to me.

Thank you to every scholar of American Jews who came before me.

And to my wonderful University of Florida students in the "Post-Holocaust American Jews" course: thank you for your insights and enthusiasm for this material!

I'm delighted to have landed in the religion department at the University of Florida and to have Anita Anantharam, Robert Kawashima, Ali Mian, Vasu Narayanan, Terje Ostebo, Anna Peterson, Mario Poceski, Erin Prophet, Ben Soares, and Bron Taylor as colleagues. At the Bud Shorstein Center for Jewish Studies, I'm grateful to Jack Kugelmass for hiring me, and to Norman Goda for continuing to make our center a dream academic environment for pursuing research and teaching innovative courses. Getting to know Buddy Shorstein and experiencing his friendship and support, not to mention his enthusiasm for "Gator Nation," has made Gainesville life more fun and meaningful.

I am thankful to Oxford University Press and to my editors, Cynthia Read and Theodore Calderara, for their staunch support of this project and to the anonymous reviewers of this manuscript. Teddy Reiner's cheerful shepherding of my manuscript through the editing process is much appreciated. My book was improved as a result of Timothy DeWerff's copyediting and Enid Zafran's indexing. My deep appreciation to Ganga Balaji for her careful work in the production of this manuscript.

My family has given me so much more than I can acknowledge here. My parents' reading of countless drafts is only one of many ways they wholeheartedly supported this project. Thank you, Mike and Iz, for being wonderful brothers and for enlarging our family to include Shifra, Abby, Elisha, Abner, Yemima, Noa, Eli, and Maya. In so many ways, my husband, Yaniv Feller, made this book better. That is not in the least surprising, because he makes everything better.

Introduction
Popularizing Judaism

Postwar Stories in 1940s America

When we first meet Phil Green, the non-Jewish reporter in the 1947 novel *Gentleman's Agreement*, he has recently moved to New York City and is about to receive an assignment from his editor. That mission—which Phil reluctantly accepts—is to write a magazine article about antisemitism. The task sends Phil on an American odyssey through the everyday encounters of Jews with racial slurs, social and professional exclusion, and emotional pain. Not long after Phil's first meeting with his editor, we find him hunched over his typewriter, cigarette dangling from his mouth, trying to find a new angle for the old story of antisemitism. Finally, it hits him. Phil decides, "I'll be Jewish! I'll just say it—nobody knows me—I can just say it."[1]

When Phil is out and about, pretending to be Jewish, *Gentleman's Agreement* delivers its most serious emotional punches. In these scenes, we watch Phil do what no actual 1940s Jew in his right mind would have done: announce to the world that he is Jewish to discover what antisemitism might come his way. Moral outrage ensues, and in *Agreement* it is served up with a side of Phil's boyish confusion that the world would be so cruel to people just because they happen to be Jewish. Over the course of his journey through the heart of 1940s antisemitic darkness, Phil hears disparaging comments about Jews, and most disturbingly, he finds his young son in tears after being called a "dirty Jew." There is also the quiet rage that overtakes Phil in a hushed hotel lobby after a heated exchange with the manager about whether his is a restricted hotel that bars Jews. And then there are the uncomfortable, intimate moments with his girlfriend, Kathy, when her liberal mask slips, and Phil worries that he detects antisemitism in the woman he loves.

All of this made *Gentleman's Agreement* absorbing as a novel and film. But it wasn't enough to make it everyone's idea of a satisfying postwar Jewish story.

Postwar Stories. Rachel Gordan, Oxford University Press. © Oxford University Press 2024.
DOI: 10.1093/9780197694367.003.0001

On a cold Sunday morning in 1948, in a radio sermon, Boston rabbi Joshua Loth Liebman gave voice to that dissatisfaction.[2] At the time, Liebman was one of the most famous rabbis in America.[3] Two years earlier, he wrote the bestselling *Peace of Mind*. Now he was speaking about another bestseller—Laura Z. Hobson's novel, *Gentleman's Agreement*.

In his radio sermon, Rabbi Liebman explained Phil's realization that "it is not enough to sit back and to be passively acquiescent in the presence of evil; one has to affirm himself and his beliefs when bigotry against the Jew, the Negro, the Catholic, or the Protestant manifests itself." Connecting antisemitism to a family of hatreds, Liebman placed Jewish concerns within a much larger battle against racism and bigotry.

Liebman continued: "We have to show the character that is within us by saying the courageous word against prejudice in a jeering social gathering, daring to be a nonconformist, a minority of one if need be." Liebman hoped a story like *Gentleman's Agreement* would guide readers toward such independence of thought.

On air, Liebman praised the novel, explaining that it "highlights both the good and evil in our present-day culture. It throws its beam of truth upon the pathetic snobbishness of the Darien, Connecticut set, the ungentlemanly set, the un-American and un-Christian set." In other words, the novel did a good job of portraying antisemitism as vulgar behavior. And yet, *Agreement* had "distinct limitations," according to the rabbi. "There is, for example, nothing in the whole of 'Gentleman's Agreement' that would give the sympathetic Christian awareness of the moral vitality of the Jewish spirit or the spiritual majesty of Jewish life and history."[4] Liebman had particular insight into the motivations behind such books. His *Peace of Mind* was in the vanguard of the "Introduction to Judaism" genre of nonfiction articles and books about Jewish religion that blossomed in the postwar years.[5]

Changing Attitudes during the Uneasy 1940s

The thesis of this book is that two midcentury genres popularized the idea of Judaism as an American *religion* and not a race. The 1940s anti-antisemitism literature, a genre of which *Gentleman's Agreement* was an exemplar, helped to cement this view of American Judaism, which was elaborated upon in what I call Introduction to Judaism Literature, including Liebman's *Peace of Mind*. By using the argot of American religion—particularly terms such as faith, belief, spiritual, communion, and creed—rabbis, novelists, and other writers translated Judaism into an American idiom, making it acceptable in the public sphere.[6] In the process, both genres contributed to a new form of Jewishness—shaped by popular culture and designed to fit the reigning myth of postwar America as a tri-faith (Protestant-Catholic-Jewish) nation.[7] A new confidence in revealing Judaism's divergences from Protestant understandings of religion also became apparent in this genre. These postwar narratives about Judaism informed American Jewish self-perceptions as well as gentile expectations of Jewish neighbors.

Both anti-antisemitism literature and Introduction to Judaism literature represent vital movements in the postwar transformation of American Judaism: first, a public denunciation of antisemitism as un-American, and second, a clear explanation of Judaism as a religion at a time when Cold War American citizenship seemed to require denominational affiliation. The two movements expressed by these genres—fighting antisemitism and making Judaism respectable and understandable as an American religion—supported Judaism's ascent.

This period of significant change in American attitudes toward Judaism were also years of change for American media. When Rabbi Liebman gave his sermon in the winter of 1948, radio was still the thing. Lucille Ball was known to Americans as the star of a popular CBS radio program called *My Favorite Husband* that would soon become *I Love Lucy*.[8] And Americans had yet to be seduced by television, which seemed, as *Time* reported, a recent and clumsy affair.[9] Sitting in the darkness of a movie theater remained a once or twice a week occurrence for many, with the big screen romantic romps of Humphrey Bogart, Lauren Bacall, Veronica Lake, and James Stewart continuing to enthrall, even as the era's film production code ensured that, at least in the movies where no hint of sex was allowed, married couples retired to twin beds.[10] There were limits to what popular culture could portray.

In these last years before TVs took over living rooms, Americans sated their desire for stories through magazines, movies, radio, and books. When *Gentleman's Agreement* premiered in November 1948, one entertainment industry magazine declared of Gregory Peck's performance that he "put so much emotion and sincerity" into his role as a young reporter determined "to present a difficult subject with honesty that it can be said with no fear of contradiction that he does the finest work of his career."[11]

Treating a difficult subject with honesty was rarer in the late 1940s than we might realize today. With the onset of the Cold War political and military rivalry with the Soviet Union, McCarthy-era anti-Communist suspicions pressured Americans not to raise fears of disloyalty through their behavior. The United States was moving swiftly into a period when revealing uncomfortable truths was to be avoided at all costs.[12] But by the 1950s, messy realities were difficult to postpone; men returning from war had been exposed to new cultures, and television increasingly brought the outside world into American homes. One chronicler of reading culture observed of the 1950s: "Suddenly America was a fact-minded nation. Non-fiction was king."[13]

The unease of these postwar times was surprising. In many ways, the country was healthier than ever. As *Time* noted in 1948, while Western Europe was wracked by Communist violence and food shortages and England's economy was in the first stage of convalescence, the "rich and powerful US" was "untouched by violence and unhurt by want."[14] As usual, *Time* had white, middle-class Americans in mind. More babies were born and fewer people died as life expectancy rose from age forty-nine in 1900 to age sixty-eight in 1950.[15] To observers, there appeared to be little of the cynical disillusionment of earlier decades. Writing about postwar Americans marrying in the late 1940s and 1950s, the editor of *Harper's* observed in 1952, that unlike young people of previous generations, "They did not regard marriage as a bourgeois expedient for enforcing a conventional monogamy upon free spirits."[16] Young people were making more money, marrying younger, eating better, and living more comfortably than their parents.[17] The 1950s version of the house with a white picket fence included babies and a flood of new postwar appliances, such as Polaroids, vacuum cleaners, and freezers, along with the other trappings of suburban domesticity.[18] By the mid-1950s, 65 percent of all new homes included family rooms—the better to accommodate the increased fertility rate approaching 3.8 children per woman.[19] But according to *Time*, the country was "full of vague fears and a lack of confidence."[20] The population was "producing more than ever before and had more money to buy things than ever before, yet the country still did not have the happiness its boom seemed to offer."[21] Grave social problems were apparent amid the economic prosperity.

One element of these anxious times was the country's continued antisemitism, which persisted despite stirrings of progress in fighting bigotry.[22] For example, in the immediate post–World War II years, the racist and antisemitic Senator Theodore Bilbo of Mississippi was blocked by his liberal colleagues on the Senate floor from assuming a third term, even as "a fringe political party called the Christian Nationalist Party nominated Gerald L. K. Smith, a pastor with pro-Nazi sympathies."[23] The same party would also adopt an antisemitic, anti-Black platform that called for the deportation of people with whom it disagreed. With these political winds, one rabbi in Springfield, Massachusetts, couldn't help wondering if an official "Week of Hate" should replace Brotherhood Week as a means of exorcising hostility within the community. The rabbi explained: "It would be much better to have the one week in 52 dedicated to hate, a week when we would all be able to get the hate out of our systems, treat each other as badly as we know how, and then observe the remaining 51 weeks as Brotherhood Weeks."[24] Even among clergy, it was not clear how postwar Americans should deal with the hatred in their midst.

In the more stylish reaches of society, Barbara "Babe" Cushing Mortimer Paley was embarking on her own version of a *Gentleman's Agreement* experience. Daughter of the renowned neurosurgeon Harvey Cushing, and one of "the fabulous Cushing sisters" of Boston, Babe had just wed her second husband, CBS president William Paley, in 1947. All of the Cushing sisters married Astors, Whitneys, and Roosevelts, prompting *Life* magazine's observation that the Cushing sisters had "married wisely and well every time."[25] Babe's 1947 nuptials to a Jew broke new ground—and it cost her. A regular on the country's "best dressed" lists, Babe continued to be photographed for *Vogue* and the society pages as Mrs. William Paley.[26] Despite Bill Paley's wealth and power, the Paleys were excluded from fashionable clubs and resorts, on account of Bill's Jewishness.[27] To outsiders, it likely seemed a small price to pay, considering the Paleys' lavish lifestyle. But this social exclusion had become part of the American Jewish experience, defining the limits of Jews' acceptance.[28] A decade earlier, a study of minority groups concluded of Jews in America, "Probably no other white minority group which has sufficient money and cultural polish to fit into the accepted standards of vacation life is absolutely barred from the ordinary summer resort."[29] In truth, the matter of Jews' whiteness was still up for debate among 1940s Americans. As one of the most popular novels read by World War II Armed Services put it, "They ain't no such thing as a white Jew."[30] That Betty Smith's *A Tree Grows in Brooklyn* (1943) included these lines and other disparaging comments about Jews did not detract from the bestselling novel's immense success during a war that Americans would come to regard, in part, as a war to defeat Nazism.[31]

On the bigotry front, there continued to be successes among liberals. Jackie Robinson broke the color line in Major League Baseball in 1947, even as whites and Blacks remained segregated. When Ed Sullivan appeared on CBS in 1948, the showman fought racial discrimination and antisemitism by inviting Blacks and Jews as guest performers on his show. But Americans had reason to wonder: were these goodwill gestures real, or just a veneer? What did it even mean to be committed to fighting bigotry against Jews, and did it have anything to do with understanding Judaism as a religion?

Here was a tension at the heart of this postwar American liberal culture: increasing prioritization of pluralism, coupled with a dawning awareness of what would become known as the Holocaust, helped shift progressive-leaning Americans toward a climate of public *anti-*antisemitism, even as comprehension of Judaism remained low. The Nazi counterexample motivated many Americans to oppose antisemitism, at least publicly and in popular culture. But new sympathy toward Jews also highlighted the ignorance of the American public about Jewish religion. What did Jewish people believe? And after triumphing over Hitler, how should Americans regard antisemitism?

In offering answers to these kinds of questions, writers increasingly centered religion in their postwar presentations of Judaism. Explaining Jews and Judaism through the language of religion, rather than as a race, nationality, or as a problem—understandings that had all been common, previously— allowed authors to present Jews in acceptable ways for Cold War readers.[32] That several books and magazine articles addressed these subjects during the late 1940s and 1950s is one clue that Jews and Judaism formed a thick strand of the postwar cultural conversation.

Becoming an American Religion

As historians have shown, the nineteenth century had also witnessed efforts to remake Judaism into an American religion.[33] But these earlier desires to recreate Judaism as an American religion were largely *Jewish* desires. In contrast, in the late 1940s and 1950s, influential non-Jews, including politicians, businessmen, clergymen, publishers, editors, movie producers, public intellectuals, and writers, broadcast their vision for integrating Judaism into the country's religious landscape.[34] And while nineteenth-century efforts to create an American Judaism focused on increasing the decorum and dignity of Jewish religious life by bringing it into harmony with the standards of Protestantism, post–World War II efforts sought to explain the distinctiveness of Judaism at a time when acceptance of religious difference, albeit of a limited kind, seemed like a hallmark of postwar American society, in contrast with Nazi and Communist enemies.[35]

Among the motivations that inspired these twentieth-century efforts to create a postwar American Judaism was the destruction of Jewish life during the Holocaust. The Nazis' racial persecution led to both a push to define Jewishness as a religion, and a post-Holocaust embrace of Jewishness that included much more than religion. It was not always a conscious move on the part of writers and editors, but in homage to the religious and cultural life destroyed in Europe, post–World War II American Judaism largely retained its ethnic flavor, reminding Americans that Jews were not only members of a religion—they were also an ethnic group with a shared linguistic and cultural background, and a national group with sentimental and political ties to the new Jewish state. Jews were connected not only by religion, but also by history, memory, language, cuisine, humor, and politics. This broad conception of Jewishness contrasted with the goals of nineteenth-century Jewish reformers who, in the eyes of one post-Holocaust observer, had "aspired to liquidate the ethnic problem" of Jews—a goal accomplished by distancing their brand of Judaism from that of Eastern Europe.[36] It was these kinds of nineteenth-century desires to divorce American Reform Judaism from the Jewishness of recent Russian Jewish immigrants that led the Cincinnati-based Reform rabbi Isaac Mayer Wise to observe of the recent Russian-Jewish immigrants: "We are Americans and they are not. We are Israelites of the nineteenth century in a free country, and they gnaw the bones of past centuries. . . . The good reputation of Judaism must naturally suffer materially, which must without fail lower our social status."[37] By the post–World War II era, with growing awareness of what befell the Jews under Hitler, it was no longer acceptable for rabbis to voice such sentiments. A warmer embrace of Eastern European Jewishness was only one of the signs that the war had altered how American Jews conceived of Jewishness.[38] It also indicated that Jewishness as religion would continue to coexist with the idea of Jewishness as culture and ethnicity.

Authors of Introduction to Judaism texts were motivated, too, by the realization that American Jews themselves, not just non-Jews, were often ignorant about Judaism. Second-, third-, and fourth-generation American Jews stood at a remove from the religion of their ancestors, often due to ignorance.[39] With the back winds of the Cold War exerting new pressures on religious affiliation, a lack of religious literacy was increasingly judged a liability in Cold War America. Some of the writers profiled in *Postwar Stories* sought to rectify that Jewish illiteracy.

Postwar Jews ignorant of their Judaism were like "orphans in history," as the *Village Voice* writer Paul Cowan put it in his 1982 memoir.[40] In Cowan's case, his family's quick ascent of the socioeconomic ladder (his mother was an heiress to the Spiegel mail-order company, and his father was a CBS president) had entailed jettisoning Jewishness and their original last name of Cohen, along the way. Cowan's memoir subtitle, *One Man's Triumphant Search for His Jewish Roots*, might not have made sense to earlier generations. Before the midcentury, Jews were either very much aware of their Jewishness, or not seeking to re-engage with it, with the exceptions proving the rule. A variation on the Introduction to Judaism genre, *An Orphan in History* explained the Jewish religion Cowan adopted as an adult. The memoir recalled Cowan's "homecoming to a home he never really knew," as the *New York Times* called it.[41] The same year that Cowan published his memoir, novelist Ann Birstein also published a book about her Jewish roots. *The Rabbi on 47th Street* told the story of Birstein's father. Despite having grown up in an Orthodox family, Birstein prefaced her book with an author's note explaining, "Like many Jewish women of my generation, I know less about Orthodox ritual than I ought to because for the most part I wasn't included in it."[42] Cowan may have felt orphaned from his Jewish heritage, but women such as Birstein knew from childhood that they were excluded from Judaism by virtue of their gender. *Postwar Stories* illustrates gender exclusion, particularly in the Introduction to Judaism genre, while also revealing how women found ways to participate in the telling of postwar Jewish stories. As the following chapters demonstrate, a later-in-life embrace of Judaism such as Cowan's would become more familiar to postwar Jews encountering Introduction to Judaism literature in the 1950s and beyond.

The World around the Books

That postwar acceptance of Jews and Judaism was one goal of the anti-antisemitism and Introduction to Judaism literatures is evident when examining the correspondence between the authors of these books and their readers. From private musings to public grandstanding, this book follows conversations between writers, editors, and readers, exposing the inspirations and challenges behind this literature. We also discover how

INTRODUCTION: POPULARIZING JUDAISM   9

publishers and other culture gatekeepers negotiated with authors to produce Jewish stories that could speak to modern American readers.

What exactly did "American religion" mean to midcentury Americans? The writers profiled in this book were trying to figure out what this classification implied for their explanations of Judaism. As is true for most writers, they figured it out through writing—and in dialogue with others.

As literary scholar Josh Lambert observes, "What we read (and write, edit, publish, and review) has to do with who we are and who we are connected to."[43] The pages that follow confirm Lambert's observation that reading provides identity and community. Since the 1920s, book clubs such as the Book-of-the-Month Club and the Literary Guild guided readers aspiring toward an educated middle-class identity.[44] "How to get rid of an Inferiority Complex," read a 1930s advertisement for the book series, "Dr. Eliot's Five-Foot Shelf of Books," which promised to elevate a reader's status through its selections by the esteemed former Harvard president Charles Eliot.[45] The full-page advertisement explained the importance of a "liberal education at your fingertips" through the story of an employee's inferiority complex quickly resolved upon discovery of the "Harvard Classics."

The desire to compensate for the educational and cultural deficits of one's background through books was familiar to many working-class Jews, particularly during the first half of the twentieth century when so many other avenues for cultural and educational advancement were still blocked by antisemitism. Growing up in the 1930s working-class town of Lynn, Massachusetts, Al Silverman, future vice president of the Book-of-the-Month subscription club, recalled an aunt—a working, single woman without dependents—who could afford to purchase books. What a feeling they provided! "Books in the home were the symbol of a better life ahead."[46] Merely by their presence, books suggested possibilities for advancement.

Affordable books were especially important during the 1930s when they were "a boon for those who have always relied on reading for solace and stimulation but have been scuttled by the depression," the *New York Times* noted in 1938.[47] The paperback revolution, begun in the late 1930s, was well underway by the postwar era, increasing the number of low-cost books in circulation still further.[48] Simon & Schuster's 1939 launch of Pocket Books forever changed reading in America, with their 4-by-6-inch books priced at 25 cents.[49] With the size and price trending downward, books became cheap and disposable. A bus ride or a drugstore counter became perfectly acceptable environs for displaying one's literary enthusiasms. In such settings it was easy to project a persona onto the world, in between sips of a soda.

During the immediate post–World War II years, to display a readerly interest in Jews was increasingly to express an open-mindedness grounded in Judeo-Christian morality. This virtue signaling often had a religious or ideological dimension for both Jewish and non-Jewish midcentury readers. Matthew Hedstrom has shown how "participation in religious and spiritual life happens through commodities bought and sold, and for much of the twentieth century the most significant of these religious commodities was the book."[50] Purchasing, owning, or reading a particular book were ways of showing an appreciation or commitment to the themes espoused. To read anti-antisemitism or Introduction to Judaism texts was to place oneself within a community of readers of such literature.

Writers' communities were also evidenced in their work. Jewish novelist Laura Z. Hobson's familiarity with the work of anthropologists such as Ruth Benedict and Gene Weltfish influenced how she understood antisemitism. Similarly, Rabbi Milton Steinberg's mentorship of a young Arthur Cohen informed the latter's perception of Judaism and Herman Wouk's feelings for his Orthodox rabbi grandfather colored his views of Jewishness.

Religion—and the Need to Have One

Along with a midcentury need for explanations of Judaism, a prevailing vagueness in matters of religion in public life made it easier for writers to fit Judaism into the era's capacious and often fuzzy understanding of religion.[51] As one journalist put it in 1954, it was an age when Americans expressed "faith in faith." "What was revived," one historian observes of the postwar era, "was not so much religious belief as belief in the value of religion" at a time when Americans' Soviet enemies rejected religion.[52] Americans may not have been highly knowledgeable about religion—a shortcoming underscored by the decisions of both *Look* and *Life* magazines to publish special issues about world religions, in 1955—but they knew they had to have one, precisely because their Cold War enemies did not. Religion was an essential ingredient of what many considered the superior American way of life.[53]

One of the surprising ways in which this postwar primacy of religion manifested was in a 1958 Gallup poll in which Americans were asked, "If your party nominated a generally well-qualified man for President" and he happened to be "Catholic," "Jewish," "Negro," or "Atheist," would you vote for him? The only question to which Americans responded "no" at a rate significantly higher than 50 percent was the question regarding atheists. More than 74 percent of Americans answered that they would not vote for an atheist president (24% answered no to a Catholic, 27% answered no to a Jew, and 52% answered no to a Black).[54] Despite deep prejudice against Jews, Catholics, and Blacks, Cold War distrust of nonbelievers—at least in the context of choosing the nation's leader—was even higher. By the mid-1950s, American patriotism and religiousness had become nearly synonymous.[55]

A famous quotation from President Eisenhower captures the religious sensibility of the era. In 1952, in the context of the Cold War and the Soviet rejection of religion, Eisenhower declared: "In other words, our form of government has no sense unless it is founded in a deeply felt religious faith, and I don't care what it is. With us of course it is the Judeo-Christian concept but it must be a religion that all men are created equal."[56]

With this statement, Eisenhower broadened American religion to include Catholics and Jews, even as he lowered the bar for doctrinal specificity. Eisenhower and those who supported this definition of Judeo-Christianity were cementing an exclusionary basis of American religion. That only *white* Americans of Protestant, Catholic, and Jewish faiths were welcome did not need to be spelled out in these midcentury declarations of tri-faith America. But some writers did make their conditions explicit. After one interaction in which the limits of tolerance were clarified, Phil Green, the protagonist in *Gentleman's Agreement*, grasps a harsh truth: "That was it, then. They were O.K. Jews; they were 'white' Jews."[57] Here, Phil marked a crucial distinction between the marginalization of Jews and Blacks: with the right behavior and self-presentation, Jews could be considered white. As we will find in readers' letters, however, the anti-antisemitism novels also pointed to the connections between the discrimination against Jews and Blacks, for as Judith Smith has shown, these 1940s novelists often "hoped that a challenge to the fascist racialization of Jewishness would reveal the fallacies of racialization in general."[58] Both anti-antisemitism and Introduction to Judaism literature evidenced the ways that people of color—of any faith—continued to remain outside the midcentury tri-faith circle of acceptance.[59] Another kind of "gentleman's agreement" was thus being described. It was one in which Jews were accepted so long as their behavior comported with the standards of white, middle-class religion.

Religion's Midcentury Moment

Several events indicated that the mid-twentieth century was a time of greater salience for religion in American public life.[60] It was in the 1950s that the phrase "under God" was added to the Pledge of Allegiance (1954); "In God We Trust" became the national motto (1956), while the idea of Judeo-Christianity as the antidote to totalitarian regimes gained widespread currency in the 1940s and 1950s.[61] Judaism and popular culture played a surprisingly central role in the cultural shifts that made religion prominent after nearly two decades of what felt like years of spiritual depression, in addition to economic depression, to many in the Northeast where much postwar Jewish literature was created.[62] Indeed, *Gentleman's Agreement* and Joshua Liebman's *Peace of Mind* were stars in a constellation of midcentury Jewish popular culture that, taken together, both drove and reflected a recasting of American Judaism.

While the aftermath of this midcentury transformation has been explored in scholarly investigations of the Judeo-Christian tradition, there has been far less attention to the way popular culture participated in this change.[63] Historians focusing on postwar American Jews have yet to fully answer the question of how Judaism achieved its postwar status as an American religion.[64] This question is one that already intrigued postwar observers. In the mid-1950s, sociologist Nathan Glazer mused:

> It would be an interesting essay in the history of ideas to determine just how the United States evolved in the popular mind from a "Christian" nation to a nation made up of Catholics, Protestants, and Jews. The most interesting part of such a study—which I do not plan to undertake here—would be to discover how it came about that the Jewish group, which through most of the history of the United States has formed an insignificant percentage of the American people, has come to be granted the status of "most favored religion."[65]

The tectonic shift that Glazer observed is at the heart of *Postwar Stories*, which argues that authors of popular culture participated in the transformation in the status of American Judaism.[66] As part of an efflorescence of postwar Jewish popular culture, these writers offered Jews new ways of understanding their identities while also reaching broader American audiences who, in accordance with their pro-democracy and anti-fascist worldview, embraced the postwar American decorum of eschewing antisemitism.

Even as Americans rose to the theme of *anti*-antisemitism, they knew very little about Jews and their religion. In response to this ignorance about Jewishness, writers sought to educate Americans by simultaneously reminding them of the deeply un-American nature of antisemitism and instructing them in the key attributes of Judaism as a religion. Acceptance of Jews as members of an American religion involved some level of rejection of the notion that Jews composed a distinct and inferior race, inherently worthy of marginalization. Recent scholarship on Jews and race, which shows that American perceptions of Jews moved away from an emphasis on racial categories during the 1940s, has focused on the transformation of postwar Jews into mainstream white Americans.[67] *Postwar Stories* explains how Jewishness moved from race to *religion*—and the role of two genres of popular Jewish literature in that shift.

The Midcentury Jewish Middlebrow Moment

If the midcentury was a "religion moment" of the American Jewish experience, it was also a middlebrow moment.[68] The anti-antisemitism and Introduction to Judaism genres are part of a larger trend of midcentury Jewish middlebrow in which popular books, movies, television, and print culture played the roles of engine and mirror to the transformation of American Jews and Judaism.[69]

The terms "highbrow" and "lowbrow" emerged in the early twentieth century and were rooted in the pseudoscience of phrenology, which posited a connection between skull size and mental capacity.[70] What is now considered bad science thus helped facilitate this stratification of culture into "brows." By the 1950s, the term "middlebrow" was not only a cultural category, as Christina Klein explains, "but also a cultural formation: a more or less self-conscious movement of artists, writers, and intellectuals who shared an aesthetic sensibility and were loosely connected through personal relationships and through an institutional infrastructure of magazines, publishing houses, book clubs, reviewers and other organizations."[71] Jews played a large role in both the general postwar American middlebrow culture and in the Jewish counterpart examined in this book. Even in Jewish middlebrow culture, however, a network of Jews and non-Jews created these books and articles. Non-Jews edited, published, produced, and as chapter 7 shows, sometimes wrote texts about Jews. Non-Jews were involved in other ways, too—as editors and readers who reviewed, applauded, and critiqued this literature.

The middlebrow category first appeared in the 1920s, and as Beth Driscoll notes, defining it was always a contentious matter. Middlebrow "emerged to complicate the binary between highbrow and lowbrow in the early-to-mid twentieth century, a period when critics were confronted by both the emergence of Modernism and the increased production of mass culture."[72] Driscoll observes that while hostility toward the category was rampant and often fierce, definitions remained scarce. The term was frequently aimed at cultural products seen as too easy, insular, and smug.[73] Driscoll's study leads to her definition of the middlebrow as "middle-class, reverential towards elite culture, entrepreneurial, mediated, feminized, emotional, recreational, and earnest."[74] Because feminine characteristics were often ascribed to Jews, many of these qualities also made middlebrow seem Jewish.[75] The highly visible marketing of middlebrow, from subscriber book clubs to bestseller lists, also tainted this literature as commercial. It was one thing to *have* money. To be actively trying to make money—and from literature, no less—was suspect behavior in the eyes of the Protestant establishment.[76]

The middlebrow category was revived at midcentury by a lighthearted *Harper's Bazaar* article about "brow" categories, which was reprinted in a 1949 *Life* magazine, alongside a pictorial chart that allowed readers to classify people into one or another "brow" culture.[77] Like a twenty-first-century quiz used by readers to determine their Harry Potter character or Hogwarts House, the chart provided a fun and permissibly judgmental means of categorizing oneself and others. For instance, an Eames chair and a Kurt Versen lamp were considered highbrow furniture, while a "mail order overstuffed chair [and] fringed lamp" were labeled as lowbrow. And "a Highbrow is the kind of person who looks at a sausage and thinks of Picasso," while a Middlebrow, this same commentator observed, thinks fine sculpture is the kind on display in his front yard.[78] This brow-categorizing carried over into midcentury American Jewish culture. Writers such as Herman Wouk, Jo Sinclair, Joshua Loth Liebman, Laura Z. Hobson, Philip Bernstein, and Milton Steinberg were classified as middlebrow by other writers who considered themselves higher up on the brow chart.[79]

Cultural happenings during the late 1940s and 1950s made it hard to miss the swirl of Jewish middlebrow culture, including the radio and television versions of the immensely popular show *The Goldbergs*, produced by Gertrude Berg; the many openly Jewish comedians appearing in American living rooms, shortly after the birth of television, on shows such as *The

Ed Sullivan Show, Milton Berle's *Texaco Star Theater* and Sid Ceasar's and Imogene Coca's *Your Show of Shows*, the 1950s Broadway and cinematic productions of *The Diary of Anne Frank*, and Harry Golden's books—the bestselling *Only in America* and *For 2 Cents Plain* from Golden's *Carolina Israelite* columns.

While Jews were central to American popular culture during the early decades of the twentieth century, playing outsize roles in vaudeville, Broadway, and Hollywood, they were generally discreet about their Jewishness. As Rebecca Davis observes of the difference between earlier and post–World War II era Jewish stars: "Listeners who heard Benny Goodman on the radio in the 1940s might not have known that he was Jewish, but everyone who encountered the brilliantly profane comedy of Lenny Bruce in the 1950s and 1960s knew that he was. . . . These midcentury celebrities made Jewishness part of their public identities as their careers ascended."[80] This change in how celebrities negotiated Jewishness is an important consideration in any assessment of the pivotal midcentury.

Popular midcentury books and movies, while briefly mentioned in most histories of the Jewish 1940s and 1950s, are rarely treated seriously as a significant factor in the reshaping of the postwar American religious and cultural landscape.[81] Critics have judged middlebrow to be an undesirable cultural standing, regarding it as unserious and apologetic.[82] This book takes a different perspective, exploring the important cultural work of two neglected streams of midcentury Jewish middlebrow. In its moment, this literature helped readers understand how Jews—once considered threatening foreigners—belonged in the United States. While the key to that belonging was primarily to define Jewishness as a religion, it also depended on a concerted effort to discredit antisemitic attitudes.

Jewish *middlebrow*—and not Jewish *popular culture*—is the term used in this book because it is indigenous to the midcentury, when essays and charts of what constituted middlebrow were published in magazines, and because of the term's emotional valence. Middlebrow is rarely a neutral term. (Virginia Woolf famously declared, "If any human being, man, woman, dog, cat or half-crushed worm dares call me 'middlebrow' I will take my pen and stab him, dead."[83]) Its tendency to connote insult or disparagement of the consumer or culture it describes helps us understand why the genres investigated in this book have heretofore remained so invisible, despite their wide readership and popularity. Middlebrow's accomplishments lie in the way it normalizes and uplifts, making readers and viewers feel comfortable with what once seemed unacceptable. This is also why middlebrow is criticized: its blatant efforts to make readers feel good.

The power of midcentury Jewish middlebrow books and essays lay in making Jews and Judaism into subjects that Americans could understand and accept. As noted above, before World War II, many Americans viewed Jewishness as a threat, a liability, or, at best, a curiosity. In the immediate postwar years, Jewishness was on its way to becoming an identity fostering pride. Likewise, Judaism shifted from "the least understood of all major religions," as described by one midcentury American scholar, to a mainstreamed, third-faith status.[84] At midcentury, establishing a newfound sense of acceptance of Jews and Judaism required dismantling entrenched, denigrating attitudes toward Jews imbibed during the previous decades and replacing them with positive associations. Affirming popular culture played a key role in this shift.

Among the factors that made the midcentury an opportune time for a shift in American sentiment was a new sympathy and interest in Jews, evident by the late 1940s. At the start of the decade, President Roosevelt had to all but swear that if the United States entered the war, it would not be to save the Jews—so unpopular was that cause with most Americans.[85] By helping to defeat the Nazis, Americans were cast in the role of saviors of Jews. Despite the reluctance of news sources to name Jews explicitly as Hitler's victims, articles and photos in middlebrow magazines and in newsreels in the spring and summer of 1945 showed that the nearly dead who had been liberated from concentration camps were, for the most part, Jews.[86] By the end of the 1940s and the onset of the Cold War, however, the Judeo-Christian tradition was at high tide, and in the writing and reading of *anti*-antisemitic literature, Americans began to make psychic reparations for what had happened to European Jews.

Americans may not have wanted to enter the war, but having won it, and basked in American soldiers' reflected glory, they could see a new postwar reflection of themselves. Unwittingly, they had become allies of the Jews. It was a stunning turnaround in orientation—and one that required a new conception of Jews and Judaism. Visibly Jewish Holocaust survivors, particularly *haredi* (strictly religious, or literally, "trembling before God") Jews who immigrated to the United States in the 1940s and 1950s, contributed to the need for more explanations of Jews and Jewishness. In the late 1940s and 1950s, middlebrow writers were at the ready, with answers to questions only beginning to be asked.

Two Genres at Work

At a time when print media were the primary vehicles for popular culture, interest in a new topic meant visiting the card catalog or browsing the relevant library bookshelves. These were years when many Americans had never entered a Jewish home or even met a Jew; it was not uncommon to base understandings of Judaism on the Hebrew Bible. For these Americans, the story of modern Jews was first made vivid through stories in popular books and magazines. Their power relied on clear, accessible writing, rather than literary greatness. It was a power of simplicity. Both of the genres at the center of *Postwar Stories* showed readers that Jews engaged in many of the same kinds of religious behavior as Christians. Jews attended synagogue. They prayed to God. They gathered with family and friends for holidays. They married and were buried in religious fashion.

The Introduction to Judaism literature made Judaism part of the story of American religion, filling gaps in readers' comprehension of Judaism and satisfying readers' desires to make Judaism—a tradition so recently decimated by a horrific European tragedy—fit into a modern American religion context. In explaining Jews, Judaism, and antisemitism, midcentury Jewish middlebrow literature taught readers how to feel about Judaism and antisemitism, by offering the kind of "vicarious experience, understanding, and wisdom" that could teach readers how to feel right about Jews.[87] Sentimental education was a large part of this midcentury middlebrow moment.[88]

The immediate postwar era provides an illuminating moment for thinking about how Jews chose to pitch themselves to an American audience, although it was hardly the first time Jews engaged in such explanations of themselves. As Lila Corwin Berman observes, "In the modern era, in a more sustained fashion than any other historical period, explaining—or presenting—Jewishness to non-Jews became a political necessity and an act of Jewish survival."[89] During the late 1940s and 1950s, an emerging sociological discourse around Jewishness as ethnic identity appealed to academically inclined rabbis and public intellectuals. But it was presentations of Judaism *as a religion* that enjoyed a broad middlebrow audience in the 1940s and 1950s.[90]

Certain features define each of the genres. The anti-antisemitism novel accomplished what journalism, nonfiction, and film about antisemitism often could not through its inclusion of the interior lives of multiple characters; individuals repeatedly learning lessons about Jews as members of a religion, not a race; and the novel itself serving as a confessional for the revelations of true feelings about Jews and antisemitism, allowing the novel to expose "before and after" views showing how *anti*-antisemitism transformed individuals.[91]

Introduction to Judaism literature relied on a Protestant conception of religion as the standard against which to compare Judaism.[92] Authors were thus rarely writing on a blank slate, but on a palimpsest of theirs and their readers' ideas about Christianity. Like Christianity, Judaism was presented as a choice, rather than an arbitrary fact of birth. If once Jews believed that God chose them, now they seemed to be in the business of choosing God. Broadly speaking, the genre was divided into two categories: those with a *how-to* approach and those with a *why-to* approach to explaining Judaism.

While Protestantism provided the template for religion in these Introduction to Judaism books and essays, Catholicism—often portrayed as a less democratic religion by Cold War Jewish writers—was the foil beside which the superiority of Judaism (a religion without a pope, as authors were quick to remind readers) could be made evident. Here, Jewish writers tapped into Protestants' fear of Catholic domination.[93] The Catholic Church's commitment to what many Protestants deemed undemocratic political beliefs, coupled with the large Catholic US presence, meant that Catholics loomed as a threat to American Protestantism.[94]

The shining star among the archive of anti-antisemitism novels is *Gentleman's Agreement*, which attracted an unusually large audience as a bestselling novel made into a film.[95] A few of the Introduction to Judaism titles were first published as essays in popular magazines, such as *Life* and *Harper's*. Some, including Nathan Glazer's *American Judaism* and Milton Steinberg's *Basic Judaism*, became staples of college courses, seminaries, and conversion classes.[96] The authors of both genres were part of an educated cultural elite and largely resided in the Northeast. Interestingly, while several popular anti-antisemitism novels of the 1940s were written by women, the postwar Introduction to Judaism genre was almost entirely authored by men. Or, rather, men's names appeared on the title page. Women contributed as spouses who read, edited, encouraged, and wrote parts of manuscripts, but they were almost never listed as authors.[97]

A rare find: "Midwife to a Novel," a 1940s essay by Edith Alpert Steinberg, wife of Milton Steinberg, detailed her involvement in the writing of her husband's 1939 novel *As a Driven Leaf*.[98] From the Steinbergs' letters, it seems that Edith also participated in Steinberg's writing of books about Judaism, including his 1947, *Basic Judaism*. As discussed in chapter 5,

Edith's essay draws back the curtains on what was usually an invisible process of collaboration between husbands and wives. Whether anyone ever considered including Edith's name as a coauthor (or the names of other wives and secretaries who made significant contributions to books) had much to do with the gendered nature of authority. The authority required to be taken seriously as an author of nonfiction was still largely the preserve of male authors, especially when the subject was Judaism, a tradition in which the highest levels of religious education continued to be restricted to men.[99]

The latter chapters of this book show how Cold War American masculinity informed the creation of this first generation of postwar Introductions to Judaism, particularly as authors centered their personal stories. One example is Herman Wouk's 1959 Introduction to Judaism, *This Is My God*, discussed in chapter 8.[100] Wouk's most recent novel, *Marjorie Morningstar* (1955) was imbued with the masculine quality of Cold War Judaism. Listening to her brother's bar mitzvah Torah reading, Marjorie muses, "This religion was a masculine thing, whatever it was. . . . The very Hebrew had a rugged male sound to it. . . . It sounded like some of the rough crashing passages in Macbeth which she loved."[101] The Jewish religion touched Marjorie, but she does not embody it as her brother does as he chants Hebrew before the congregation. That gendered view of Judaism would find expression in *This Is My God*.

In contrast to the Introduction to Judaism genre, the moral authority required to write an anti-antisemitism novel, or any social protest novel, was largely the domain of women, as it had been since the days of Harriet Beecher Stowe's *Uncle Tom's Cabin*.[102] In the 1940s, sentimental education remained the work of women writers. And it was effective. As their letters reveal, readers felt outraged and united in fighting antisemitism after reading anti-antisemitism novels.[103] Women may not have been credible experts on Judaism, but they could write believably about their experiences with antisemitism.

For the 1940s cohort of women anti-antisemitism writers, the nation's unusually politically attuned First Lady was a prominent role model. Unlike impressive career women such as journalist Dorothy Thompson, who was married and divorced several times in an era when divorce was frowned upon, Eleanor Roosevelt's developing political consciousness occurred while she appeared to be adhering to ideal feminine behavior, making her example more difficult for social conservatives to dismiss.

The distance that Eleanor Roosevelt traveled in her attitudes toward Jews was itself a transformation worthy of treatment in an anti-antisemitism novel. As a young woman, ER, as her biographers refer to her, participated in the antisemitism of her upper-crust upbringing, gamely joining her mother-in-law, Sara Delano Roosevelt, in antisemitic repartee. "The Jew party [was] appalling. I never wish to hear money, jewels, or sables mentioned again," she wrote after one social occasion.[104] To ER, her husband's advisor and future Supreme Court justice, Felix Frankfurter, was "an interesting little man but very jew." It was during World War II that ER's attitudes began to evolve.

Named "the world's foremost female political force" by *Time* magazine in 1939, ER expressed her *anti*-antisemitism and anti-racism in her nationally syndicated column, "My Day," on multiple occasions during the 1940s and 1950s.[105] As a columnist, she was able to publicize "many conditions which need airing and which can be corrected by simply giving them publicity," as a 1942 magazine profile of the First Lady observed.[106] Days after Pearl Harbor, ER's column expressed her indignation on behalf of Japanese Americans whose loyalty to the United States was unfairly questioned. She also used the opportunity to condemn antisemitism.[107] A fan of *Gentleman's Agreement*, ER wrote in a 1947 column: "this book is stimulating and thought-provoking, and should be widely read both in the United States and other countries, for we have travelled down a road of unthinking prejudice."[108] That the highborn wife of a president openly expressed such views provided a model for how respectable women of a certain age and class could become voices of protest against racism and antisemitism. As the following chapters demonstrate, women readers were often unofficial but important book promoters, long before the work of cultural influencers was widely recognized.

Whether Jewish or gentile, women authors of anti-antisemitism literature drew on their own lives—their experiences with Jewish lovers, colleagues, and friends, as well as their own brushes with antisemitism. Fictionalizing such autobiographical details could be an effective strategy for midcentury women writers to express their personal truths. Another middlebrow Jewish novelist, Anzia Yezierska, would discover the dangers of writing autobiographically when she published her memoir, *Red Ribbon on a White Horse*, in 1950.[109] In a *New York Times* review, Orville Prescott praised the "intense, emotional, extraordinary in its self-revelation" memoir but ultimately used Yezierska's self-revelations against her. "Miss Yezierska's self-portrait," Prescott concluded, "indicates that she was supersensitive, self-centered, tactless, bitter, confused and unsure."[110] Woe to the midcentury woman writer who dared to reveal her feelings! Real life nonetheless had a way of bleeding into fiction, as Laura Z. Hobson and her fellow anti-antisemitism novelists would find.

The 1940s cohort of anti-antisemitism writers embraced a diversity of members that midcentury American Judaism did not accommodate. The largely homosocial nature of the "thinkers and writers" of American Judaism was not deemed a problem during the 1940s and 1950s. Still, this gendered division of writers may have affected the paths of thoughtful readers. Readers turning to Introduction to Judaism literature found few examples of women who thought and wrote about Judaism. If anything, this literature confirmed suspicions that it was men who steered the course of Judaism. While men and women continued to take part in the writing of social protest literature, American Judaism may have lost a generation of postwar female contributions in intellectual and leadership positions as midcentury Introduction to Judaism literature modeled a community of men thinking and writing about Judaism.

The prominence of both genres in mid-twentieth century American popular culture was a new phenomenon, yet the 1940s and 1950s were not the first time that *anti*-antisemitic views were expressed in fiction or that Jewishness was presented as a religion in American middlebrow culture.[111] The extensive contributions of the bestselling, Pulitzer Prize–winning writer and playwright Edna Ferber's extensive contributions to literature bring to mind the important Jewish middlebrow culture of the early twentieth century, as does the earlier fiction of Emma Wolf.[112] Middlebrow Jewish culture of these earlier eras was not as plentiful as it was in the 1940s and 1950s. With a few exceptions, these earlier middlebrow writers did not portray Jews as members of a middle-class American religion, but rather as marginalized, immigrant "others." Earlier middlebrow culture also lacked the support from society at large that its midcentury counterpart enjoyed during the heightened postwar popularity of the Judeo-Christian tradition.[113]

That such views were expressed before—and would be expressed again—is a reminder of the abiding possibility to mount a principled moral critique of antisemitism as un-American, and that the United States was a comfortable context for explaining Jewishness as a religion.[114] Despite the rise of bigotry and discrimination between the late nineteenth century and the 1940s, Jews' civil and legal equality was not endangered. Jews' participation in American life as citizens, voters, and economic actors provided reassurance, and for many, a belief in their country's immunity from serious Jew hatred.

Antisemitism would thus remain "a social force in America without any significant legal power."[115] That reality would continue to inspire Americans in their efforts to fight the antisemitism they did encounter.

The Power of Midcentury Jewish Middlebrow Culture

The dynamic of middlebrow culture as mirror and engine of societal change is familiar to many. In the largely white suburbs of Boston where I spent my childhood, my only regular exposure to African Americans was a popular television show about a Black middle-class family featuring a doctor father and a lawyer mother. I didn't recognize it at the time, but *The Cosby Show* (in spite of its creator's subsequent disgrace) taught me how to think about Blacks in contemporary America. In a way that parallels the middlebrow Jewish culture of the mid-twentieth century, the TV show prepared me to be accepting of a certain kind of upper-middle-class Black family, while providing no map of behavior and attitudes for interacting with African Americans outside of these boundaries.[116] Sitcoms like *Will & Grace* or *Modern Family* similarly helped change American ideas about gays and lesbians, and films such as *Philadelphia* (1993) instructed Americans to feel empathy for victims of HIV/AIDS.

This is not to say that middlebrow literature *caused* societal change on its own.[117] Rather, the books and magazine articles analyzed in *Postwar Stories* furnished an arena for articulating and questioning explanations of postwar American Jews and Judaism. Readers of Introduction to Judaism literature wrote to authors and editors, affirming the explanations offered, providing their own interpretations, or requesting clarification. They also spoke to their friends and families about what they read. In this way, Jewish postwar stories became part of readers' encounters with Jews and antisemitism, functioning in conversation with other texts and experiences. For Jewish readers, the literary genres analyzed here provided the experience of having their identity recognized by popular culture. As Charles Taylor observes, "we are formed by recognition," and thus, identity is "partly shaped by recognition or its absence, often by the *mis*recognition of others, and so a person or group of people can suffer real damage, real distortion, if the people or society around them mirror back to them a confining or demeaning or contemptible picture of themselves."[118] As we will discover, the depictions of Jews in anti-antisemitism and Introduction to Judaism literature were capable of reassuring or harming Jewish readers, depending on the associations and emotions they evoked. For young people coming of age in the late 1940s, reading a popular novel about antisemitism that became an Academy Award–winning film, or encountering a *Life* magazine story about Judaism could make a strong impression on their understanding of the significance of antisemitism and Judaism in American culture. As Melani McAlister has shown in her scholarship about the Middle East, popular culture matters when studying American attitudes because books, magazine articles, and films provide an intimacy to otherwise foreign subjects, making them personally meaningful to readers and viewers.[119]

As Jews moved from a status of marginalized racial group to being perceived as members of an American religion, several observers noted the role of popular culture.[120] Two such commentators, Marshall Sklare, a sociologist of Jews, and Ted Solotaroff, an editor and critic, observed:

> Not so very long ago . . . books that dealt with Jewish characters and themes went begging for publishers; today there is reason to assent to the frequent observation, most recently made by Robert Lowell, that "Jewishness is the theme of our literary culture in somewhat the same fashion that Middle Western and Southern writing occupied this position in earlier decades." Nor is this merely a matter of the Bellows and Malamuds and Roths; the popularity of Harry Golden a few years ago as a native American wit, a sort of Jewish Will Rogers, the movement of Jewish theater from Second Avenue to both Broadway and off Broadway, as well as the staggering sales of pop fiction, such as *Marjorie Morningstar* and *Exodus*, are perhaps even more decisive examples of a public acceptance that borders on courtship.[121]

The courtship did not last, however, or at least not with the ardor that had characterized the two decades following World War II. In the 1950s, some Americans may have patted themselves on the back for recognizing that Jews and Catholics deserved a place at the table of American religions, but by the late 1960s, they also realized that a mainstream made up of white Protestants, Catholics, and Jews was not nearly sufficiently inclusive to accommodate the country's diversity. If each generation's maturity is achieved, in part, by recognizing lies propagated by preceding generations, the last third of the twentieth century inherited, and began to untangle, a thorny mess of midcentury myths. Those myths included the ones suggested by the nation's vaunted Judeo-Christian heritage and its message that Jews and Christians had always made up the religious mainstream of America.[122] *The Myth of the Judeo-Christian Tradition*, published first as an essay in 1969 and written by Arthur A. Cohen, profiled in chapter 8, was one of several signs that the national mood was shifting.[123] Ideas that seemed capable of uniting the country at midcentury, such as organized religion, American exceptionalism, and Judeo-Christianity, had become divisive. By the late 1960s, the civil rights movement, the 1965 Immigration Act, a changing perception of Israel in the wake of the 1967 Six-Day War, American Jewry's more solidly middle-class profile, and a societal centering of radicalism rather than liberalism affected understandings of pluralism in America, and Jews' position therein.[124]

Nathan Glazer's sly observation about the status of Judaism as a "most favored religion" was only slightly hyperbolic in its day. Seventy-plus years later, in the wake of a marked increase of antisemitism, Glazer's characterization of American Judaism has slipped into the realm of history. It is a reminder that the midcentury was a very different period in American religious history. And yet, the midcentury's legacy affects our contemporary moment, in part because of the work performed by Jewish middlebrow.

At a time when Americans still turned to books and magazines such as *Time* and *Life* to learn about the world, middlebrow writers created new texts for those interested in learning about Jews. A glimpse at how this midcentury Jewish literature changed American attitudes can be seen in the letters to the editor that appeared in the summer of 1955 after *Life* ran its most extensive photo essay about Judaism. The very fact of a major photojournalistic article about Judaism, with a full cover-page image, should be cited as evidence of a transformation in popular media's attention to Jews.

It bears noting that both Jews and non-Jews wrote to the magazine to express their appreciation, criticism, and questions about the article. The Orthodox rabbi and president of Yeshiva University Samuel Belkin praised it, as did a Jewish housewife in Cleveland, Ohio, who wrote, "It gave me great pleasure to read Life's article on Judaism. I felt at home with all the rituals and ceremonies you described and it gave me a warm feeling to be part of such a great history."[125] The reader articulated what many writers of middlebrow hoped to elicit: identification and reassurance.

Even when readers disagreed with the article, their criticism furthered the public discussion of Judaism, pushing the magazine toward greater specificity and accuracy, as when the Orthodox rabbi Hayim Donin of Detroit, Michigan, wrote to correct *Life* on their explanation of the Jewish laws of Kashrut:

The supreme motive behind the dietary laws is described in the words of Maimonides: "The Dietary Laws train us in the mastery over our appetites; they accustom us to restrain both the growth of desire and the disposition to consider pleasure of eating and drinking as the end of man's existence."[126]

The meaning behind Kashrut and the teachings of Maimonides had not previously been a topic of discussion in the pages of *Life*. But now they were. And in the coming decades, Donin would go on to write his own Introduction to Judaism books, including *To Be a Jew: A Guide to Jewish Observance in Contemporary Life* and *To Pray as a Jew: A Guide to the Prayer Book and the Synagogue Service*. Had the 1955 *Life* Judaism article served as inspiration for the Detroit rabbi? Rabbi Donin was one of many readers discovering through midcentury middlebrow Jewish literature that Americans were interested in stories about Jews and Judaism.

1
From Race to Religion and the Challenge of Antisemitism

To understand the rise of the two genres at the heart of *Postwar Stories*—1940s *anti*-antisemitism novels attacking discrimination against Jews and Introduction to Judaism genres explaining Judaism—it is helpful to comprehend the attitudes they were combating. During the first decades of the twentieth century, antisemitism in its many variants was the major impediment to recognition of Judaism as an American religion. For the non-Jewish majority culture, Jews represented one of several obstacles to the United States' fully realizing its promise as a Christian country.

With World War I and the shock of entering an international conflict, Americans donned a new patriotic garb. It was one of conformity and 100 per cent Americanism.[1] Americans of the 1910s and 1920s took to blaming others for World War I and seeking stability in isolation.[2] Rejecting the recently founded League of Nations and working to end immigration became means of cutting ties with foreign lands.[3] In this post–World War I context of distrust, "the Jew was not only a Christ-killer or a boor or a Semite," one rabbi observed in the early 1920s, "he was also an alien and a radical, an international banker and an enemy of gentile civilization."[4] Feelings of disillusionment from World War I and the "100 percent Americanism" generated by the passions of war galvanized nationalism and suspicion that erupted in the Red Scare of 1919–1920, the Henry Ford mania, the rise of the Second Ku Klux Klan, and anti-radicalism.[5] The international ties of Catholics and Jews, and the charge of "race suicide" among "old stock" Americans, became common in the wake of the First World War, along with urban race riots.[6]

By this point, negative images of Jews had long been in circulation. Even in the 1850s, Rabbi Isaac M. Wise explained that one of his motivations for publishing his magazine, the *American Israelite*, was that the image of "a rascally Jew" could be found "in every cheap novel, every newspaper printed some stale jokes about Jews to fill up space, and every backwoodsman had a few jokes on hand to use in public addresses; and all this called forth not one word of protest from any source."[7] These negative stereotypes of Jews were revived in the early twentieth century when the Jew was seen as "the international banker, but also the inflamed radical responsible for Communist revolution in eastern Europe. Above all, he was the agent of a vast conspiracy designed to enslave America."[8]

Such images suggested that in the view of antisemites, Jewishness was more of an economic identity than a religious one.[9] As anti-immigration activists argued for the restriction of Eastern and Southern European immigration during the early 1920s, they pointed to what they perceived as the purely economic motivations of the new immigrants: a reporter for the *Saturday Evening Post* opined in 1921 that "the tremendous movement of peoples from Europe to America which is in progress . . . is purely, simply, and solely an economic movement. It is a movement that must not be misrepresented by sentimentalists and near-Americans as being a movement of oppressed people in search of religious or any other freedom."[10] The ancestors of legitimate Americans were inspired by the higher principles of religious freedom, ran this argument. Jews were motivated by money.

With the rise of eugenics and racialized thinking, Jewish difference was "increasingly articulated in racial terms as a hard boundary set in body and blood."[11] As anti-immigrant sentiment mounted in the 1910s and 1920s, white Protestants' desire to preserve their vision of America took center stage. "The question of restriction is not selfishness at all," Congressman Albert Johnson, a coauthor of the 1924 Johnson-Reed immigration law, asserted. "It is the law of self-preservation."[12] His, as it turned out, was also the law that prevented many European Jews from preserving their own lives during the 1930s and 1940s.[13]

After the drafting of the 1924 immigration act, Jews and other opponents challenged its definition of Americanism. "Were Jesus and his twelve disciples on earth today, they would have to cast lots as to which one of them would have the privilege of coming to the United States," Rabbi Stephen S. Wise declared in a January 1924 address.[14] But these voices of dissent merely sounded un-American to those who believed in their mission to "keep America American," as President Calvin Coolidge's campaigning famously phrased the effort to keep immigrants out of the country.[15] Such efforts to free the country from immigrants were nothing new. This xenophobia was "not the occasional mild fever in the US. It was a chronic, debilitating illness," as Thomas Leonard observes.[16]

When the headline "America of the Melting Pot Comes to an End" appeared in the *New York Times* in the spring of 1924, the article explained the positive consequences of the new legislation: "It will mean a more homogenous nation, more self-reliant, more independent and more closely knit by common purpose and common ideals."[17] The statement revealed the premium placed on conformity. In the coming decade, that impulse to safeguard white Christian America led to charges of "Bolshevist," "un-American," and "alien" being leveled at President Roosevelt's New Deal, or what was sometimes referred to as his "Jew Deal," because of Jewish involvement in the government program.[18]

The Great Depression and the country's need for scapegoats spurred a national antisemitic mood. Within a decade, surveys of American attitudes in 1938 and 1940 found that the most prominent among Jewish stereotypes was that of the Jew as an economic man: "an individual desirous and well qualified to get ahead financially, eager to compete in the race for economic success and willing to employ all possible means toward this end."[19] Popular culture cemented these disparaging associations. As Michael Dobkowski has argued, negative stereotypes of Jews were presented in respectable publications in a spirit of objectivity by influential individuals, thus serving as "a catalyst for the proliferation of anti-Jewish manifestations in America."[20]

During the first four decades of the twentieth century, when many Americans had never met an actual Jew, there were too few countervailing images to balance the barrage of antisemitism permeating American culture. A generalized fear of immigrants as agents of crime, immorality, and radicalism often focused on Jews, especially in cities such as New York, where Jews were more conspicuous than other immigrant groups, because of language, religious practice, and garb.[21] When Nazism rose in Europe in the 1930s, Americans had reached a point of acceptance and even approval of antisemitism.[22] In this context it was nearly unthinkable to accept Jews as members of a religion with moral precepts the equal of Christianity.

When Antisemitism Was Part of the Novel

The view of Jews as an alien threat to good Americanism found plenty of literary expression during the first half of the twentieth century. A keen observer of high society, bestselling author Edith Wharton imbibed Old New York's desires to keep its gates closed to Jews, the better to safeguard its age of innocence from rapacious arrivistes. In her 1905 novel, *The House of Mirth*, Lily Bart recognizes that no matter his wealth, Mr. Rosedale, as a Jew, would remain forever "the same little Jew who has been served up and rejected at the social board a dozen times within her memory."[23] In the 1920s, the upper crust continued to excel at snobbish xenophobia, in reality and in fiction. An example was F. Scott Fitzgerald's 1922 novel, *The Beautiful and the Damned*, in which the moneyed Anthony Patch discerns the threat of a growing urban Jewish population while reading "a dozen Jewish names on a line of stores; in the door of each stood a dark little man watching the passers from intent eyes—eyes gleaming with suspicion, with pride, with clarity, with cupidity, with comprehension.... The slow upward creep of this people—the little stores, growing expanding."[24] Fitzgerald's more famous novel, *The Great Gatsby* (1925), bore witness to a Jewish threat to Protestant women whose insecurity made them susceptible to the seductions of wealthy Jewish men.[25]

In 1929, William Faulkner's commercially successful *The Sound and the Fury* suggested that while some Jews might be considered faithful adherents of the Jewish religion, a more accurate conception of Jews was as members of a parasitic race. In a conversation about farmers, a character wonders why farmers work so hard. "And what for?" He asks. "So a bunch of dam eastern jews [*sic*] I'm not talking about men of the jewish religion.... I've known some jews that were fine citizens." He clarified, "'I have nothing against jews as an individual.... It's just the race. You'll admit that they produce nothing. They follow the pioneers into a new country and sell them clothes.'"[26] Echoing nineteenth-century European disparaging views of ghetto Jews—that helped to birth the Zionist idea of the New Jew—Faulkner's characters concluded that real Americans plowed the land, while the Jewish race made money off them.[27] Faulkner thus made his own entry into the 1920s discussion of Jewishness as race. In his formulation, individual religious Jews deserved respect for having overcome the negative characteristics of the Jewish race.

Tellingly, it was in the postwar years—coinciding with the attitudinal changes described in this book—that critics re-examined some of these literary expressions of antisemitism in light of shifting sensibilities. In 1947, Milton Hindus, a literary scholar at the University of Chicago and soon to be one of Brandeis University's first faculty members—published his essay "F. Scott Fitzgerald and Literary Anti-Semitism: A Footnote on the mind of the 20's" in *Commentary*.[28] Hindus analyzed Fitzgerald's portrayal of his Jewish character, Meyer Worsheim, concluding that Fitzgerald did not allow any redeeming characteristics into his Jewish gambler, "not even so much redemption as Shakespeare allows to Shylock in his dominantly villainous portrait."[29] But it was not as simple as *The Great Gatsby* being a "piece of propaganda against the Jews," Hindus explained.[30] Hindus wanted to set the record straight: "*Anti-Semitism is a component part of the novel*," he wrote.[31] And Hindus wasn't the only one who felt the time was right for reassessing antisemitic classics of the 1920s. Arthur Scott, a Princeton-educated English professor, penned an "In Defense of Robert Cohn" essay in 1957.[32] Scott's essay offered a corrective to the antisemitism that Ernest Hemingway displayed in his portrayal of Robert Cohn in *The Sun Also Rises* (1926). Reminding readers that as a Jew, Hemingway's character, Robert Cohn "suffered the anguish of the socially displaced," Scott explained that Cohn deserved sympathy—if not in 1926, when the novel was published, then a generation later when Scott's essay was written. Midcentury changes in attitudes toward Jews affected even literary criticism. Scott also noted that the first Bantam paperback edition of *The Sun Also Rises* in 1949 deleted all the antisemitic comments about Cohn from the original Hemingway novel. It was a stark example of the new standards of permissible commentary about Jews in the postwar era.

Not Quite Religion

Even with an ocean separating them from Hitler, American Jews felt newly visible as a minority group during the 1930s and 1940s, as news of Nazi persecution heightened their sense of kinship with European Jews.[33] The stirrings of pride evoked by the establishment of the state of Israel in 1948 added to a feeling of a shared communal experience with Jews around the world that did not necessarily require religious affiliation.[34]

In both midcentury Jewish middlebrow genres, this not-just-a-religion quality of Jewishness coexisted alongside authors' efforts to make the case for Judaism as an American religion. Characters in anti-antisemitism novels discussed the complicated nature of Jewishness, and Introduction to Judaism books presented multiple ways of defining Judaism, as when Milton Steinberg began *Basic Judaism* (1947) thus: "Sometimes it denotes a full civilization.... In this significance, it embraces secular as well as sacred elements, for example, the love songs of medieval Hebrew poets, the folk music and dance of East European Jewries, social institutions of all sorts and much else." In his Introduction to Judaism book *What Is a Jew?* (1953), Morris

Kertzer wrote: "It is difficult to find a single definition of a Jew," and then proceeded to define cultural, ethnic, and religious definitions of Jewishness, finally adding that, "*The Jews are not a race*" (emphasis in the original).[35] For Kertzer as for other authors, this matter of what Judaism was not—a race— was an important point to impart to readers.

The meaning of race changed over time, but during the first half of the twentieth century, it was used interchangeably with categories including ethnicity, nationality, type, stock, and group.[36] In this book, "race" refers to the human categorization that Americans deemed scientific during the first half of the twentieth century.[37] In the 1920s and 1930s, Americans viewed human races as observable from the look of someone's hair, skin, nose, and lips and analogous to animal pedigrees and stocks. But race wasn't only a matter of appearance. As Charles King observes, "Every race seemed to come prepackaged with its own ways of speaking, eating, dancing, and dressing."[38] Physical ability, intelligence, language, and level of civilization were also connected to race, with inequalities between the races taken for granted. By the late 1930s, it was clear, too, that Americans associated race with persecution. Midcentury social scientists found that in avoiding close personal relations and intermarriage with Jews, Americans treated Jews "not like Frenchmen or Methodists"—and therefore, not as members of a nationality or religion—"but like Negroes," and therefore Americans saw connections between Blacks and Jews because both were members of marginalized groups.[39] The treatment of Jews by the larger society thus influenced American perceptions of Jews as a race.

In the 1920s and 1930s, immigration restrictions, university quotas, and hiring discrimination impinging on American Jewish life had little if anything to do with a Jew's religious observance. It was ethnic, national, tribal, and especially racial categorization of Jews that had the most practical meaning for Jews. "More than any other term for self-definition," it was race that provided a "feeling of community and connection to other Jews, something that they sorely needed in times of greater tension and uncertainty," historian Eric Goldstein observes.[40] In the wake of communal experiences during the first half of the twentieth century, midcentury Jews felt the relevance of categories including, culture, nation, and race. But by the late 1940s they could also read the writing on the wall: postwar Americans clearly favored religion as the category by which to define acceptable difference. Had not President Roosevelt spoken movingly of the freedom of worship as one of the "four freedoms" in his 1941 State of the

Union Address?[41] The trope of religious freedom was evident throughout World War II, with the nation's commemoration of the 1942 sinking of the courageous "four chaplains"—two Protestants, a Catholic, and a Jew—aboard the SS *Dorchester* sounding another note in support of the idea of the United States as a tri-faith nation.[42] With the onset of the Cold War, American Jews understood which part of their identity to accentuate, as the rhetoric of religious freedom helped Jews "escape the stigma of racial minority status and eased their acceptance into the racial privileges of whiteness in American life," in the words of one religion scholar.[43] The language of religion enabled Jews to exercise their advantages as white Americans: to secure respectability for their distinctive heritage.[44] The opportunities that flowed from being considered an American religion were unmistakable; all other categories raised the specter of more threatening kinds of Jewish differences.[45]

The mid-twentieth-century recasting of Jewishness as religion came, like its nineteenth-century American and European emancipation-era precedents, with its own pitfalls. As Tisa Wenger has shown, religious freedom was a double-edged sword for minority groups such as Jews and Indigenous Americans: "It worked against other models for being Jewish, such as the emerging framework of ethnicity."[46] Alternative ways of understanding Jewishness did not disappear in the late 1940s and 1950s. Jewishness as nationality, ethnicity, culture, and even racial identity continued to surface, reminding readers of the ways Jews were different.[47] But the tenacity of these other ways of categorizing Jews also pushed writers—and sometimes readers—all the more strongly, to insist on the religion designation. By the 1950s, assimilatory factors made religion the preferred category, leading to the conclusion by one midcentury sociologist that "collectively, American Jews regard themselves as first of all a religious community."[48]

For Jews unsure about their commitment to Judaism, the religion category had the benefit of being associated with freedom of choice. Choice fit the American context, for the United States was a country without an established church, and where "One was not born into a Jewish community, as in Europe, but affiliated—or not—with a particular synagogue. Religion was less a heritage carried with little reflection from generation to generation than a conscious voluntary choice," as Michael Meyer observes.[49] By the late 1950s, that shift to thinking about *why* one should be a Jew left its mark on Introduction to Judaism literature, which previously had focused on answering questions such as, "*What* is Judaism?" Like other educated choices of democratic citizens, choosing Judaism—or choosing to it practice in a particular way—required its own literature.

Overcoming Race

Decades of seeing the world through the lens of race permeated midcentury Americans' thinking about Jews. It was not that religion played no part in American conceptions of Jews prior to the midcentury. The interfaith Goodwill Movement of the 1910s and 1920s that birthed the National Conference of Christians and Jews, for example, was informed by a religious conception of Judaism.[50] But in these early decades of the twentieth century, Americans promoting tolerance between Protestants, Catholics, and Jews—such as the "Tolerance Trios" of ministers, priests, and rabbis traveling the United States during the 1930s—were consciously moving against a tide of public opinion that perceived Jews as members of an inferior race.[51]

Even in the 1940s, as eugenics was taking on a malodorous reputation in light of Hitler's racial laws, the pseudoscience lingered in American culture and thought. In 1942, President Roosevelt assigned a Smithsonian scientist to work on a study of the effect of racial crossing. The scientist, a Czech anthropologist, "fielded the President's questions about Japanese 'racial characteristics'—nefariousness, for example, and trickiness, and ruthlessness—and was only too eager to reinforce FDR's notion that the development of the Japanese cranium accounted for these traits."[52] In 1944, "Eugenic factors for mate selection" was listed as a topic of instruction in *A Design for General Education for Members of the Armed Forces* issued by the American Council on Education Studies.[53] And a *New York Times* book review with the headline, "What You Should Know about Eugenics," suggested that there were still important things to understand about this fake science.[54]

Race-thinking also affected Jews' understandings of their Jewishness. When, in 1933, Reform rabbi Stephen S. Wise reflected on his inability to focus on the religious aspects of Judaism—because of the greater urgency of racial persecution of Jews in both Europe and the United States—he lamented that racial identity had eclipsed religious identity for American Jews.[55] "I have as much right to be a teacher as has Dr. Holmes, Dr. Fosdick, the Cardinal or the Bishop," Wise remarked, referring to his fellow New York City clergymen.[56] "But I am obsessed by an attitude of self-defense forced on me by the Nazi persecution. I cannot think. I cannot meditate. I am a teacher forced to be an unarmed policeman defending my German coreligionists." Nazi persecution of Jews had pressured rabbis such as Wise into focusing on communal self-defense, often at the cost of making religion their primary concern, which now seemed a luxury reserved for white, Christian clergy. And yet, resentment about not being able to focus on Jewish religion demonstrated awareness of the multiple ways to think about Jewishness.

Striving to Move beyond Negativity

The writings examined in the rest of this chapter demonstrate the difficulty of being Jewish during the 1920s and 1930s without feeling the despair that came from contemplating denigrating views of Jewishness. The psychosocial dynamic of absorbing and reacting to discrimination was not confined to the midcentury, nor to Jews.[57] As a discourse it was timeless and protean, responding to different historical and cultural settings. In the 1920s, 1930s, and 1940s, but also in the postwar era, and on into the twenty-first century, American writers described the process of experiencing antisemitism, in fiction and in nonfiction. The language changed over time: "alienation," "marginalization," and "stigmatization" were among the terms employed at different points in history. But as this chapter demonstrates, this theme was especially salient between the 1920s and the 1940s.[58] By the 1940s and 1950s, authors of anti-antisemitism and Introduction to Judaism texts sought to free Jews from demeaning self-images. Their attempts did not always succeed.

But it wasn't only antisemitism itself that was so dispiriting; the solutions offered by American Jews were themselves discouraging. Large segments of American Jewry seemed to believe that they could act their way out of antisemitism. If they were only *not quite so Jewish*, ran this logic, they might earn gentile praise.

Rabbi Milton Steinberg (1903–1950) was one Jewish leader grappling with the emotional experience and existential questions that antisemitism raised. Steinberg's 1936 article "The Jew Faces Anti-Semitism" addressed a problem he saw devastating American Jews like a plague. Although much was written about antisemitism, Steinberg reflected, Jews' emotional response to the "all-enveloping hostility" directed at them was too often neglected.[59] This was a typical Steinberg concern: the emotional lives and psychological well-being of Jews. Steinberg explained that one of the dangers of antisemitism is "what it does to the Jew as a human being, in its effects on his morale, self-respect and sense of worth."[60] Steinberg detailed the American Jewish experience of antisemitism: "Except for their Jewishness the student might be admitted to a school of medicine, the instructor might be a professor, the little girl would be enrolled in a fashionable finishing school, and the suburbanites might be members of the local golf club."[61] He concluded, "Were they not Jews, they would have lived a fuller, freer life."[62]

How did Jews respond to this predicament? To Steinberg's consternation, he found they became overly self-conscious. Feeling that "they must acquire impeccable manners," such Jews believed that "Once their etiquette is beyond reproach, their problem will be solved. The Gentile, no longer annoyed by exhibitions of vulgarity, soothed now by the smooth, easy graces of the refashioned Jew, will decide that Jews are decent, well-behaved human beings."[63] If only they could change Jewish behavior, such Jews reasoned, they might lessen the blows of antisemitism. Steinberg lamented this over-scrutinizing of Jewish comportment, for "it means that Jews will be unable to live naturally. Nor can Jews be expected to maintain a wholesome regard for themselves if they are convinced that Jewishness is something unpleasant, something to be toned down, suppressed and sloughed."[64]

The strategy of Jewish self-improvement was not without basis. Even liberal non-Jews conceded the point. In the pages of *The Nation*, a leading left-wing magazine, a non-Jewish writer elaborated on the implicit compromise that society demanded of Jews during the 1920s:

> With a quite unconscious arrogance the friendly non-Jew has tended to demand more and more from the Jew, as though the bargain could never be complete. He has said to the Jew; "Now that you are free from the restrictions and the terrorism of the Ghetto, you must put aside as rapidly as you can your queer Ghetto ways, your absurd and inconvenient taboos, your un-Western legalistic religion. . . . If you can manage it, you'd better 'reform' your synagogue even though it is the most ancient of all living institutions; or better still, perhaps you can manage to forsake the synagogue and drift into one of the numerous minor groups in which we peculiarly abound, like Christian Science or the Ethical Culture movement."[65]

Had they been "true liberals . . . instead of pseudo-liberals," the writer admitted, the proper response to Jews would have been to fight "for a place for him in Western Society unassimilated; we should have said (what is only the truth) that the pattern of modern life would be richer because of the Jew, and that his right to be Jewish and colorful and different was just as sacred a right as any other."[66] But this was a minority view, and its public utterances were rare.

As depressing as it was, this "doctrine of Jewish salvation according to the revelation of Emily Post," as Steinberg called the American Jewish concern to behave right, referring to the nineteenth-century-born socialite and writer of etiquette guides—was not all that surprising.[67] In the pages of the *Atlantic Monthly*, a Jewish writer put the matter in the negative: "Let us face realities. A single Jew has the power to cast odium on the whole race. A single Jewish banker lends credence to the absurd notion that all Jews are rich; a single Jewish Communist gives rise to the cry that all Jews are bent on destroying the government."[68] Jews seemed to be at fault for their own persecution.

A Fake Science to Fuel the Fire of Bigotry

During the first four decades of the twentieth century, most Americans did not regard antisemitism as a national problem. Until the second half of the twentieth century, it was not at all clear that Americans believed that victims of antisemitism deserved sympathy—much less that integrating Jews into the American mainstream might benefit the nation as well as the Jews. In the early 1940s, Jews continued to receive reminders that they were not even considered fully human. In 1943, Reform rabbi and scholar Joshua Trachtenberg observed that the success of contemporary antisemitic demagogues rested, in part, on the idea that the Jew is "less than human, indeed, antihuman."[69] Trachtenberg related a friend's recent experience with North American prejudice: the friend parked his car in a small French Canadian town when two children approached and peered into the car windows. "'C'est un Juif,' declared the older and wiser, after a moment's consideration. 'Mais non,' protested the other in his innocence, 'Ce n'est pas un Juif; c'est un homme.'"[70] It was demoralizing for intellectuals such as Trachtenberg to discover that their very humanity was in question. But this was far from the only maleficent thought directed at Jews. Indeed, in the mid-1940s, social scientists found that Americans blamed the increase in antisemitism "mainly on the Jews' own supposed characteristics."[71] Greed, dishonesty, and excessive power, especially in the economic field, were among those characteristics.[72]

Even the war itself and revelations about the Nazi horrors did not influence American attitudes toward Jews, leading one group of social scientists to conclude that "the wartime revelations concerning Nazi persecution of Jews ... seem to have had no lasting effect on the attitudes of the public toward Jews. As the horrors receded in time, their impact, such as it was, evoked less and less sympathy for the Jews."[73] A 1946 study of American attitudes revealed that "the war made us conscious" of Jews.[74] But this spotlight on Jews may have actually encouraged hostility.

That Jews were categorized as a racial group in addition to a religious group compounded Americans' lack of empathy. In the minds of many gentiles, Jews' racial otherness overshadowed their religious affiliation. Thus, antisemitism abutted racism at a time when racism was deemed socially legitimate and supported by the science of eugenics, particularly in the early twentieth century. "Eugenic ideas were politically influential, culturally fashionable, and scientifically mainstream," Thomas Leonard observes of the first three decades of the twentieth century.[75] Biology curricula at all levels included eugenics and "the elite sprinkled their conversations with eugenic concerns to signal their *au courant* high-mindedness."[76] Embedded in American thought, this faux-science fueled antisemitism and racism into the 1930s and beyond.[77]

Like anti-Black racism, racist antisemitism found cultural backing in the idea that Jews, like Blacks, were racially inferior to the Anglo-Saxon establishment.[78] In the 1940s, Rabbi Milton Steinberg looked back on the particular appeal of racist antisemitism in the preceding decades:

> It is perfectly suited to the purposes for which it was designed. It converts an irrational prejudice into a kind of social hygiene. It transforms the anti-Semite from a hoodlum into a physician fighting a dread disease. . . . It is in sum, in everything except truthfulness and tenability, the perfect apologia for anti-Semitism, that ideal rationalization after which the hate driven have been groping for a century and more.[79]

The American eugenics movement behind this racist antisemitism created *believers*, not evidence, as Ibram X. Kendi writes of the 1910s.[80] Americans were already discriminating against people due to their race, gender, or class and were seeking external reasons to support the regnant social hierarchy. The North proved fertile ground for the white supremacist terrorist group Ku Klux Klan to expand its racism beyond Blacks to include those with immigrant backgrounds in ways that dated back to the nativist political party, the Know Nothings of the mid-nineteenth century (named for their response to outsiders' questions about their activities). In the 1920s nativist worldview, Jews were cast as threats to American values, "diabolically clever communists even as they were rapacious money-grubbers squeezing money out of virtuous Protestants."[81] Jews at the time were strongly associated with radical politics, communism, and inner-city immorality, which further exacerbated bigotry. Even stories of exceptional Jews, such as Louis Brandeis, Felix Frankfurter, and Oscar Straus, seemed to reinforce the idea that most Jews could *not* make it in America during the first half of the century.

The prevalence of what today is called a "blame the victim" mentality in American culture—spanning everything from rape, bullying, and domestic violence—bolstered this entrenched antisemitism as Jews were seen as deserving their low status and abuse.[82] "Where there is so much smoke, there must be some fire," the Jewish writer Ludwig Lewisohn explained of gentiles' attitudes toward antisemitism, with their intimations of Jewish responsibility for having provoked the ire of non-Jews.[83] Public opinion polls showed that Americans agreed: a 1938 Gallup poll revealed that nearly two-thirds believed that European Jews were at least partly responsible for their persecution under the Nazis.[84] In considering the impact of 1947 films exposing the evils of antisemitism, the American Jewish Committee expressed concern that "Throughout history the popular response to highlighting the Jews as the outstanding victims of intolerance has been: 'Such unpopularity must be deserved; millions of critics can't be wrong.'"[85] Sensitive to the country's ambient antisemitism, Jews absorbed the message that they were likely to be blamed for the hatred directed against them. When Rabbi Steinberg surveyed common Jewish responses to antisemitism in the early 1940s, he observed: "Common to all the folk strategies are a premise and an inference: the premise that Jews are themselves responsible for the ills they endure, and the inference that their position can be improved only by modifying their behavior."[86]

That observation held true for a 1940s Jewish mother writing in the pages of the middlebrow *Parents'* magazine during World War II. She wanted her children to consider the possibility that criticism of Jews might be based on reality, and that they could change these unflattering truths. Teaching her children that criticism sometimes merited consideration, she posed the rhetorical question, "Do we really talk too much, dress too ostentatiously, go around with chips on our shoulders? Perhaps we do. Perhaps we should let ourselves be instructed in ways more attractive to the general community; perhaps that would be an important step in breaking down the barriers between us."[87] In the spirit of "the doctrine of Jewish salvation according to the revelation of Emily Post," she advised her children that Jews could improve themselves, for "manners spring from life itself; ours are the result of the nervous tension in which our race has been forced to live; and some day when we have less to worry us, we will be calmer, more casual, more like people who have led easier lives than ours for generations."[88] With more empathy than the gentiles who applied similar logic, she explained to her children that Jews' painful history was the unfortunate cause of their bad behavior.

Where there was an understanding among Jews that self-improvement could lessen the hatred directed against them, there was also a belief that they could leave behind their victim status. This desire for betterment would find its way into the anti-antisemitism literature of the 1940s.

A Discourse of Illness and Disability

To be seen as "less than" is often to experience oneself in the same negative light. These feelings of Jewish inferiority were a popular subject for rabbis, Jewish communal leaders, and writers to address. "Because of our Judaism we must be prepared to give up some of the world's goods even as we must be prepared to make sacrifices because of other disadvantages with which we may happen to be born," Harvard professor Harry Wolfson wrote in 1921— as though Judaism were analogous to a birth defect.[89] Wolfson may have meant this only half seriously, but that half is important. His is a powerful and early twentieth-century expression of Jewishness as illness.

In his accomplishments and career, Wolfson was unusual. Born in Ostrin, Lithuania, in 1887 and educated at the Slabodka Yeshiva, he emigrated with his family to the United States at age sixteen. Continuing his education at New York's Rabbi Isaac Elchanan Theological Seminary, he went on to teach Hebrew school in Scranton, Pennsylvania.[90] At age twenty-one, he arrived at Harvard, where he earned his undergraduate and doctoral degrees. In 1915, Wolfson joined the Harvard faculty and spent the rest of his career there. He had left a traditional Jewish upbringing to pursue academics and achieved unusual success.

Wolfson's experience of antisemitism differed from that of urban, early twentieth-century Jews who spent their entire lives in more densely Jewish settings. Even by 1950, the *American Jewish Year Book* reported Jews' tendency to seek employment from other Jews and from employers known to be friendly to Jews, rather than in the gentile milieus that characterized Wolfson's academic career.[91] In a 1921 essay for the *Menorah Journal*, a leading American-Jewish literary and intellectual magazine founded in 1915 by Jewish Harvard students, Wolfson described the loneliness and despair of Jews who had abandoned religious homes only to find themselves spiritually adrift in an unfriendly world.[92]

In his 1921 essay, Wolfson wrote, "All men are not born equal. Some are born blind, some deaf, some lame, and some are born Jews."[93] His writing offers a window onto the feelings of Jews who had attained the highest levels of secular success and yet found themselves searching for guidance to cope with the ramifications of their Jewishness. Their accomplishments did not end their struggles with antisemitism. Reaching a professional zenith brought more acute awareness of the unlikeliness of finding acceptance as a Jew. Wolfson's writing is a reminder that the dynamics at play among Jews in the mid-twentieth century were not unprecedented. American Jews reflected on antisemitism and its effects before the 1940s, as Wolfson's example shows, although the midcentury witnessed broader societal reckoning with antisemitism than earlier eras.

It is almost painful, today, to read Wolfson's dim view of Jewishness. But his was not the first metaphor of Jewishness as disability. As Charles Silberman observed, the comparison was made a century earlier by the German Jewish writer Heinrich Heine, who wrote, "Those who would say that Judaism is a religion would say that being a hunchback is a religion. Judaism is not a religion but a misfortune."[94] When Wolfson compared Jewishness with a disability in 1921, his words captured the experience of Jewishness as burden and illness that was not uncommon, even among those who, like Wolfson, achieved both secular success and a deep understanding of Judaism by virtue of an in-depth religious education. For the young, intellectual Jews in Wolfson's orbit, Jewishness was a problem that required a solution. Although Wolfson titled his essay "Escaping Judaism," he espoused resignation and acceptance of Jewishness. "Are we willing to submit to Fate, or shall we foolishly struggle against it?" Wolfson rhetorically asked his Jewish readers.[95]

During the 1920s, Jewish readers may have recognized themselves in Wolfson's words and in his description of the "adulation of and yearning for Christianity," typical among intellectual Jews in his orbit. But his essay also looked to deeper causes. Wolfson concluded that the yearning to escape Jewishness arose from the difference between the "incomplete, chaotic, and frayed life of the Jew of today" and "the peaceful, harmonious and normal Christian life around us."[96] The problem, as Wolfson saw it, was that serenity was associated with Christianity. In this era before Judaism and Jewishness were mainstreamed and normalized, in part through middlebrow culture, "Jewish life in the modern Gentile world is an anomaly," he noted, resulting in a host of negative feelings about Jewishness.[97]

In the first half of the twentieth century, the discourse of Jewishness as illness and liability was pervasive, with examples coming from the pens of rabbis, Jewish writers, gentile observers of Jews, middle-class Jews seeking name changes, and wealthy Jews.[98] Understandings of Jewishness, race, and pluralism would change during these four decades, but the metaphors of disability showed surprising staying power. Even in the late twentieth and early twenty-first centuries, novelists, social scientists, and historians of Jews would employ this discourse in discussions of Jewishness.[99] Jewish novelist Emma Wolfe (1865–1932) used a similar metaphor in her novel *Heirs of Yesterday* (1900), in which being born a Jew is referred to as a "life-sentence," and "a misfortune."[100] A 1908 *Atlantic Monthly* article, "The Social Disability of the Jew," described a "racial disability" leading to social exclusion.[101] Rabbi Mordecai M. Kaplan observed in his 1934 book *Judaism as a Civilization* that "in accounting for this sense of inferiority and self-contempt which is eating like a canker into the Jewish soul, it is usual to point to the fact that Jews find their Jewishness a handicap to them in all walks of life."[102] Kaplan recalled a "prominent American Jewish woman," who said, "I would have asked God to make me a Gentile, but since I had no choice I pray to Him to help me be a good Jew."[103] In 1930, when two non-Jewish journalists embarked on *"Christians Only" The Story of Anti-Semitism in America*, a study of American antisemitism, the authors turned to the same discourse of Jewishness as disability: "What terrific obstacles the Jew has to overcome. He starts out with the knowledge that he is gravely handicapped because he is a Jew and he realizes that he must try doubly hard to get a break to balance against his handicap."[104] Edna Ferber's semi-autobiographical 1917 novel, *Fanny, Herself*, included an exchange with a friendly priest in which Fanny acknowledged her Jewishness by saying, "Yes, I've got that handicap."[105] The discourse of disability also resonated with philosopher Horace Kallen, when he observed Jewish college students during the 1930s: "They give signs of an anti-Semitism peculiar to themselves; a hatred of that in themselves which handicaps them, so that they reject it with hearts and heads, even though they cannot in fact separate themselves from it, or it from themselves."[106] The novelist Herman Wouk could not ignore the discourse of disability either. Born in 1915, Wouk's long life afforded him a rare perspective on the changing American Jewish experience. When Wouk wrote *This Is My God*, in the late 1950s, he took note of a new Jewish pride, "despite the disabilities that come from many decades of ostracism."[107]

The rabbinate, too, registered this discourse. The writer and rabbi Mortimer J. Cohen of Philadelphia's Congregation Beth Sholom gave a 1933 address titled "Christian Only—Jewish Disabilities in the Modern World," in which he named antisemitism as the major disability Jews faced.[108] Rabbi Milton Steinberg, mentioned earlier, was also well acquainted with his congregants' perception of Jewishness as sickness: "Occasionally one meets a Jew in whom the malady is virulent, a Jew who literally hates Judaism, other Jews and himself," he wrote.[109] As historian Susan Glenn observes, Jewish self-hating discourse proliferated by the 1940s, becoming what some called "the neurosis" of the wartime generation, and a frequent topic of fiction.[110] In the early 1940s, the Jewish Reconstructionist movement defined its platform in response to the "malady of doubt and discouragement" among American Jews concerning their Jewishness.[111] Henry Morgenthau III, the son of FDR's Secretary of Treasury, recalled his parents' view of Jewishness as "a kind of birth defect that could not be eradicated, but with proper treatment, could be overcome, if not in this generation then probably in the next."[112]

Morgenthau's Jewish upbringing was very different from Wolfson's, but what they shared as adults was their experience of Jewishness as illness and burden. Wolfson's story is relevant because it shows both successes and low points experienced at a time when Jewishness was viewed as a burdensome fact of birth.[113] Quotas instituted in the 1920s made Jewish students at Harvard something of a rarity, and those who succeeded, as Wolfson had, in academic careers were even more unusual.[114] Wolfson's understanding that he was an acceptable Jew at Harvard so long as he conformed to unspoken rules was the norm among an elite minority. They had made it, yet they did not find social acceptance among gentiles. Aware that he was there under sufferance, Wolfson "went out of his way to prevent any embarrassment for Harvard University," never taking a public stand on issues, even when Harvard failed to welcome refugee professors during the Nazi era.[115] Neither did Wolfson risk exposing himself to judgment, personally or professionally—a difficult feat to pull off in academia. Wolfson "sought no honors, entered no competitions, but went his way. He would be the friendliest, and most courteous, and most cooperative of men if others sought him out. But he avoided occasions where he might put himself at the risk of personal rebuff."[116] A former student recalled Wolfson's habit of self-withdrawal: "Somewhere and sometime he had felt so rejected that he hesitated ever to commit his feelings fully."[117] Wolfson limited his relationships and possibilities. Such were the consequences of his Jewish disability.

Those close to Wolfson felt his stress. "Sometimes the strain of being 'the Jew' on the Harvard College faculty would wear on him, and he would occasionally yield to moments of bitterness. He would write a book someday, he would say, about all the injustices he had seen at Harvard; he would talk of friends I never knew, of a man Zimmerman who had finally become insane," one of Wolfson's former students recalled.[118] But part of what made Wolfson successful at Harvard was that he was the type of person who would never publish a book about the injustices he experienced and witnessed. He was willing to be the Jew at Harvard who observed but did not disturb the status quo.

Wolfson did publish a sympathetic account of the internal ruminations of American Jews moving in educated circles. His 1921 essay "Escaping Judaism" painted a dismal portrait of a discontented people, badly scarred by a hostile environment. "We Jews, only too conscious of our faults, seem to see only the virtues of Christianity, and we are gradually drifting toward an uncritical adulation of Christianity at the expense of our esteem for Judaism."[119] He did not delve into the reasons Jews were so conscious of their faults, but he noted the depressing results of this low self-regard: "the mind of the modern Jew is restless, agitated, uprooted, and is longing for a haven of refuge, which he does not find among his own people."[120]

Sympathetic to the yearnings of young Jews, Wolfson reasoned that, "broken in spirit and failing in hope," Jews could not help but be "overcome by a longing for the triumphant Christian God and would turn [their] backs upon [their] own discomfited, helpless, poverty-stricken Jehovah."[121] He understood, too, the youthful urge to move beyond the expected path. But it was typically not Christianity that these young Jews truly desired, Wolfson insisted. What they truly sought was "life, contentment, friends, and a desire to belong somewhere."[122] Horace Kallen (1882–1974), another talented Jewish academic, also wrote about the spiritual ennui of the academically inclined, young Jew: "He was stranded, alone, between the Jews he could not warm to and the Christian who could not warm to him."[123] It was those Jews who were insecure about their Jewishness about whom Wolfson and Kallen were writing.

Suggesting a remodeling of Judaism as a solution, Wolfson acknowledged that reformers had already begun such renovations, often attempting to make Judaism resemble Christianity. But Judaism was not a religion like Christianity, Wolfson admonished. Rather, Judaism was "a form of life," with a set of laws to uphold that life. Here, Wolfson foreshadowed the critique some Jewish thinkers would level at midcentury Judeo-Christianity: in its true form, Judaism was not a mirror image of Christianity, as the term "Judeo-Christian tradition" suggested to some.[124] Rather, Judaism contained many elements that would always seem foreign to Christians.

As Wolfson put it in "Escaping Judaism," there was no way around the Christian view of Judaism as legalism (because of Judaism's commandments—as opposed to Protestantism's promise of salvation through faith alone)—"however we may fret under this designation" of Judaism as a sclerotic legal system, ill-suited to modernity.[125] "We can explain and justify Jewish legalism," Wolfson wrote, "but we cannot deny it."[126] And while law and discipline could be a fine influence on life, "law which is foreign and imposed upon life is a burdensome yoke," as in America, where Talmudic backgrounds were scarce. Yes, one could make minor adjustments to Judaism with the goals of decorum and modernization, but how much of Judaism could be extracted, while still retaining something meaningful? "There will always be a residuum of Judaism that will make you uncomfortable and demand some sacrifice," Wolfson concluded.[127] He knew well the embarrassing stigmata of Judaism and the urge to brush them aside, to be done with the black leather straps of *tefillin* and the *tzitzit* hanging beneath men's clothing, and the restrictions of Kashrut and shabbat observance. But think forward, Wolfson beseeched his readers. *How will you feel when it is all gone?*

> You may abolish the obligatory green thatched booth on the Feast of the Tabernacles, and of your own free will you will adorn your temple pulpit with evergreen as a mere ceremonial. You may do away with the blowing of the ram's horn on New Year's Day, and out of a mere feeling of propriety you will reproduce its thrills on the temple organ as a reminiscence. But how long will you subsist on these empty husks of religion? . . . How long will your soul be satisfied with this disembodied ghost of religion? You may succeed in preserving Judaism as a faint reminiscence of ancestral pride, or as a mere obstinate refusal to join other religious bodies, but of what worth will such a Judaism be to you and to the world?[128]

There was only so much of Judaism that could be changed or abandoned before there was nothing left to provide spiritual sustenance.

Thinking with Wolfson in the 1950s

A generation after "Escaping Judaism," Wolfson's questions about the limits of religious reform remained relevant. It would have been difficult for the 1920s Wolfson to imagine how the American scene would change for Jews by the 1950s. Midcentury Jews grappled, sometimes communally and sometimes individually, with adapting Judaism to their altered postwar circumstances. For example: should 1950s Jews be allowed to drive to synagogue, even though driving was prohibited under the laws of Shabbat observance? Given the reality of suburban living, the Conservative movement's Committee on Jewish Law and Standards ruled automobile travel allowable if the distance between home and synagogue was too far to walk.[129] Less formally, Jews made decisions about how to observe holidays and kashrut in ways that did not risk negative judgment from middle-class, Christian neighbors. Christmas trees in midcentury Jewish homes signaled participation in what many perceived to be a civic holiday. The expression "Happy Holidays," a more inclusive alternative to "Merry Christmas," came into common usage in the 1940s, ushered in by the song of that title (written by Jewish songwriter Irving Berlin for the 1942 film, *Holiday Inn*—the same film for which Berlin wrote the song, "White Christmas").[130] The greeting exemplified Jewish efforts to negotiate participation, without undue compromise, in the country's religious and civic life.

Part of what *had* changed by the 1950s were the feelings surrounding Jewishness in America and Judaism's new status. Even the very word, "Jew," required a makeover in its meaning and the associations it elicited among Americans. Cynthia Baker writes about the word "Jew": "'The Jewish Question' that haunts the modern era is, in some measure, the question about the possibility and means of turning this name for other, a name that denies, *de*legitimates, and *de*nounces, into a name for self, a *pro*nouncement about identity, connection, and the contours of 'legitimate' difference."[131] Opposition to antisemitism during the late 1940s paved the way for "Jew" and "Judaism" to become labels for legitimate and positive difference. The 1950s positioning of Judaism as "equal to" Christianity—different from it, but in an acceptable way—was a result of the popular culture examined here and the Judeo-Christian tradition, even as that Judeo-Christian discourse excluded other traditions.[132]

In his 1921 essay, Wolfson did not foresee a proud Jewish identity for Americans. In his view, Judaism could not be brought into alignment with modernity. He wrote of the limited choices for Jewish life: "You may succeed in preserving Judaism as a faint reminiscence of ancestral pride, or as a mere obstinate refusal to join other religious bodies, but of what worth will such a Judaism be to you and to the world?"[133] For Wolfson, widespread positive feelings about Jewishness was still difficult to imagine.

Moving toward Pride

During the first half of the twentieth century, Jewishness was often experienced as a significant and burdensome difference from the Christian norm. Moving from Jewishness as handicap to Jewishness as positive identity was far from a seamless process. "We often use *illness* to disparage a way of being, and *identity* to validate that same way of being," the writer and activist Andrew Solomon noted in his 2012 book *Far from the Tree: Parents, Children, and the Search for Identity*.[134] Solomon examined how families of children with cognitive, psychological, and physical impairments regard those distinctions, but his central question of orientation toward difference is applicable to Jewishness. Rabbi Milton Steinberg understood these antithetical orientations that a Jew might take toward Jewishness when he observed: "It is an elementary principle of psychology that a person must approve of himself if he is to be happy and creative."[135] The phrase "proud Jewish identity" was not yet widely employed, but it was what Steinberg envisioned.[136]

Half a century later, that healthier spirit was still elusive to Andrew Solomon, who was gay and Jewish. Andrew Solomon's case is worth considering because it resonates with some of the examples in this book, and it demonstrates that antisemitic challenges to positive feelings around Jewishness persisted, despite gains made in the immediate postwar era. His story is also a reminder that the affirming work of midcentury middlebrow Jewish culture was not a balm for all Jewish wounds, and that the pain caused by antisemitic rejection was not confined to the first half of the twentieth century. Notwithstanding a privileged 1960s and 1970s Manhattan childhood, Solomon absorbed his family's anxieties about Jewishness. He explained why his mother had found Jewishness undesirable: "She had learned this view from my grandfather, who kept his religion secret so he could get a high-level job in a company that did not employ Jews. He belonged to a suburban country club where Jews were not welcome."[137]

These were familiar circumstances for Jews attempting to succeed in the secular world. It seemed that the Solomon family had arrived in affluent society. Andrew Solomon was educated at Horace Mann, and at Yale; his father was the chairman of a pharmaceutical manufacturer. But emotional scars from the past lingered. Solomon's mother's broken engagement to a gentile ("His family threatened to disinherit him if he married a Jew," Solomon relates) before her marriage to Solomon's father contributed to her interpretation of Jewishness as disability. "For her, it was a trauma of self-recognition, because until then she had not thought of herself as a designated Jew; she had thought she could be whomever she appeared to be."[138] Solomon absorbed his mother's view of Jewishness as an unattractive, heritable trait. With few positive associations, and several family stories about being the target of antisemitism, Jewishness was an inherited liability—not unlike being gay. It was yet another identity to keep in the closet.

The dynamic of experiencing and responding to antisemitism remained relevant in later generations, and at many stages of a Jewish life. A young person's consciousness of the restrictions and hurts imposed by antisemitism arrived at different points of development. Childhood might bring playground taunts about Jews killing Jesus, and the frank and uninhibited statements that young children specialize in, often parroting their parents' views. Harsh discoveries of antisemitism continued as teenagers learned which camps, colleges, sororities, and social clubs were unlikely to accept Jews, as well as who was willing to befriend, date, or hire a Jew. Before the postwar era, when topics deemed unpleasant were judged inappropriate for discussion—as opposed to our own therapeutic culture, in which distress caused by a topic often signals a need for discussion—these realities of antisemitism often went unsaid, even as they were keenly felt.

Contemporary willingness to discuss antisemitism in America has some of its origins in the 1940s culture of anti-antisemitism. That era's genre of anti-antisemitism fiction helped open a national conversation about domestic antisemitism, offering glimpses of what it might mean to reckon with American prejudice.

2
The Roots of 1940s Anti-Antisemitism Fiction

In December 1947, Henry Seidel Canby, founder and editor of the *Saturday Review of Literature* and the first editor in chief of the Book-of-the-Month Club, surveyed a spate of recent novels about American antisemitism and racism. The success of this new fiction, he wrote, "both through critical recognition of their merit and through the less academic standard of the cash-register, is a phenomenon worth thinking about."[1]

Americans were buying books that attacked racism and antisemitism, Canby noted. With cautious optimism, Canby, like other observers, posited that these 1940s novels, "may mean that the conscience of America is awakening."[2] The 1940s crop of novels exposing North American antisemitism included Gwethalyn Graham's *Earth and High Heaven*, Margaret Halsey's *Some of My Best Friends*, Josephine Lawrence's *Let Us Consider One Another*, Jo Sinclair's *Wasteland*, Arthur Miller's *Focus*, Saul Bellow's *The Victim*, Laura Z. Hobson's *Gentleman's Agreement*, Norman Katkov's *Eagle before My Eyes*, Mary Jo Ward's *The Professor's Umbrella*, and Burke Davis's *Whisper My Name*.[3]

Was Canby's observation about the country's awakening conscience true? When it came to antisemitism in America, he was on to something. But the shift in attitudes that Canby noted had begun earlier in the decade, leading to a culture of anti-antisemitism that found expression in 1940s middlebrow anti-antisemitism fiction.[4]

After aviator Charles Lindbergh's infamous September 11, 1941, speech at an America First rally in Des Moines, Iowa, public discourse about the former hero reflected changing attitudes toward Jews. Lindbergh, who was one of the biggest celebrities of the first half of the twentieth century, gained a new kind of renown as an isolationist through his vocal support of America First, an influential pressure group of about 800,000 members controversial for its antisemitic and pro-fascist views.[5] In his Des Moines speech, Lindbergh blamed three groups—the British, the Jews, and the Roosevelt

Postwar Stories. Rachel Gordan, Oxford University Press. © Oxford University Press 2024.
DOI: 10.1093/9780197694367.003.0003

administration—for "pressing this country toward war."[6] Lindbergh was not the first or the only person to scapegoat Jews for the deepening crisis in Europe. Such accusations circulated in private conversations, behind closed doors, and on the radio through Father Charles Coughlin's antisemitic sermons.[7] But Lindbergh's September 11 speech had apparently gone too far. "The dog whistle was too loud," Sarah Churchwell observes of Lindbergh's remarks. "Codes don't work if what is supposed to be covert becomes overt."[8]

In the wake of his Des Moines speech, Lindbergh was immediately and roundly censured by politicians and newspaper editors around the country for his "race prejudice."[9] President Roosevelt's administration was quick to compare Lindbergh and Hitler, with White House Press Secretary Stephen Early remarking on September 12, "You have seen the outpourings of Berlin in the last few days. You saw Lindbergh's statement last night. I think there is a striking similarity between the two."[10] Writing to his Treasury Secretary Henry Morgenthau, President Roosevelt confided, "I am absolutely convinced that Lindbergh is a Nazi," and to his former secretary of state Henry Stimson, Roosevelt lamented, "What a pity that this youngster has completely abandoned his belief in our form of government and has accepted Nazi methods."[11] Newspaper editorials echoed Roosevelt's condemnation.[12] "The voice is the voice of Lindbergh, but the words are those of Hitler," opined the *San Francisco Chronicle*.[13]

Lindbergh's broadcast remarks—portraying Jews as warmongers—and their aftermath were dramatic events that took root in the mind of novelist Laura Z. Hobson. Hobson was spending the summer and fall of 1941—the last few months of a pregnancy hidden from all but her closest friends—in Noroton, Connecticut. *Gentleman's Agreement*, Hobson's novel about antisemitism in America, would not be published until 1947, but as Hobson listened to Lindbergh's speech on the radio, she found herself filled "with a necessity to do something, to decide something and do it right away."[14] The fact of her pregnancy, and the vision of bringing a child into a bigoted society, may have motivated Hobson's concern. Cut off from her usual activist options of organizing with friends, Hobson was "alone in a little house in Noroton with no access to the Fight for Freedom Committee or any other group I could appeal to, to raise money for a public protest or even a few major newspapers." She turned to writing as a sphere of activity in which she could workshop her response to Lindbergh's antisemitic speech.

The idea of anti-antisemitism, if not the phrase, crystallized in the 1940s, after receiving impetus from events such as Lindbergh's Des Moines speech and the backlash it provoked. Social scientists found that "Lindbergh's charge against the Jews attracted more public attention than the other parts of his threefold indictment."[15] Many Americans sought to distance themselves from Lindberg's accusations, based on an October 1941 survey, which found that only 6 percent of the sample spontaneously named Jews as a group trying to get the country into the European war.[16]

A few months later, the Japanese attack on Pearl Harbor strengthened the culture of anti-antisemitism as Jewish interests aligned with the country's defense imperatives.[17] "Is Lindbergh a Nazi?" read the title of a 1941 pamphlet raising the question, sparking a turn in public opinion against the national hero.[18] In the Lone Star State, "Stay Out of Texas, House Roars Out to Lindbergh," read a typical headline.[19] At Notre Dame, philosophy professor Francis McMahon denounced Lindbergh for his "un-Christian" and un-American attack upon "our Jewish people," declaring, "I cannot remain silent while you foment the spread of anti-Semitism at a moment when the Jewish people sustain one of the supreme agonies of their history."[20] Lindbergh's antisemitic remarks occasioned an outpouring of public statements that, in effect, reversed the content of the Des Moines speech.

This kind of editorializing about Lindbergh suggested an early, albeit limited, public reckoning with prewar antisemitism in America.[21] Even the America First committee deemed it necessary to issue a statement declaring that they "deplore the injection of the race issue into the discussion of war or peace."[22] This led the *New York Times* to editorialize, in passing, on the subject of Jews and race, a topic the newspaper likely would have avoided were it not for the need to criticize Lindbergh: "Passing over the question whether a religious group whose members come from almost every civilized country and speak almost every Western language can be called a 'race,' let us examine what Mr. Lindbergh actually said."[23] Similar to the declarations coming from other newspapers, the *Times* firmly stated that "We do not believe that anti-Semitism will ever gain ground in this country so long as the masses of our people are true to the great tradition on which this Republic was founded and for which such a multitude of known and unknown heroes have labored, sacrificed and given their lives." In suggesting that *real* Americans did not engage in anything resembling Nazi behavior, such statements made clear that Hitler had introduced a new standard for what counted as serious antisemitism.

By blaming Lindbergh for singling out Jews and for his sympathy for the Nazis, these public denunciations may have inadvertently diminished perceptions of the seriousness of America's own regnant antisemitism. At least on the level of publicly stated ideals, prominent Americans would not abide such blatant antisemitism as Lindbergh's. The *Christian Century* noted the cognitive dissonance that Americans appeared willing to bear: "One hundred clubs and hotel foyers rang with denouncement of Lindbergh on the morning after his Des Moines speech—clubs and hotels barring their doors to Jews."[24] American media coverage coded the Nazis' racist and violent antisemitism as consummate evil, while native antisemitism often went unmentioned.

But there were also small steps forward. Lindbergh's speech ironically led to Jewish pride over the level of American outrage incited, as Jewish newspapers listed the names of "notable American men and women who ... assailed, in no uncertain terms, Charles A. Lindbergh's attempt to inject race prejudice into the politics of this country."[25] American Jewish organizations seized on the public uproar as an opportunity to broadcast their vision of the Jewish position in America. As the American Jewish Committee (AJC) and the Jewish Labor Committee denounced the "unsupported and unsupportable charge impugning the patriotism of Americans of the Jewish faith," in Lindbergh's speech, they stated "our interests and those of our country are one and indivisible."[26] The AJC proclaimed that "the overwhelming denunciation with which the charge has been met from coast to coast by the press and by leaders of all faiths, places it in the category in which it belongs. It is not a serious argument but only another example of the now familiar tactics of the Nazis to divide the country by stirring up religious and racial hatreds and setting group against group."[27]

Relief came to liberals who opposed American Firsters, in seeing Lindbergh's position publicly labeled as fringe and un-American.[28] Republican Wendell Willkie criticized the speech as "the most un-American talk made in my time by any person of national reputation. If the American people permit race prejudice to arrive at this critical moment, they little deserve to preserve democracy."[29] Lindbergh's Des Moines gaffe was a godsend to interventionists, as Lynne Olson observes: "Neither Roosevelt nor Harold Ickes made a public comment, but then they didn't have to; the national reaction was already one of outrage."[30] With Lindbergh's speech reported and countered all over the country, it was as though the mask had slipped from the former national hero. And to Jews, the important thing was that their fellow citizens realized there had been a mask in the first place—that anyone who harbored such feelings about Jews was not truly an American hero.

Writing against the Tide of Antisemitism

"Anti-antisemitism," a term used in the 1940s, is the one employed in this book to capture a 1940s liberal sentiment.[31] It was a convenient term to signal America's desired distance from European and fascist bigotry without having to say too much about actual Jews. Jeffrey Alexander observes of the sudden popularity of anti-antisemitism in the 1940s: "It was not that Christians suddenly felt genuine affection for, or identification with, those whom they had vilified for countless centuries as the killers of Christ."[32] Rather, the Nazis were declared America's enemies, and "if Nazis singled out the Jews, then the Jews must be singled out by democrats and anti-Nazism." As one historian put it, World War II "saw the merging of Jewish and American fates" as Hitler became the greatest enemy of both Jewry and the United States.[33]

In view of the pervasiveness of antisemitism earlier in the century, this 1940s reversal was dramatic, and it affected liberal Americans' self-understanding. During the war, the Nazis were sheltered under the titles of "Axis" and "enemy." Victory in Europe, however, brought more than simple, joyous relief to the Allies. Shocking images of the concentration camps brought home incontestable evidence of the unprecedented horror of Nazi brutality. As a result, postwar Americans sought to reject earlier racist, discriminatory policies and ideas—or at least those that applied to Jews.

During the 1940s, anti-antisemitism found expression in literary and popular culture, with an increase in books, both fiction and nonfiction, about antisemitism.[34] "Jews emerged as the social minority ... by which to measure the purity of American democracy," literary historian Gordon Hutner observes of the surprising number of books about antisemitism published in the 1940s.[35] Not only *Gentleman's Agreement*, which was made into a film shortly after the novel's publication, but also *Crossfire*, another movie about American antisemitism, received multiple nominations during the 1948 Academy Awards, with *Agreement* winning the award for best picture.[36] Its prominence as a theme at the 1948 Oscars was one of several indications that anti-antisemitism had become central to the country's postwar liberal creed and part of America's global moral leadership.[37]

This change in ideals is not to be confused with the disappearance of antisemitism. Discrimination toward Jews in the form of university quotas, housing covenants, restricted country clubs, and hiring discrimination continued well past the 1940s. And as the war raged, antisemitism was actually on the rise, even as the ideal of anti-antisemitism developed among liberals.[38] A decade later, the 1958 bombing of Atlanta's Hebrew Benevolent Congregation served as a reminder that the 1940s culture of anti-antisemitism had not ended antisemitism. Antisemites found new causes for their hatred, such as Jewish activism on behalf of integration during the civil rights movement. As usual, everyday behavior, and especially that which occurred on the other side of closed doors, lagged behind progressive values.[39] But shifting national ideals were significant. They pointed to liberal aspirations and curtailed public bad behavior.[40]

More frequent messaging about the need to fight discrimination against Jews suggested a changing culture. During the first half of the twentieth century, particularly the 1920s through the early 1940s, overt and covert antisemitism in the United States was so ongoing and pervasive in the non-Jewish majority that it often seemed neither worthy of discussion nor, because it was so unpleasant to its targets, a topic fit for polite conversation. Indeed, when *Gentleman's Agreement* was published, one review explained the novel's premise of a non-Jew pretending to be Jewish, and that "He had the usual experiences."[41] It was not even necessary to spell out "the usual experiences"—so well known were the antisemitic slights Jews faced. Experiencing antisemitism often seemed like part of what it meant to be Jewish. This is not to say that individual Jews did not feel indignation, or that they lacked agency in the face of such discrimination. But there was an element of acceptance of antisemitism as though it were part of the air one breathed.[42]

Twenty-first-century Americans speak of sporadic antisemitic *incidents*, with the Squirrel Hill synagogue shooting the most violent.[43] For typical American Jews of the 1920s and 1930s, antisemitism affected nearly every aspect of life—housing, educational opportunities, profession, recreational activities, social clubs, dating, and friendships.[44] Accepted as a matter of course, discrimination against Jews shaped an individual's aspirations and dreams, determining what a young Jew believed was possible. This largely taken-for-granted quality of antisemitism, by both its perpetrators and victims, was punctured at midcentury with the rise of *anti*-antisemitism.

The 1940s thus evidenced increased discussion of antisemitism in mainstream media and popular culture. One historian notes that, "After decades of only episodic public discussion of anti-Jewish quotas" in colleges and graduate schools, for instance, "magazine and newspaper articles of 1945–1947 exposed in detail the practice of excluding Jews."[45] These years saw the publication of important nonfiction books about antisemitism, written by non-Jews, such as Isacque Graeber and Steuart Henderson Britt's *Jews in a Gentile World* (1942), which the *Atlantic Monthly* praised for showing that "Antisemitism and the American Constitution are wholly incompatible."[46] The 1943 publication of investigative reporter Arthur Derounian's book *Under Cover: My Four Years in the Nazi Underworld of America* followed Derounian as he "became the intimate and trusted friend of leaders in such groups as the Bund, the Christian Front, the Silver Shirts, and America First."[47] It's worth noting that in the same issue of the *Atlantic Monthly* that reviewed Derounian's book as an enlightening read, a review of an academic study of the Confederate statesman Judah P. Benjamin referred to the subject as "a dumpy little Jew."[48] In the early 1940s, cracks in the antisemitic façade were beginning to show, but the framework was still largely in place, as old worldviews and habits of speech endured.

Discussion of antisemitism continued in the latter half of the decade.[49] The American edition of Jean-Paul Sartre's *Anti-Semite and the Jew* was published in 1948, as was Carey McWilliams's *A Mask of Privilege: Anti-Semitism in America*. *Commentary* magazine brought antisemitism into the center of 1940s literary discussion when the magazine published a symposium on "American Literature and the Younger Generation of American Jews."[50] One of the questions posed to a group that included writers Alfred Kazin, Howard Fast, Lionel Trilling, and Muriel Rukeyser was whether their perspective as "artist and citizen" had been affected by antisemitism. Answers varied, but the writers voiced optimism. As Isaac Rosenfeld, then an assistant editor at the *New Republic*, put it, Jews had become specialists in alienation, "the one international banking system the Jews actually control," and as a result of antisemitism, they had a unique perspective on societal shortcomings.[51] "No man suffers injustice without learning, vaguely but surely, what justice is," Rosenfeld continued, explaining that "The desire for justice, once it passes beyond revenge, becomes the deepest motive for social change. Out of their recent sufferings one may expect Jewish writers to make certain inevitable moral discoveries. These discoveries, enough to indict the world, may also be crucial to its salvation."[52] Along with acknowledgment and discussion of antisemitism came recognition of its implications for creative minds.

Bestselling Jewish novelist Edna Ferber was in the vanguard of this literary anti-antisemitism with her 1939 autobiography, *A Peculiar Treasure*. When she wrote, in the opening pages, "I should like, in this book, to write about being a Jew. All my life I have been inordinately proud of being a Jew," it signaled a divergence from the "Jewishness as misfortune" trope of so much earlier American Jewish writing.[53] Ferber's statement, "I can't account for the fact that I didn't resent being a Jew," it may have read like a challenge to the status quo—verily, a countercultural pronouncement—as Ferber went on to explain that despite her upbringing in an antisemitic midwestern town, she had always felt her Jewishness was a "privilege. Two thousand years of persecution have made the Jew quick to sympathy, quick-witted (he'd better be), tolerant, humanly understanding."[54] Publicly calling oneself a proud Jew was a much more revolutionary act in the 1920s and 1930s than simply being a Jew. The latter was about ancestral identity and could be hidden. The former faced pushback both from many Jews—whose attitude was, often from bitter experience, that their Judaism was a handicap and best hidden—and from the general non-Jewish population, who on the whole disdained Jews and might find the claim laughable.

Similar to the anti-antisemitism novelists of the 1940s discussed in the next chapter, Ferber based her anti-bigotry narrative on the country's democratic ideals—an argument that previous generations of American Jewish writers, including Emma Wolfe and Emma Lazarus, also employed.[55] If Americans would only tend to the garden of the "Soul and Spirit of America," Ferber explained, they might cut down the weeds of bigotry and racism that had become overgrown and keep the country true to its democratic ideals.[56]

To understand the transformation in attitudes that *anti*-antisemitism brought about, consider the first half of the twentieth century: in the early, nativist-imbued decades of the twentieth century, the country's mission was aptly encapsulated by President Calvin Coolidge's slogan to "Keep America American," by preserving its old, white, colonial stock, as some described the preferred ancestry of American citizens.[57] Even in the late 1930s, when news of Hitler's persecution of Jews, if not its full scope, reached the United States, Americans persisted in their xenophobia. Two months after the November Pogrom of 1938, when a poll asked Americans if the United States should accept 10,000 Jewish children from Europe, 60 percent answered no.[58] In the next year, the SS *St Louis*, with more than 900 Jewish passengers fleeing the Nazis, was turned down by immigration authorities in Miami after being refused entry to Cuba.[59] Finally, they were forced to return to Europe, where Belgium, France, Holland, and the UK took the refugees in. More than 250 of those originally on board the ship would eventually be killed by the Nazis.[60]

It did not seem to matter to the vast majority of the nation's elite that the inscription on the Statue of Liberty, by Jewish poet Emma Lazarus, expressed values contrary to these more restrictive ones: "Give me your tired, your poor, Your huddled masses yearning to breathe free, The wretched refuse of your teeming shore. Send these, the homeless, tempest-tost to me."[61] These words may have been on Liberty's pedestal, but they had not penetrated the hearts of much of the country's social and governing elite.

Shifting tides of opinion arose, in part, from the fear of failing to live up to American ideals. During the 1930s and 1940s, a few articulate voices exhorted Americans to beware of how easily public opinion might slide toward Nazi ideology. *It Can't Happen Here*, Sinclair Lewis's 1935 dystopian novel, was one popular example of this crying out in the wilderness. But on a smaller scale, so was a 1940 editorial in the Louisville, Kentucky, *Courier-Journal*.[62] "We Are Lost If We Accept This Crime," ran the headline, noting Americans' acceptance of Hitler's persecution of Jews.[63] Observing the contrast between the noble ideas engraved on the Statue of Liberty, and recent remarks of Charles Lindbergh, the editorial concluded, "We have failed. We have failed miserably; but we have not yet denied the dream." Lofty American ideals still existed, even if they were floating high above ground. Failure could always be redeemed, the editorial reminded readers. "Even with the Negro, where our failure has been most base, we still hope and we still slowly improve.... Anti-Semitism is the entering wedge for racism. And racism once accepted, America becomes an impossibility." These were cautionary voices reminding Americans not to lose sight of their democratic path.

By the mid-1950s, awareness of the dissonance between the nation's ideals and the reality of American racism and xenophobia had grown.[64] The Anti-Defamation League invited a Massachusetts senator who was a descendant of Irish immigrants to write a book about immigrant contributions to America. In his 1958 book, *A Nation of Immigrants*, Senator John F. Kennedy suggested a few lines might be added to the Statue of Liberty's pedestal, for greater accuracy: "as long as they come from northern Europe, are not too tired or too poor or slightly ill, never stole a loaf of bread, never joined any questionable organization, and can document their activities for the past two years."[65] That a Catholic politician with his sights on the White House was willing to publish this critique of America's restrictive immigration policies may have been a sign that the mainstream appraisal of the country's restrictive immigration policy was changing. By the 1950s, a culture of anti-antisemitism, fueled by Americans' postwar sense of themselves as the opposite of Nazis—an irony, to be sure, considering the Nazis learned much from American racism—collided with older, nativist views of immigrants, sometimes leading to criticism of the racist attitudes of previous generations.[66]

While there were no silver linings to be found in the rise of Hitler, his regime "more clearly than ever before in the history of the Jewish problem identified the cause of antisemitism with the forces of political reaction, corruption and aggressive war," as historian Koppel Pinson put it in 1945.[67] By making antisemitism the ideological cornerstone of Nazi domestic and world policy, Hitler's atrocities against the Jews had a reverse effect, in that, "for all opponents of Nazism there developed a greater awareness of the dangers of antisemitism."[68] Once it became firmly associated with the Nazis, antisemitism was easier to call out as unacceptable among Americans. As scholars have shown, this nascent change had more to do with American triumph over Nazism than with recognition of Jewish trauma from the Holocaust.[69] But alongside this sentiment, *anti*-antisemitism became central to good Americanism. As Pinson wrote in 1945, it was as though the rise of Hitler had introduced a novel equation to supporters of democracy: the Enemy = Nazi = Antisemite.[70] The corollary was that midcentury Americans should be *anti*-antisemitic.

A Choice for Gentiles

When Laura Z. Hobson found herself preoccupied with Charles Lindbergh's remarks, in September 1941, she began to formulate her response in a draft of an essay that she titled "Choice—for Gentiles." With signs of her growing confidence in broaching the topic of antisemitism—a boldness that came, in part, from observing the public's reaction to Lindbergh—Hobson presented readers with a choice. "There are 122 million Gentiles—you are strong, you are many. There are 7 or 8 million Jews, of which I am one. You can drown us, shoot us, poison us all and have done forever with the Jewish problem."[71] They were harsh words. "Go ahead, get on with it," she wrote:

> Be efficient as Americans are, clean us out, neatly, nicely, but with no weeping in the night. And then pay your price, like men. Pay it fully, pay without whining or regretting. . . . Say farewell forever to your beautiful phrase about life and liberty and the pursuit of happiness. And to that other, that all men are created equal. . . . Among you let all Catholics or Mormons or Seventh Day Adventists quit feeling safe, secure. For never again could any religious minority feel secure to worship their God as they wish. . . . Yes, the price would be big. The price would claw to bits America's monumental

history, lay waste her simple, most noble concept of democracy. The full price would break most American hearts. Either pay it like men, or have done with the tawdry torture of antisemitism.[72]

Hobson tried to publish the essay. She sent it to her friends, Time Inc. publisher Henry Luce and journalist Dorothy Thompson. In 1934, Thompson became the first American journalist expelled from Nazi Germany after she published critical comments about Hitler. During the 1940s, Thompson wrote a monthly column for *Ladies' Home Journal*. It was through her ex-husband, publisher Thayer Hobson, that Laura Z. Hobson became friendly with Thompson and her then-husband, Pulitzer Prize–winning novelist, Sinclair Lewis. That personal friendship with Lewis gave Hobson confidence in her own novel-writing, as she later recounted in her autobiography.[73]

Neither Luce nor Thompson replied to Hobson with a publication lead—a response that may have indicated Hobson's writing expressed too much raw anger at the Protestant establishment. This failure to publish Hobson's harsh words is also a reminder of how easy it was for those who considered themselves liberals to abdicate responsibility for actively fighting antisemitism. That, too, was a lesson that Hobson incorporated into her novel. Still, both Luce and Thompson replied to Hobson in solidarity. "One should have watch-dogs against intolerance—and thank God, the dogs barked plenty last week," Luce wrote to Hobson in reference to the uproar over Lindbergh's Des Moines speech.[74]

Although it was disappointing not to have the essay published, the act of writing helped Hobson clarify her response to antisemitism. It also illuminated a truth that would become central to the plot of *Agreement*: antisemitism was not solely a "Jewish problem." The majority culture, Hobson would show in her novel, was the group most responsible for effecting change. This was the powerful anti-antisemitic lesson at the center of *Gentleman's Agreement*.

3
When Women Made Anti-Antisemitism Fiction Popular

When Laura Z. Hobson pitched her idea for *Gentleman's Agreement* to her friend and publisher, Richard Simon, in 1944, she wrote him of her hopes for what she and other novelists might achieve: "Maybe six other authors are right this minute finishing novels on the same subject—maybe not one will do much by itself, but perhaps all together those authors could become a kind of force for ending the complacency of uncomfortable or scared silence which defaults to the rantings of the bigots, who don't practice that conspiracy of silence at all."[1]

Several writers were, in fact, working on anti-antisemitism novels. Hobson had recently heard that her writer-friend Margaret Halsey had published *Some of My Best Friends Are Soldiers* (1944), a novel attacking racism and antisemitism.[2] As Hobson wrote to Simon, she was also excited by the news of Toronto novelist Gwethalyn Graham's *Earth and High Heaven* (1944), a popular anti-antisemitism novel, being serialized in *Collier's* magazine. And although Cleveland-based novelist Jo Sinclair was farther afield from Hobson's New York literary circles, by 1946 it would be difficult for Hobson to miss the many *New York Times* references to Sinclair and her award-winning anti-antisemitism novel, *Wasteland*.[3]

As she worked on *Gentleman's Agreement*, Hobson discovered that she was part of a group of 1940s anti-antisemitism novelists that included Halsey and Graham. So were Arthur Miller (*Focus*, 1945) and Saul Bellow (*The Victim*, 1947). Bellow and Miller are among the best known of these novelists, but it was a small group of women writers who made the genre popular in the 1940s. Their middlebrow fiction received attention from the popular press, and in some cases, consideration for film treatment. Hobson did not know all her fellow anti-antisemitism novelists, personally.[4] But, even in 1944, she understood the significance of their work. "How does one fight such things?" she wrote to Simon about antisemitism. "Each in his own way—and any serious author who attempts the fight, might just be lucky enough to chip off a bit here and there from this growth, if it's only by opening the thing to table-talk and woman's club discussions, as I'm sure Peg Halsey's book and Gwethalyn Graham's Earth and High Heaven are bound to do."[5] At a time when many Americans wondered what they could possibly do to fight bigotry and racism, anti-antisemitism novelists grasped an inspiring truth: popular stories sparked reflection and conversation among readers.

In part, what Hobson described to Simon was her understanding of the power of midcentury middlebrow Jewish culture. A generation earlier, Edna Ferber had been a strong, but relatively isolated, middlebrow Jewish author attempting to portray Judaism as mainstream in her 1917 novel, *Fanny, Herself*. At midcentury, several writers worked toward mainstreaming anti-antisemitism. Among them, Hobson's was the most star-studded path: she eventually collaborated with producer Darryl Zanuck and screenwriter Moss Hart and saw her name on the silver screen. The inspiration that Hobson found in the success of other women writers lit her path, reminding her that she was part of an anti-antisemitism movement extending from publishers and writers to readers.

Hobson's Journey to Anti-Antisemitism

Laura Z. Hobson never planned to write an important Jewish book. And yet, *Gentleman's Agreement* became the most celebrated and widely reviewed of the 1940s anti-antisemitism genre that indicated both a new openness toward the topic of antisemitism and a muted literary response to the Holocaust.[6]

Agreement tells the story of Phil Green's efforts to write a magazine story about antisemitism. "Over and above what any normal man thinks about it, what must a Jew feel about this thing?" Phil asks himself.[7] To answer that question, he goes undercover as a Jew, so he can think "himself into the very brain of another human being."[8] Phil's girlfriend, Kathy Lacey, a liberal Manhattan divorcee, is quickly implicated in the story. Kathy originally suggested the idea for a magazine story about antisemitism to her uncle, Phil's editor. But her own latent antisemitism soon emerges, providing Phil with insight into the ways that even "good liberals" might unknowingly become carriers of antisemitism. "You really do think I'm an anti-Semite!"[9] Kathy finally explodes at Phil, after one too many of his intimations that her thinking on the subject is not quite kosher. In response, Phil explains his new perspective to Kathy, providing a lesson in proper feelings that was a specialty of sentimental fiction: "It's just that I've come to see that lots of nice people ... are ... unknowing helpers and connivers. People who'd never beat up a Jew or yell kike at a child. They think antisemitism is something way off there, in a dark crackpot place with low-class morons. That's the biggest thing I've discovered about the whole business."[10] Here was an important truth of *Agreement*: one need not enter the tenebrous dens of lunatics to find dangerous antisemites. They are all around us. If one isn't actively combating discrimination, Phil teaches Kathy, passivity helps the cause of antisemitism.[11]

By enlarging the circle of those concerned with antisemitism, *Agreement* helped transform what had been a Jewish problem for defense organizations and rabbis to worry over into an American problem requiring an American solution.[12] Just as the French philosopher Jean-Paul Sartre argued in his book *Anti-Semite and the Jew* (1946) that antisemitism was the invention of the antisemite—a passion arising from the bigot's fears and needs—Phil makes a similar discovery about gentile responsibility for antisemitism.[13] Phil's development as a character hinges on his acknowledgment of this truth: "It had never been a Jewish problem, for Jews alone could never solve it," Phil realizes. "It was a nonsectarian problem. And because of the simple thing of majority, it was mostly a Christian problem. He'd always known that. But now he was a different sort of Christian. Now he was one of the Christians able and ready to act. On whatever front the thing showed itself."[14]

This kind of obfuscation—calling antisemitism "the thing"—was typical of Hobson. Decades later, when writing her autobiography, Hobson looked back at her early drafts of *Agreement*. The word "antisemitism" never appeared. "Why?" Hobson asked herself. "Why was I delaying page after page? Was I, like my Phil, afraid that nobody would want to read anything about antisemitism?"[15] Having undergone psychoanalysis in her thirties, Hobson was trained to explore her avoidances.[16] Realizing that she had "avoided that word that was so central to the entire book," Hobson revised her manuscript. She felt relief upon writing *antisemitism* into her first chapter, "right up front." While *Agreement* explicitly chronicled Phil and Kathy's growing understanding of antisemitism, it also marked Hobson's coming to terms with an issue that plagued her, and which she had struggled to address in her writing.[17]

Hobson's desire *not* to be passive in the face of antisemitism motivated her writing *Agreement*. Previously, Hobson had shown little interest in what were referred to as "Jewish affairs," such as Zionism, the plight of Jewish refugees, or Jewish communal self-defense. "It's the whole thing, not the poor, poor

Jews," the Jewish character Dave Goldman, who has just returned from military service, explains to Phil Green in *Gentleman's Agreement*.[18] Here, Dave voices Hobson's views on antisemitism: true, Jews suffered most directly from antisemitism, but in the end, all of society paid a steep price for injustice. Such views had roots in the postwar turn toward universalism, and in Hobson's parents' vision of the United States.[19]

Hobson described her parents, Michael and Adella Zametkin, as "Russian and Jewish, and old-fashioned socialist, and agnostic, and internationalist, and non-sectarians, and pro-labor and antimilitarist, and hotly opposed to every form of oppression, injustice, exploitation, infringement of freedom to speak out, to write, to vote to oppose."[20] Michael Zametkin helped to found the *Jewish Daily Forward* newspaper in the late nineteenth century, and Adella Kean Zametkin wrote a woman's column for the Yiddish daily *Der Tog*.[21] During her childhood, Hobson's parents moved from New York City to Brooklyn and finally to Jamaica, New York, to give Laura and her twin sister what they deemed a more American upbringing. "The whole point was to bring up their children as total Americans, with no trace of foreign accent, no smallest inflection or gesture that was not native to this their beloved country," Hobson later recalled.[22] The Zametkin home combined immigrant radicalism and conformity to American ideals.[23]

Immigrants with enormous hope that their socialist vision could be realized in the United States, the Zametkins passed on much of that faith to their daughter, Laura (Laura's twin, Alice, would take her parents politics in another direction, joining the Communist Party with her husband).[24] While a feeling for Judaism did not motivate Hobson's writing of *Agreement*, she may have been inspired by an impulse toward activism inherited from her parents. Hobson's father was famous for his soapbox speeches; for Hobson, it was her writing that communicated her vision for a society in which Jews were not considered racially other, and religious differences were immaterial.

After graduating from Cornell, Hobson worked in advertising, journalism, and then at Time Inc., where she was among the few women or Jews in a non-secretarial or photographer position during the 1920s and 1930s. Employee and friend to Henry Luce and his second wife, Clare Boothe Luce, Hobson would be described in a Luce biography as a "dynamo" and "hard-driving and ambitious" who "had no hesitation telling Harry exactly what she thought about anything."[25] That straight-talking fed into Hobson's fiction-writing.

Hobson dropped her Russian-Jewish surname, Zametkin, in favor of more Anglo-sounding names that included, at different points in her life, her mother's maiden name (Kean) and a boyfriend's last name (Mount).[26] Eventually, she kept the name of her non-Jewish husband, publisher Thayer Hobson, to whom she was married for five years. These name adjustments illustrate Hobson's struggle to declare who she was in the world. Was she a divorced Jewish woman? The wife of a WASP publisher? Or her mother's daughter?

The character Phil Green was not the child of Russian-Jewish immigrants. But he, too, realizes the benefits of name tweaking. Phil explains to his editor that professionally, he used his mother's last name, Schuyler, as his first name, because it "Sounded ritzier to me, I guess, than Philip—like Somerset Maugham instead of William, or Sinclair Lewis instead of Harry."[27] He then realizes that "Philip" is helpful for passing as a Jew.[28] By portraying her gentile, male hero altering his name, Hobson normalized name-changing, despite the Jewish taint surrounding this form of identity-modification at midcentury.[29] As one 1940s *Atlantic* article put it, Jews were known to change their names "as a prop to their teetering little souls: because they are socially insecure or are ashamed of their birthright."[30] Decades later, when Hobson was writing her autobiography in the 1980s, she would claim pride in having never discarded Zametkin, keeping it as a middle initial throughout her life.[31] But there was a big difference between keeping the middle initial Z and keeping Zametkin. Hobson's pride over her roots was likely truer in the 1980s than when she was a young woman trying to establish her career in 1930s Manhattan. By that point, Hobson had felt the sting of antisemitism in a series of coming-of-age experiences that taught her how a Jewish name might impede her social, academic, and professional success.

As a Cornell undergraduate, Hobson's professor of Greek seemed intent on pronouncing Zametkin in every conceivable way other than the correct one, prompting Hobson's bold words: "Sir, if we're supposed to pronounce names like Clytemnestra correctly, and Iphigenia and Agamemnon, and Aeschylus, don't you think you could say Zametkin?"[32] It is difficult to imagine a female college student addressing her male professor this way in 1920, although Hobson recorded it in her autobiography. Whether or not this was apocryphal, Hobson still remembered her anger at what seemed so intentional a mispronunciation. Among her other college encounters with antisemitism was Hobson's discovery that she was only welcome in the Jewish sorority, Sigma Delta Gamma, known on campus as Seven Doity Gews. Hobson had no interest: "Apparently, I knew even then that I didn't want to belong to anything that was all-Jewish."[33]

But it was her exclusion from Phi Beta Kappa, despite having the grades for it, that was "the great wound of my youth."[34] Harry Caplan, a Cornell scholar of classics angry about the antisemitism he saw poisoning campus life, informed Hobson about the bigotry behind her Phi Beta Kappa rejection. According to Caplan, the administration felt there were "too many greasy little grinds from New York," and as a result, he described "a Jew clean-up" extending even to Phi Beta Kappa.[35] Having never learned about her Jewish heritage, Hobson lacked perspective on the benefits of Jewishness. But she was getting a pretty good education on the drawbacks.

Reclaiming Moral Indignation

An attraction to literary people endured throughout Hobson's life, leading to friendships and occasional romances with writers, publishers, and editors, many of whom were not Jewish. Male Jewish authors of her generation were rarely as enveloped in WASP society as Hobson. Even her Manhattan address set Hobson apart from most midcentury Jewish intellectuals and writers. For much of her adult life, Hobson made her home on the fashionable Upper East Side rather than the more Jewish West Side. As a result of these circumstances, Hobson often witnessed subtle and non-violent forms of antisemitism in which gentiles engaged in private.

Hobson also stood at more of a remove from Jewish religious and communal life than many of the male Jewish writers of her generation. A secular Jew, Hobson did not belong to any established Jewish community, nor did she inhabit the thickly Jewish, urban enclaves familiar to male, Jewish writers of her generation. Hobson's social circles were largely made up of Ivy League–educated, Anglo-Saxon Protestants, as well as Jews in publishing and the news media, including *Time* magazine writers and editors. Based on Hobson's correspondence, it seems that hearing about secular or non-Jewish middlebrow women writers and their successful novels about antisemitism and racism was more meaningful to her than hearing about Jewish male authors, such as Arthur Miller and Jerome Weidman, who occupied different spheres of literary and Jewish culture.[36] Based on the historical record, Hobson's memoirs, and the memories of her family including her sons, it seems that Hobson never attended synagogue, a Shabbat dinner, or a Passover

Seder. She had done very little to signal Jewish affiliation prior to *Gentleman's Agreement*. Although her close friends were largely aware of her Jewish roots, most of her 1940s readers were not. Upon publication of her first novel, *The Trespassers* (1943), a novel about non-Jewish refugees from wartime Europe, the *New York Times* reviewer Marjorie Farber expressed skepticism that this "former wife of Thayer Hobson," who was also an "American copywriter and promotion chief" at *Time* magazine, could have had much experience "with the tragedies of immigration" described in her novel.[37] With her name and author profile, Hobson appeared far removed from the immigrant experience. Farber was not the only one to make that mistake.

Hobson's assimilation brought her the kind of career and social success that made her Jewishness nearly invisible to the public. Some readers of *Agreement*, assuming that the author was not Jewish, wrote to Hobson to express incredulity and gratitude that a gentile woman could write so movingly about antisemitism. Masha Leon (1931–2017), a Holocaust survivor and longtime writer for the *Jewish Forward* (the same newspaper that Hobson's father had helped establish) would later recall her excitement upon discovering *Gentleman's Agreement* as a teenager: "Only in America could there appear a best-seller attacking anti-Semitism. And written by a non-Jew (so I thought). When the film, starring Gregory Peck . . . hit the screens of the world, I was ecstatic. Now millions of *goyim* will get an inkling of what it is like to be Jewish in a non-Jewish world."[38]

Ironically, given that the theme of *Agreement* was antisemitism, it seems probable that Hobson's novel benefited from her ambiguous identity. Had readers known *Agreement* was written by a Jew, it would likely have been dismissed by many as special pleading by a Jewish writer. It was precisely this kind of scenario that Hobson wrote into *Agreement*. At the end of the novel, when Phil considers compiling his magazine articles about antisemitism and publishing them as a book, he meets a publisher who warns him not to send his manuscript "to the wrong house" and thereby attach "a neat handicap to the book."[39] When Phil asks what he means, the publisher explains that the wrong publisher would be a Jewish publisher, for "if one of the Jewish houses put their imprint on it, people might think it was just special pleading."[40] Phil is horrified by this argument.

Here was evidence of the logic of creating a non-Jewish protagonist: Phil's shock—and Hobson's ability to portray righteous indignation as the proper response to antisemitism—works because Phil had *not* spent his whole life as Jew. Coming from a Jew, such moral outrage would have been less credible, if only because Jews were seen as inured to antisemitic slights. Phil's non-Jewish colleague, Anne, voices this expectation when she finally learns Phil is not Jewish: "I did want to say a couple of times, 'For heaven's sake, how've you lived this long, spending this much juice on it all the time?' "[41] Because he is awakening only now to harsh antisemitic realities, Phil's response is to repeatedly denounce antisemitism in tones of moral outrage. Phil's earnestness may have caused a bit of eyerolling among Jewish readers and viewers, but it was generally appealing as the embodiment of a postwar American conscience. In contrast, the Jewish character Dave Goldman is portrayed as hardened to antisemitism—a reaction duly noted by Phil. In a restaurant scene in which a drunk calls Dave a *yid*, "fury tears through" Phil. But Phil takes note of "the control in Dave's impassive face," whose eyes are "hard" and whose "mouth bore a sardonic twist."[42] If Dave experiences anything like Phil's raw anger, he has learned to stifle it. Thus does Hobson teach readers another side effect of antisemitism: it dulls Jewish expressions of righteous indignation. Only a *non*-Jew can believably express such outrage. And only a gentile passing as a Jew who can always reclaim his non-Jewish identity has the courage to speak his mind. To his credit, Phil recognizes his privilege. Shortly after patting himself on the back for his feelings of identification with Jews over their suffering, Phil realizes that "in a way he was kidding himself. . . . He knew that for him it would come to an end when he gave the word." Phil can always stop pretending to be a Jew. It's much harder for Jews, Phil realizes, since "he alone had an escape clause."[43] In his conversation with the publisher who has warned him against Jewish publishing houses, Phil replies, archly, that he's "never heard of 'Christian publishing houses' and 'Jewish houses' except in the Third Reich. . . . Even firms run by men who are Jewish—we just call them 'publishing houses.' In a way, that's what the whole series is about."[44] And in a way, it was what *Gentleman's Agreement* was about, too.

In the language of twenty-first-century activists, Phil awakens to his identity as an ally to the Jewish cause. Although some reviewers criticized Hobson's focus on non-Jews, this narrative strategy of centering gentiles enabled more readers to identify with the process of becoming *anti*-antisemitic as they recognized themselves in Phil.[45] "One learns how to be oneself by taking one's cue from others who are doing the same," Rita Felski observes of the reader's experience of identifying with a character.[46] In the opening pages of the novel, Phil's relatability is established as he is introduced as a sympathetic widower recently moved to New York with his young son and mother. Phil's morality is evidenced by the fact that he feels an "uneasy sadness" for his son growing up without siblings or a mother, and a "sharp distaste" for his own bachelorhood—an often suspect status in Cold War America—all of which signal that Phil is the right kind of American, the kind deserving of empathy.[47] And although Hobson sets *Agreement* in Manhattan, she is careful to present Phil's reactions to the city as those of someone more at home in the heartland: Phil is less accustomed to "living in a rectangular shelf of space rather than in a house set to the earth among bushes and trees."[48] Like many American readers of *Agreement*, Phil is only mildly interested in antisemitism at the start of the novel; his first emotions upon receiving his antisemitism assignment are anger and frustration, as well as an anticipation of boredom as he contemplates the research he'll have to do.[49] Readers continue to discover Phil's down-to-earth humanity as he initially judges the sophisticated New Yorker, Kathy, as too snobby. He finds her gestures "absurd and artificial." Quickly, and as a result of physical attraction (another sign of his heterosexuality) and open-mindedness, he warms to her, allowing himself to bond with a woman who is genuinely interested in him.[50]

Identifying with Phil allows readers to bring their recognition of his moral outrage back to themselves. Readers wrote to Hobson about this experience of internalizing the problem of antisemitism. A New York lawyer attested: "It brings home the fact that anti-semitism is an American problem—and a world problem—which threatens to infect our social system beyond repair."[51] Feeling the urgency of Hobson's lessons in the novel, he added, "I believe the message of your story and its manner of presentation should be read by every adult in America today."[52] Another appreciative reader put Hobson's contributions this way: "May I commend you on the superb job you have done, and tell you how glad I am to hear another 'voice crying in the wilderness' of intolerance and prejudice. The battle against the Nazi spirit is the battle of our century."[53] That "Nazi spirit," the reader explained, could be found in "those unwarranted feelings of superiority among friends, and relatives" that were so disheartening to discover. "Then someone like you, or Margaret Halsey speaks up—and it is good to discover another articulate intelligence on the side of decency." Hobson replied that she had "read your letter to Margaret Halsey who happens to be a close friend of mine so you cheered two authors instead of just one."[54]

It was in this way—fans engaging with a community of readers and authors—that anti-antisemitism novels became part of postwar Americans' response to Hitler's atrocities. This literature made space for novelists and readers to unite in common cause against prejudice. When one fan wrote to

Hobson that she, too, was in the fight, Hobson replied, "You wrote that you were involved in the fight against prejudice from a different angle—the political battlefield—but I think if you look over your left shoulder you will find me right beside you. I think we are nice company, don't you?"[55] *Agreement* rallied readers and modeled moral outrage as the proper American response to bigotry and discrimination. Just a few years earlier, while World War II was raging, it had not been at all clear whether Hobson would be able pull this off.

The Great Jewish Book Corresponding to *Strange Fruit*

In early September 1944, Hobson wrote to Richard Simon about her excitement at seeing novelist Gwethalyn Graham's anti-antisemitism novel, *Earth and High Heaven*, serialized in *Collier's*. The first Canadian novel to reach number one on the *New York Times* bestseller list, *Earth and High Heaven* was written by the non-Jewish, divorced, Canadian-born, Smith College–educated Gwethalyn Graham.[56] There was talk of a possible Hollywood movie adaptation.[57] Betty Smith, the bestselling author *A Tree Grows In Brooklyn*, and a Yale Drama School–educated playwright, was even interested in adapting *Earth and High Heaven* into a play.[58]

"Have you read *Earth and High Heaven* in *Collier's*?" Hobson wrote to Simon.[59] "Have you heard that Nunnally Johnson wants to make a picture of it? It's all so new a departure—both for magazines and for film, that it fascinates me. Did it do good or harm in *Collier's*—I don't imagine anyone can tell yet." Hobson was encouraged by this news about another female writer, whose anti-antisemitism novel was serialized in a popular glossy magazine and receiving Hollywood consideration. It made it easier to imagine those possibilities for herself.

Hobson was not alone in her surprise that antisemitism had become a viable theme for fiction.[60] Recalling his 1945 anti-antisemitism novel, *Focus*, Jewish playwright Arthur Miller later reflected, "As far as I knew at the time, anti-Semitism in America was a closed if not forbidden topic for fiction—certainly no novel had taken it as a main theme."[61] Miller further explained that it was difficult for him to write about antisemitism because it was so entangled with all of his experiences, and because the subject inevitably led to his own resentment and defensiveness. In a 1947 speech, Miller remarked, "Instantly, therefore, and inevitably, when I confront the prospect of writing about Jewish life my mood is defensive, and combative. There is hardly a story or play I could write about which would not have to contain justification for behavior that in any other people need not be justified."[62] In *Gentleman's Agreement*, the non-Jewish protagonist, Phil, similarly discovers the challenges Jews face in responding to antisemitism after watching his friend, Dave Goldman, react to an antisemitic comment. Phil reflects on the Jew's burden in such moments: "The anti-semite offered the effrontery—and then the world was ready with harsh yardsticks to measure the self-control and dignity with which you met it. You were sensitive or too sensitive; you were too timid or too bellicose."[63] It is a measure of Phil's empathy that he perceives this inner Jewish turmoil.

Signs of a new market for fiction attacking antisemitism and racism inspired Hobson in her writing. In one of her letters to Simon, in the fall of 1944, Hobson referred to her friend Margaret Halsey: "I'm eagerly waiting for Peg Halsey's book—no book store has it yet. I didn't know it dealt with this subject at all."[64] Margaret or "Peg" Halsey was the ex-wife of Richard Simon's brother, Henry. Before marrying into the Simon family, Halsey was an entry-level employee at Simon & Schuster. A winner of an early National Book Award (before the National Book Awards were abandoned during World War II and then restarted in 1950), for her humorous bestseller *With Malice Toward Some* (1938), Halsey's writing continued to garner high praise. Her 1997 *New York Times* obituary would recall Halsey as "a witty writer with an acute social concern," comparing her to Dorothy Parker.[65]

The Halsey book that Hobson anticipated reading—*Some of My Best Friends Are Soldiers*, published in 1944—focused on race relations and antisemitism. The *New York Times* reviewer expressed surprise that a writer known for her sense of humor was taking on such serious topics, observing, "Although suggestions on interracial dealings seem a rather profound undertaking for Miss Halsey's equipment," the novel "is entertaining for those who must have their pocketful of wisecracks."[66]

The subjects of Halsey's books during the 1940s were the result of her own change in attitudes. As an adult Halsey realized that she had been "brought up to be anti-Semitic," at a time when "Jews were usually referred to as kikes," and the remark, "That's the Jew of it for you," was "current and prevalent."[67] Invoking the Charles Dickens character considered an archetypical Jewish villain, Halsey described her 1910s and 1920s childhood in Yonkers, New York, as a setting in which "it was taken for granted that the Jewish confraternity consisted of a threatening multiplicity of Fagins whose aim in life was to humiliate and destroy the seraphic congregation of the Gentiles."[68] Halsey recognized that she imbibed these messages from the adults around her, who were "not evil people. . . . They were simply passing on what they themselves had never heard questioned. The anthropologists call it cultural conditioning."[69] As an adult living in Manhattan, Halsey's views evolved. Halsey recalled moving to New York City as a young woman and meeting other gentiles "whose opinion I valued and who disapproved of anti-Semitism." It made a difference in her own thinking.

As a writer, Halsey performed a bit of her own cultural conditioning as she modeled progressive attitudes and behavior through her popular books. After earning readers' respect through her perceptive and witty observations, Halsey demonstrated anti-antisemitism in her writing. "My early training in anti-Semitism had been external and more or less automatic, and since I came from the sheltered and non-embittered middle class, I had no pressing emotional reason for clinging to it."[70] Halsey's reflections suggest a condescension toward lower-class Americans, illuminating how writers utilized middle-class respectability to present antisemitism as socially unacceptable behavior. Gentiles like Halsey—and the character Phil Green—provided alternative, anti-antisemitic ways of being American.

Halsey amplified her anti-racist themes in *Color Blind: A White Woman Looks at the Negro* (1946), in which she attempted an honest examination of her adult interactions with Blacks, beginning with Jeannette, the first maid Halsey hired. Halsey later realized, "I knew nothing at all about Jeannette qua Jeannette. To me, she was the entire Negro race, and I was going to make up to her for all the indignities which had been visited on her section of the populace over a period of seven hundred years. Disastrous is not the word for what this little project turned out to be."[71] As focused on the "Negro Problem in America" as she was in *Color Blind*, Halsey looked to Europe and Hitler's antisemitism as the exemplar of absolute evil. In writing about the white supremacist Mississippi senator Theodore Bilbo, Halsey posited, "The point is not whether Bilbo is like Hitler, but whether we are like the Germans—passive, sheeplike and very, very easily bluffed." Halsey believed Americans could do better. It was true, Halsey conceded, that "We are not functioning brilliantly as a democracy."[72] But democracies never do. "Brilliance is not an attribute of democracies—which when they cease to bumble and fumble and lurch and sprawl toward their goals, also cease to be democracies."[73]

Although *New York Times* reviewer Orville Prescott found Halsey's "girlish style" of writing "marvelously irritating"—demonstrating a typical highbrow reviewer's condescension for the feminine middlebrow—he judged *Color Blind* valuable for its list of practical steps to fight racism and because "each book, play, or public address which arouses sympathy and interest in persons who have not considered the matter before strikes a blow in a common cause."[74]

It was in the epistolary novel, *Some of My Best Friends Are Soldiers*—which Hobson read when she was beginning to write *Agreement*—that Halsey focused more on antisemitism. A reviewer for *Opportunity: Journal of Negro Life* commented that it was not the racist episodes in the novel that made *Some of My Best Friends* exceptional, "for they are, unfortunately, commonplace."[75] It was Halsey's humor and wit that made her anti-racism and anti-antisemitism lessons easily absorbed by readers.

Hobson was a fan. As she informed Simon, "I got and read Peg Halsey's book. Though I think it is too slight and at many points artificial . . . I'm very much for it. I think it will do some good even, only a jot of good maybe, but a starter." As she noted in that same letter, Hobson had also recently read Graham's serialized *Earth and High Heaven*. "I felt that about the Collier's serial—and the fact that it is bought for movies by Sam Goldwyn for 100 grand knocks me over and makes me feel that maybe the conspiracy of silence *is* ending. Which I approve of. And selfishly perhaps, I feel that things like these pave the way for other books which will perhaps be deeper and truer in some ways at least."[76] Not every anti-antisemitism novel had to be top-notch, Hobson implied. Some of these novels would simply prepare the ground for others—hers, for instance—that might go "deeper and truer" on the subject.

But going deeper and truer was a difficult goal, especially when the lessons imparted by anti-antisemitism novelists were countercultural. In Halsey's *Some of My Best Friends*, the main character, Gretchen, a volunteer in a serviceman's canteen, hears an antisemitic remark from a wealthy patron that offends Gretchen's Jewish friend. The incident was based on one that Halsey witnessed as a volunteer at the Stage Door Canteen that caused Halsey to reflect that " 'Jewboy' was Standard English for many of the soldiers who came to the Canteen," despite the fact that these American soldiers were at war, defending democracy.[77] Halsey later observed in her autobiography that "There seemed to be room for a restatement of what in those days we called 'tolerance' for minorities and if such a restatement could be sugar-coated with humor, it might persuade people who would never dream of reading a tract." After the antisemitic episode, Gretchen muses: " 'Sticks and Stones may break my bones, but names will never hurt me.' Only names do hurt people."[78] That names *do* hurt people was one of the themes of anti-antisemitism novels. The old children's rhyme, accepted wisdom and central to childrearing, was overturned in the anti-antisemitism literature of the 1940s. Barbs and slurs and discriminatory remarks did matter. They did their own kind of emotional damage, even if the marks they left were not always visible.

Exactly how discrimination mangled the insides of a person might have been the specialty of another midcentury middlebrow novelist. Lillian Smith, the bestselling author of the interracial romance *Strange Fruit* (1944), wrote about the permanent emotional and psychological scars that discrimination left on all races. The *New York Times Book Review* referred to *Strange Fruit* as "one of the most rewarding first novels to come out of the South in years," adding that "America's peculiar dilemma has waited a long time for understanding—and for a two-sided fictional treatment."[79] Despite being banned in Boston for obscenity, *Strange Fruit* sold a million hardcover copies, topping the bestseller list and surprising the publishers who had rejected it.[80] In the mind of Hobson's publisher, Richard Simon, *Strange Fruit* provided a model for what an anti-antisemitism novel might achieve in terms of popularity. Although Simon was skeptical of Hobson's plan to write a novel about antisemitism, he looked to *Strange Fruit* for evidence that a novel exposing prejudice might succeed.[81] When Simon wrote to Hobson in late September 1944, he shared his belief that novels about bigotry were not effective in combating antisemitism, but added: "By all this I do not mean that we're against publishing books about refugees or jews [sic] or Negroes or any of the other problems which so many people would rather not face or think about or hear about. But we do know that in order for those books to do any good they have to be extraordinarily well done and plausible."[82]

There were good reasons for Simon's skepticism. When Simon wrote to Hobson in September, 1944, he referred to the commercial disappointment that was her first book: " 'The Trespassers' did not achieve the hundred thousand or more which we had hoped for because not enough people found that—for whatever reason—it rang a bell in their hearts." Simon turned to another social ill—racism—for an example of the potential of an anti-antisemitism novel. "On the other hand, 'Strange Fruit' did ring that bell and so did 'Native Son' and so did 'Under Cover.' The great Jewish book corresponding to 'Strange Fruit' has yet to be written. Perhaps you are the one to do it."[83] Frustrating as it was at the time, Simon's challenge inspired Hobson.

Without *Strange Fruit* it would have been difficult for Simon to imagine a novel like *Agreement* becoming a hit. These connections between the two novels in the minds of a publisher and his author illuminate the complexity of the relationship between antisemitism and racism. It was not simply that the culture of 1940s anti-antisemitism helped pave the way toward the civil rights movement.[84] The larger issue of racism in America provided examples and lessons for Jews and writers. As Hobson's and Simon's letters reveal, efforts to combat racism through literature inspired anti-antisemitism novelists. Indeed, Hobson inscribed this inspiration into her novel, in a scene in which Phil's colleagues discuss the popularity of the recent novel *Strange Fruit*.[85]

In October 1944, Hobson's letters to Simon revealed connections she was making between antisemitism and other forms of discrimination. Hobson was temporarily living in California while writing for film studios to supplement her income. The West Coast provided Hobson with a new perspective on antisemitism: "I'm plenty frightened about what antisemitism and antinegroism [sic] is growing up into for the country," she wrote to Simon.[86] Away from New York, where Jews constituted more than a quarter of the city's early 1940s population and the city's largest ethnic group, Hobson likely experienced antisemitism in a new way.[87] As a Jewish woman, Hobson felt a heightened sense of her minority status in California. "Out here it seems more rampant to me than in the circles I knew at home, perhaps because the widespread and almost unargued Anti-Jap feeling here makes so sturdy a base for all other racisms to flourish on."[88] Hobson experienced firsthand how antisemitism and racism thrived and built upon each other.

From Antisemitism to Anti-Racism

It wasn't only the anti-antisemitism in Hobson's proposed novel that elicited Richard Simon's skepticism. The central premise of a gentile pretending to be Jewish struck him as implausible. "Readers will not believe that a gentile would pose as a Jew," he wrote to Hobson in a discouraging letter, in August 1944.[89] Who would voluntarily become a Jew? was the implication. It was the old Harry Wolfson understanding of Jewishness as burden—something that one couldn't help but hope to escape. Jewishness was far too undesirable, Simon suggested, to be presented as a choice. Yet Hobson's novel imagined a society in which Jews were perceived as ordinary Americans, just like

Christians. With Hitler's focus on racial differences as their counterexample, midcentury liberals perceived blindness to difference as a preferable stance. Frank Sinatra's 1945 film short, *The House That I Live In*, captured this sentiment. During Sinatra's teachable moment with a group of schoolboys who had been taunting a Jew, Sinatra lectures them: "Religion makes no difference. Except maybe to a Nazi, or somebody that's stupid. Why, people all over the world worship God in many different ways. God created everybody."[90] The lesson was clear: good postwar Americans paid little attention to the differences between Christians and Jews. It's unlikely that Hobson believed in this reality—why else would she have changed her name, at different points in her life, to something less Jewish-sounding than Zametkin? And why bother writing anti-antisemitism fiction if Americans already fully subscribed to the equality of Christians and Jews? That Jews should be treated just like Christian Americans was Hobson's wish for her country. This vision is on display at several points in the novel including a party scene in which Phil surveys a room full of writers, artists, and scientists and thinks to himself, "Here was a world where a man's name, the shape of his nose, the religion he believed in or the religion he did not believe in—where none of it counted."[91] Was there really such a world? Phil's attraction to it made readers want to live there too.

This religion-blind ideal, implying that all religions, or at least all three "American religions," were regarded equally was more aspiration than reality. It also ignored a truth of Jewish experience: Jews did not always experience their Jewishness primarily as a religion, at least not in the Protestant sense of religion as an internal faith and a separate sphere of life.[92] Further, as midcentury sociological studies of Jews acknowledged, what mattered to Jews in their religion differed from what mattered to Christians. Beliefs and creed, these midcentury explanations of Judaism explained, were not as central to most Jews' experience of their Judaism as community and deed.[93] But these specifics of Jewish religion were not the primary concern of anti-antisemitism fiction.

Eight years before Will Herberg's *Protestant-Catholic-Jew* (1955) explained that "To be a Protestant, a Catholic, or a Jew are today the alternative ways of being an American," Hobson's novel had a very similar thesis at its core.[94] Phil Green explained to his young son, one morning, "You can be an American and a Catholic, or an American and a Protestant, or an American and a Jew."[95] Hobson prefigured Herberg's sociological thesis, and taught readers that Jewishness was one of three valid ways to be an American. In *Agreement*, after witnessing this breakfast table interaction, Phil's mother congratulates Phil on a parenting job well done. She tells him, "Just using the three together every time, as a group. Catholic Protestant Jew, like apples pears peaches. That's a good start."[96]

Phil's explanation of the three religions was a good start because it marked a shift away from seeing Jews as members of an inferior race, or dangerous "other," to seeing Jews as members of an American religious tradition on par with Christianity.[97] Identity thinking, explains the philosopher Kwame Anthony Appiah, includes the rise of considering diverse labels (such as Protestant, Catholic, and Jewish) *as things of the same kind*. Grouping Judaism alongside other mainstream American religions, as though it were simply another variety of American religion, evidenced a change in thinking. Before the era of *Gentleman's Agreement*, racial thinking about Jews dominated, and Judaism seemed mysterious and unknown, a relic of the ancient past.

Portraying Jewish identity as an antidote to antisemitism was also the approach of anti-antisemitism novelist Jo Sinclair (1913–1995). Unlike more famous examples of the genre, such as *Gentleman's Agreement*, or more highbrow examples, such as Arthur Miller's *Focus* and Saul Bellow's *The Victim*, Sinclair's *Wasteland* is less well-remembered today despite including what is considered the "first full, loving portrayal of a lesbian in twentieth century American fiction."[98]

In *Wasteland*, the Jewish lesbian character Debby explains to her brother Jake that seeing a psychiatrist helped her overcome insecurities. "Before I went, I used to feel that awful shame. Of what I was. . . . I'd be so hurt all the time, so ashamed of being different, that finally I just couldn't make sense of anything."[99] Debby is ashamed of her Jewishness, her poor immigrant parents, their shabby home, and, perhaps most ambitiously for this 1940s popular novel, her lesbianism. The last point received scant attention from many of the 1946 reviews of *Wasteland*, suggesting that while public discussion of antisemitism and Jewishness increased during the 1940s, lesbianism was still an identity that dare not speak its name.[100]

Sinclair's linkage of antisemitism and homophobia showed how fighting antisemitism became associated with attempts to make postwar America safer for multiple kinds of difference. In response to Jake's deep uneasiness over his Jewishness, Debby explains how his pain might lead to insights about other kinds of suffering. She tells Jake, presumably referring to her newfound comfort in her lesbianism, although Sinclair's unwillingness to name it as such reveals the limits of 1940s acceptance of homosexuality: "I can feel how

I'm part of a person they call nigger, or dirty Jew, or cripple. Maybe it takes hurt to understand hurt, I don't know. But it's like I can understand all kinds of hurt now."[101] In Sinclair's novel, forging a Jewish identity meant building awareness of the marginalization of others.

In *Gentleman's Agreement*, this connection between antisemitism and other hatreds is accomplished in service of a different goal: deflecting victimhood away from Jews. When Phil initially brainstorms ideas for how to write about antisemitism, he jots down connections to other prejudices: "Link up with growth of anti-alien feeling, anti-Negro, anti-Catholic, all minority. (Threat to US most serious, not to Jew.)"[102] While Sinclair used the parallel between antisemitism and other bigotries to show how experiencing antisemitism might lead to empathy, Hobson aimed to shift attention away from Jewish victimhood.

In anti-antisemitism novels, readers' sensitivity to the psychological experience of overcoming antisemitism was cultivated through specific narrative strategies, including a literary "confessional." Main characters divulged their latent or former bigoted feelings—sometimes in conversation with another character, and at times in interior monologues—and then, through character development, overcame their former antisemitism to arrive at a position of *anti-*antisemitism. In Jo Sinclair's *Wasteland*, the confessional act occurs through Jake Braunowitz's conversations with his therapist. In Margaret Halsey's *Some of My Best Friends*, Gretchen's transformation becomes apparent through her letters to her brother. In *Earth and High Heaven*, Gwethalyn Graham shared her characters' inner thoughts with readers, thereby illuminating shifts in attitudes. In *Agreement*, Phil Green's conversations with his girlfriend, family, colleagues, as well as his interior monologues, reveal changes in Phil and those close to him. Skillful novelists thus presented "before-and-after" views of character development, demonstrating that there were constructive ways of responding to bigotry and overcoming it within oneself.

The year before *Gentleman's Agreement* was published, *Wasteland* made an unexpected literary splash. In January 1946, Sinclair's editor, Edward Aswell, wrote to Sinclair: "Never in my editorial career, I think, has any event given me greater pleasure than your winning the Harper Prize Novel contest with your first novel, Wasteland. When I announced the news to you over the telephone, you said you couldn't believe it. Perhaps the enclosed check for $10,000 will at last convince you that it is real."[103] The *New York Times* reported that Sinclair was "happy, naturally, about winning, but was anxious to let it go at that," declining a trip to Manhattan and a party in her honor.[104]

Sinclair's success as a writer may have depended, in part, like Hobson's, on her name-changing. Born Ruth Seid to Russian-Jewish immigrant parents, Sinclair adopted a pen name after discovering that the magazine *Esquire* published male authors, exclusively.[105] In moving from *Ruth* to *Jo*, Sinclair may have been aiming toward a less feminine-sounding name, but it was no coincidence that she chose an Anglo-sounding surname as a replacement for *Seid*. Sinclair's early discomfort in her poor, immigrant roots, coupled with her coming to terms with her homosexuality, inspired *Wasteland*.

Readers of all backgrounds felt moved by Sinclair's story of young people overcoming disadvantaged backgrounds. Plenty of non-Jews, including Richard Wright and the short-story writer Nolan Miller, found a universal message in *Wasteland*. Miller wrote to Ed Aswell, shortly after *Wasteland* was published, "It is far better written than FOCUS and MRS. PALMER'S HONEY, two other books I have read recently which, in their way, treat the same theme."[106] Proving that Jewish writing about antisemitism was not always dismissed as "special pleading," Miller added, "Most important to me is that it is a novel about a Jew, written by a Jew. It is, then ... close to the living nerve of her heart, and it is splendid that she has been able to be so courageous, for I do think this: WASTELAND is one of the most courageous books I have read since Joyce's PORTRAIT OF THE ARTIST AS A YOUNG MAN."[107] That courage to write honestly about feelings of shame spoke powerfully to all kinds of readers.

But for some, *Wasteland* was a distinctly Jewish story. In the Cleveland weekly Yiddish newspaper, *The Jewish World*, reviewer Isidore Schoen explained that *Wasteland* could *only* be considered a Jewish story, and that reviewers claiming otherwise were mistaken.[108] Taking issue with one such review that averred, "The story of this novel could very easily be told about a family of any other nationality than Jewish, regardless of religion or creed," Schoen explained that "such a mental revolution as Jake goes through can only happen in a Jew." It was more than twenty years since Harry Wolfson had written "Escaping Judaism," but its core message–that American Jews wished they weren't what they were–continued to feel, to many, like a distinctly Jewish experience. Schoen did not blame Jews for their psychic struggle, stating, "Maybe it is not so much our own fault as the fault of the Diaspora, which implanted to us an inferiority complex, and the Jake Browns are the results of thousands of years of pogroms, sufferings and tortures."[109]

Claiming *Wasteland* for Jews may have been Schoen's goal, but the novel, in fact, had much wider appeal, stemming from multiple factors: the connections that Sinclair made between antisemitism and other forms of discrimination; Sinclair's deft use of the relationship between her main character, Jake, and his psychiatrist (the doctor's notes are included in the novel); and Jake's search for identity. As a result, readers wrote to Sinclair with their own stories of internal growth, or even with questions about how to find a psychiatrist as supportive as the one in her novel.[110] More than a few readers found a lifeline in the lesbian character, Debby. "I hope I'm not prying," a Betty Breaux wrote to Sinclair, "but your book and characters were so interesting and understanding, I was wondering if you know a 'Debby'—I would like to know all about her."[111] A Francis Cohen admitted in her letter that "I've never written to an author in my life. I don't know why I am now." But of course she knew why: "Maybe it's because of Debby. Yes, I think it's Debby alright. Once while I was reading the book I put it down for a second and said how funny it seemed to come across a character in a book and wish like all hell you could get to meet that person."[112] Sinclair had given many readers their first exposure to a positively portrayed lesbian.

Ed Aswell praised Sinclair's moving vision of a more inclusive America, explaining in a letter to Sinclair, "The theme of it is the best possible doctrine for the time we live in, because, in addition to being a fascinating story, a brilliant delineation of characters, it is a plea for tolerance and understanding of minority groups everywhere—a plea for the abolition of a waste land in all the areas of American life."[113] But Aswell was not Sinclair's only important supporter.

Richard Wright, author of the bestselling *Native Son* (1940) and one of the most successful Black writers in 1940s America, expressed deep appreciation for Sinclair's writing.[114] At Aswell's request, Wright had read Sinclair's manuscript, and his recommendation was influential in her winning the 1946 Harper's Prize. As Aswell communicated to Sinclair a few weeks prior to her novel's publication, "Wright phoned me this morning in great excitement. I had sent him proofs of WASTELAND, and he said to me that nothing he had read since THE DUBLINERS had moved him so deeply."[115] As a newcomer in the land of published novelists, Sinclair had much to gain from Wright's praise and generous mentoring. Wright would continue to support Sinclair by advising her on issues relating to contracts, royalties, taxes, and agents, assuring her, "If I can be of any help in this matter—in terms of letting you know what is usually done and what to expect as your rights—I'll be more than glad to do so."[116]

In *Wasteland*, Wright found the fulfillment of his hopes for a novel exploring the psychology and prejudices of the white immigrant in America. Wright had observed such prejudice in his own Jewish mother-in-law: "I'm sure when Ellen's mother was a peasant in Russian Poland, she did not hate so many people of other races; but since coming to the land of the free and the brave she has had a lot of trouble keeping her sons and daughter from marrying Negroes, Japanese, and what not, folks whom she has learned to hate since coming to our great and noble land ... she swapped her ancient age-old culture for the American cult of material success and its parallel of color hate and moral imperialism, and it has not worked out. Oh boy, what a theme for a novel! She has come to worship what she is now hating in this land. Why don't white writers write these things up?"[117] To Wright, Sinclair was the rare white author willing to examine the process by which individuals came to loathe themselves and others. The Jewish writer Judd Teller similarly picked up on Sinclair's penchant for reaching into the heart of the matter. He called *Wasteland* "One of the few honest novels about Jews ever written by an American writer."[118]

In their fan mail, readers, too, expressed appreciation for Sinclair's honesty of emotion. "You will probably hear from many Jewish readers who, like the girl I was just having lunch with, will tell you that you have gone to the heart of their innermost trouble and have illuminated it as they never hoped," one non-Jewish aspiring novelist wrote to Sinclair, adding, "I venture to predict that you will receive equally as many letters from non-Jewish readers."[119] An admiring Harvard undergraduate wrote, "You went deeper than outward appearances."[120] He compared Sinclair favorably with other popular Jewish writers. "You went to the roots of their behavior and explained just why it is that Jews of that class and of my class live the way they do." Another reader expressed gratitude for Sinclair's message, despite her very different background: "I grew up through a similar pattern of emotional tension such as you portray in your story. Yet my family are not Jewish, nor are we negroes, but we were labeled 'Bohunks,'" the woman explained of her Czechoslovakian immigrant family.[121] Sinclair's metaphor of a mental ghetto in *Wasteland* was one that the letter-writer seized on to describe her own experience: "My ghetto existed just as firmly and seemingly impenetrable as did Deborah's. I have broken it down by patient toil and growth of spiritual understanding. I look at some members of my family and see that they are still living within the walls of their ghettos and my heart aches for them." Musing on the stifling nature of societal expectations and stereotypes—a dynamic at the heart of *Wasteland*—the letter writer shared views that Sinclair would have understood: "It is so strange how we accept the opinions which society imposes and we do not question the authority, be it right or wrong—we merely accept." Just as Jake learns from his psychiatrist to question his assumptions about his family, the writer added: "Only when we begin to question (as you and I and many others have done) then do we begin to grow."[122] The reader understood her freedom to question, reject old assumptions, and to grow spiritually as the results of her American environment. She wrote to Sinclair of her "gratitude, when I realize my 'Freedom to Question,' to analyze and particularly to express. This privilege, of course, is 'America' and though I have parents who unintentionally failed me and my brother and sisters, I have awakened enough to say to that parent, 'I love you and thank you for having come to America—you made me an American!'"[123]

This focus on the American context as crucial to personal transformation held true for the anti-antisemitism novels of Hobson, Sinclair, and Halsey, suggesting that fighting antisemitism and arriving at a healthy identity were victories contingent on American values. In *Gentleman's Agreement*, Phil completes his writing assignment and realizes that waning antisemitism is connected with other important changes, such as making society safe for more types of people: "Other centuries had had their driving forces. Perhaps the twentieth would have its own singular characteristic as men looked far back to it one day. . . . Perhaps it would be the century that broadened and implemented the idea of freedom, all the freedoms. Of all men."[124]

Unlike Sinclair, Hobson avoids specifics about this postwar vision of an America made safer for a wider circle of people. But the suggestion is made, in the novels of Hobson, Sinclair, and Halsey, that there is a link between fighting antisemitism and fighting other kinds of bigotries. Anti-antisemitism novels helped to bring about an awakening among readers, illuminating the rampant discrimination in their midst and allowing them to imagine new possibilities for societal change.

4
The Limits of Anti-Antisemitism Literature

"It may not be an 'Uncle Tom's Cabin' in the popular conception of propaganda literature," Dorothy Fletcher of Ridgewood, New Jersey, wrote to novelist Laura Z. Hobson in the spring of 1947, "but, to me and to those of my friends who have already read it, it seems about the most honest and perceptive as well as the most entertaining and interesting piece of a social-political nature in current literature."[1] One of many fans who penned admiring letters to Hobson, Fletcher explicitly linked *Gentleman's Agreement* to a tradition of middlebrow social protest literature that stretched back to Harriet Beecher Stowe's nineteenth-century anti-slavery novel and extended forward, in the coming decades, to include Harper Lee's Pulitzer Prize–winning 1960 novel *To Kill a Mockingbird*.

Like these other examples of social protest literature, *Agreement* offered its own interpretation of American exceptionalism.[2] Hobson reminded readers that their country was different. True, the United States was not free of antisemitism. But in the shadow of Hitler's atrocities, American religious bigotry appeared benign. When *Agreement* became a film within nine months of the novel's publication, critics interpreted its Hollywood success as further evidence of the country's democratic values and desire to improve itself. In her glowing review of *Gentleman's Agreement*, film critic Cecelia Ager (niece of the Jewish writer Anzia Yezierska), put it this way: "It is wonderful that it was made. It is more wonderful still that it has turned out to be such an astoundingly good picture. But the most wonderful thing of all is that it reminds us that only in an alert, vigorous democracy forever striving to attain the democratic ideal, could it, or would it, ever have been made at all. Oh, it makes one proud!"[3] Among fans, *Agreement* occasioned a round of applause for American moral superiority.[4]

Even as she shone a spotlight on American prejudice, Hobson revealed her belief in the country's ability to right its wrongs. It was a classic posture for authors of social protest literature. As Zoe Trodd observes, "Protest writers have long asked America to *be* America."[5] Not every anti-antisemitism novel hit this sweet spot of readers' desire for self-scrutiny, combined with the self-congratulations that came with expressions of American exceptionalism. But neither was every author so inclined toward this target. Arthur Miller's 1945 anti-antisemitism novel, *Focus*, portrayed an ominous wartime national culture. Tormented by the local antisemitic Christian Front organization, a Jewish character is flummoxed by his neighbors' refusal to recognize the dangers in their midst, asking: "How many wars we got to fight in this world before you will understand what they are doing to you?"[6] Miller's story of "man's inhumanity to man," as the *New York Times* described *Focus*, did not share *Agreement*'s optimistic view of the country's capacity to improve.[7] It is only in the final scene that the gentile protagonist yearns for the kind of societal change that *Focus* presents as nearly impossible: "a swift charge of lightning that would with a fiery stroke break away the categories of people and change them so that it would not be important to them what tribe they sprang from."[8] Unlike Miller's chilling portrait of 1940s Brooklyn, Hobson's hopeful 1940s Manhattan remained hitched to the dream of a better tomorrow. *Agreement* offered a particularly gratifying combination for readers seeking the satisfaction of confessing their sins—absolution was achieved through the purchasing, reading, and discussion of such social message books—alongside reassurance that they were already doing something to right the wrong of antisemitism: Look, they were reading *Gentleman's Agreement*!

But some readers were on to Hobson. Two years after *Agreement* was published, *Partisan Review* published novelist James Baldwin's essay "Everybody's Favorite Protest Novel," in which Baldwin criticized and rejected the genre. The essay took direct aim at *Uncle Tom's Cabin* and *Native Son*, the recent novel of Baldwin's former mentor, Richard Wright. But Baldwin did not spare *Gentleman's Agreement* in his critique of books in which "whatever unsettling questions are raised are evanescent, titillating; remote, for this has nothing to do with us." Baldwin imagined readers experiencing "a very definite thrill of virtue from the fact that we are reading such a book at all. This report from the pit reassures us of its reality and its darkness and of our salvation; and 'As long as such books are being published,' an American liberal once said to me, 'everything will be all right.'"[9]

The false sense of reassurance that the genre provided, according to Baldwin, is worth keeping in mind when considering the merits and limits of 1940s *anti*-antisemitism fiction. Ironically, the very existence of novels illuminating antisemitism and racism may have been among the reasons—along with a booming economy and a national politics of consensus—that midcentury Americans were content to slumber on, in spite of the nation's continued inequality.[10] As a result of recent revelations about Nazi atrocities, readers instinctively understood the gravity of antisemitism. But Hitler's racist and murderous antisemitism also explains readers' challenge in taking their own American antisemitism seriously. Nazi Germany made it easy to dismiss American prejudice as relatively inconsequential.

The white liberalism fueling anti-antisemitism fiction of the 1940s fell short, failing to move beyond condescension to nonwhite subjects.[11] As Gregory Jay argues, the "liberal race novel," landmarked by *Uncle Tom's Cabin*, and including mid-twentieth-century novels such as *Gentleman's Agreement*, *Strange Fruit*, and *To Kill a Mockingbird*, "struggled to criticize racism, call for social and political change, and promote liberal philosophies of freedom and equality."[12] While novelists' strategies included tapping into readers' emotions, they also worked within an understanding of the narrowness of liberal sympathies. As this chapter shows, 1940s anti-antisemitism novels reified the US racial order at the same time that they argued for moving Jews from the racial to the religious category, a process that entailed whitening Jews.[13] But race was not the only arena in which anti-antisemitism novels demonstrated limited tolerance. By displaying the varieties of acceptable Jewishness, anti-antisemitism novels made clear which kinds of Jews were eligible for integration into mainstream society. In the case of *Gentleman's Agreement*, religious Jews, poor Jews—and really, everyone outside middle- and upper-class circles—were unwelcome.

Achieving Jewish Identity within a White Racial Order

Anti-antisemitism novels provided Jewish readers with a guide for embracing Jewishness as part of a comfortable American identity—something that, in the early 1940s, many Jews still had trouble conceptualizing. For example, the story of growth at the center of Jo Sinclair's *Wasteland* portrayed Jake, with the help of a psychiatrist, beginning to question his old assumptions about Jewishness. The discovery that his non-Jewish psychiatrist is familiar with Passover, Jake's favorite holiday, is a watershed moment as Jake hears, for the first time, the rites of his family's holiday table described by an educated American in dignified terms—a foreshadowing of midcentury Introduction to Judaism texts. Hearing the doctor tell him, "In your mind, then, the Seder supper is tied to words like family, like Jewish history and culture, security, strength.... And behind your family, tens of thousands of Jewish families, going through the dignity and beauty of each of these prayers" makes Jake newly aware of the grandeur of Judaism, which he had associated with the shame of his family's poverty and immigrant roots.[14] Shifting his understanding of Jewishness from marginalized racial group to respected religion affords Jake new self-esteem. As Jake recounts his family's Passover Seder, he realizes that despite his secular life, he *does* have a religious sensibility. "You may not be religious in the sense that your father is," the psychiatrist tells him, referring to Jake's father's Orthodoxy. "But that Passover ritual and promise, that holding out of spring and hope, are religion to you, John. Just as surely as if you prayed in Hebrew. They're your sense of God, your clasped hands in prayer. Other men get it from music. Or from poetry."[15]

Relying on the psychiatrist's American understanding of religion, with its hints of Christianity ("clasped hands in prayer"), Jake recognizes his own potential for spirituality. This more capacious understanding of religion is apparent in another significant American ritual in the novel. After both Jake and his sister, Debby, have successfully completed therapy, they donate blood for the war effort. Their donations represent their new feelings of belonging in America, as Jake's psychiatrist notes: "Jewish blood, in his mind not too long ago a despised thing, has been accepted and now flows in the mixture of American blood."[16] Pride in Judaism is presented as the antidote to the experience of racial antisemitism, even as Jake's "blood thinking" about Jewishness persists.[17]

In the aftermath of World War II and the Nazis' racist antisemitism, there is a new potency to this blood-thinking about Jews. That Jake and Debby's blood donations occur in the context of the Red Cross segregating Black and white donations (a policy initiated in 1942 and discontinued in 1948) raises the stakes higher.[18] Debby explains to Jake while they are on their way to donate: "You know, where we're going now they keep Negro and white blood separate.... They make little ghettos for a thing like blood. When I give my pint, Jack, it's against that. Dead against it. Some day they'll know they can't do a thing like that. Part of my blood will show them that some day."[19] Debby contributes to the American war effort with her Jewish blood in silent protest of the country's racist policy, and with hopes that Black blood will soon be accepted. There is no indication that Jake feels similarly.

Sinclair's message about Jews and race is thus mixed.[20] Jake ultimately feels accepted by American society as a result of his gift of blood. However, this acceptance is predicated on a racial order that segregates Black blood. As the psychiatrist's notes acknowledge, Jake gave his blood as a Jew and an American, but most importantly, "he gave as Everyman. He wanted to be the anonymous man of America, the man who is as same as the next man, with as much to give and as much to be reckoned with." The doctor notes that an "Everyman, in other words, is not, and cannot be, a part of a wasteland."[21] While Jake's blood donation allows him to feel that he belongs in society, the country's policy of blood segregation ensures that Blacks cannot find the same acceptance. In the 1940s racial order, a Black man cannot be an Everyman. As the *Journal of the American Medical Association* put it in their 1942 statement of opposition, blood segregation was "not only unscientific but is a grievous affront to the largest minority group in our country."[22] Jake's self-satisfaction after his blood donation suggests his unthinking willingness to uphold America's racial order.[23]

Similar to Phil Green's desire for acceptance of Jews such as his friend Dave Goldman—in other words, non-objectionable Jews who can pass as gentiles—Jake seeks acceptance as a Jew who might be mistaken for any other white guy. In both novels, Jewish masculinity is on the line. Jake and Dave are counted as real American men, so long as they conform to gentile standards. Dave Goldman's status as an American is affirmed through his resemblance to the gentile, Phil Green, and because he fits into the era's structure of American manhood: he is a soldier, husband, father, and breadwinner.[24] Toward the end of *Wasteland*, after Jake's blood donation, the psychiatrist notes of Jake's masculinity that his "new dominance has been accepted."[25] Prior to this resolution, Jake's shaky masculinity is represented by his bachelorhood, a suspect status in midcentury America, where marriage and fatherhood constituted the masculine ideal.[26] After his blood donation, Jake's manhood is finally secure, in large part because America's postwar racial order accepts Jews, unlike Blacks. Meanwhile, it is Debby, not Jake, who opposes racism because it segregates people into isolated "wastelands" where human connection and creativity cannot be cultivated. Jake does not share these progressive views. In fact, early in the novel, he feels "the shame of Debby associating with Negroes."[27] Later, Jake is more open to hearing Debby's views. At one point, when the siblings discuss the old neighborhood their family abandoned—anticipating Jewish postwar participation in urban white flight—Debby gently guides Jake through an examination of their family's racism. "Any idea what we were trying to escape from?" she asked softly. "Was it really the Negroes? Or was it fear; and of course we pinned the word Negro to the fear, didn't we? Did we really think the Negro would contaminate us, or was it some old, secret nightmare we could name nigger now? ... It's easier to run away from something with a name, isn't it?"[28] The novel does not show Jake making the leap to Debby's anti-racist views. Instead, there is the suggestion that Jewish masculinity may be too important—and too fragile—for Jewish men to risk their white masculinity by working on the problem of racism. Sinclair does not seem to critique these gender norms. As a writer and a lesbian (a stand-in for Sinclair) who falls outside postwar gender norms, Debby is better positioned to tackle such problems. She has less to lose.

In *Gentleman's Agreement*, too, the message on race is mixed. Jewishness retains its racial aspect in parts of the novel, with characters described as displaying Jewish characteristics. Professor Lieberman is depicted as a secular Jew whose Jewishness is a matter of appearance. For 1940s Americans, race was something that could be discerned from appearance. And so, Lieberman is described as having "the face of a Jew in a Nazi cartoon, the beaked nose, the blue jowls. And the curling black hair."[29] In spite of this portrait of Lieberman, Phil argues against this outmoded racial conception of Jewishness. As Matthew Jacobson observes, "the text is at war with itself in a way that wonderfully demonstrates the character of racial categorization itself as ideology deeply entrenched."[30] *Gentleman's Agreement* made the case for Judaism as an American religion while allowing readers to hold on to what likely felt like a more emotionally satisfying way of thinking of Jews—as not quite, or not just, a religion. Other anti-antisemitism novels similarly revealed the persistence of racial discourse around Jewishness, even as these novels explicitly presented Jewishness as a matter of religion.[31] In Gwethalyn Graham's *Earth and High Heaven*, Marc Reiser contemplates, "What is a Jew?" and considers the term's racial and religious meanings.[32] In Arthur Miller's *Focus*, characters are described as Jewish because of their appearance and because they display what antisemites consider racially Jewish characteristics.[33] For example, "Jew had always meant imposter" to the gentile protagonist, Newman.[34] The very humanity of Jews is in question: "However close to being human a Jew might seem," Newman realizes, non-Jews do not value Jewish life.[35] In Saul Bellow's *The Victim*, a Jew is "a man of wrong blood, of bad blood."[36]

These mixed messages about Jews as members both of a religion and of a race matched American attitudes. The continuation of race-thinking about Jews appeared in a 1947 *Seventeen* magazine story about six female college students touring the country—they were "so concerned about prejudice that they took a semester's leave from UCLA this spring to go on a country-wide tour of the nation's high schools and colleges to discuss it."[37] Among the questions posed to the Jewish member of the tour was whether Jews were a religion, race, or a nationality. The Jewish student answered that Jews were primarily a religion, adding that because of their "long cultural heritage," Jews were also "more than a religious sect."[38] As would continue to be true, it was difficult to answer the question, *What exactly is a Jew?*

Learning about Race while Un-learning Jewishness as Race

Anti-antisemitism novels continued the racial conception of Jews, along with portraying ambivalence about defining Jews strictly as members of a religion. In Gwethalyn Graham's *Earth and High Heaven* (1944), the Jewish character Marc Reiser is at Yom Kippur services when he considers the categories by which he might define his Jewishness, and "realized that his sense of identity" with those around him was more a matter "of race, of race suffering and race achievement, than of religion."[39] But race, too, is quickly disposed of, "for even supposing there had been such a thing as a specifically Jewish race," the sociologists and anthropologists had mostly rejected such notions, Marc reasonably concludes.[40] Although the idea of Jewishness as race has an instinctual hold on him, Marc cannot accept it intellectually. Graham showed readers that racial categorization of Jews was incorrect even as she highlighted its tenacity—and offered the alternative category of religion.

Two years later, in Jo Sinclair's *Wasteland*, the Jewishness of Jake Braunowitz's poor immigrant family is also described in racial terms. It is with his psychiatrist that Jake learns to think of Jewishness as religion. Like Marc Reiser in Graham's novel, Jake is a secular Jew who appreciates that Jewish ritual connects him with family and community. A year later, *Gentleman's Agreement* included multiple teachable moments and conversations about Judaism as a religion. So strong was the instinct to categorize Jews as a race that Hobson seemed to need to emphasize her point about religion. In one scene, Phil Green discusses the meaning of Jewishness with Professor Lieberman, a secular Jewish scientist. Lieberman explains, "You see, Phil, I have no religion, so I am not Jewish by religion. Further, I am a scientist, so I must rely on science which tells me I am not Jewish by race since there's no such thing as a distinct Jewish race."[41] There's little substance to Lieberman's Jewishness, beyond what others perceive as his Jewish appearance.

In another scene, Hobson delivers a heavy-handed teachable moment about the proper categorization of Jews. By revealing Kathy's thoughts, Hobson showcases common mistakes and lessons learned about discourse surrounding Jews: "That time after he'd gone to see Professor Lieberman and she'd said something perfectly casual about 'the Jewish race.' Phil had explained once or twice that the phrase was based on old misconceptions which were completely disproved by modern anthropologists. But she'd said it—it was just habit. She wasn't fighting the scientists when they said there was no such thing. She knew perfectly well that the three great divisions of mankind were the Caucasian Race, the Mongoloid, the Negroid. She remembered his finger pointing out a phrase in a pamphlet written by leading anthropologists 'There is no Jewish "Race."'"[42] Hobson highlighted the ingrained habit of race-thinking in a way that comforted readers with the knowledge that even good liberals such as Kathy made this mistake—and were capable of correcting it.

The pamphlet that Phil and Kathy consulted—found among Hobson's papers at the Columbia University archives—was "The Races of Mankind," written by two women anthropologists, Ruth Benedict and Gene Weltfish.[43] Published in 1943 by the nonprofit Public Affairs Committee, "The Races of Mankind" explained how the war against the Nazis could be fought on the home front through scientific facts combating dangerous untruths about race advanced by Hitler (even as the pamphlet upheld a myth of "three great divisions of mankind").[44] "Aryans, Jews, Italians are *not* races," wrote Benedict and Weltfish.[45] They were speaking Hobson's language. The pamphlet further explained that "Jews are people who acknowledge the Jewish religion. They are of all races, even Negro and Mongolian."

Hobson's inclusion of the "The Races of Mankind" in *Agreement* was one of the ways she enlisted science as a bulwark against antisemitism and Nazism. Professor Lieberman, the rational, secular Jewish scientist with whom Phil finds intellectual fellowship, was another. In *Gentleman's Agreement*, scientists are depicted as prophets of truth in a secular milieu.[46] That it is Professor Lieberman who voices anti-Zionist views, telling Phil, "I can't really talk to a positive Zionist any more than to a confirmed Communist," allowed Hobson to portray anti-Zionism and anti-Communism as the perspectives of an educated scientist.[47] At that point in her life, Hobson viewed both Zionism and Communism as threats to good Americanism.[48] By the 1970s,

Hobson's feelings about Israel shifted again, but she remembered the 1940s as a time when "I still was idealist enough to believe that the only true search for an end to the 'Jewish problem' was for the opening of all those closed doors, so that Jews everywhere could go on thinking of themselves as Frenchmen, Germans, Italians, Americans or whatever—with Judaism their religion, but not their state."[49] For Hobson, categorizing Jews as a religion was a practical step toward Jewish integration.

In *The Races of Mankind*, Benedict and Weltfish presented the challenge of their times: "With America's great tradition of democracy, the United States should clean its own house and get ready for a better twenty-first century. Then it could stand unashamed before the Nazis and condemn, without confusion, their doctrines of a Master Race."[50] According to the scientists—and Hobson—accepting Jews as members of a *religion* was part of America's cleaning its own reputation on race relations. That Blacks, Asians, and other people of color remained outside this circle of inclusion did not seem to concern Hobson.

Unlike the anthropologists who authored educational pamphlets for the public, some academics found it difficult to relinquish the language of race, as it applied to Jews. "The Idea of 'Race' Dies Hard," a 1949 *Commentary* article by the Jewish sociologist and Princeton professor Melvin Tumin, explained that despite postwar discrediting, race-thinking—not to mention explicit racism—persisted. We cannot entirely reject the idea of race, Tumin asserted, because it still *feels* true. During the 1940s, social scientists acknowledged this pull toward racial categorization. Among the FAQs posed in "Sense and Nonsense about Race," anthropologist Ethel Alpenfels's 1946 pamphlet for adolescents, was the question: "If there is no Jewish race, why can I always tell a Jew when I see one?"[51] These frank misperceptions provided opportunities for writers such as Alpenfels to explain the social and historical factors behind group identities, and to declare unequivocally that "Judaism is a religion not a race." Tumin also conceded the realities of physical appearance: "The persuasive argument of science which emphatically denies the popular notion of race . . . has constantly yielded to the more clearcut evidence of people's senses that a Negro *is* different from a Chinese, that a Spaniard *can* be set apart from an American Indian—that, in truth, it is often possible to tell a Jew from a Gentile, *just* by looking at him."[52] In 1940s America, race still seemed discernible from one's appearance.

Even in universities, the process of moving away from racial discourse was slow. Tumin's article revealed that, as early as 1949, college students had been learning "for two decades now" that the racial categorization of mankind was false. The findings of social scientists such as Franz Boas, Ruth Benedict, and others, Tumin explained, were marshalled to teach students to "apply the doctrine of cultural relativity to human affairs to understand thereby that the habits of different human groups are worthy of respect—and in any case are not fixed by biology."[53] Despite all this "pedagogical effort" in the classroom, Tumin reported, "there has as yet been no apparent popular tendency to stop using the traditional term 'race' (with all its inevitable trail of biased overtones), or to stop thinking of mankind as divided into three basic groups: white, black, and yellow."[54] Even as academics, novelists, and Jewish communal leaders argued against it, racial discourse endured. This was not surprising given that racism did not receive serious legal challenge during the 1940s.[55]

"Jew" and the "Average American"

To the consternation of some anti-antisemitism novelists, popular media also resisted altering racial discourse. In the mid-1940s, *Time* magazine continued to use "Jew" to denote a racial meaning. As a result, Hobson and her writer-friend Margaret Halsey wrote to *Time* in 1946 in protest. In reply, the editorial staff explained that as long as Americans talked about Jews as a race, *Time* would do the same. The editors explained:

> We certainly grant that whenever a writer uses the term "Jew" in other than its religious sense, he is apt to become enmeshed in semantics and end up in an untenable position. However, to limit the word strictly to religious matters and discussions, leaves one without any brief, usable term to designate those who are not Judaists but who, because of their background and culture, consider themselves and are considered by others as a group with special problems and interests in common.[56]

Here was a definitional quandary. The word *Jew* clearly connoted an identity that did not necessarily pertain to religion, but this non-religion meaning raised the specter of dangerous Nazi race-thinking. Further, as a middlebrow publication, *Time* was primarily interested in how the average American used the word. Referring to Webster's Dictionary, the *Time* editor replied to Halsey's letter, "In defense of Mr. Webster (whose definitions

TIME defers to as standard reliable criteria for editors), we would like to say that common usage determines the meanings which philologists set down. And while anthropologists do not use 'Jew' except when speaking of a person whose religion is Judaism, the average person does."[57] The average American, *Time* observed, had not shifted to thinking of "Jew" as only pertaining to members of a religion. "When most people stop doing so, philologists and writers will too. Our editors are, however, very conscious of the danger of inflaming racism by injudicious inclusion of the words Jew or Jewish in news reports, and are careful to avoid using them unless they have a definite news bearing on the story." *Time* recognized that they were wading into dangerous waters when it came to "Jew," but they were unwilling to change their locution until there was evidence of a widespread societal shift in usage. *Time*'s editor conceded: "It all boils down to this—Time strives for directness and brevity."[58] Surely, *Time*'s reply suggested, this logic made sense to intelligent readers?

Well, no. Directness and brevity should not be *Time*'s only goals, argued Hobson and Halsey. Through their correspondence, the two writers demonstrated their two-pronged approach to combating race discourse. First, they portrayed its common but inaccurate usage in their novels—and corrected it. Second, they took offending wordsmiths to task, often through letter-writing. As a popular magazine, Halsey asserted in her letter, *Time* should be a leader in promoting new ideas. "You defend Time's unscientific and inaccurate use of the term 'Jew' on the ground that the average person is also unscientific and inaccurate," Halsey wrote. "But where is Time [sic] supposed to stand in relation to the average person—ahead of him or behind him?" The dynamic between *Time* and its readers was not one-way, Halsey exhorted. She encouraged *Time*'s editorial staff to take seriously their responsibility to model enlightened discourse: "It is certainly true that a magazine cannot help but be molded by the pressures of the culture in which it exists. But it is also true that it can mold that culture, as well as be molded by it." The relationship between middlebrow literature and its readers was dynamic, Halsey explained. "The magazine and the culture should interact. If you really mean what you say . . . then you are picturing Time as having the helpless passivity which generally characterizes the inhabitants of bassinets." *Time*, Halsey insisted, should assume greater responsibility toward its readers. "It seems to me that if Time had given more conscious thought to its relationship to the culture and to the average person in that culture, it would not now find itself defending the contention that religion is biologically transmissible."[59]

Halsey's letter to *Time* delineated the pedagogical relationship that anti-antisemitism novelists imagined with their readers: one of responsible teaching, modeling, and guiding readers toward more enlightened attitudes and behavior. Although these novelists did not use the phrase *activist-writing*, the term captures the culture-shaping they envisioned. By depicting relatable (i.e., non-Jewish) characters who opposed antisemitism and rejected racial categorization of Jews, these novelists sought to influence readers. At times that influence extended to their correspondence, as when Hobson responded to a fan with a brief lesson about race and Jews. Self-consciously taking "on the role of school teacher," Hobson brought the Nazis into her lesson as she explained, "Hitler was wrong, as he was about everything else, about the Jews not being Nordics. To anthropology the word 'Nordic' means a biological type—blonde, blue-eyed. . . . There are plenty of Englishmen, Hollanders, Swedes, and other Nordics who are also Jewish."[60] It was another example of the way anti-antisemitism literature provided an arena for novelists to respond to the Holocaust and to mold its lessons for readers.

Even when she received glowing reviews, Hobson did not hold back from offering polite corrections to a reviewer's racial language. Hobson wrote to one reviewer of *Gentleman's Agreement*, whom her publisher planned to excerpt: might they tweak his phrases referring to "racial discrimination" to refer to "racial or religious" discrimination? There were good reasons for her persnickety request, Hobson explained. "My point is that since one of the myths to fight is that there is such a thing as 'a Jewish race'—that the phrases are not really precise in talking about a book which is mostly about anti-semitism."[61] Like other activists, Hobson seized every opportunity to press her point.

In spite of these efforts, race-thinking continued, often as a result of the experience of Jews in Europe during World War II. In the pages of the middlebrow magazine *Woman's Day*, Elinor Rice, future novelist and biographer of suffragettes, wrote about Jewishness and race in her own life.[62] When she was in her forties, a gentile friend asked Rice why she continued to call herself a Jew, when she was not religious and when she obviously understood that Jews were not a race. If not by religion or by race, then in what way was she a Jew? Rice answered: "It is because when *you* hear about Jews in Europe being marched into gas chambers or, more recently, having no homes and living years huddled in barracks, you say 'Poor fellows.' I say 'There but for the grace of God go I.'" She told her friend that "according to Hitler's racial law, I'm Jewish. . . . While there are people who make such laws or people who would like to make them, I and many others like me will continue to be Jewish."[63] It was a negative reason, but the Nazis' racist antisemitism determined Rice's own sense of Jewishness. By the late 1940s, attitudes had changed since the days of Harry Wolfson's resigned acceptance of the burden of Jewishness. Among the connections with that earlier era was how little choice Jews still felt they had in the matter of defining their Jewishness. The choices that anti-antisemitism fiction presented were largely the choices of gentiles. Non-Jews could choose to change their antisemitic behavior. But in 1940s anti-antisemitism fiction, Jews were stuck with their Jewishness.

"Propaganda of the most artful kind"

How to encourage readers to make changes in their thinking and behavior was a question for anti-antisemitism novelists. But it was critics who voiced the strongest views on the matter. A *Saturday Review* critic of anti-antisemitism literature took a stab: "It is futile to appeal to the intellect, to discuss anti-Semitism from the platform or in solemn books which are read by people who mentally agree with every sentence, and yet who continue to behave according to the old platform."[64] Instead, "The appeal must be made to man's heart, to his conscience, and to his instinctive sense of justice in a way that only the novel and the drama can achieve, for there a man can see himself mirrored on the page or on the screen."

In the 1940s, reviewers seemed to recalibrate standards for these female-authored, social message novels, suggesting that literary greatness was not the goal so much as effective teaching of lessons.[65] The *New York Times* review of *Agreement* delivered a backhanded compliment to Hobson in this vein, when it called *Agreement* a "Grade-A tract ... cleverly camouflaged as a novel," even as the reviewer praised the "brilliance" with which Hobson pulled it off, categorizing *Agreement* as "required reading for every thoughtful citizen in this parlous century."[66] Similarly, the *Saturday Review* assessment of Gwethalyn Graham's *Earth and High Heaven* opened with: "One of the hardest tasks to do successfully is the thesis-novel. At some point the thesis is apt to get out of hand and then the novel ceases to be a novel and becomes a tract. It all turns into a message and trips the reader up as obviously as the word Moral tacked on at the end of a nineteenth century story." But *Earth and High Heaven* had passed the test. The reviewer concluded: "It is to Miss Graham's credit that she has accomplished this difficult task expertly."[67]

Novelists felt pressure to produce something reviewers would not dismiss as merely propaganda. As Hobson began drafting *Agreement*, she worried over how to avoid didactic writing. As Hobson confessed in a September 1944 letter to Richard Simon, "one of the major issues in my mind now is a purely literary one—can I get enough story-line, emotional interest etc into it to save it from being a lecture or a tract?"[68] She explained to Simon that she would need to write a few chapters before she knew if her goals were achievable. In time, readers' letters affirmed that Hobson was at least partly successful. The National Director of Friends of Democracy, Inc., wrote to Hobson of his hope that *Agreement* might awaken more readers to its cause: "I wish it might be possible to require every Christian in the country to read 'Gentleman's Agreement.' It might jolt some of our benighted Christian brethren out of their complacency." He explained that it "would do them good to read 'Gentleman's Agreement,' and besides, they would be interested and enlightened."[69]

Others were more pointed about *Agreement*'s teaching methods: "It is propaganda of the most artful kind," one reviewer observed.[70] "Women who wouldn't touch *The Nation* or *The New Republic* . . . with a ten foot pole are going to read 'Gentleman's Agreement' as they sit under the dryer, and they're going to urge their husbands to read it."[71] This midcentury gender logic indicated that sentimental literature was the kind of emotionally manipulative reading that appealed to women, who in turn would influence their husbands.[72] These gender stereotypes suggested that women were more likely to be emotionally moved by fiction, and that they could be counted on to advocate for such novels.

Fan mail showed that there was truth to the idea that women shared news of good fiction. In March, 1947, Hobson told a reporter from the *New York Herald Tribune* about how word of *Agreement* traveled between woman friends. Hobson had heard from an Evanston, Illinois, reader in whose social circles "someone said something about 'the chosen people.' One of the women there—it was she who wrote the letter—looked at another who also had just finished reading Mrs. Hobson's serial. 'Gentleman's Agreement,' she said cryptically. 'What do you mean?' the other wanted to know. Then the talk began about the theme of the book." Hobson was delighted that she "had created a handy phrase that will be used significantly as 'Lost Week End' has been used," referring to her friend Charles Jackson's recent novel.[73] It was a sign of *Agreement* having achieved a level of cultural saturation.

Similarly, a San Francisco woman wrote Hobson that the only reason she had heard about *Agreement* was because a friend who subscribed to *Cosmopolitan* sent her the first installment. She assured Hobson that "I and many others I have talked to about your story think the writing and content are excellent. We are writing the editor of the magazine."[74] A woman from Islip, Long Island, wrote to Hobson of her intention to purchase copies of *Agreement* and mail them to her acquaintances. "They need to read it."[75] Similarly, a Mrs. Liebeskind of Brooklyn wrote that "I have just finished my copy of your book and have already passed it on to my eager friends."[76]

It turned out that it wasn't only that postwar Americans liked *Gentleman's Agreement*. They *liked* liking *Gentleman's Agreement*. In progressive circles, it said something complimentary about a reader that she appreciated *Agreement*. The novel provided what James Baldwin had referred to as "a very definite thrill of virtue from the fact that we are reading such a book at all."[77] That pleasure of engagement with a text critiquing antisemitism while flatteringly reminding readers of their personal commitments to social justice has a history landmarked by the Puritan jeremiad.[78] It was the pleasure of castigation that motivated self-improvement—a special kind of American heartbreak that resulted from believing in the possibility of getting it right next time. In social protest literature including anti-antisemitism novels, pointing out societal flaws in a way that oriented readers toward avenues for betterment was a time-honored tradition that managed to provide affirmation of American ideals. Whether it was a matter of "virtue signaling," as twenty-first-century observers might regard it; a sincere desire to be part of a community of anti-antisemitism readers; or enthusiasm to share good fiction with friends, readers enjoyed recommending a novel that attacked antisemitism. Declaring oneself a fan of the novel was a way to self-identify as a good liberal without necessarily committing to action.

Acceptance within Reason

When it came to anti-antisemitism literature, fandom meant participating in a postwar project to distance Americans from Nazi intolerance. Expanding the categories of once-marginalized groups to be integrated into the American mainstream was a slow process that began, for some, by reading a fictional account of such tolerance. Yet, not all kinds of Jews were acceptable, as anti-antisemitism literature made clear.

"Americans without Distinction" was the title of Diana Trilling's critical review of *Gentleman's Agreement*, because of what Trilling saw as Hobson's inability to allow significant differences into her liberal worldview. "If *Gentleman's Agreement* regards Jew and Gentile as but two profiles of the same face," Trilling observed, "it is because Mrs. Hobson recognizes no valid differences between them."[79] Where were the *religious* Jews in this novel? Trilling asked in her review. For that matter, where were the religious Christians? In Hobson's fictional world, no religious, noisy, or angry Jews need apply.[80] This lacuna in postwar Americans' supposed commitment to protecting minorities is apparent in *Agreement* when Phil concludes that he and his Jewish friend, Dave Goldman, are essentially the same kind of person, despite their sectarian differences. If the phrase had been available to him (and to Hobson) in the 1940s, Phil might have said, "Our core is the same."[81]

What Phil does say shows his resistance to recognizing Dave's Jewish particularity: "Dave was like him in every essential, had the same boyhood patterns, the same freedom from either extreme of poverty or wealth, the same freedom from any creed-bound faith. They had both grown up in a generation when religion did not work itself very deep into life." Phil takes comfort from the thought that "whatever Dave felt now—indifference? Outrage? Fear? Or contempt?—would be the feeling of Dave as a man, and not Dave as a Jew. Dave as citizen, as American, and not Dave as a religious being. That, Phil was sure of. And that was good."[82]

What was good was the lack of meaningful difference that Phil saw between himself and his Jewish friend. Phil (and Hobson) have gone so far as to suggest that Dave the American and Dave the Jew are separate parts of the same person. And that his Americanness was the more important part—indeed, the part that compensated for the Jewishness. As would become clear as the Cold War intensified, sexuality—and specifically, heteronormativity—was capable of securing American identity.[83] Dave's marriage and, later in the novel, his attraction and flirtation with Phil's non-Jewish colleague, Anne Dettrey, establish his bona fides as a red-blooded, heterosexual American man. But in Hobson's worldview, it is also Dave's secularism, or shallow religiosity, that evidences his good, liberal Americanness. His "freedom from any creed-bound faith" might have seemed like no kind of freedom at all, to Hobson's religious readers. For a secular Manhattanite like Hobson, however, this liberation from creed was a prerequisite for good citizenship.

That religiousness might even pose a risk to good citizenship is integral to Phil's thinking. Dave is as fully an American as Phil precisely because neither was the type to let "religion work itself very deep" into their lives. Phil realizes that "It was more valid to think of someone like Dave, the kind of man he himself would be if he were a Jew. He could not 'think into' a deeply religious old Jew in a prayer shawl, or into the poor, ignorant Jewish peddler behind a pushcart on the East Side, or into the wealthy tycoon in business."[84] Thus did Hobson demarcate what constituted an acceptable American Jew: "The deeply pious, the truly ignorant, the greatly powerful of any creed or religion were beyond his quick understanding."[85] *Belong to a religion* was one part of Hobson's lesson to readers. But *do religion in moderation* was another part. As Hobson explained in a letter, in addition to combatting antisemitism, *Agreement* was an attempt to fight the religion labels that divided people— the "old business of pigeonholing human beings in separate boxes marked 'Jewish,' 'Protestant,' 'Catholic,' or whatever."[86] There was no sense in making such distinctions among Americans, Hobson believed. In *Agreement*, Phil modeled this open-minded approach, as when he remarked that "to talk of a man in the vocabulary of religious distinctions would go against" his principles.[87]

While Hobson portrayed Phil Green—a stand-in for 1940s liberals— as not the type who delved deeply into religious and cultural differences, she also showed that Phil was complicit in another set of stereotypes that excluded Jews outside middle- and upper-class respectability. For critics such as Diana Trilling, this refusal of the "liberal ideal" to recognize real difference evidenced a lack of tolerance. Trilling hoped that this kind of intolerance might motivate some "to underscore rather than eliminate minority differences."[88] In the coming years, as we will see in subsequent chapters, Trilling's plea for greater attention to the religious and cultural particularities of minority groups would be realized by authors of Introduction to Judaism texts.

In drawing such a small circle of tolerance, Hobson awakened readers to the harsh limitations of so much 1940s tolerance discourse. Examples of religiously observant protagonists in the anti-antisemitism literature of the 1940s are indeed rare. The secular Labor Zionist journal *Jewish Frontier* judged this lack of diversity of Jews within Hobson's novel as its own kind of gentleman's agreement among liberals: only the "good Jews," who resembled liberal Protestants, were granted acceptance.[89] It was an irony that the genre itself reflected on, as in Graham's *Earth and High Heaven*, when the

Protestant Erika Drake muses that she had been "taking refuge in the comfortable delusion that even if these prejudices and restrictions were actually in effective operation, they would only be applied against—well, against what is usually designated as 'the more undesirable type of Jew.' In other words, against people who more or less deserved it."[90] *Agreement*, too, commented on this tendency to distinguish between good Jews and those who deserved discrimination because of their objectionable religious and cultural differences. At work, Phil hears a Jewish colleague express annoyance with a group of rich Jews who have "set up a snazzy golf club of their own," in which Jews of German and English ancestry "blackball guys of Polish or Russian-Jewish stock. Meaning, anybody who looks good-and-Jewish."[91] In *Agreement*, this exclusiveness is rendered as snobby Jewish behavior. The *Jewish Frontier* suggested that Hobson herself was guilty of such snobbishness in their critique of *Agreement*: "We know of Jews in Brooklyn who have beards, who not only look different, but live differently. These Jews are in need of real tolerance, because they have had the courage to keep up their own character and culture." Homing in on the sins of *Gentleman's Agreement*, the reviewer charged: "These Jews Laura Z. Hobson would not dare bring into the picture, because she doesn't believe in this type, because she herself is not tolerant of this type."[92] In truth, Hobson may not have identified with religious Jews. With an awareness of readers' prejudices—and her own—she was downplaying Jewish particularity in her novel.

Garish and uneducated Jews posed another kind of problem. Hobson's views would evolve over the course of her lifetime. But in the 1940s her attitudes—born of her child-of-immigrants experiences overcoming the stamp of foreigner through her careful self-presentation—might have aptly been labeled "Acceptance, within reason."[93] Hobson's unwillingness to offer more unconditional acceptance surfaces at multiple points in the novel. One of these moments that is especially revealing of Hobson's gendered perspective on antisemitism and assimilation occurs while Kathy is on a ski holiday. When she encounters two young women on the slopes, Kathy sees their "glittering costume jewelry . . . the frozen beads of mascara at their eyes, the gleam of eye shadow, the thick lipstick, congealed and cracked," and hears their coarse language. The reader understands that the two women are Jewish, as Kathy thinks to herself, "Why do they *do* it? She thought miserably. Why do they make themselves so noticeable? It's awful. It's just awful."[94] Kathy is an attractive, liberal Manhattanite; indeed, it was even Kathy who originally suggested the idea of an antisemitism article to her uncle who is

Phil's editor. Kathy also undergoes the greatest character development in the novel as she eventually recognizes her own latent antisemitism. But Kathy cannot abide the kind of garish Jews she meets in this scene. It is an example of middlebrow fiction policing class boundaries, as female characters such as Kathy revealed a preoccupation with proper middle-class behavior and self-presentation.[95] Miss Wales, Phil's Jewish secretary, who passes as a gentile in order to find employment, also expresses repugnance for loud, pushy Jews whom she calls "kikey" Jews, reminding readers that both gentiles and Jews may harbor antisemitic attitudes.[96]

The ski scene illuminates Kathy's moral limitations, raising the specter of intolerance from those who consider themselves "good liberals." Having spent her adult life among educated, liberal Manhattanites, many of whom were gentiles, Hobson's experience primed her for sending a coded message to her Jewish readers: even the good Americans, like Kathy, might judge Jews harshly. Even someone who wanted to be *anti*-antisemitic, whose desire to feel right about Jews is intertwined with her desire for Phil, faced challenges when confronted with Jews who did not conform to society's gendered expectations. Kathy risks losing Phil if she does not change her attitudes. But Jews, Hobson's novel subtly teaches, risk losing the Kathys of the world if they do not change their supposedly offensive behavior. In *Gentleman's Agreement*, Hobson offered lessons for both Jews and non-Jews about right behavior and attitudes. As much as the anti-antisemitism literature exposed antisemitism to Americans—making it a topic of discussion and consideration—it also provided a guide for how the normalization of Jews and Judaism might occur, and exactly which kinds of Jews were eligible.

Not all Jewish readers were receptive to such messages. "Is it being tolerant to concede the right to be different only to somebody who is exactly like yourself?" The *Jewish Frontier* reviewer insisted, "this is precisely the make-believe tolerance of Laura Hobson."[97] Thinking back to the bleak days of Harry Wolfson and his 1920s "Escaping Judaism" pamphlet, the reviewer elaborated on the changed circumstances of American Jews: "Twenty years ago, Jewish parents in America had only one goal: to give their children happiness by disembarrassing them of their Jewish heritage, by encouraging them to escape." But "today it is different" the reviewer asserted in 1947:

And that's why *Gentleman's Agreement*, a novel full of generous aspirations, a book that arouses the better side of man, fails to satisfy us. For hundreds of thousands of Gentiles [sic] will soon have read it, and in them it can only awaken a mock tolerance, a superficial, weak brotherly goodwill toward one sort of Jew, the sort that has clipped its wings in order to fit in; a brotherly goodwill toward upper-class Jews who were always accepted in pre-Hitlerite Germany, for whom it is easy to escape race-hatred, and to whom they say: "If all the Jews were like you."[98]

Hobson wrote *Agreement* from the perspective of an assimilated Jew who had grown up in the early twentieth-century melting-pot culture, but the novel was being read, as the *Jewish Frontier* made clear, through a post-Holocaust lens.[99] And it wasn't only leftist Jews who saw the dangers of Hobson's lesson of sameness. *Life* magazine also wondered if efforts such as Hobson's to combat antisemitism were, in fact, "obscuring the central point?"[100] *Life*'s message of acceptance of Jews in all their particularities (and in all of the ways Hitler had not accepted them) was actually at odds with Hobson's central point—indeed, her personal credo—that Jews were just like everybody else.

"Well, they are and they aren't," the *Life* editorial asserted, explaining that "to insist only on the likeness"—as Hobson did—"is to insist that the only solution to the Jewish problem is for Jews to be assimilated into the dominant white Protestant American culture." That was not actually a realistic solution for all Jews, *Life* maintained. Quoting Elliot Cohen, founding editor of *Commentary*, *Life* explained, "We will be a less tolerant and a poorer country unless we learn not only to permit but to prize the variety and values of the kind of American who never appears in advertisements—the Pole, the Italian, the Irishman, the Seventh Avenue dress manufacturer and the bearded orthodox rabbi, the grimy, sweaty workman and the men of other eye-slants and skin colors." By referring to the "kind of American who never appears in advertisements," Cohen made his own plea for more inclusive American culture.

Proclaiming Jewish religious and cultural distinctiveness was not actually the goal of most 1940s anti-antisemitism literature, however much some readers yearned for it. A Frances Grossman of New York City wrote to Jo Sinclair to ask why, in response to the antisemitism the Braunowitzes experienced, *Wasteland* had not offered more positive explanations of religion: "Why didn't Jake and Sig attend Hebrew School or have the Rabbi come to the house and give them instruction in Hebrew and whatever else is necessary to confirm them, I think about the age of 13, into the Jewish faith."[101] Grossman added, "If my question is a foolish one, try to understand it springs from ignorance of the Jewish religion, for though I come from a home that is Jewish by heritage, it has always been pseudo-Gentile in thinking so that consequently I now must spend a great deal of time learning about the religion and faith that is my birthright—and there is so much to learn." Grossman's defensive tone reflected awareness of the unusual nature of her request as well as her desire for information on Judaism. Indeed, Grossman's query about Jews being "confirmed"—a rite more common among Christians than Jews outside the Reform movement—suggested ignorance. As Grossman and other readers discovered, anti-antisemitism novelists, who were mostly secular in orientation, showed limited interest in writing about Jewish religion.

The Gentleman's Agreement of American Religion

The role of Judaism in anti-antisemitism novels was largely to portray Jews as members of a respected American religion. This function of religion is captured in one of *Agreement*'s most famous scenes, mentioned earlier. At the breakfast table, Phil explains to his son, Tommy, that Jews are members of a *religion*: "You can be an American and a Catholic, or an American and a Protestant, or an American and a Jew." So there's no confusion, Phil adds, "Or you could be French or German or Spanish or any nationality at the same time you're Catholic or a Protestant or a Jew." Phil tells Tommy that one thing is your country, "But the other thing is religion if you have any, or your grandfather's religion, like Jewish or Catholic or Protestant religion. That hasn't anything to do with the country or the language. . . . Get it? . . . Don't ever get mixed up on that. Some people are mixed up."[102]

Religion is something one might or might not have or inherit, Phil teaches Tommy, and there were but three choices: Protestantism, Catholicism, and Judaism. None of these religions should ever be equated with nationality, Phil explains. This disavowal of Jewishness as nationality represented another opportunity for Hobson to voice her anti-Zionist views. When Tommy asks his father why some people *are* mixed up, Phil replies: "Oh, they talk about the Jewish race, but never about the Catholic race or the Protestant race." There is still a lot of confusion around the meaning of Jewishness, Phil informs Tommy, suggesting that it is a sign of enlightened and progressive American values to understand that Jewishness is considered a matter of religion. This may be another "gentleman's agreement" in the novel (in addition to the term's meaning in relation to restrictive housing covenants): good, postwar liberals accepted Jews as members of an American religion—a dramatic shift from previous decades, when they were viewed as members of an inferior race.[103] Although the midcentury process of Jewish integration into the American mainstream was not a legal process, it parallels the eighteenth- and nineteenth-century European Jewish emancipation, when European Jews sought to show their "sameness" to other Europeans, by presenting Jewishness as just like Christianity.[104] In return for acceptance as members of one of the big three American religions, midcentury Jews were expected to fit themselves neatly into the religion category and to behave as good, white, middle-class Americans.

Connecting Jews and Others

Despite the vast gulf between treatment of Blacks and Jews, both Black and white readers found connections between the discrimination exposed in anti-antisemitism literature and the racism directed against African Americans. It helped, too, that Hollywood had "entered the fray of discussion and debate about civil rights and the relationship of race to national identity in the wake of America's experience in World War II with such vigor that one commentator characterized the industry as being on a crusade."[105] Many in the film industry and among its observers were blunt about the fact that more than altruism motivated these "social problem" films addressing race, such as *Home of the Brave* (1949), *Lost Boundaries* (1949), and *Pinky* (1949). As Hobson's publisher Richard Simon learned, such engagement with religious and racial discrimination could be good business.

What form the connection between antisemitism and racism would take in fiction was up for negotiation during the 1940s. In 1947, John Harold Johnson, a Black businessman and publisher of *Ebony*, *Jet*, and *Negro Digest*, wrote to Hobson, suggesting she write "a piece for *Negro Digest* along the same theme as 'Gentleman's Agreement,' only as applied to Negroes." Johnson explained that he found Hobson's treatment of subtle, nonviolent antisemitism especially relevant. "It seems to me that with race hate in its most virulent forms coming more and more under the eye of the federal government . . . with lynching and race rioting decreasing, that Jim Crow, as we know it, is taking on more subtle form."[106] Johnson believed that with Hobson's "excellent work in exposing the anti-Semitism on the part of so many people, we are certain you could do a really excellent job on the equally subtle forms of anti-Negro discrimination, which I am sure that you are familiar with." Johnson assured Hobson that she had a large Black fan base, as a result of *Gentleman's Agreement*, and urged her to make racism a priority in her writing. Perhaps because she was a single parent of two young boys, and perhaps because, like many novelists, Hobson followed her own writerly interests, Hobson did not take Johnson up on his suggestion. She begged off in her reply to Johnson, explaining, "I find myself in a state bordering on collapse and completely stripped of the leisure or the energy to work on my third book which I have barely begun."[107]

It was not until the end of a fan's letter that one June Gilliam of Cleveland revealed her Black identity—"p.s. Hey, I'm a Negro (did you guess?)"[108] In her letter, Gilliam explained the connections she discerned between anti-Black racism and the antisemitism that Hobson described in *Agreement*. "I know all about the 'shakiness in the knees' when you take a stand, and the feeling of nastiness . . . and the 'backed up violence' of frustration. . . . You've really pinned down the snide and nasty crack and the hedging and the stupid 'I don't want to play with you'. [sic] All of it of a piece with the stuff in my experience. You've hit it. Over and over again. The plucking at Phil's raw nerves echoes the age-old tune played on mine. It's neat and a good clean package. But brightest of all, it's not preachy." Gilliam took up Hobson's call in *Gentleman's Agreement* to make theirs a century for all people—and not just the "American Century," as Henry Luce labeled it. "It's time. This is the century," Gilliam wrote to Hobson. "This, by God, is the place, and if only many more of the Kathy's could start being Phil's or Anne's and many more like me could be you, then nothing atomic or otherwise could destroy this wonderful, half-baked country (world) of ours." Hobson had won over another fan. "I'll save a few pennies for your next," Gilliam wrote. "Please don't stop now."[109]

The connections between antisemitism and other forms of bigotry and racism would be strengthened in the developing civil rights movement in the next decade. As Supreme Court Justice Hugo Black observed in 1950, segregation was "Hitler's creed—he preached what the south believed."[110] Justice Black was not alone in drawing this parallel. During the war, this moral equivalence between Nazism and American racism was frequently made. "Are you for Hitler's way?" read the flyers that Howard University students distributed at their 1940s restaurant sit-ins.[111] And in 1946, when Tennessee State troopers shot at African Americans during "racial disturbances," the NAACP, through their special counsel, Thurgood Marshall, called the action "closer to the action of the German storm troopers than any recent police action in this country."[112] The *New York Times* headline read: "NAACP Tells Truman Shooting of 2 by Tennessee Troopers in Jail Was Worthy of Nazis."[113] Even when Jews were not the persecuted group in question, Nazism was the measure of absolute evil in postwar America.

Anti-antisemitism became braided into the thick strand of postwar liberalism that opposed racism and would, in the coming decades, take on additional injustices, in opposition to which liberal Americans defined themselves. It was certainly more comfortable for Americans such as Justice Black to link the persecution of Blacks to Nazism than to acknowledge the deep entanglement of racism in American history.[114] Americans may have triumphed over Hitler, but theirs was a victory accomplished with racially segregated armed forces. Observers noticed the stain that racism continued to leave on America's moral record. The Swedish sociologist Gunnar Myrdal's 1944 book, *An American Dilemma: The Negro Problem and Modern Democracy*, a social scientific study of race relations, served as a "moral wake-up call," reminding readers that, unless corrected, mistreatment of Blacks would continue to impede America's ability to fully realize its democratic ideals of equality. As the Myrdals wrote in the 1940s, it was difficult to imagine that "the German Reich should have called in a foreign researcher to make an unbiased report on the country's most serious race problem—the Jewish question."[115] Americans at least demonstrated a degree of self-awareness and transparency, the Myrdals maintained. Anti-racism and anti-antisemitism novelists of the 1940s largely shared this optimism about Americans' potential for self-improvement.

Ten years after its publication, *An American Dilemma* was cited in *Brown v. Board of Education* as social scientific evidence in the Supreme Court's decision that what had been deemed separate but equal education for black children was, in fact, harmful to their development. The Court ruled: "Segregation of white and colored children in public schools has a detrimental effect upon the colored children. The effect is greater when it has the sanction of the law, for the policy of separating the races is usually interpreted as denoting the inferiority of the negro group. A sense of inferiority affects the motivation of a child to learn. Segregation with the sanction of law, therefore, has a tendency to [retard] the educational and mental development of negro children and to deprive them of some of the benefits they would receive in a racial[ly] integrated school system."[116] The old "sticks and stones" shibboleth was being overturned. It was not only physical violence that damaged people. Words and actions marking inferiority were finally called out by the Court.

Pervasive and deeply rooted in American history, racism was the 1940s moral dilemma that most exposed the gap between American ideals of equality and everyday reality. As Myrdal observed, the "Negro problem . . . suggests something difficult to settle and equally difficult to leave alone. It is embarrassing. It makes for moral uneasiness."[117] Yet, for all of the moral ambiguity that racism introduced into American society, it was not the moral problem that 1940s Americans were prepared to tackle. As a group much smaller in numbers, Jews presented a more manageable problem. As Myrdal observed, "The Jew is discriminated against in America, but there is a quantitative difference between this and the discrimination against the Negro which is so great that it becomes qualitative."[118] In a way, Jews benefited from the smallness of the problem they presented; with their limited numbers, their difficulties appeared solvable. The anti-antisemitism of this era was a first step in that direction. With the end of World War II, and the images of Allied soldiers liberating concentration camps, it became easier to believe in a progressive narrative in which Americans were already helping to improve the Jewish plight.

Confronting antisemitism through books and popular culture during the 1940s likely eased the consciences of many Americans even as racism continued to fester. Discrimination toward Jews persisted well past the 1940s.[119] As with contemporary social movements, such as #MeToo and Black Lives Matter, anti-antisemitism did not end the bad behavior that it was intended to call out. But this middlebrow literature impacted conversations about antisemitism, even as these novels offered limited possibilities for acceptance of difference.

Americans were accustomed to understanding discrimination against Jews as a fact of life. But within the structure of a novel, writers clearly cast antisemitism as an evil requiring heroes to defeat it and psychological strength to overcome it within oneself, thereby motivating readers to take a stand. As seen from readers' letters, fiction humanized the fight against antisemitism. Fiction also allowed a writer like Hobson to turn her anger into a cause that readers could join—or push back against. Even dissatisfied readers discovered that the anti-antisemitism genre clarified what they truly desired from postwar Jewish stories.

5

How Basic Is *Basic Judaism*?

Not everyone was pleased with the way Jews and Judaism were presented in the anti-antisemitism literature of the 1940s. In a February, 1948 radio broadcast, Rabbi Joshua Liebman of Boston's Reform Temple Israel gave *Gentleman's Agreement* a mixed review. His remarks included this criticism of the novel-turned-film: "There is ... nothing in the whole of 'Gentleman's Agreement' that would give the sympathetic Christian an awareness of the moral vitality of the Jewish spirit or the spiritual majesty of Jewish life and history. The author, Mrs. Hobson, apparently has little awareness of the positive and creative aspects of Judaism."[1]

Liebman was not off base. Reviewers—both Jewish and non-Jewish— noted that one finished *Agreement* with no more understanding of Judaism than at the start. John Mason Brown, of the *Saturday Review*, shared some of Liebman's views. After reading Hobson's novel and seeing the film, Brown concluded, "In both instances I am conscious of having been presented with no more than a laundry list of indignities to which Jews are submitted. . . . Although happy to have such dirty linen aired," Brown wished Hobson had also shown "the many sources of rightful special pride to the Jews, no less than the humiliations to which they are exposed by Gentiles who fancy themselves democrats."[2] Brown's criticism was shared by the secular Jewish writer Diana Trilling, who had not appreciated Hobson's homogenized portrayal of American Jews. In their generally positive review of the film, the Catholic liberal magazine *Commonweal* expressed a related regret about *Gentleman's Agreement*—that it did not portray Jews feeling "proud of their Jewishness. . . . This is a feeling that the non-Jewish Phil Green could not experience."[3]

In effect, Hobson was criticized for the very strategy that made *Agreement* successful—its foregrounding of the non-Jewish experience of antisemitism. Phil Green, the reporter who goes undercover as a Jew to investigate antisemitism, spends no time in synagogues, engages in no Jewish ritual, nor is he exposed to Yiddish or Hebrew. "In Mrs. Hobson's novel about the Jews," Trilling wrote, "their cause is both explained and fought for them by Gentiles—especially by the hero, who spends eight weeks masquerading as a Jew in order to learn what it feels like to be discriminated against."[4] Trilling's point was: *Where are the real Jews and Judaism in this story?* Anti-antisemitism novels succeeded in bringing bigotry to the attention of readers, but they did so with minimal information about Judaism. For some readers, these unsatisfying depictions of Judaism whetted their appetite for the more positive content of Introduction to Judaism literature.

Postwar primers on Judaism found authors in all the major movements of midcentury American Judaism. Prominent examples included *Basic Judaism*, by Conservative rabbi Milton Steinberg, and *What the Jews Believe*, by Steinberg's cousin, Rabbi Philip Bernstein. The Modern Orthodox, Pulitzer Prize–winning novelist Herman Wouk's 1959 book, *This Is My God*, was another Introduction to Judaism with a long life, as decades of American Jews received the book as a bar mitzvah or confirmation gift.[5] Over forty such Introduction to Judaism books and essays would be published in the period between 1945 and 1960.[6] Mostly middlebrow, the genre included academic examples such as Nathan Glazer's *American Judaism*. Published by the University of Chicago Press, *American Judaism* was part of a series that also included *American Protestantism* and *American Catholicism*. During the 1950s, the "religion bookshelf" served to reinscribe tri-faith America, as middlebrow publications that listed the year's "Best Religion Books," referred primarily to books from "the three chief American faiths."[7] Glazer's *American Judaism* became the Introduction to Judaism book most often assigned to college students.[8] When Columbia University professor Salo Baron reviewed Glazer's manuscript for the University of Chicago Press, Baron opined, "From the standpoint of sales, I have no doubt that it will appeal to a fairly large audience, Jewish and non-Jewish." Baron wrote, "There has been considerable interest in religious revival and the new religious questions within the younger generation, and there really is no satisfactory literature available in the field."[9]

By the time Glazer's book was published, the 1954 tercentennial celebration of American Jewish settlement provided another rationale for the publication of Introduction to Judaism books. The *Saturday Review*, a weekly middlebrow magazine, described the tercentennial as a celebration enacted through the publication of books about Jewish history and heritage, "as befits the People of the Book."[10] More literary examples of the genre included Abraham Joshua Heschel's 1950s books: *The Sabbath* (1951), *Man Is Not Alone* (1951), and *God in Search of Man* (1955). That the publisher, Farrar, Straus & Giroux, believed they could sell Heschel's intensely Jewish books suggested their confidence in the market.[11] "Like every product of his pen," Harold Ribalow observed of Heschel's books, "'God In Search of Man' is beautifully written, well organized, and surprisingly clear, even to the lay reader."[12] Heschel's midcentury publications found prominent Christian boosters, including Reinhold Niebuhr, who called Heschel "a creative interpreter of religious life and thought whose books have had an increasing hearing among both Jews and Christians."[13] Purchasing, reading, gifting, and reviewing books about one of the Judeo-Christian religions were ways to express interest and affiliation with these traditions.[14]

* * *

The connections between the lack of Judaism in anti-antisemitism literature and a desire for more thorough explanations of Jewish religion were voiced by two prominent midcentury rabbis: the aforementioned Liebman, and Conservative Rabbi Milton Steinberg, of Manhattan's Park Avenue Synagogue, who is the focus of this chapter.[15] In 1939, Steinberg published *As a Driven Leaf*, a novel based on an archetypal Jewish heretic, the second-century Elisha ben Abuyah, and his struggle to reconcile Rabbinic Judaism with Hellenistic society. In a way, the novel was "intellectual penance," as Steinberg's former student Arthur Cohen later called it.[16] Steinberg originally intended to write a doctoral dissertation at Columbia University about the parallels between Greek and Roman cultures and Judaism, but he never completed the thesis. Instead, using notes from his dissertation research, Steinberg wrote his first novel.[17] As Steinberg related to Cohen in 1946, "I'm not at all perturbed at the fact that the book [*As a Driven Leaf*] is nontechnical. While all of us who have been extensively exposed to academic procedures tend to value scientific work more highly than popular, I for one have increasingly freed myself of late from that obsession. That is why my thesis is still unwritten, whereas other things have been finished and are in process."[18] For generations to come, *As A Driven Leaf* found many more readers than would likely have a doctoral dissertation.

Despite the ancient setting of his first novel, Steinberg, a former student of Mordecai Kaplan, was preoccupied with contemporary Jewish concerns.[19] In a 1947 synagogue bulletin, Steinberg wrote of *Gentleman's Agreement*: "Mrs. Hobson ... sees only the surface of the problem of anti-Semitism; she does not see Judaism at all."[20] To Steinberg and others, *Agreement* evidenced a lack of appreciation for Judaism, even as Phil championed Judaism as an American religion.

It is not surprising that Liebman and Steinberg expressed impatience with a novel that bore so directly on the Jewish experience and yet resisted Judaism so thoroughly. But *Agreement*'s lack of Jewish religion was true to Hobson's experience as a secular Jew reared in an agnostic home. The novel's inclusion of dialogue about Judaism showed that Hobson understood the practical value of Judaism's new postwar status in tri-faith America even as religion held no personal significance for her. *Agreement*'s treatment of sectarian differences fit the observations of midcentury sociologists who noticed that American Jews found utility in framing their Jewishness in terms of religion. As sociologist Marshall Sklare observed in his postwar study of Conservative Judaism, "the designation of the Jewish group as constituting a denomination is a highly convenient fiction which it is wise to cultivate."[21] Sklare found that there were many who "because of public relations considerations" (and despite weak religious affiliations) "feel that it is essential that Jews stress the religious designation."[22] Similarly, sociologist Nathan Glazer observed that "American Jews, if they believe in anything, believe in the instrumental efficacy of religion, as do, of course, most American Catholics and Protestants."[23] When Will Herberg wrote that "Americanness today entails religious identification as Protestant, Catholic, or Jew in a way and to a degree quite unprecedented in our history," he described an association with unique benefits for Jews who recognized that religious affiliation established their Cold War American bona fides.[24]

In this regard, Hobson was like many midcentury American Jews who did not experience Judaism as their faith but nonetheless recognized the value of naming it as such. Over time, referring to Judaism as an American religion in both middlebrow genres had the effect of helping to make Judaism into an American religion in the minds of Americans. It was another example of the engine of middlebrow culture facilitating new ideas about Jews.

Writing about Jewish *Religion*

The emaciated conception of Jewishness in *Gentleman's Agreement* may not have been the story of Judaism that Liebman, Steinberg, and other rabbis, for that matter, wanted told to postwar Americans, but it was the way Judaism was often portrayed in popular fiction in the 1930s and 1940s.[25] Perhaps partly as a response, nonfiction primers emerged as a genre for positive midcentury depictions of Judaism as a religion.

Even before the post–World War II flourishing of the Introduction to Judaism genre, rabbis and Jewish leaders realized that the responsibility for rebuilding postwar Judaism would fall to Americans. The editor of the 1941–1942 *American Jewish Year Book* reflected: "Although grateful for its immunity from the plague which has virtually destroyed Jewish life in Europe," American Jews realized "they have been spared for a sacred task—to preserve Judaism and its cultural, social and moral values . . . and to prepare themselves . . . when the way will be open for them to . . . rehabilitate the survivors of the unspeakable disaster which has temporarily prostrated them."[26] The task of preserving Jewish heritage became especially visible in the realm of book culture. A bestselling book provided a unique opportunity to showcase what many considered the treasures of Judaism—its literature, rituals, history, and festivals.

Few midcentury rabbis understood that literary goal as well as Liebman and Steinberg. Liebman was the first American rabbi to publish a bestseller about Judaism. His 1946 *Peace of Mind* sold more than a million copies in its first three years and remained among the top ten on the nonfiction bestseller list when Liebman died of heart failure in 1948, at age forty-one.[27] His book set out to explain how Judaism, combined with the latest insights from psychology, could improve readers' lives. Liebman's success provided a model to Milton Steinberg, whose review observed admiringly that Liebman managed to make his subject accessible without diluting its Jewishness. "At no point does Doctor Liebman make the slightest effort to elide his Jewishness or the Jewish sources of his inspiration," Steinberg observed.[28] "To the contrary, he speaks readily, naturally, forthrightly as a Jew, a rabbi, an advocate of the Jewish tradition." Steinberg hoped to accomplish something similar in *Basic Judaism*, which he published a year later.

Tellingly, *Basic Judaism* opened with these lines: "This is a book about the Jewish religion. Not about Jews, or Jewish problems, or Jewish culture, or Zionism, but about those beliefs, ideals, and practices which make up the historic Jewish faith." As Steinberg explained to his editor, he wanted to make his subject perfectly clear to all those readers who "didn't want to read another book on Zionism"—a subject that was both much in the news and did not always feel pressing to Jews focused on cementing their status as Americans.[29] Unlike Zionism, Judaism as a religion felt like a relatively fresh angle in the 1940s, after a decade of "spiritual depression," coupled with the economic depression during the 1930s.[30] As rabbi-writers such as Steinberg and Liebman wrote their Introduction to Judaism books, they were responding, in part, to larger conversations about Jews from the preceding decades that seemed to concern everything *except* Jewish religion. Jewish *problems*, not Jewish religion, were paramount during the 1920s and 1930s. As the author of one Introduction to Judaism book put it, Americans seemed to think of Jews in terms of "Hitlerism, refugees, anti-Semitic propaganda, and Jewish counter-propaganda," such that Jewish religion slipped out of many Americans' perceptions of Jews.[31] More than rabbis' sermons, which reached a relatively small audience, popular books about Judaism affected how midcentury Americans thought about Jews and Judaism at a time when Americans still turned to card catalogs in libraries when interested in a subject.

Non-Jewish readers were especially unaccustomed to thinking about Judaism as a contemporary, modern religion. During the first half of the twentieth century, it was not uncommon for Americans to base their understanding of Judaism on the Bible.[32] As a result, during the 1930s and early 1940s educated Americans wondered, for example, if Jews continued to sacrifice animals.[33] Conservative Rabbi Louis Finkelstein experienced this jarring contrast between his own understanding of Judaism and that of non-Jewish society when he published a book about Judaism in the late 1940s. A group of marketing experts met with Finkelstein to explain their reservations about his proposed title, *Judaism and the Jews*: "For the reading public, they argued, Judaism has merely archaeological interest, having ceased to exist more than eighteen centuries ago, with the fall of Jerusalem at the hands of Titus. In contrast, they said, the Jews are a contemporary phenomenon, of perennial interest."[34] Before 1950, large segments of Christian America had little understanding of Judaism as a modern religion that had undergone extensive modification between Titus and Bolshevism. *Jews*, on the other hand, were a group associated with current events and problems. Finkelstein, incidentally, took this lesson to heart. Realizing how little Americans understood about Judaism, Finkelstein's tenure as head of the Jewish Theological Seminary included a full range of cultural programs, such as establishing a radio and television department, designed to introduce Judaism to Americans.[35] For 1950s Jewish communal leaders, Judaism as a "living faith" became a popular descriptor, employed with the aim of educating Americans who perceived Judaism as an ancient religion.[36]

Steinberg had been an active participant in the earlier discourse about Jewishness as problem. During the 1930s, he published *Atlantic Monthly* essays about the challenges Jews faced. Steinberg also wrote for Jewish journals and magazines, such as the *Reconstructionist*, which Steinberg helped to found with Rabbi Mordecai Kaplan and Kaplan's son-in-law, Ira Eisenstein. Steinberg's friendship with the founders of Reconstructionism was not unusual. At midcentury, Reconstructionism was considered more of a perspective within Conservative Judaism than its own movement (Reconstructionists did not establish their own seminary until 1968).[37] Many midcentury Conservative rabbis were friendly with Kaplan, who was their former Jewish Theological Seminary professor and mentor. One Jewish thinker observed in 1960 that "Mordecai Kaplan has been, for more than forty years, the escape door of the Jewish Theological Seminary. Had it not been for the inventive and imaginative techniques which he devised to rationalize the Judaism into which the Seminary was inducting its students, it might have lost—in those years of religious attrition, the late twenties, thirties, and early forties—literally scores of future rabbis."[38] Kaplan helped rabbis-in-training believe in the possibility of a modern Judaism.

"This is the kind of book that should sell forever."

Steinberg's relationships bolstered his confidence that there was a market for books about Jews and Judaism. In 1945, Steinberg's editor at Harcourt Brace, Lambert Davis, a Southerner whose authors included Robert Penn Warren and Eudora Welty, wrote to Steinberg about his proposal for a book about Judaism.[39] "As for the Primer on Judaism," Davis wrote to Steinberg in the spring of 1945. "The more I think of it, the more I believe it is an extremely sound idea. It is a book that I would want to read myself, even though I've had the best teacher on the subject," Davis wrote, referring to Steinberg and adding: "It is a book that ought to be written."[40] Steinberg was buoyed by the encouragement of his non-Jewish editor, who was well positioned to provide reassurance of a wider audience for his writing.

But Steinberg wasn't only contemplating his writing for the sake of writing. The struggle to support his family on Manhattan's Upper East Side meant that Steinberg could not afford *not* to think about finances.[41] "I am sure of its commercial possibilities," Steinberg wrote to Davis of *Basic Judaism*, explaining that "There never has been a simple vivid presentation of Jewish beliefs and ideals. A crying need exists for one among and for Jews and, I believe, to a lesser extent among non-Jews." Imagining *Basic Judaism*'s future, he elaborated, "This is the kind of book that should sell forever. It will be presented as a confirmation gift, to settle arguments, and as a means of persuasion by Jews who wish to win over other Jews to a positive position on Judaism."[42] *Basic Judaism* would go through thirty-nine editions between 1947 and 2004, suggesting that Steinberg's predictions were not far off the mark.

Steinberg's confidence in the market for his book may have been inspired, in part, by reactions from his more moneyed congregants and readers, such as the Morgenthau family. After Steinberg's *The Making of the Modern* Jew was published in 1934, a handwritten note arrived from Helen Morgenthau Fox, the sister of the Secretary of the Treasury, Henry Morgenthau Jr.[43] A botanist, Fox was in the process of designing the Metropolitan Museum's Cloisters herb gardens when she wrote to Steinberg, "It is the kind of book that I am going to give as a present."[44] In her letter, Fox named the men in her life to whom she planned to gift Steinberg's book. Interestingly, while Fox judged Steinberg's book "exciting," she also found it "so tragic and anguished," given "present day conditions and my own history in relation to being a jewess [sic]," that she felt the need to take breaks from reading it, as she recounted to Steinberg. Despite her assessment that the book's somber subject was best suited for male readers, Fox's enthusiasm translated into her desire to promote *The Making of the Modern Jew*. That kind of interest was valuable to authors like Steinberg. Publishers, too, appreciated this word-of-mouth publicity. A 1940s *Harper's* article about publishing noted that "Publishers nowadays are beginning to send the important books on their lists to a growing list of influential readers, to start the conversation even before publication."[45] The article continued, "Everyone in the book trade agrees that one of the most potent factors in book sales is talk among readers. Someone reads a book and likes it and tells a friend about it; the friend decides that he ought to buy it, and the circle expands."[46] Women readers such as Fox served as this kind of helpful advocate of books to which they felt an emotional connection. Fox's letter is also a reminder that while Steinberg was changing Park Avenue Synagogue—indeed, the congregation shifted from Reform to Conservative under his leadership—Park Avenue Synagogue was also changing Steinberg. He was being introduced to Jews whose affiliations with Judaism were often expressed materially, through the purchase of books or Judaica objects. That, too, may have affected the value Steinberg placed on his writing.

Steinberg's musings about the potential market for *Basic Judaism* showed the enjoyment he found in the business of books. He delighted in thinking with friends about their writing projects and helping them make relevant connections with editors and agents. In this vein, Steinberg wrote to a literary agent-friend at the firm Russell & Volkening, inquiring, "Is there a book in the reminiscences of a delicatessen keeper who has simply fabulous experiences with his customers but doesn't know how to get them down on paper and would need a good ghost writer?" Steinberg also found an outlet for his sense of humor within his writing social circles. "He does have a title, which Edith and I adore," Steinberg wrote the agent. "It is 'Ham on Rye.' "[47] For friends such as Grace Goldin, a writer and wife of Steinberg's longtime friend Judah Goldin, Steinberg regularly read drafts, offering generous encouragement and commiseration.[48] The business of books was interesting, fun, and a source of new kinds of relationships for Steinberg.

One of those new kinds of relationships was with his wife. As discussed in the Introduction, Steinberg's book-writing opened a new door inside the Steinberg marriage; husband and wife entered the realm of collaborators, as Edith Steinberg recounted in her essay "Midwife to a Novel."[49] In describing how she and Milton worked on his first novel together, Edith's cheeky sense of humor was on full display: "To encourage naturalness in the dialogue," Edith explained, "I developed the practice of testing the lines by declaiming them out loud. Cornelia Otis Skinner had nothing on me as I acted out all the characters in a dramatic sequence in an effort to discover the right words and the right behavior. I even managed the love scenes with the correct fervor and delicacy." Edith did not hide the messiness of spousal collaboration, explaining that "at least once a week our raised voices stopped the piano player next door who doubtless still entertains her own theories as to what goes on in our apartment. The temptation to throw things was at times very strong," she added. "And recurrently one or the other of us stalked out of the room in a huff, finished with the book forever, only to be recalled and placated. It was jolly fun." Not shy about detailing how transformative the collaborative process had been, Edith wrote that working on *As a Driven Leaf* "had the most salutary effect on me." Going on to explain her exhilaration in partnering with Milton, she confided that "We shared a sense of achievement. It was very much like a roller coaster, up with success and down with failure. But high or low, we were in it together, up to our necks; and the togetherness was exciting." That meaningful experience of collaboration between husband and wife extended to the writing of Steinberg's other books, including *Basic Judaism*.

It was true, as Steinberg realized, that American, English-language primers about Judaism were few in number. By the time that Davis and Steinberg corresponded about *Basic Judaism*, publishers were beginning to appreciate that a market for such books existed. A decade later, Nathan Glazer observed: "Commercial publishers found it worth their while to publish books on Jewish theology."[50] Previous decades had seen a few American-published primers on Judaism (Orthodox Rabbi Leo Jung's books about Judaism in the 1920s and 1930s), and German Reform Rabbi Leo Baeck's 1905 *The Essence of Judaism* was the best-known, internationally, of such primers, in the early twentieth century.[51] While Baeck's book was first translated into English in 1936, in England, it was not until 1948, with the rise of the American genre of introduction to Judaism books, that it was published in the United States, indicating the growing American market for such primers.[52] By the end of the twentieth century, Anita Diamant and Rabbi Irving Greenberg were among those who found success in the genre.[53]

Transitioning from Problem to Religion

During the 1930s, when Steinberg began writing for the popular press, interest in Jews among readers stemmed from the news, rampant worldwide antisemitism, and war. In the summer of 1933, both of Steinberg's articles, "How the Jew Did It," and "How the Jew Does It," appeared in the *Atlantic Monthly*, becoming the basis for his book, *The Making of the Modern Jew* (1934). Largely a response to antisemitism and ignorance about Jews, these publications treated Jews as "the riddle among the peoples of the world," requiring illumination.[54] The Harry Wolfson view of Jewishness as unfortunate tragedy also shaped Steinberg's 1934 book, as he described the contemporary situation as one in which "the catastrophe of Jewishness ... can not be escaped and which is nevertheless empty of all satisfaction."[55]

Today, we forget how much mystery once surrounded Jews and Judaism. By the second half of the twentieth century, attending a bar mitzvah, a Jewish wedding, a Passover Seder, and even a circumcision became more common social and cultural experiences for non-Jews in some regions of the United States. But the first few decades of the twentieth century were still years when non-Jews rarely encountered even the externalities of Jewish religion, let alone an actual Jew.[56] In accordance with this reality, Steinberg's writing evidenced the self-consciousness of a Jew accustomed to being misunderstood. It had become natural for Steinberg to see himself both as the "alien other" that Christians saw in him, and as he understood himself. Like the double consciousness that W. E. B. Du Bois described in *The Souls of Black Folks* (1903), Steinberg's writing showed the strain on Jews of always looking at one's self through the eyes of the antisemitic majority culture. It was a way of experiencing one's Jewishness that was not uncommon for an elite group of well-educated, intellectual Jews accustomed to moving in gentile circles and negotiating gentile prejudices. "In the eyes of the world he may be a living anachronism, a vestigial survival of mediaevalism," Steinberg wrote in the *Atlantic Monthly*. "In his own eyes he is a loyal Jew, obeying God's will as revealed on Sinai, and finding it graceful and lovely."[57]

As Steinberg wrote, "Of all the prophecies of Scripture concerning Israel, one has been fulfilled, even if not in its original connotation: 'And ye shall be unto me a *peculiar* people.'"[58] It was as though Steinberg felt the need to reassure his gentile readers: *You are not strange for thinking us strange. We are strange!* Steinberg described the image of the Jew as a mythical, mysterious figure: "His folk ways, compounded of strange customs and unreasonable ceremonials, smacked suspiciously of black magic and the sorcerer's craft; his books, written in illegible characters, suggested the wizard's talisman.... The Jew was strange, he was different, he was incomprehensible, and, most bewildering of all, he could not be persuaded to die."[59]

By the mid-1940s, Steinberg's approach to writing about Jews was shifting, along with the broader American conversation about Jews. As though tiring of the earlier 1930s discourse about Jews as problem, Steinberg, paraphrasing Ecclesiastes, wrote in 1945, in *A Partisan Guide to the Jewish Problem*, "Of making books on the Jewish problem there has been in recent years almost no end."[60] For Steinberg, as for other rabbis, the mid-twentieth century witnessed a transition in what it meant to write about Jews. Steinberg took part in this new paradigm by rehabilitating an idea that now seemed both old and new: Judaism as a compelling modern faith.

Coming to Judaism from the Outside

When Steinberg was drafting *Basic Judaism* in the mid-1940s, he was already a published author of fiction and nonfiction. He had written and thought deeply about Jewish suffering, Jewish religion, and the challenges facing contemporary American Jews. But like many to whom he ministered, Steinberg came to his love of Judaism from the outside, with a path that included time as a secular Jew. For authors who lacked religious upbringings, the secular parts of their biography were vital to understanding how to effectively pitch Judaism to the uninitiated. Their books became expressions of their own life choices, offering testimony on the meaning of engaging with Judaism.

Unlike rabbis born into religious homes, Steinberg's writing reveals his familiarity with secular Jewishness. "Many a Jew now living can recall the time when he helped arrange a dance for the eve of the Day of Atonement in the conscious desire to torment the benighted faithful," Steinberg wrote in his first book.[61] Few rabbis would have referenced this desecration of Yom Kippur as a typical youthful experience, but these were Steinberg's roots. It was his maternal grandmother's attachment to Judaism and her Sabbath preparations that provided the warm glow of Jewishness as religion during Steinberg's childhood. There were also fond memories of attending socialist lectures with his father that translated into an enthusiasm for intellectual debate and passion for justice that found expression in Steinberg's religious life.[62]

Synagogue attendance had not been a regular part of Steinberg's childhood, but his friends would change that. As a teenager, Steinberg and his family moved from Rochester, New York, to Jewish Harlem, where Steinberg attended DeWitt Clinton High School. Classmate Lionel Trilling remembered Steinberg as a "respectable citizen and a prig," who was somewhat "separated from the boys" because of his intellectual and academic powers.[63] Steinberg found friends in brothers Myron and Ira Eisenstein, who would help found Reconstructionist Judaism with Mordecai Kaplan. Following the Eisensteins to Congregation Anshe Chesed, then located in a middle-class Jewish Harlem neighborhood, the teenaged Steinberg became a more regular *shul*-goer.

At City College, as Steinberg's philosophy professor, Morris Raphael Cohen, hurled challenges and insults at religion, Steinberg turned to his Anshe rabbi, Jacob Kohn, for information and support. When it came to defending his own religion, the young Steinberg realized he knew far too little and lacked the kind of American, English-language books that could explain Judaism to him. His conversations with Kohn provided the Jewish education Steinberg needed for his classroom verbal spars with Professor Cohen.[64] Steinberg's time with Kohn affected him deeply as he moved toward greater ritual observance, replacing the agnosticism of his youth with new interest in Judaism. With Kohn, Steinberg also experienced a rabbi's guiding influence. Within a few decades, a generation of young Jews would feel something similar about Steinberg's mentorship. "At the time of his early death in 1950," the Zionist thinker Ben Halpern would later recall, Steinberg "had perhaps the deepest personal influence of any rabbi in America."[65] Students and colleagues remembered Steinberg as an unusually strong and affirming presence in their lives.

At the Jewish Theological Seminary, Steinberg valued the sociological and philosophical insights of Mordecai Kaplan, even as he felt the inadequacy of Kaplan's conception of God. Kaplan enabled a generation of rabbis to make Judaism more acceptable to modern Jews desiring Jewish community and Jewish outlets for their creative, artistic, and recreational needs. But Kaplan had not, Steinberg believed, sufficiently responded to Jews seeking spiritual sustenance in a hostile world. It was to these Jews that Harry Wolfson addressed his 1921 "Escaping Judaism" pamphlet. Wolfson counseled dignified resignation to the handicap that was Jewishness. Steinberg felt there were better options to be found within Judaism.

In his advice to a young Arthur Cohen, Steinberg revealed the strengths and weaknesses he found in Kaplan's thinking: "When you read Kaplan," Steinberg wrote to the twenty-year-old Cohen, "read him for his theory and program of Jewish life, not for his theology. A man can't be a theologian who lacks metaphysics and that is Mordecai Kaplan."[66] The comment highlighted Steinberg's desire for more discussion of faith and God in modern Judaism. Cohen would later reflect about his mentor, "Essentially what Reconstructionism lacked—poetry and philosophy—was precisely what Milton demanded."[67] Still, Kaplan was a savior for Steinberg during his difficult years at the seminary, where he, like other rabbinical students, struggled to find an understanding of Judaism they could preach to contemporary Jews. (In a 1948 letter to the wife of a close friend, Steinberg referred to JTS as "that great fountainhead of theological evasions which is your husband's Alma Mater and mine."[68]) Cohen wrote, "What Mordecai Kaplan had to teach ... Milton Steinberg never forgot: Judaism had to be worth the struggle to preserve it."[69] But what Steinberg thought was worth preserving turned out to differ from Kaplan's teachings.

Jews who took the time to learn about Judaism, Steinberg posited, would discover that Jewishness did not need to be experienced as a liability. As Steinberg sermonized: "A Jew who feels himself enriched and stimulated by Judaism, who senses that his intellectual horizons have been widened by it, will spontaneously be ready to identify himself with Jewish life."[70] Deeper understanding of Juda*ism* (the Jewish religion as well as its written and oral traditions) would lead to more positive feelings about Jewish*ness* (the state of being Jewish). As a rabbi, Steinberg worked in both directions: combating negative feelings around Jewishness, so that Jews might have more energy for Judaism, was one path. Showing congregants the meaning and joy to be found in Judaism, in order to diminish their negative feelings toward Jewishness, was another path.

Feelings about Jewishness were a constant concern for Steinberg. In a 1941 sermon about "First Principles for American Jews," Steinberg spoke about the reality of antisemitism, observing of the Jew that "how well he can 'take it' will depend in very great measure on his attitude toward Judaism."[71] Steinberg observed that "their courage in their future lot" is "in all actuality, being determined at this moment by the disposition which they are making of their Jewish heritage."[72] In a February, 1945 sermon, Steinberg discussed the short supply of "Indignation" among American Jews. Too many Jews were "taking anti-Semitism lying down on the ground when they ought to be on their feet fighting back," and Steinberg felt that American Jews lacked a sense of self-worth.[73] He added that antisemitism diminished Jews' appreciation for Judaism: "We never enjoy Judaism—we only suffer for it and even then not heroically," Steinberg lamented.[74] "It is the first function of a human being to respect himself, to stand erect and foursquare before the world . . . to be in sum, a man." Steinberg's words addressed Jewish men, but there's evidence that his messages and example made an impression on women. One woman—the wife of publisher Ogden Reid—who later spoke at a memorial service for Steinberg, would eulogize the late rabbi as having "flaming courage in an age of fear and easy silence. He rescued the fine art of indignation."[75]

Steinberg's attention to feelings about Jewishness extended to all areas of life. "I wish to urge those few persons in the Park Avenue Synagogue who have made it a practice to send Christmas greetings to their Jewish friends to desist from doing so in the future," Steinberg wrote in a 1947 synagogue bulletin. He explained: "I never get a Christmas card from a Jew without being plunged into the most painful reflections over the spiritual gaucherie of which otherwise cultivated people are sometimes capable; over the capacity of Jews to overlook . . . a festival as lovely and significant as Hanukkah."[76] To some Park Avenue Synagogue members, Steinberg's attention to such details may have felt intrusive and controlling. But Steinberg took seriously his ministering, understanding his role as exerting "influence on the persons whose souls are supposedly in my care."[77] For those who felt unmoored as Jews, Steinberg's attentiveness provided comfort and ballast.

Steinberg's often concrete guidance for leading a positive Jewish life showed the influence of Mordecai Kaplan. Like Harry Wolfson, Kaplan was sensitive to the suffering of those who experienced their Jewishness as a burden. Kaplan's response was to launch a new program for creative Jewish life. Steinberg's positive approach may have been the result of his opposite route toward Judaism: unlike Wolfson, Steinberg had journeyed *toward* Judaism, from secular Jewishness. He wanted more Jewishness, more Jewish ritual, more Jewish community, more Jewish religion. In typical Steinberg fashion, when he was consulted in 1942 about naming a new, Jewish-sponsored university in the Boston area, Steinberg responded that he thought "Brandeis," the last name of the first Jewish Supreme Court Justice Louis Brandeis, was insufficiently Jewish. He advised, instead, "either a Jewish historical place name of universal import, or the name of some Titanic Jewish personality," such as Sinai University, Isaiah University, or Maimonides University.[78]

From his pulpit at Park Avenue Synagogue, Steinberg could see that there were many congregants who, like him, had grown up with only dim understandings of Judaism. He understood what it was to be a young Jew, "groping to establish rapport with the Jewish Tradition, standing at the synagogue's doors 'heart in, head out.'"[79] "Empty vessels" was what Steinberg called these Jews.[80] Such Jews were "ignorant of their own past," but they represented potential to Steinberg. In moving from his first pulpit in Indianapolis, to Manhattan's Park Avenue Synagogue on the Upper East Side of Manhattan, Steinberg hoped to reach larger numbers of undereducated Jews. Upon hearing of Steinberg's new position in 1933, Reform rabbi and Zionist leader Stephen S. Wise wrote to a colleague, "I rejoice to think that he is to be in New York and that his strength and courage and devotion are to become a part of the common assets of the Jewish life of the largest Jewish community in history."[81] Steinberg felt similarly.[82] As he wrote to his cousin, Philip Bernstein, shortly after accepting the Park Avenue Synagogue pulpit: "I have a feeling that I am stepping into something which can be tremendous if I have the ability to swing it."[83] Writing important, middlebrow books would be part of Steinberg's next chapter.

The Irony of the Genre

The very title of Steinberg's 1947 Introduction to Judaism text suggested the needs and the failures of late 1940s Jews. What did it say about American Jews that there was a market for a book titled *Basic Judaism*? As Steinberg wrote Arthur Cohen about the enthusiastic reception of his book: "On the reaction to Basic Judaism which you described, you are quite right in saying that the favorable impression it has made is a reflection upon the religious illiteracy of the American Jewish community."[84] The irony of midcentury Introduction to Judaism literature was that its success as a genre of books was a reflection of the failure of Jewish education. The situation of uneducated Jews may have been dispiriting for those who valued high levels of Jewish education, but it also represented potential to authors such as Steinberg.

As Steinberg explained in *Basic Judaism*, the book was intended to help readers fill their gaps in understanding and to educate Jews who did not yet know what they did not know about Judaism. One reviewer observed that the purpose of *Basic Judaism* was "to set unsynagogued Jews like myself to thinking about the Jewish religion and their relationship to it."[85] Steinberg posited that *Basic Judaism* offered something new because it was "written from within Judaism and hence sympathetic to it, concerned with it for its own sake and not as a foil for something else, unencumbered with details and as free as possible from doctrinal and ritualistic dissensions."[86] Still, Christianity, and Catholicism in particular, was clearly on Steinberg's mind in *Basic Judaism*, as when he explained Jewish views of sin, the body, sexuality, freedom of thought, and the good life.

Rabbis like Steinberg may not have admitted it, even to themselves, but using Christianity and, specifically, Catholicism as a foil for Judaism was a helpful strategy for defining Judaism as a democratic faith. These Jewish writers constructed their own hierarchy of religions, in which Judaism was a "good religion," a status earned, in part, through its commonalities with liberal Protestantism, while Catholicism was judged "bad religion."[87] Even critics of *Basic Judaism* generally agreed with this presentation of Judaism, as when Irving Kristol exclaimed in his review of *Basic Judaism*, after describing Jewish views of sexuality, "How far is this from the Catholic mind!"[88] Today, Kristol's comment reads as anti-Catholic sentiment, but for Jews like Kristol, who grew up with stories, if not personal experiences, of Catholic bullies taunting young Jews for being Christ-killers, such anti-Catholic statements likely did not register as bigotry. In the American Jewish imagination of the 1930s and 1940s, Catholics—a much larger and more powerful group—were the bullies, and Jews were the victims.[89]

Steinberg had been reading popular books about religion for well over a decade before publishing *Basic Judaism*. As a result, he had a clear idea about what made for a good Introduction to Judaism, and was ill-disposed to books that treated religion as "an unpleasant, but by very virtue of that fact, a salubrious medicine."[90] Steinberg sought to clearly communicate the joys and benefits of religion. With an understanding of the value of middlebrow books that reached more readers than would ever hear one of his sermons, Steinberg surveyed the field of moralistic literature in 1946 and observed that these kinds of books "tend to be either very bad or very good."[91] To be in the latter group, Steinberg posited that such a book "must be earnest, not glib, never underestimating the difficulty and the painfulness of man's lot," and that it must bring "some new knowledge or conception to bear on the riddles of man's existence." In reviewing a successful example of middlebrow Introduction to Judaism literature—Liebman's bestselling *Peace of Mind*—Steinberg observed that "Rabbi Liebman feels at first hand the texture and the dimensions of the internal dilemmas, intellectual and emotional, of man's nature and experience."[92] Steinberg hoped to accomplish something similar in his book. Confirming that he had been successful, the *New Yorker* reviewed *Basic Judaism* as "a brief and unentangled explanation of the origins, practices, and aspirations of the Jewish faith, particularly successful because of the author's rare ability to stick to unadorned information, instead of wandering off into the fascinating but convoluted alleys of theological controversy."[93]

In *Basic Judaism*, the reasonableness of Judaism—what Steinberg called its "mellower" and more realistic view of man—usually implied a comparison with Christianity. Steinberg wrote about Judaism with the consciousness that Christian ideas shaped readers' understanding of religion. The words "Talmud" and "Halakhah" were absent in Steinberg's six pages on Jewish law, despite being integral to Judaism, but they were also foreign-sounding to Christian readers. Then, too, the six pages in *Basic Judaism* about the Jewish view of Jesus are probably out of proportion to the importance of Jesus in Jewish religious life, but less so in the context of Steinberg's presentation of Judaism as shaped by Christian assumptions and expectations. Although Steinberg's editor urged him to shorten his discussion of Jesus, Steinberg explained in a letter to a friend:

HOW BASIC IS *BASIC JUDAISM*? 123

I think that gentiles who are interested in getting the Jewish view of jesus [*sic*]—if there are such—ought to get it fairly straight and not in the garbled, saccharined misrepresentations of a Sholom Asch or of a Werfel. An intelligent goy ought have an opportunity to find out approximately what Jews of good will and favorable disposition think about Christianity and about Jesus.[94]

The Jesus discussion stayed in the book. Using the device of an imagined Christian interrogation of the Jewish view of Jesus, *Basic Judaism* explained how Jews viewed Jesus:

Let it be conceded that Jesus is neither God, nor uniquely His Son, nor the Messiah, nor a moral prophet, nor even an impeccable human being. Certainly he was, despite his defects, a great man, a gifted and exalted teacher. Will not the Jews accept him as such? To which the answer of Jews runs: "Have Jews, except under the extremest provocation, ever quarreled with such a presentation of him?"[95]

* * *

A decade after *Basic Judaism* was published, the tone of such an imagined face-off between Judaism and Christianity would have shifted. But with Charles Lindbergh's speech and isolationist sentiment, as well as Father Charles Coughlin and the activities of the pro-Nazi Christian Front, in recent memory, the mid-1940s was a considerably more anxious time for Jews than the late 1950s. When Steinberg wrote *Basic Judaism* he was still defending the right of his co-religionists not to be Christians. Often, in *Basic Judaism*, the comparisons between the two traditions were made explicit, as when Steinberg wrote: "The tension between body and soul which so harrowed first the pagan world and then the Christian is relaxed in Judaism. To the age-old question: which shall a man gratify, his flesh or his spirit, Judaism answers simply, 'both.'"[96] On the topic of man's capacity for goodness, Steinberg explained that in Judaism, "Perfection is not a human trait," adding that, "there are religions which insist that he achieve it or be lost."[97] Steinberg clearly had Catholicism in mind as he explained that "certain religions," which, "having set an unreachable standard" for man, "they foredoom him to damnation, from which only divine grace can deliver him."[98] Switching over to Protestantism, Steinberg commented that since predestination meant that "grace by definition is conferred, not won, God's intervention on his behalf comes out in the end unpredictable, even capricious. In this respect Judaism is mellower, more realistic."[99] That Jews "are not only congregants of a church," they were also part of a culture, meant they "are Jews for other reasons than doctrine alone. Which takes some of the strain off doctrine in Judaism."[100]

These multiple meanings of Jewishness made room for Zionism in Steinberg's account: "Judaism, the faith of Israel, includes also a faith *in* Israel," Steinberg explained.[101] The land of Palestine and the Hebrew language were sacred, because of their associations: "It was in the Holy Land and in Hebrew that revelations came to the prophets. . . . Palestine was the site of many of the supremely memorable incidents in Jewish history, and Hebrew was the medium for most of the precious utterances of the Jewish soul."[102] Land and language were crucial to the Jewish future in Steinberg's formulation. For centuries, Steinberg explained, dispersion and persecution hampered the growth of Judaism. "But when a Jewish Commonwealth has come into being, when outcast Jews have found peace, when the Hebrew language and literature have taken root in their native soil, the Tradition will have a fresh chance at free, spontaneous unfolding."[103] Such circumstances are favorable for Jews all over the world. "For Palestine then will be an unfettered heart pumping the blood of health and vigor to all the Jewries of the dispersion." Steinberg believed it a certainty that "the Jewish people everywhere will be the stronger for the Homeland and its revived Hebrew culture, and therefore the better able to labor for the advent of that ideal society which it was the first to project and after which it has striven so long and mightily."[104]

Tolerance of doctrinal difference was inherent in Judaism, in Steinberg's formulation, as were intellectual inquiry, debate, and the right to make up one's mind. "Where other historic religions have busied themselves with doctrine first and ethic second, Judaism has done just the opposite," Steinberg wrote. "It has concentrated its attention on giving men specific instructions on how they ought to comport themselves, especially in their dealings with one another."[105] The centuries-old antisemitic portrayal of Judaism as preoccupied with legalism was overturned in *Basic Judaism*, to reveal an emphasis on ethical living and non-dogmatic religion. Whereas Christianity was sclerotic and enforced conformity, Judaism promoted open debate.

Judaism's approach to other religions proved its liberalism, in Steinberg's portrayal. "Anyone may become a Jew, but no one has to do so in order to be saved," Steinberg explained.[106] In Christianity, meanwhile, Steinberg explained that Paul's teachings revealed a more exclusive worldview: "There is neither Jew nor Greek, there is neither bond nor free . . . for ye are all one in Christ Jesus"—did not actually apply to anyone who was not a professing Christian. To Christians, Steinberg reminded readers, if you were not Christian, you were damned. In Judaism, the righteous of all peoples have their share in the world to come.[107] To Steinberg, this "readiness to recognize that others aside from Jews possess spiritual merit sufficient for salvation constitutes an instance of liberalism almost unique in western theology."[108] While overtly making the case for Judaism's liberalism—and the respectful view of other traditions that it engendered—*Basic Judaism* included reasons for believing in the superiority of Judaism. It was as though Steinberg were thinking back to his days in the college classroom with Professor Morris Raphael Cohen. He understood what it meant to be a young Jew seeking proof of his religion's validity.

A Judaism for Main Street America

Although Steinberg would be remembered as an important midcentury rabbi, he was not part of the New York Jewish intelligentsia—a group of anti-Stalinist Jewish intellectuals that included Irving Kristol, Lionel Trilling, Diana Trilling, Alfred Kazin, Clement Greenberg, Midge Decter, Irving Howe, Hannah Arendt, Nathan Glazer, and Philip Rahv.[109] This cohort of writers and editors—most of whom were educated at City College and Columbia—is strongly associated with the publications its members founded, edited, and contributed to, including the *Partisan Review*, *Public Interest*, *Commentary*, *Dissent*, and *New York Review of Books*. When it came to their attitudes toward Jewishness, they were known for a posture of alienation and ambivalence.[110]

Steinberg's distance from these Jewish intellectuals became apparent in the reception of *Basic Judaism* among highbrow Jewish writers.[111] Intellectuals' criticism proved their engagement with the new Introduction to Judaism literature. Jewish intellectuals might not have approved of Steinberg's book, but they were not ignoring it, either.

In the pages of *Commentary* magazine, the writer and future neoconservative Irving Kristol weighed in: "If we tolerate such concepts as basic Judaism, basic Christianity, basic Buddhism, and so on, why should we not settle for basic religion—in which everything is so watered-down and vague that no one's religious sentiments are excluded from participation?"[112] Where Steinberg sought to show unity between the different branches of Judaism, Kristol saw shallowness. He judged Steinberg as accommodating "his religious views with facility to the outlook of an American 'Main Street' in its New Deal variant."[113] To Kristol, such views represented the problems of the American Jewish community. "It results in the perversion of the Jewish religion into a doctrine of social (and sociable) principles, the transformation of Messianism into a shallow, if sincere, humanitarianism, plus a thoroughgoing insensitivity to present day spiritual problems."[114] After the war and Hitler, Kristol implied, how could Steinberg take such a benevolent view of man, who was clearly capable of so much evil?

In resisting recent trends in neo-Orthodox theology, Kristol asserted, *Basic Judaism* displayed intellectual timidity.[115] Jewish theology should move away from certitude and complacency, Kristol maintained, and toward a "theology of crisis." But Steinberg viewed the neo-Orthodox theological trend that emerged after World War I in reaction to nineteenth-century modernist liberal theology as an obsessive search for evil. When Steinberg's young friend Arthur Cohen wrote to Steinberg of his attraction to Reinhold Niebuhr's theology of crisis, Steinberg replied wearily: "The problem of evil looms very large.... I wonder however whether it isn't looming too large. Niebuhr stands to Judaism very much as a hypochondriac stands in relation to a person who is a realist about his lot but healthy minded.... That doesn't mean we have to be Pollyanna about it, but neither ought we be nervous Nellies."[116] Steinberg did not completely reject Niebuhr's neo-Orthodoxy, but he saw it as foreign to Judaism: "It is nothing less than a historic pattern of thought and feeling. To one reared in the Jewish tradition, something of morbidity seems to pervade this motif in Protestantism."[117] Steinberg saw himself as an optimist who hoped to steer Jews such as Cohen toward a more balanced view of Judaism. Thus, Steinberg preached the remarkable functionality of Judaism in America. He wrote: "English is my first language, and that of my children.... The history of America is my history. I mean it when I sing 'Land where my fathers died.' But Jewish history is my background, too." Steinberg modeled an American Jewishness that sacrificed neither Jewish nor American traditions or heroes. "Lincoln and Jefferson are my heroes together with Rabbi Akiba and Moses Maimonides. The four get along in my imagination most companionably.... I sing Negro spirituals, American ballads, and Hasidic or Palestinian folksongs with equal vigor and tonelessness." There was no need for Jews to shun American ritual and celebration, Steinberg asserted: "On the Fourth of July I set off fireworks and attempt to transmit to my children my appreciation of the significance of the holiday. With equal earnestness I kindle Hanukkah lights.... At no time am I conscious of strain between the two worlds. I move from one to the other with such naturalness I am scarcely aware of the change in spiritual locale."[118]

Did 1940s readers believe that Steinberg really moved so seamlessly between American and Jewish traditions? Steinberg laid out the dream of many, even if it was not their lived reality. Reading this vision of a robust American Jewish life articulated by a respected rabbi was likely inspiring. In *Basic Judaism*, Steinberg's folksy humanity covered well-trodden ground as he made the case for harmony between American and Jewish traditions. He wrote: "Both are democratic. Both emphasize the worth of the individual and his right to freedom. In both there is passionate devotion to the ideal of social justice. And the vision of the more abundant life is a secularized parallel of the ancient Jewish dream of the Kingdom of God on earth."[119] When Judaism thrives, Steinberg posited, it showed the United States was living up to its democratic ideals.[120]

Steinberg's book and others like it provided fodder for a younger generation to criticize. The problem with *Basic Judaism* and books like it, according to critics, was that they rendered Jewish religion far too simple. These intellectuals insisted that there was more to Judaism, even as they admitted their own religious illiteracy. But here was also a hidden benefit to the middlebrow primers. It was true, as Steinberg confided to Arthur Cohen, that the success of a book titled *Basic Judaism* proved the sad state of American Jewry. But the effectiveness of Introduction to Judaism books, with titles such as *Basic Judaism* and *What Is a Jew?*, in announcing their accessibility indicated that it was perfectly acceptable—and completely American—to need an introduction to Judaism. The result was a broadened conversation about Judaism. Their titles and approachable style announced that these books and essays were open to all comers, and that one did not need to be a scholar or an Orthodox Jew to join a conversation about Judaism.

Steinberg's *Basic Judaism* challenged others to go further in their presentations of Judaism. A dozen years later, in the *Saturday Review*, a writer reflected on the "unfortunate tendency, especially in recent years, to publish popular handbooks on Judaism that reduce the subject far below its intrinsic depth, a kind of 'Judaism Made Easy,' which is insulting to the reader and misleading in its intent. Judaism is not easy. No serious way of life is."[121] In that 1959 review essay, the reviewer pointed readers toward multiple new English-language guides to the Talmud, including Morris Adler's *The World of the Talmud* and Louis Ginzberg's *On Jewish Law and Lore*, marking a new chapter in the Introduction to Judaism genre.[122] Previous Introduction to Judaism books, including *Basic Judaism*, rarely included extensive discussions of Talmud.[123]

Disappointment over this early generation of Introduction to Judaism books did not shut down the genre; instead, criticism inspired new variations on the theme. In multiple ways, middlebrow simplification of Judaism had worked its power: some readers felt ownership of a tradition that previously seemed esoteric and foreign, while others, such as Kristol, began to demand a more challenging Judaism. Both responses showed engagement. While Introduction to Judaism books like *Basic Judaism* did not meet the needs of every reader, these 1940s publications began the postwar trend of American Judaism primers. Jewish religion was becoming understandable to Americans who were more receptive than ever to learning about it, to judge from the interest of mainstream publishers and editors. In the 1950s, the project of explaining Judaism as an American religion would be further aided by mainstream middlebrow institutions, such as Time Inc. The reflection of their religion that Jewish readers found in the pages of middlebrow publications such as *Life* magazine was not always a pleasing one, but it did capture Americans' attention.

6
Philip Bernstein and the 1950s Religious Revival

September 11, 1950, was a proud day for Rabbi Philip Bernstein. His article "What the Jews Believe" was featured on the cover of *Life*, a magazine read by 13.5 million people.[1] Of all of the publications in the Time Inc. parent company, *Life*, with its mission to show readers the news through photographs, was the magazine intended for the widest readership. It had become a national arbiter of what counted as part of the American Way of Life, and this issue, appearing on newsstands just before the Jewish New Year, was no different. Its pages contained photographs ranging from the frontlines of the Korean War to Hollywood. An article titled, "Extra Chins Help Irene Dunne Portray Victoria" showed the actress trying on a "cosmetic latex chin-piece."[2] Photographs and texts combined, in *Life*, to educate readers about events they might never encounter in their daily lives. Bernstein's "What the Jews Believe" followed this pattern. It offered readers a clear explanation of a religion with which many Americans were only vaguely familiar.

As if taking cues from *Gentleman's Agreement*'s Phil Green and his limited interest in Jewish religion, the essay portrayed Judaism cautiously, and with Christian expectations in mind. Although the *Life* editor instructed the rabbi-author not to write his article as a retort to antisemitism, that was difficult advice for a rabbi who came of age during the 1920s and 1930s. Explaining Judaism to such a large middlebrow readership—still unusual for a rabbi—was, like most early postwar Introduction to Judaism literature, inherently an act of *anti*-antisemitism. Writers such as Bernstein sought to present Judaism sympathetically, and with understanding of readers' biases. Introduction to Judaism literature thus overlapped with anti-antisemitism literature in its goals of combating antisemitism. But the genre went much further down the path of explaining Jewish religion in its particularities.

During this early era of postwar Introduction to Judaism texts, American society was undergoing a religious revival that was perceptible by the late 1940s—and undeniable by the late 1950s.[3] The uptick in religious activity

Postwar Stories. Rachel Gordan, Oxford University Press. © Oxford University Press 2024.
DOI: 10.1093/9780197694367.003.0007

was evident in a number of areas including the publication of Bibles and religious books, and construction of religious buildings.[4] Bernstein's 1950 Introduction to Judaism in the pages of *Life* appeared at an early stage of the revival, while Judaism was gaining its footing as a postwar American religion, and as middlebrow cultural institutions such as Time Inc. were figuring out how to portray Jews. The very presence of an article about Judaism in *Life* indicated new cultural winds affecting religion and Judaism.

A New Popularity for Judaism

In 1950, novelist John Hersey's *The Wall*, a fictional account of the Jewish resistance to the Nazis in the Warsaw ghetto, became a *New York Times* bestseller, and the Israeli song "Tzena, Tzena" hit number two on the Billboard charts. It had just been recorded by a new folk singing group called the Weavers, featuring singer-songwriter Pete Seeger.[5] One reporter described the surprising and sudden ubiquity of the Israeli import: "You get off at a whistle stop in Wisconsin to get a cup of coffee and out of the juke box comes Tzena, Tzena. In Atlanta, Ga., you listen at midnight to the radio disc jockey and it's Tzena, Tzena. You go in New York to the Radio City Music Hall and what is the finale number? Yes, it's Tzena, Tzena, again."[6] Danny Kaye, born David Kaminsky of Brooklyn, one of many celebrated Jewish comedians of his time, was being hailed as "the best young comedian we have around" in the *New Yorker*.[7] In the same month that Bernstein's *Life* article appeared, the middlebrow women's magazine *Redbook*, for the first time, featured a six-page spread about the Jewish high holidays.[8] Jews and Judaism enjoyed a new postwar popularity.

But it wasn't only a new vogue of Jews and Judaism that led to the Time Inc. treatment. In the postwar years the widely held perception of a national religious revival provided another impetus for such publications. As Stephen Whitfield has pointed out, the United States was unique among Western nations in its experience of so dramatic an upsurge of postwar piety. During these early Cold War years Americans' religious beliefs were likely intensified by the "the need to combat a political system that was, above all, defined as godless."[9]

In sermons and in newspaper editorials, ministers and commentators expressed their belief that national commitment to religion was growing. The Reverend Norman Vincent Peale's *The Power of Positive Thinking* was not published until 1952, but the book's message that individuals could overcome negativity and achieve faith in God had already entered the zeitgeist. There was an element of hoping to make it so by saying it, in these written and oral pronouncements about the religious surge. "Perhaps the belief that there is a revival of religion rests primarily upon a priori judgment," Reinhold Niebuhr remarked in 1950.[10] "It is generally assumed," Niebuhr explained, that "periods of crisis are conducive to a revival of religion; and this assumption encourages the conviction that an age of crisis, such as our own, must therefore be more interested in religion." In a 1948 *Time* cover story, writer and former Communist Whittaker Chambers reflected on Niebuhr's role of bringing a preoccupation with sin back into style. By reminding Americans that "life is inevitably tragic," Niebuhr worked against the tide of easy postwar optimism, in which religion's primary purpose was to provide reassurance.[11] Under *Time*'s cover image of Niebuhr, the caption read, "Man's story is not a success story."[12] That message fit Niebuhr's neo-Orthodox goals of serving as a troubler of easy consciences. But it was not a message that many American Jewish leaders of the late 1940s and early 1950s felt called to preach. After the Holocaust it did not seem particularly necessary to point out to Jewish communities that man was capable of evil.[13] To provide spiritual sustenance for the rebuilding of world Jewry after the greatest catastrophe of modern Jewish history, authors of Introduction to Judaism books crafted uplifting messages about Jewish religion and culture. The president of New York's Jewish Theological Seminary, Rabbi Louis Finkelstein, who would appear on the cover of *Time* magazine in 1951, spoke of a new concern about "spiritual values" among a younger generation, with noticeably more cheerfulness than had characterized Niebuhr's brooding theology in *Time*'s cover story. Finkelstein told a laymen's religious institute, "Indeed, the whole American people is waking up to the fact that it needs religion."[14]

After two decades that felt like an era of growing secularism, the long marriage between American culture and religion was revived again during the 1950s. Even outsiders noted the change. "The first thing that has struck me is how America is now more religious than Britain," Dr. Alec Vidler, an editor of the Anglo-Catholic British monthly *Theology*, told *Time*, while visiting the United States in 1948.[15] "People here go to church much more." The British clergyman stopped short of expressing sincere admiration of the American scene, explaining his reservations by drawing a comparison to the "prodigious religiousness" of nineteenth-century Britain: "All that business and efficiency in organizing religious services and activities, served, I am sure, as a cushion against the hard impact of the living God. Our churches were like comfortable and well-managed religious clubs, in which we felt nicely at home, in which we felt good, in which we even wanted to be better, at least on Sunday evenings when singing particularly lush hymns."[16] In the United States, Vidler observed wryly, religious efficiency and prosperity was "still doing its comfortable, but fatal work."[17] Not everyone assessing the increased religious activity judged it true piety.

Supporters of 1950s religion urged its benefits as a prophylactic measure against communism and other potential crises. As one historian observed of 1950s American religious behavior, "The ordinary customers understood quite well that . . . religion was not only a faith choice but a rational choice; it could defend togetherness better than the psychoanalysts or the communists."[18] Contemporary observers also admonished religious Americans to be on guard. "We reject the communistic teaching that Christianity is untrue; that religion is unnecessary," President Truman wrote to the Eighth World Baptist Congress, in the summer of 1950.[19] "I believe there is no problem, moral or economic, in the field of our national sphere or among the nations of this troubled world, that would not yield to the intelligence, the courage and the faith of free men if those who seek solution, approach the problem in the spirit of the Sermon on the Mount." For Truman, the country's Judeo-Christian religion was mostly Christian. In the pages of *Redbook*, J. Edgar Hoover's 1949 essay "God or Chaos" warned his largely female readers of the communists' recruitment efforts: they tried to fool potential recruits with the line that communism "is a kind of religion."[20] In fact, Hoover wrote, communists were enemies of religion. As to suspicions of Jewish proclivities for radicalism, Hoover offered defense of *religious* American Jews: "Actually, very few Jews belong to the Communist Party in the Soviet Union. In America, there are names of Jewish origin on the membership rolls of the Communist party; but a Jew who follows the teachings of Judaism could never be a Communist."[21] Hoover proffered his own *anti-antisemitic* defense of American Judaism, in service to Cold War American values.

For Orthodox Jews, the era called for cautious optimism about their movement's ability to win and retain souls. When the Orthodox Jewish journal *Tradition* was founded in 1958, the journal explained its mission: "to discuss, interpret, and illustrate the basic tenets of Judaism in such a way as to meet the doubts of the modern mind and strengthen the faith of modern man."[22] The president of the Orthodox Rabbinical Council of America wrote in that first issue: "We hope it will dip into the treasure of the Jewish spirit and uncover its ancient fabulous jewels, refurbished to sparkle even in an atmosphere of modernism, materialism, and doubt."[23] In the past, *Tradition*'s editors explained, Orthodoxy faced too many obstacles in communicating its main ideas. According to *Tradition*'s editors, these challenges included:

> Yiddish instead of English, the foreign accent, European mannerisms, the lack of education, the abrupt cultural discontinuity, and the inability and apparent unwillingness to re-express valid truths in a contemporary idiom—these were problems of communication, not of basic philosophy. And it was this lack of communication which left so many Jews ignorant of the light that the tradition could shed on the basic problems of the modern world. Thus, Orthodoxy was not tried and found wanting but—to paraphrase a famous writer—it was not tried in the first place by great numbers of people as a working philosophy in the context of modern life.[24]

As the founding editors of *Tradition* articulated communication challenges, they were also expressing one of the primary functions of midcentury Jewish middlebrow literature: conveying the riches of Judaism in a modern American idiom. As the next chapter shows, this attention to the difficult task of communicating their goals would bear fruit for the movement's future.

A Mirror to the Middle Class

To Time Inc. publisher Henry Luce, religion was also personally important. Considered one of the most influential Americans of his day, and a friend to midcentury US presidents, Luce was a Yale-educated son of Presbyterian missionaries and a man motivated by what one historian calls an "imperialism of the spirit, with its imperative to change the world," although Luce was upfront about his vision for the world.[25] "I am," Luce said of himself, "a Protestant, a Republican, and a free enterpriser, which means I am biased in favor of God, Eisenhower, and the stockholders of Time Inc.—and if anyone who objects doesn't know this by now, why the hell are they still spending 35 cents for the magazine?"[26] In his 1941 "American Century" *Life* editorial, Luce called on Americans to take the reins of world leadership: "We must undertake now to be the Good Samaritan of the entire world."[27] Such responsibilities required understanding of world events, including those relating to religion.

Unlike the *Saturday Evening Post*, another influential midcentury middlebrow magazine, *Life*, along with the rest of Time Inc., was based in New York, where it was difficult to ignore Jews. The *Post*, with its famous Norman Rockwell covers, seemed to have "always been the sort of magazine that was read by Richard Nixon's mother," in which every piece "had to be understood in Fargo, South Dakota [sic]," in the words of journalist Pete Hamill.[28] Meanwhile, Luce's publications reflected a more sophisticated middlebrow perspective. *Life*, which Luce bought and made part of Time Inc., in 1936, shifted the traditional balance between text and image in journalism. Older magazines like the *Post* had used drawn images to illustrate a story, but *Life* made its images "the principal subject of a magazine."[29] And unlike the *Post*'s reliance on illustrations, *Life* shunned them, in favor of what looked like the future—photography, suggesting a superiority over older magazines, as "photographs had the advantage of instant authority (see for yourself). And they were sexy (showing skin)," as Deborah Solomon observes.[30]

Life was, indeed, the visual embodiment of the middle class, as its photographs made clear who belonged and who, by their absence, did not.[31] Income or occupation alone did not guarantee middle-class status. Race and, in some regions, religion could obstruct one's ability to participate in the structures of middle-class life, notwithstanding high incomes or professional status. Higher salaries, educational opportunities, and the Servicemen's Readjustment Act of 1944 eased the way of white GIs, including Jews, into the middle class. In the 1950s, Blacks could not find themselves portrayed as middle-class Americans in *Life*'s pages. But Jews could now see themselves reflected back in articles such as "What the Jews Believe" (1950), "Life Goes to a Bar Mitzvah" (1952), and a June 1955 cover story about Judaism, discussed in the next chapter.[32]

Still, Jewish access to the 1950s American Way of Life remained limited by quotas, real estate covenants, and rampant discrimination in hiring that did not truly abate until the last third of the twentieth century. Jews were *becoming* middle class in the 1950s. But like their racial status, their socioeconomic standing felt shaky. If their chances of being admitted to an Ivy League college or a professional school, of landing a dream job, of gaining membership in a fancy country club, or even of purchasing a home in a desirable suburb were limited, to what extent were they truly part of the middle class, and the sense of possibility it represented?[33] As *Look* magazine described the situation in their 1955 article "The Position of the Jew in America Today," to be a Jew was to "feel that you belong here in America—up to a point."[34] Social acceptance was the rub. As one 1950s Jew put it provocatively, "I sometimes feel like a prostitute. They'll call on me to lead their Community Chest campaign or help on the Red Cross. But when it comes to the country club, I'm not good enough for them."[35] Such comments suggested the need to provide a special service, or to be unusually talented in the manner of an Albert Einstein or Yehudi Menuhin, to be a valued midcentury Jew. To simply be a Jew was not enough. As Hobson's *Gentleman's Agreement* intimated, postwar Jews had the *potential* of gaining social acceptance if their behavior warranted it. But not if they offended gentile sensibilities. Then, they were like the girls Kathy met on the ski slopes: not the "right kind" of Jews. This feeling of being judged not quite good enough for meaningful personal relationships with gentiles was another sign of the glass ceiling limiting midcentury Jews' ascent.

Religion in *Life*

Convinced of the global importance of religion, Luce directed *Life* toward exploring the "World's Great Religions." In a mid-1950s letter to *Life*'s deputy editor, he observed, "Religion-in-America is today such a tremendously interesting Topic. It is of course interesting to Americans. But Religion-in-America is also beginning to be of considerable interest to people overseas—in fact Europeans are beginning to be somewhat amazed by it." Luce's wide-ranging intellectual pursuits led to the creation of magazines reflecting these interests (*Fortune, Time, Life*). Religion was another such weighty topic. In the winter of 1955, *Life* began a series of special issues on "The World's Great Religions," including Hinduism, Buddhism, Islam, Judaism, and Christianity. Three years later, the issues were made into a book of the same title.[36]

"Religion does not explain everything about a people's behavior," *Life*'s editors wrote in their first religion issue, "but, as the mother of morals and definer of justice, it has ever been a chief arbiter of man's conduct."[37] To understand why people do what they do, *Life*'s editors suggested, it was important to understand their religious beliefs and practice. As Luce saw it, *Life* was riding a wave of postwar American engagement with religion. By 1958, Luce looked back over the past dozen years and wrote in a Time Inc. internal memo: "As it turned out, Religion was a more-than-ordinarily high-priority subject in America in the post-war years. There set in a huge revival—at least in the sense of church membership."[38] Luce reflected that the "climax of our efforts" at Time Inc. "and in a sense, of America's interest in Religion" was *Life*'s Christianity issue and the Great Religions Books subsequently published. By 1958, although Luce sensed that "the tide of 'religious interest' in America may have passed its peak," he wrote to his editorial staff that "the wave is still high—and man is a religious animal."

To Luce, there was no getting around the inherent interestingness of religion. At the bottom of his memo, he jotted down: "The Christianity issue did not exhaust the subject; it just exhausted us."[39] In memos to his editorial staff, he made clear that there were still plenty of Christianity and religion topics for *Life* to cover. As Luce reminded his editors, when it came to religion, "We as Americans are more or less used to it. People my age or older remember 30 or 40 years ago when religion seemed to be on the decline and then in the last 10 years when it has been on the rise."[40] As a publisher attuned to major trends and events, Luce saw potential in the topic and its contemporary revival in America. It was in this context that *Life* gave unprecedented attention to contemporary Judaism.[41]

To inaugurate its engagement with Judaism, *Life* assigned the article that would become "What the Jews Believe" to Reform Rabbi Philip Bernstein, of Rochester, New York. Like his cousin, Milton Steinberg, Bernstein was the child of immigrants. He grew up in a home in which his mother was more religiously observant than his father.[42] Following college at Syracuse University, Bernstein graduated with the first class at the Jewish Institute of Religion, a New York City seminary founded by Rabbi Stephen Wise, a Reform rabbi and Zionist leader whom Bernstein admired. Along with his fourteen classmates, Bernstein was "drawn to study with Wise, who modeled the possibility that progressivism, Jewish nationalism, and religious life could co-exist and promised that, together, they could lead a renewal in American Jewish life."[43] A Guggenheim Foundation fellowship in 1925–1926 granted Bernstein half a year at Cambridge University, followed by European travel and six months in Palestine, studying at the newly founded Hebrew University.[44] Bernstein's rabbinical career included leadership roles in the Central Conference of American Rabbis (CCAR), Reform's national rabbinic organization. From 1942 to the end of the war, Bernstein served as executive director of the Committee on Army and Navy Religious Activities (CANRA), helping to find homes for Europe's displaced Jews.[45]

By the time of his 1950 *Life* article, Bernstein had published articles on Jewish topics in *Harper's*, the *Nation*, and the *New Republic*, and he had made wartime radio appearances, including several on the "Message of Israel" program, in which he addressed the parents of servicemen.[46] Milton Steinberg, who died six months before "What the Jews Believe" was published, provided Bernstein a model of making writing part of one's rabbinical career. As young rabbis in the early 1930s, they kept each other informed of their publications and extended invitations to speak at their pulpits. By the late 1940s, both Steinberg and Bernstein understood there was a market for English-language explanations of Judaism.

"Not only good journalism, but also good citizenship"

Because community and ritual often felt more central than belief to Jews—a point made frequently in midcentury primers on Judaism—"What the Jews Do" might have been a more accurate title of Bernstein's essay. But the *Life* article—as was evident from the directions provided by the magazine's editorial director, John Shaw Billings—was intended, primarily, for a Christian audience. Billings instructed Bernstein: "The article, for authority, should be written by a rabbi, but it is addressed to the non-Jew. Unless the non-Jew understands it and accepts it and warms to its exposition of a faith not his own, the article is a failure." Billings further explained that "The article we are looking for is primarily theological. It is not political; it is not cultural; it is not sociological. It answers in the simplest (and loftiest) terms the Christian questions 'What is a good Jew? What does he believe? Why does he believe it?'"[47] *Life's* editors felt they would achieve an authentic explication of Judaism by asking a rabbi to write the article. The editors made clear that they were not interested in those parts of Judaism unrelated to religion.

According to Billings, the author of such an article "must go on the assumption that the reader knows practically nothing about the subject and must be almost led by the hand through what to the good Jew would seem to be the most elementary and fundamental material."[48] The test to determine whether the article would be published, Billings wrote to Bernstein, would be the "clarity and interest with which the article describes and explains the fundamental religious beliefs and practices of the American Jew." Billings cautioned: "The article should not argue with Christianity. It should not be defensive in temper, as if it were retorting to anti-Semitism."

Bernstein's correspondence with Billings shows that he viewed *Life's* invitation as an honor and an opportunity to become a spokesperson for

American Judaism. In this way, he was well-suited to his task. In his initial letter to the Rochester rabbi, Billings wrote, "I gather you have much the same feeling we have here that such an article would be not only good journalism, but also good citizenship in that it would help dispell [sic] ignorance where bias breeds."[49]

Whether or not it was true that education cured bigotry, Bernstein's prior interfaith activities trained him to think this way. Bernstein's name was suggested to *Life* by the Reverend Daniel Poling, a fellow clergyman involved in the war effort. Poling's son, Clark Poling, was among the celebrated four chaplains who drowned when the SS *Dorchester* sank, in 1943. Poling wrote his own *Life* essay, about Christian belief, in 1949. In that essay Poling explained: "Christianity is first of all a faith, not an institution or even a way of life. It is a belief." To inspire his readers, Poling added, "if ever again Christians believe hard enough they may accomplish in their time a world revolution as complete as that which followed the conversion of the Roman emperor Constantine in the 4th Century."[50] If Poling's essay sought to awaken the piety of his Christian readers, Bernstein's essay had a more elementary starting point: remedying ignorance about Judaism among all Americans, while steering clear of "Jewish problems." Zionism and the situation of Jewish Displaced Persons need not be mentioned, Billings wrote to Bernstein.[51] He guided Bernstein in presenting a Judaism free of political entanglements.

A month after Billings's initial letter to Bernstein, the editor cautioned the rabbi not to rush his writing, for "This is a great and timeless subject," and *Life* was prepared to wait for the right essay. Bernstein's Reform temple had recently conducted its annual Institute for the Christian Clergy, providing Bernstein with an opportunity to query ministers in attendance about their congregants' most-asked questions about Judaism. They included: Why did Jews reject Jesus as the Messiah? What is the attitude of Liberal Judaism toward Jesus? Do the Jews still consider themselves the chosen people? Do Jews use the New Testament? Do Jews anticipate rebuilding the Temple? The questions revealed that Christians sought commonalities with Jews, as well as understanding about their differences.

Bernstein's resultant essay took seriously the questions from Christian clergy and the directions he received from Billings. It opened with, "The Jew has no single organized church. He has no priests. The concept of salvation by faith is alien to his mind. Yet he has deep religious convictions which run like golden threads through all Jewish history. For him Judaism is a way of life, here and now. He does not serve his God for the sake of reward, for the fruit of the good life *is* the good life."[52] From this start, Bernstein established essential differences between Judaism, a way of life, and Protestantism, a belief in salvation by faith.

The article went on to explain that Judaism was not a monolith. "Judaism around the world is marked by diversity of practice and latitude of faith.... The Jew acknowledges no supreme ecclesiastical authority, but rather it wells up from the depth of the Jewish heart."[53] Countering the antisemitic view of Judaism as emphasizing law and lacking in spirit—and capitalizing on anti-Catholic prejudice against the papacy—Bernstein portrayed the diversity of Jewish practice as a virtue: "The congregation's rabbi is a teacher, not a priest. Without any vested ecclesiastical authority, he is not even necessary to the functioning of the synagogue. Any male Jew with sufficient knowledge of the prayers and the laws can conduct a religious service, officiate at marriages and bury the dead."[54] Unlike *certain traditions* (read: Catholic), ran this logic, Judaism was democratic and lay-led.[55]

Instead of *Life*'s usual photographs, Bernstein's essay was illustrated with images by the German-born, Jew-turned-Quaker, wood-engraver Fritz Eichenberg. For some *Life* readers, Eichenberg's evocative black-and-white portrayals of Jewish rituals, such as the Passover Seder and the sukkah, may have brought to mind the Christian images that Eichenberg created for his friend, Dorothy Day's newspaper, *The Catholic Worker*. For others, the powerful images may have reminded them of Eichenberg's Works Progress Administration artwork. For many readers of the Bernstein essay, the absence of photographs of real people allowed them to consider its subject, Judaism, without having to think about actual Jews. In 1950, *Life* was at an in-between stage in its presentation of Judaism: the magazine no longer treated Jews as a race, as in the days when novelists Margaret Halsey and Laura Z. Hobson took Time Inc. to task for its race discourse. But neither was it ready to include photographs of modern Jews living robustly Jewish lives in America.

At several points in the essay, Bernstein responded directly to ancient Christian challenges to Judaism, by explaining that Torah was more than a source of narrow and rigid moral laws: "the religious Jew finds much more in the Torah than burdensome legalism," and, "Jews never regarded the codification of law as a strait jacket." Bernstein defined the Jewish view of Jesus: "Although Jews are able, if they wish, to understand Jesus, the Jew of Nazareth, they have never been able to understand or accept the idea of the Trinity."[56] In his *Life* essay, Bernstein wrote that Judaism "offers no easy way to God. No son has been sent down to lead us to Him. No mediator intercedes for us. In the final accounting there is a purely personal relationship between the individual and his God."[57] More than Christianity, Bernstein suggested that Judaism allowed for direct communication with God.

Bernstein did not shy away from the deicide accusation integral to the education of generations of Christian children. Rather, Bernstein gently reminded readers that the Romans had power at the time of Jesus's crucifixion: "Those were very turbulent times. The Jews, under the heel of Rome, were seething with discontent. Zealots rose all over the land. To break the spirit of rebellion, Emperor Tiberius sent his most ruthless procurator, Pontius Pilate, to enforce order and obedience of the Jews. The records show that he put thousands of Jews to death for actual or potential rebellion."[58] The question of whether Jews killed Jesus was clearly still a sensitive point of contention between the two traditions.

Certain stereotypes of Jews proved useful to Bernstein's presentation, such as a Jewish "love of learning." He described the Jewish custom of placing honey on a Jewish child's first page of Jewish learning: "thus beginning an association of pleasantness which is expected to last through life. When most of the world was illiterate, every Jewish boy could read and by 13 was advanced in the study of a complex literature."[59] In describing the Jewish affinity for learning, Bernstein provided reasons for Jewish pride, and helped to weaken some of the less flattering stereotypes surrounding Yeshiva boys and their bookish habits. Although a Reform rabbi, Bernstein portrayed a more observant Jewish lifestyle in parts of his essay, as when he wrote that a religious Jew "Begins and ends the day with prayers. He thanks God before and after every meal, even when he washes his hands. All his waking day the traditional Jew wears a ritual scarf beneath his outer garments as a reminder of God's nearness and love. There are prescribed prayers for birth, circumcision, marriage, illness, and death. Even the appearance of a rainbow evokes an ancient psalm of praise."[60] Many Jewish readers would not have identified with this description of Jewish religious practice, but the essay served its intended effect of showing that Judaism *was* a religion.

Drawing harmonious parallels between Judaism and Christianity was one of Bernstein's strategies. In explaining the significance of Torah, Bernstein described the 1908 fire in which his Rochester congregation's building had burned down, and "an Irish policeman dashed to the ark and seized the Torah. He handed it to the rabbi rushing up to the building. 'Here,' he said, 'I saved your crucifix.'"[61] Bernstein added: "Well, the Jews have no crucifix, but the policeman had the right idea: the scrolls are the most sacred symbols of Judaism."[62] It was a story that might have offended some Jews through its suggestion that the Torah was analogous to the crucifix, but it exemplified one meaning of midcentury Judeo-Christianity: these were two religious traditions that shared some common religious values.

In contrast, sinfulness was a topic that allowed Bernstein to reflect on the relative benefits of Judaism and to showcase "Judaism's balanced interpretations of the nature of man. On the one hand there are no perfect saints in the Jewish tradition. Even Moses, the greatest Jew of all time, was denied admittance to the promised land because he disobeyed God. But Judaism, on the other hand, does not regard man as inherently sinful or depraved."[63] It was possible, Bernstein demonstrated in his discussion of good and evil, to show Judaism's advantages over Christianity. "Our instinctive drives are considered good because God gave them to us. There is no asceticism in Judaism, no retreat to monasteries. Celibacy is not required of the rabbis. The rabbis of the Talmud maintain that much good has come from our so-called 'evil desires.' They say that our sex drive has produced love, marriage, the family, the perpetuation of the race. Without the acquisitive instinct, they claim, homes would not be built, fields would not be tilled."[64] A reasonableness pervaded Judaism, according to Bernstein. Instead of the Christian doctrine of man's fall in the garden of Eden, "in the Jewish religion, sinning is simply a wrong which the individual may or may not commit, depending upon his character and free choice. As the rabbis say, everything is in the hands of God but the fear of God." In Bernstein's formulation, Judaism, unlike Christianity, was not a religion obsessed with sin.[65]

After publication, Bernstein's flattering portrayal of Judaism was roundly applauded. In *Life*'s "Letters to the Editors" section and in correspondence addressed directly to Bernstein, Jewish readers expressed gratitude for what was previously unavailable: a dignified, accessible explanation of their tradition. From Miami, a reader wrote that "I have taught the tenets of the faith and have read most of the leading texts on the subject, but no book or article I know attains the beauty, the completeness and the accuracy of Rabbi Bernstein's contribution."[66] "What the Jews Believe" could make a Jew proud, readers attested in their letters. A Melvin Gladstone wrote to the editors that "as a Jew who has long neglected the significance of our Holy Days, I wish to thank *Life* and Rabbi Bernstein for affording me a most inspirational and liberal re-education. As a father of two young boys, I find the contents of this article will inform my sons of the basic principles of Judaism and the great heritage to which they are heir."[67] A New York City reader wrote that Bernstein's article "was so informative and objective—I was filled with a renewed sense of pride in being a Jewess after reading it. Several of my non-Jewish friends have commented most favorably as a result of reading your masterly dissertation on 'What the Jews Believe.' The article will, I believe be invaluable in creating understanding and appreciation of our great heritage."[68] For Jews who had grown up during the first half of the twentieth century, when positive portrayals of Jews and their religion in popular culture were scarce, the effect of Bernstein's article in *Life* is difficult to overestimate. In the twenty-first century, Bernstein's essay reads as obvious and pedantic; in 1950, it was a novel, dignified, and uplifting summary of modern Judaism.

Rabbis and leaders in the Jewish community expressed gratitude for what Bernstein had accomplished. Israel G. Jacobson, the executive director of the Association for Jewish Children of Philadelphia, congratulated Bernstein for his important effort on behalf of interfaith relations and Jewish self-respect:

> Frankly, I think it contributes more to decent self-respect among the Jews and positive understanding among the non-Jews than any other article I have ever read. I have gotten this from people who are somewhat tied in with the Council for Judaism, as well as from strong Zionists, and there is a unanimity among those whom I have met who are Orthodox, Conservative, and Reformed [sic] with regard to the excellence of your contribution.[69]

Jacobson described a woman he knew who expressed regret about being born a Jew because, "in her opinion, Christianity and Hinduism, were superior religions." Yet, Bernstein's article "made her change her point of view—she is now proud that she is a Jew."[70] Part of what Bernstein achieved, Jacobson made clear, was to provide reasons for Jews to shift from the Harry Wolfson mentality of Jewishness as illness, and toward a more positive understanding of Jewishness. A Reform rabbi in Montgomery, Alabama, felt himself to be just such a beneficiary. He wrote to Bernstein that "a great many Christians in Montgomery have discussed it with me and they too feel it was a fine explanation of Judaism. I am going to make it required reading for my confirmation class."[71] The National Director of the Anti-Defamation League wrote to Bernstein: "I can't think of any instance where Jewishness and Judaism have been explained more simply and with greater clarity for the edification of non-Jews. Sincerity and dignity shines out in every paragraph. The article is a major contribution to adult education in this field and it is an inestimable service in the cause of obtaining a better understanding of Jews among our non-Jewish fellow citizens."[72]

The response from non-Jews suggested that Bernstein met *Life*'s goals for the article. "Most informative and inspiring," a minister from Woodstock, Connecticut, wrote to *Life* of Bernstein's article.[73] Another reader detailed his circumstances: "Your article in the September 11th issue of Life Magazine was just such an explanation of the Jewish faith that I have been wanting.... Many of my Jewish customers are personal friends.... I am more than grateful to you for this opportunity to understand my friends' customs, traditions, and faith."[74] A reader from Hollywood, California, echoed this praise: "Please accept my applause for the fine article you wrote.... My Christian friends and myself not only enjoyed the article, but were enlightened.... Acquainting our neighbors of such religion as you so beautifully explained it, will do more for erasing prejudice than any other means."[75] Readers' expressions of gratitude revealed their sense of fulfilling a "good citizen" deed in reading and discussing an Introduction to Judaism.

Still, "What the Jews Believe" had its detractors. In the pages of the Labor Zionist journal the *Jewish Frontier*, Will Herberg criticized the essay for being "misrepresentative of authentic Jewish faith," a curious phrase, considering Will Herberg's secular, Marxist past and his earlier desire to convert to Christianity.[76] It was Herberg's engagement with Reinhold Niebuhr's writing in the late 1930s that tempted him toward conversion. But after the two men met, Niebuhr convinced Herberg to explore his own Jewish tradition.[77] In spite of these roots, by the 1950s it seemed that Herberg had anointed himself an arbiter of true Judaism.

"For all the familiar phrases," Herberg wrote of Bernstein's essay, "it seems to me to bear no real relation to authentic Jewish faith." Herberg objected to Bernstein's writing that salvation by faith is alien to the Jew, because "if faith is used in its proper sense as utter trust in and fidelity to God, then Jewish religion emphatically teaches, as we shall see, that salvation is by faith."[78] Similarly, Bernstein's treatment of the hereafter had been too glib, according to Herberg, who reminded readers that Judaism taught that lack of faith was a reason for exclusion from the world to come: "Even if faith is taken in its derivative sense as belief in doctrine, 'salvation by faith' still remains significant in Jewish teaching." As to resurrection of the dead, a topic on which Bernstein wrote that "the Jews have never agreed on what happens after death," Herberg reminded readers: "But it is simple fact that the resurrection of the dead was already a cardinal Rabbinic dogma before the time of Christ, that the Mishnah excludes those who deny that 'the resurrection is prescribed in the Torah' from a 'share of the world to come.'"[79] As Herberg pointed out, Bernstein misrepresented key concepts in Jewish theology.

But the real problem with Bernstein's article and its presentation of Judaism, according to Herberg, was that it expounds "the religion of the respectable man at his ease in respectable society. It moves on the dead level of mediocrity and is utterly incapable of encompassing the heights and depths of the human spirit. It is, in short, 'bourgeois' religion, the religion of self-satisfied externality." In criticizing Bernstein's *Life* article, Herberg encapsulated what some viewed as problematic with middlebrow Jewish culture: it offered little more than "moralistic platitudes, some tepid metaphysical speculations, and the comfortable assurance that things are fundamentally all right and there is nothing really wrong with the world that just plain, wholesome goodwill cannot cure."[80] Herberg rejected what he saw as a Pollyanna interpretation of religion. But at this early stage of the religious revival, many readers likely agreed with *Time* magazine's assessment that Bernstein had provided "a lucid and readable primer of Judaism from a cheerfully humanistic point of view."[81]

Sounding the notes of a misunderstood writer, Bernstein vented his frustration over Herberg's review to a rabbi-friend. "Herberg completely misinterpreted the purpose of the article," Bernstein wrote, "which was not to preach a sermon to Jews but to tell Christians in a simple, readable way about the beliefs and practices of American Jews."[82]

Herberg's criticism of Bernstein's portrayal of Judaism echoed some of Irving Kristol's harsh 1948 review of Milton Steinberg's *Basic Judaism*, for portraying Judaism as a tradition that "permits its believers to read the *New Republic* with untroubled soul."[83] Steinberg's explanation of Judaism was permeated by his desire to conform and uplift, that Kristol viewed as typical of mainstream liberal Christianity and middlebrow culture. Kristol wrote:

> Steinberg's Judaism is obviously native American. That is to say, in its heart it has no faith in the effectuality of religion on the American scene, and hastens to adopt a vocabulary with a higher popularity rating at the first opportunity. Genial and well-wishing—appropriate company for a business man's luncheon. When he says "all good men are Messiahs," it rings with all the fervor and conviction of "any boy can grow up to be president."[84]

There was merit to this charge that rabbis such as Bernstein and Steinberg were writing apologetics for Judaism. As a result of the editorial directions they received, as well as their own experience with antisemitism, midcentury rabbi-authors of Introduction to Judaism texts *were* attempting to make their religion genial to Christian readers. But they were also trying to convey the particularities of Judaism, and to educate both Jewish and non-Jewish readers about a tradition receiving new postwar interest.

Herberg didn't see it this way. He lamented, after reading Bernstein, that a "hidden 'liberalism' permeates and enfeebles conventional Jewish religion, even the most orthodox. The dimension of depth is gone. The passion for the absolute, the sense of the grandeur and misery of man and of the utter impossibility of life without God, the fervent belief in the election and vocation of Israel, have well-nigh disappeared from the religious writing and thinking and preaching of American Jewry."[85] Herberg's criticism summarized the charges repeatedly made against midcentury middlebrow Introduction to Judaism literature: the "dumbing down" of Judaism and a resistance to anything that was not uplifting. Usually, detractors perceived themselves as defending true Judaism, but in all cases they resented the public-facing of a Judaism that appeared robbed of its grandeur and depth. In turn, authors of middlebrow introductions to Judaism smarted at criticism leveled by intellectuals whose "critical mood" toward Judaism, as Rita Felski describes this intellectual orientation, seemed to be policing serious thought and taking an adversarial attitude toward middle-class Judaism.[86]

While intellectuals and highbrow thinkers rallied around Herberg's criticism, Bernstein's supporters dismissed Herberg's review. For Reform Rabbi Albert S. Goldstein, Herberg was one of those who "boomerang into Judaism after ranging widely over alien fields and streams of thought and life remote from Judaism," Goldstein wrote, referring to Herberg's secular life and reintroduction to Judaism via the Protestant theologian Reinhold Niebuhr.[87] Goldstein continued his commiseration with Bernstein: "Herberg may find 'deplorable' the 'bourgeois, superficial, naïve, trivial, humanistic, liberal, sentimental, idealistic optimism' of what the Jews do believe." Goldstein, like other rabbis of the era, was all too familiar with Herberg's critique of 1950s suburban Judaism. "But to imagine that his curious, eclectic theology reflects anything like the belief of 'the Jews' is hallucinatory. Herberg isn't refuting Bernstein. He is tilting against the windmill of the going beliefs of practicing Jews. Herberg's essay is sequinned-o'er with quotes from Jewish authorities; but, the basic pattern of his fabric is the thinking of Kierkegaard and the

Existentialist. Perhaps the Jews ought to revere this existential patron-saint as the only Moses since Moses. The fact is that practicing Jews generally don't know the gentleman's name—as why, particularly, should they?" Particularly galling to Goldstein was the sudden authority invested in Herberg, who had come to Judaism later in life: "Is it not a trifle unseemly," Goldstein wrote to his friend, for a newly observant Jew like Herberg, "to don professional robes, get himself a lectern and hastily begin to teach?"[88] Exacerbating Goldstein's and other rabbis' irritation at Herberg's sudden expertise in Judaism was their resentment over Herberg's popularity—because of the success of *Protestant-Catholic-Jew*, which was praised by Niebuhr in the *New York Times*.[89]

With Jews and Judaism becoming more mainstream, rabbis and communal leaders found themselves vying for public attention and acclaim. For rabbis, writers, and potential spokespeople (usually men) of Judaism, the midcentury middlebrow moment in American Jewish culture brought out the usual ambitions and resentments of a popularity contest. Who would earn the chance to introduce Judaism to a newly receptive wide readership was not the sole issue. As revealed in the wake of Herberg's review of Bernstein, another important question had reared its head: what kind of Judaism should be presented?

7
Life's "Old-Fashioned Jews"

If someone had told publisher Henry Luce that the June 13, 1955, issue of his *Life* magazine—coming five years after Philip Bernstein's Judaism article—would be life-changing for a Jewish wig-stylist who had immigrated from postwar Poland, Luce might have been puzzled. But the effect on a European-born woman was only one of many Jewish reactions to the issue. The magazine's portrayal of Judaism elicited cheers from Yeshiva University and anger from Reform Jews. It even roused one Reform rabbi to a self-conscious defense of "Jews with beards." None of these responses was intended. Through their editorial perceptions about what made Judaism interesting, *Life*'s mostly non-Jewish staff created an Introduction to Judaism text that evoked surprisingly powerful emotional reactions and augured a shift in perceptions of Orthodoxy and Judaism more generally.

The 1950s was an interesting time for Orthodox Judaism to receive middlebrow treatment. It was a decade when observers still, as in most preceding decades, predicted the movement's demise.[1] Not until the late 1960s did observers regularly declare Orthodoxy as flourishing.[2] But in the mid-1950s, indications of a stronger future for Orthodoxy were discernible and seeds were being planted for what that future would be in America.[3] That tension between outsiders' expectations of Orthodoxy's decline, and the movement's leaders' desire to plan for the coming decades may have inspired their laity to take action in the direction of the leaders' vision.[4] By 1958, an underdog spirit led to significant organizational efforts, as the Union of Orthodox Jewish Congregations of America announced plans for the development of 1,000 new congregations and the doubling of Jewish day schools in America in the coming years.[5] Indeed, steps had already been taken that would make the coming years a time of growth for those who fell under the large umbrella of Orthodox Judaism. Important Orthodox Jewish day schools had been founded in the late 1930s and 1940s.[6] In 1943, Rabbi Aharon Kotler had established the Beth Medrash Govoha in Lakewood, New Jersey, and become the head of the Council of Torah Sages, positions that had allowed him to become "the driving force in the renaissance of the Lithuanian yeshiva world

Orthodoxy (also referred to as yeshivish, Right Wing, and Haredi Orthodoxy or the Torah world) on American soil."[7] In 1951, Rabbi Menachem Mendel Schneerson officially succeeded his father-in-law as the Lubavitcher Rebbe, and would become one of the most influential Jewish leaders of the twentieth century.[8] Also during the 1950s: kashrut was professionalized, and the availability of kosher-certified foods greatly increased.[9] Yeshiva University established a medical school in 1953 and Stern College for women in 1954. The Orthodox Youth movement, the National Conference of Synagogue Youth (NCSY), which began as the Torah Leadership Seminar, was founded in 1954, and the Orthodox journal *Tradition* began publication in 1958. These were midcentury bricks being laid for the path forward. The June 13, 1955, issue of *Life*, which profiled an Orthodox Jewish family, was another sign of Orthodoxy's postwar growth. It would turn out that Orthodoxy would benefit from an alliance with American middlebrow culture.

Reconstructing Time Inc.'s internal conversations through archival sources shows that in planning the 1955 *Life* Judaism issue, different kinds of Jews were up for consideration from those who appeared in the magazine's 1950 portrayal of Judaism. It was no longer Reform or those segments of Judaism resembling Protestantism that seemed most suitable for middlebrow treatment. The shallow Jewishness appealing to the *anti*-antisemitic Phil Green of *Gentleman's Agreement* already seemed too bland and boring. Now, Orthodox Judaism, along with Israeli Judaism and the religion of Eastern European–born Jews, sparked interest among producers of popular culture.

Within the decade, the Russian-born Yiddish writer Sholem Aleichem's (1859–1916) Tevye stories had important American premieres in the form of a 1953 off-Broadway play, *The World of Sholom Aleichem*, and an acclaimed 1959 teleplay.[10] In the next decade, with the phenomenal success of the Broadway musical *Fiddler on the Roof* (1964), interest in religiously observant and Eastern European Jews and Judaism grew.[11] These other kinds of Jewishness stood out to non-Jewish culture-makers. And like so much that is considered interesting, it was not sameness to America's majority Christian religion that attracted attention. It was difference. Even the mid-1950s—a decade so often remembered as a time of conformity—put a premium on acceptable rebels from mainstream culture. Middlebrow culture that reflected back images of Jewish religion intriguingly different from Protestantism had the potential of showing Jews and non-Jews that the particularities of Judaism were worth engaging. To those concerned about cultivating a robust religious life in the 1950s, it appeared that Orthodoxy had something distinctive to offer. In 1955, in the pages of *Time* magazine, for example, Reform Rabbi Jacob Petuchowski, who had grown up in an Orthodox German-Jewish milieu, explained that Orthodoxy provided a more substantial Jewish religion to converts than that of his own Reform movement. An Orthodox rabbi, Petuchowski explained, could offer the convert, "the Creed of Maimonides in one hand and the Shulchan Aruch [a codification of Jewish law] in the other. He could say to the prospective convert: 'Here is a new way of living. Take it!' And then the convert would really have taken something; he would not merely be moving from one 'branch' of universal religion to another."[12] The postwar American Way of Life made religion synonymous with good Americanism, but in diluting the particularities of so much Judeo-Christian religion, it may have also inadvertently increased the attractiveness of more ritualistic varieties of religion.

The June 13, 1955 issue broadened the genre of Introduction to Judaism to include texts written and curated by non-Jews. When popular culture about Jews is created by non-Jews, these "non-Jewish Jewish" cultural productions, by their very existence, demonstrate that Jewishness has earned the attention and interest of a wider audience.[13] In the mid-twentieth century, examples accrued, particularly in music, with the Andrews Sisters' rendition of "Bei Mir Bistu Shein" in the 1930s, Perry Como's recording of Kol Nidre in 1953, Harry Belafonte's 1950s rendition of "Hava Nagila," and the Weavers' performance of the Israeli song "Tzena, Tzena."[14] But when non-Jewish Jewish middlebrow focused on only one segment of American Jewry—Reform, Conservative, or Orthodox—it had the potential to inspire feelings of pride, envy, resentment, and shame among specific groups of Jews.

Those reactions would have been difficult to predict after *Life*'s previous engagement with Judaism. Positive response to the 1950 *Life* article "What the Jews Believe" by Rabbi Philip Bernstein had been encouraging. In 1954, as *Life* prepared for upcoming special issues on world religions, the magazine's editors looked back on mistakes from Bernstein's article. "It covered only the beliefs of the reformed [*sic*] Jews in America, and did not get at the fundamentals of orthodox Judaism at all," Luce wrote in an internal memo, reflecting views that had been expressed by Jewish readers who had written in to the magazine.[15] Luce explained the benefits of focusing on Orthodox Jews in a future issue: the Orthodox were "both more colorful and more basic, since the reformed [*sic*] Jews are a modern group that has compromised with modern life and thrown over a great many of the old beliefs that are fundamental to Judaism."[16] Orthodox Jews were thus considered more photogenic, by virtue of seeming less modern.

What did Luce mean, in referring to the Orthodox as "more colorful and more basic"? To Luce, the essence of Judaism—or the religion's "basicness"—was to be found in Orthodoxy. "I think reformed [sic] Jews could be given a couple of pages," Luce wrote. "But the main part of the essay should deal with the ceremonies, theological beliefs and daily life of the old-fashioned Jews."[17] In his view, non-Orthodox Jews were boringly similar to American Protestants. During a decade when "old-time religion" was valued, Orthodox and Israeli Judaism were perceived by *Life*'s editors as fitting these cultural desiderata better than Reform Judaism.

It is also possible that the New York–based Luce was thinking about the kinds of reports of Orthodox Jewish life that trickled into his city's newspaper of record. In the early 1950s, a *New York Times* reader might have seen the 1952 headline "Jews Revive Old Sabbatical Rite of Scroll-Reading in Holy Land."[18] The article reported on the revived custom of reading a Torah scroll as part of the "ceremony commemorating an ancient ritual performed in the days of the Hebrew Kingdom after every sabbatical year, when reigning monarchs read publicly from scrolls in the holy temple." The ceremony had last been "performed in the temple in 42 A.D. by King Agrippa in compliance with a biblical ordinance in Deuteronomy."[19] To fill out readers' imagination of this biblical tableau, the paper reported that "the proceedings were punctuated by choruses from ram horns blown by two dozen men. Some of the Orientals had long, twisted horns, while others blew the short, curved type used in the United States synagogues." Or Luce might have read about a nationwide "Torah Tour" of Orthodox rabbis in the United States, with the goal of encouraging Orthodox Jewish practice and halting trends that "tend to pave the way to assimilation."[20] Or perhaps he skimmed a story about "the ancient Jewish festival of Shabuoth, commemorating the giving of the Ten Commandments to Moses on Mount Sinai," or of the observance of "Succoth, a harvest festival stemming from Biblical times."[21] These kinds of news stories of Orthodox religious life, most of them exoticized, went beyond delivering up a vision of Orthodoxy as "Old World religion." To those unacquainted with modern Orthodox Jews, they suggested that Orthodoxy was biblical and defiant in the face of modernity.

Life's vision of Judaism was one that flourished at the intersection of the renewed old-time religious revival of the 1950s and an orientalism that viewed Eastern European and Israeli Jews as both not fully modern and more authentic than their Reform and Conservative counterparts. There was an irony in this grouping together of Eastern European and Israeli Jews, for the origins of the Jewish State included an intention to create a new kind of Jew; in contradistinction to the Orthodox Jews of the old country, the "New Jew" of Israel was envisioned as the opposite of his Eastern European Jewish ancestors.[22] But now *Life*, in their internal editorial conversation, suggested that the essence of Judaism lay with both groups: Eastern European religious and Israeli Jews. The magazine's presentation of Judaism reflected a surprising mainstream American appetite for these Orthodox and Israeli divergences from 1950s suburban American (that is, largely Conservative and Reform) Judaism.[23] In *Life*'s formulation, the "New Jew" of postwar America required the inspiration of Eastern European immigrants and Israeli Jewish counterparts.[24]

When *Life*'s Judaism special issue appeared in 1955, the magazine's circulation was over five million, making this photo essay, shot by two Jewish, European-born photographers, Alfred Eisenstaedt and Cornell Capa, one of the most widely read of postwar introduction to Judaism texts.[25] Novelist Philip Roth may have had this 1955 *Life* issue in mind when he wrote his 1959 short story "Eli, the Fanatic." Roth's story chronicled a postwar suburban Jewish encounter with newly arrived Orthodox Holocaust survivors who are building a yeshiva in town. One concerned suburban Jew tells another, "I don't know if you know—but there's talk that *Life* magazine is sending a guy out to the Yeshivah for a story. With pictures."[26] The "with pictures" was sufficient explanation of the mortification suburban Jews would suffer as a result of having survivors—with their beards and their hats and their "talking a dead language"—become the Jewish face of their town, which they previously, rather proudly considered "a progressive suburban community."[27] As in the Roth short story, after the 1955 Judaism issue of *Life* hit newsstands, emotions ran high among Jews unsettled by the magazine's presentation of Orthodox Jews.

When the Judaism issue appeared, it was still three years before the publication of *Exodus*, Leon Uris's bestselling historical novel about the founding of the Jewish state. Americans had yet to read "the story of the greatest miracle of our times," as Uris referred to his novel, which portrayed Jews as triumphant heroes.[28] In addition to being a story of Jewish suffering and restoration, Amy Kaplan observes, *Exodus* presented "the founding of the Jewish state as a universal good, as the embodiment of human aspiration and the fulfillment of the noblest impulses of mankind."[29] As Matthew Silver has shown, *Exodus* managed to "persuasively associate Israel's founding with forces of democratic freedom in the postwar world," a narrative that for the duration of the Cold War "appeared to encapsulate absolute truth about the rectitude of the Jewish state."[30] The cultural work that Uris's middlebrow novel performed was thus multivalent: the novel and film showed Americans that it wasn't solely Jews who had a stake in Israel's future, and it presented the Holocaust as a tragedy that was the precursor to the creation of the Jewish state.[31]

In the years after Israel's founding, the new Jewish state could not always compete with other world news, including the Korean War, the end of Stalinism, and the Chinese Communist Revolution.[32] Tucked deep inside a July 1949 issue of *Life*, an article about Israel described the new Jewish state, "at the age of one."[33] Disabusing readers of any notion that modern Israel "was a realization of the Old Testament dream," *Life* explained that many modern Israelis were in fact secular and that the state was anything but a land flowing with milk and honey. "Economically it is far from self-sustaining."[34] Gazing into the Israeli psyche, the magazine added, "With only a tenuous security the Israelis are almost belligerent in their pride."[35]

What might have surprised attentive readers of the 1949 Israel article was *Life*'s casual invocation of race-thinking about Jews. "Much of Israel's story is told in the faces of its citizens and its cities," the article explained, showing, through photographs, that Israelis hailed from all over the world.[36] "Sunshine, food and freedom usually quickly improve the newcomers' health and before long they are assimilated in a melting pot which has created a tanned, sturdy 'Palestinian type' closely resembling European Nordics." Less than five years after the fall of the Nazi regime, *Life* summoned to readers' minds a racial type once used interchangeably with Aryans—and tied it to the American melting pot—as an ideal to which Israelis might strive.[37] *Life* attempted to employ its own discourse of 1940s *anti*-antisemitism by reversing Nazi logic: if Nazis defined Jews as an immutably inferior race, *Life* would correct that racist antisemitism by declaring the evolving Jewish resemblance to the Nordic type. It was almost as though *Life*'s editors believed that by running the Nazi trope in reverse, their portrayal of Jews might undo the pseudoscientific underpinnings of Nazi antisemitism.[38]

And yet, to illustrate their point, the article featured six photos, taken by John Phillips, an Algerian-born photographer, of Israeli men from all over the world, whose greatest resemblance was in their bare-chestedness and the confident pose each man struck for the camera.[39] In other words, *Life*'s anti-antisemitic declaration that Jews were not racially inferior was not only about race, but about gender. It was their masculinity that proved these Israeli men did not fit the Nazis' antisemitic tropes about Jews. Powerful Israeli women did not appear in these photographs meant to demonstrate that the Palestinian type resembled the Nordics, for it was masculinity that mattered.[40] It was another sign of how race-thinking about Jews endured and was intertwined with gender-thinking.

* * *

Awareness of Israel was growing in the early 1950s, along with an interest in Eastern European Judaism. Both of these developments could be felt within the different movements of Judaism.[41] The 1950 *Life* essay had included these lines about the Reform movement's embrace of "color" and its shift toward more traditional religious observance, including more Hebrew and wearing of *kippot* (Jewish head-coverings): "Responsible leadership has awakened to the fact that a heritage so diluted cannot sustain loyalty or be effectively passed on to a new generation. Accordingly, Reform has begun to move back toward the center. Discarded traditions have been reestablished; religious warmth, color, discipline have been partly restored."[42] If Classical Reform had once seemed like the darling among Judaism's American movements, that favored position shifted to those parts of Jewish religion being labeled as "traditional," "authentic," and, although the point was often made implicitly, as bearing some resemblance to the Eastern European Judaism that had been destroyed less than a decade earlier.[43]

What had happened to *Life*'s non-Jewish writers and editors since the 1950 "What the Jews Believe" article to account for the magazine's shift away from its Reform portrayal of Judaism, and toward one that seemed more colorful and old-fashioned? The reasons for this change were not confined to the criticism and responses that *Life* received after Bernstein's article, for there had been much praise in the wake of that essay. Other events—political, cultural, and religious—were affecting how Americans thought about religion, Jews, and Judaism. There was President Eisenhower's administration, begun in 1953, which made religion more central to civic and political life. And a growing sense that a religious revival was not just in the offing, as was the case in the mid-1940s, but, as the previous chapter detailed, that America was indeed in the midst of such a revival.

When Rabbi Bernstein was invited to write his 1950 essay about Judaism, John Hersey's bestselling middlebrow novel, *The Wall*, was not yet published. A fictional account of the Jewish uprising in the Warsaw ghetto, which Hersey told through the journals of a Jewish character named Noach Levinson, *The Wall* was "the first American novel to confront the Holocaust fully and centrally."[44] It was while serving as a *Time* and *Life* correspondent in Moscow, in 1945, that Hersey first decided to write *The Wall*.[45] Like publisher Henry Luce, Hersey was the son of Christian missionaries who had spent his childhood in China before attending Hotchkiss boarding school on a scholarship and working his way through Yale. Hersey, too, was shaped by a religious upbringing, and although his adult life was largely secular, something of a religious impulse never left him, but transferred to his vocation as a writer. As historian David Hollinger writes, Hersey drew on his "missionary imperative to make things right" in his writing.[46] By the time he began writing *The Wall*, Hersey had already published *A Bell for Adano* (1944), which would earn the thirty-year-old writer a Pulitzer Prize.

In the spring of 1950, *The Wall* became a bestseller and a "literary event of real consequence."[47] Part of the momentousness was the novelty of a non-Jew of high literary status demonstrating such understanding of Jewish history and religion.[48] "The great thing to note about this astonishing and very moving book," one reviewer observed, "is the quick and affectionate understanding, the superlative human sympathy, the wealth of love itself with which Mr. Hersey has interested himself in a tradition so different from his own, to recall to the world the three million Polish Jews who were massacred during the war."[49]

Those words came from Alfred Kazin, whose review evidenced his astonishment that a non-Jew would write so compassionately about Jews and Judaism. It was another case of the influence of "non-Jewish Jewish culture."[50] Kazin, nonetheless, felt that Hersey's portrayal lacked "Jewish color," and that his Polish Jews "are entirely too middle-class and 'nice,' so one misses the verve and tang of those masses of poor laborers ... the implacable fervor and mystical intensity among the orthodox, and the mockingly ragged and marginal life of the *Luftmenschen*—Jews so poor, even for Polish Jews, that it was proverbially said they lived 'on air.'"[51] At the time, Kazin was about to publish *A Walker in the City* (1951), a book that captured the particular flavor and color of Jewish life in Kazin's childhood neighborhood of Brownsville, Brooklyn.[52]

As Kazin's review intimated, Hersey's treatment of the wartime Jewish story was an illuminating cultural moment for American readers. Hersey may have missed some of the color of Eastern European Jewishness, but he had taken seriously his research of Judaism.[53] *The Wall*'s publication and acclaim showed Americans that there was value in the European Jewish story. In the coming years, as Anne Frank's story was published in English in 1952 (with a foreword from Eleanor Roosevelt), and Abraham Joshua Heschel's books received mainstream attention, the idea developed that the experience of European Jews and their religion merited attention and respect.[54]

As the editors' letters reveal, *Life*'s choices suggested a desire for Jews to provide non-threatening color contrasted with the majority Protestant background of American religion. It was a role that Jews had been performing for decades. Sometimes, Jewish color came through in humor, sometimes in religion, and sometimes, in language, as in the fall of 1955, when the Broadway musical *Guys and Dolls* (1950) made its cinematic premiere, starring Frank Sinatra and Marlon Brando. Written by three Jewish writers (Abe Burrows, Jo Swerling, and Frank Loesser), the musical included gambler Nathan Detroit's Yiddish-inflected lines to his girlfriend Adelaide, "*Alright already, I'm just a nogoodnik. Alright already, it's true, so nu? So sue me, sue me, What can you do me? I love you.*" The musical's inclusion of a dash of Yiddish mirrored what scholars were already discovering about the function of Yiddish for American Jews: it was primarily of nostalgic value. In a 1955 academic article, sociologists observed of Yiddish: "Since the nostalgia component is so strong, there is little impetus to preserving the tongue as a lingua franca or toward instituting a concerted effort to transmit the language to the next generation. In fact, were such steps taken, the nostalgia itself might be destroyed; Yiddish would again constitute a problem."[55] Yiddish was not a "problem" so long as it was clearly part of Jews' *past*. In the 1950s, middle-class American Jews' primary relationship to the language was nostalgic, not that of daily use—what Jeffrey Shandler refers to as the postvernacular mode of Yiddish.[56] Being a Jewish audience member at a Broadway production of *Guys and Dolls* and recognizing the Yiddish lilt on stage was an experience that reflected a high level of adjustment to the American environment, now that associations with Yiddish were primarily those connected to the pleasant remembrance of things past.[57]

While viewers of American film were getting a taste of the kinds of color Jewishness might add to American stories, in more highbrow realms of American literature, Jewish color emerged as celebrated writers such as Saul Bellow, Irving Howe, and Alfred Kazin became unapologetically Jewish in their writing.[58] "Jewishness! What would postwar American fiction be with it—its color, its sharp eye, its colloquial verve, its comic passions its exuberant plaintiveness?" John Updike observed of this generation of writers.[59] Julian Levinson writes of the 1950s: "Suddenly every reader of American fiction, Jewish or not, was expected to understand a smattering of Yiddish. Terms were left untranslated, lending the same authority to Yiddish that had been previously been reserved for French, German, or Spanish. Stories about New York Jews were offered up and read as parables for the national soul."[60] These inclusions of Jewishness and Yiddish in works of fiction helped to make Jews more familiar to American readers.

And sometimes Jewish color came through quite literally, in color. Marc Chagall was praised in the American press in the postwar years as he was throughout much of the twentieth century, for the vibrancy, poetry, and passion of his compositions. "The rich color and intrinsic decorative character of his work are always in evidence," wrote a *New York Times* art critic, in February 1946.[61] Another critic of the late 1940s tied Chagall's talents to his Jewishness, drawing on the enduring power of race-thinking about Jews: "Chagall is deeply affiliated with the soil, so to speak. His spirit moves in perfect accord with that of his race. . . . He is whimsical, droll, blithely irrational, and the opulence of his imagination is given all the rein that a bewitched Pegasus could wish."[62] George Biddle, the Groton- and Harvard-educated artist and friend of Franklin Roosevelt, described his feelings of "excitement, adventure, passion and sense of the painter's sincerity" upon lingering in the "beautifully arranged exhibition of Marc Chagall's paintings, then being shown at the Modern Museum." Biddle wrote of his wish for "an American art that deeply moves me," in the way that Chagall's paintings did. In the United States, the ardor of Chagall's paintings was often associated with his Hassidic, Old World roots.[63]

The American vogue for the Russian-French-Jewish painter was strong during the post–World War II years, even reaching into middlebrow media. In December 1946, *Seventeen* magazine offered a suggestion for the perfect Christmas gift—the latest book about Marc Chagall, "one of the outstanding painters of our time," whose work was "highly imaginative, poetic yet strong—in a deceptively simple, seemingly naïve way." *Seventeen* advised, "One of your artistic friends will love you for life if you give it to her on December 25th." Similarly, when *Cosmopolitan* sought to educate its largely female readership about artistic trends, in the spring of 1948, it asked, "Does Modern Art Annoy You?" To ease frustration with modern art, the magazine guided readers through understanding a painting by "the internationally famous artist, Marc Chagall." Chagall's painting may have been based on his "memories of his childhood in a small Russian Village"—a cozy-sounding description that, unlike "shtetl," seemed to de-Judaize Chagall, but *Cosmopolitan* reassured readers that "you needn't know those memories to enjoy his color, or to delight in such whimsical images as a donkey pulling sleigh . . . or a rooster in strange juxtaposition to a Madonna." And when *Seventeen* asked, in 1952, "How Come Modern Art?" the magazine looked to teenage artists for answers. Susan Raphael of Cleveland, Ohio, explained that Marc Chagall was the artist who most inspired her: "The sensuous warmth with which he recreates the memories of his boyhood in a small Russian town and the happiness of his marriage were the keys to my own direction," including Raphael's decision to paint a portrait of her family's Passover celebration.[64] For readers of these postwar middlebrow women's magazines, European Jews and Judaism registered as culturally significant.

Life's editors were thus planning their 1955 special issue on Judaism at a time when something like an inherent allure of Jews and Judaism was becoming ever more apparent to the writers, editors, and publishers of middlebrow literary culture. In 1955, as *Life*'s editors determined a plan to focus on religious and Israeli Jews, they noted: "This would undoubtedly take us to Israel, to old Jewish colonies in Europe and to the people of Manhattan's lower East Side." Despite the geographic diversity of the photos in that issue, *Life*'s presentation also highlighted the importance of the United States. Weeks before the issue went to press, Assistant Managing Editor Philip Wootton, noting the prominence of America in the Judaism article, wrote in a memo, "The U.S., of course, is the greatest Jewish country on earth and as such our U.S. take on Judaism dominates the essay."[65] It was a measure of the unprecedented change in status of Judaism that the exceptionalist view, typical of Time Inc. publications, had come to pervade even their treatment of Jews and Judaism.[66]

It would have been difficult to imagine a 1930s Time Inc. magazine declaring that the United States was the "greatest Jewish country on earth." Indeed, when the article "Jews in America" was published in *Fortune* magazine (part of the Time Inc. media company) in 1936, its tone was bleak. Due to the news from Europe ("the unbelievable record of Nazi barbarities"), the article explained that American Jewry was in the midst of communal depression: "Misgivings and uneasiness have colored the thinking of American Jews."[67] Far from declaring the United States a great Jewish country, *Fortune* noted the Jew's status as stranger: "The Jew is everywhere and everywhere the

Jew is strange. Japanese are strangers in California but not in Japan.... The Jews are outlanders everywhere. The country of the Jew, as Schopenhauer puts it, is other Jews."[68] By the mid-1950s, when sociologist Werner Cahnman cited data from the 1936 *Fortune* article, he did so with a warning: read the *Fortune* article "with a great deal of caution."[69] The facts in the article were not the problem, Cahnman explained. It was the analysis that revealed "the subconscious antisemitism of the authors." By the 1950s, it was already clear that the previous era's discussion of Jews now failed the test of postwar sensibilities. New modes of thinking and writing about Jews were in order.

An Unexpected Win

Almost twenty years after the 1936 *Fortune* portrayal of Jews, *Life*, another Time Inc. magazine, prepared for something very different. For its 1955 special issue on Judaism, *Life*'s editors chose a theological framework, in order to make its presentation of Judaism understandable to Christian readers: "The Treatment should, I think, be from the theological standpoint, just as it has been in the previous essays," *Life* editor, Ed Thompson wrote, referring to the *Life* special issues on great world religions. Judaism was presented as the predecessor to Christianity: "The Jews are the people who invented the concept of the one, personal and semi-abstract conception of God which has been taken over by the Christians and the Mohammedans. Thus, a consideration of their beliefs is a natural preface to the essays on Christianity that would follow."[70]

The article presented the all-encompassing nature of Jewish life: "In Judaism, as God is one so is life: every part of it must be sanctified.... That is why the religious Jew moves through life on a round of blessings, which he says over food and drink, for new clothes, when he sights the sea or sees any beautiful object. That is also why the Torah ranges from minute instruction to sublime teaching." *Life*'s description of a religious orientation to the world, wherein Judaism was relevant to all aspects of life, was likely unfamiliar to most readers in the postwar years—a time when religion seemed both newly elevated in status and more separate than ever from other spheres of life. It was just this dynamic that publisher Henry Luce observed in 1955, when he referred to American religious culture as more serene and staid than that of previous decades.[71] Compare the 1950s to the Scopes trial and the debates between William Jennings Bryan and Clarence Darrow, Luce urged. Would 1950s Americans ever get as exercised over science versus religion? Nowadays, Luce observed in 1955, religion seemed to occupy its own protected and isolated sphere, disconnected from the rest of life. In contrast, in its portrayal of Orthodox Judaism, *Life* presented a religion powerfully relevant to everyday life.

Like other Introductions to Judaism of the past decade, *Life* grouped Judaism safely among the Abrahamic religions. Unlike "Oriental religion and Greek thought," the article explained that the God of the Jews "insists on his uniqueness."[72] The issue emphasized the monotheistic nature of Judaism, and its earth-centeredness and orientation toward deeds ("It looks to an after life, but its practice is not so much to prepare man for the next world as to guide him in this."[73]) But unlike most previous primers that were intended for a mixed readership of Jews and non-Jews, the *Life* issue showcased *Orthodox* Judaism.

The alliance between *Life* and Orthodoxy was not initiated solely by the magazine. After all, *Life* meant national coverage. It was a chance to tell the Orthodox story to a much wider audience than any sermon or article in the Jewish press could deliver. By the 1950s, Orthodox leaders believed there was a desire among postwar Jews for the kind of substantive Judaism that Orthodoxy could deliver—and they appreciated the value of public relations.[74]

In the pages of the Orthodox magazine, *Jewish Life*, Sam Hartstein, director of Yeshiva University's Public Relations Department, implored Orthodox Jews to take publicity seriously. In his 1949 article, "A Public Relations Program for Orthodox Jewry," Hartstein explained that public relations "is neither a cover-up for shortcomings nor a substitute for good work. It is the character of Torah Judaism believably expressed so that all may know. Not only should an effective publicity program be maintained but this service should encourage the individual groups to issue smart literature, make use effectively of radio time, magazines, the press and other media of reaching the public."[75]

By the mid-1950s, Orthodoxy would have an opportunity to make good use of print media. Word reached Victor Geller, dean of Yeshiva University's Community Service Division, that *Life* magazine was looking for an Orthodox Jewish family to profile in their 1955 special issue.[76] Geller, who had served in the infantry during World War II, was a 1948 graduate of Yeshiva College and a 1950 graduate of Yeshiva's Wurzweiler School of Social Work and would later write *Orthodoxy Awakens*, which included the story of

Geller's role in the 1955 *Life* article.[77] A decade earlier, Geller's experiences in the military explaining his religion to his fellow soldiers had been good preparation for his involvement in the *Life* article.[78]

Over lunch with *Life*'s photographer, Cornell Capa, the younger brother of war photographer Robert Capa, Geller heard about *Life*'s stipulations for the kind of Jewish family the magazine hoped to feature. The family should have three generations in reasonably good health. They should have an upcoming special event, such as a bar mitzvah or wedding, that *Life* could photograph. And the family should be economically comfortable. Capa told Geller, "It cannot be poor. This is important because we want the pictures to tell a positive story. Poverty can't be hidden from the camera. It makes even the sunniest picture a little gray."[79] The postwar era was a time when Orthodoxy appeared to be emerging from poverty.[80] *Life*'s concern to portray Orthodox Jews as financially comfortable was less a desire to capture Orthodox Jews as they really were than it was a desire to show Jews as middle class—a sign of Orthodoxy's integration in mainstream middle-class American society. In effect, *Life* was following its own *anti*-antisemitic prescription to present Jews as integrated into middle-class society.

The *Life* journalist whom Capa collaborated with on the article was a woman named Jozefa Stuart, daughter of the renowned anthropologist, Bronislaw Malinowski. Stuart was not Jewish. Cornell Capa, born in Budapest to assimilated, non-practicing Jews, described himself to Geller as "not far from a *goy* (gentile). I don't remember very much from the few years of private lessons that I had before my bar mitzvah."[81]

That Capa knew enough to refer to himself as "not far from a goy," and that he had a bar mitzvah, a religious ceremony still inaccessible to most Jewish girls during the 1950s (the girls' version—called a *bat*-mitzvah—was not common among American Jews until the 1970s and 1980s), made him more of an insider than he was inclined to admit. True, Capa had not chosen to live a religiously Jewish life as an adult, but neither had he collected a slew of marginalizing experiences within a religious community, as might have been the case were he a Jewish woman. At their meeting, Capa told Geller that he and Stuart were "coming to the story with a sense of sympathetic objectivity."[82] Capa's objectivity was of a different kind from that of his non-Jewish colleague. And although he and photographer Alfred Eisenstaedt appear to be the only Jews involved in this largely non-Jewishly created article, his own feelings about Jewishness, which seem to have been the feelings of someone distant from and untroubled by Orthodoxy, likely influenced the images he captured with his camera. His famous brother, Robert Capa, died in 1954, while Cornell Capa was working on the Judaism *Life* issue.[83] At the time of his death, Robert Capa was photographing the First Indochina War for *Life* when he stepped on a landmine. Robert Capa's feelings about Israel—which came through in the photographs he took for two books, *This Is Israel* (1948) and *Report on Israel* (1950)—probably affected Cornell Capa's feelings about Jewishness.[84] Despite the distance between the largely secular Jewish state and Orthodox Judaism, the farther one stood from Jewishness, the closer these two very disparate facets of Jewish life might seem. For secular Jews like the Capas, Israel's postwar success provided another avenue toward interest and empathy with things Jewish, even if Cornell Capa preferred to call it "sympathetic objectivity."

As Capa spoke about *Life*'s requirements for the Jewish family, Geller had an idea. Some years earlier he had worked with a Jewish family named Fink, helping them revive their local Orthodox congregation.[85] They were economically comfortable, and there were even three generations of the Fink family living in Scranton, Pennsylvania. Geller, as he would tell the *New York Times*, was "the only full-time organizer of Orthodox congregations in the country," and he frequently collaborated with Jewish families such as the Finks who hoped to organize Jewish communities beyond urban centers.[86] From his grassroots work, Geller understood that the Jewish move to the suburbs affected religious life. What had once been taken for granted, now had to be consciously built—or not built—by individual Jews: "In the city, men and women pass the synagogues by and never notice them. They're surrounded by Yiddish newspapers, kosher food—a complete Jewish environment," Geller observed. Social scientists were discovering the same phenomenon. Nathan Glazer observed in the 1950s that Jewish life had seemed to flourish naturally in the urban settings of the 1920s–1940s. In those city neighborhoods, "one could still buy kosher food at every street corner, eat in kosher restaurants, and send one's children to religious schools that met in the afternoon or to all-day schools in which a part of the curriculum was devoted to English studies, to fulfil the requirements of state law."[87] The suburbs presented a very different reality.[88] "When they get to Syosset," Geller remarked of the postwar Jewish suburban frontiers, there were no Hebrew schools or kosher butchers around the corner.[89] "Before you can stay away from synagogue in the suburbs, Geller observed wryly, 'you have to build it.'" The Finks had participated in that pioneering work of creating suburban Judaism.

There was only one problem with the Finks as a potential focus for *Life*. When Geller telephoned, requesting their participation in the *Life* story, their first response was no.

In his telephone conversation with David and Tobi Fink, Geller went into pitch mode. He later wrote that he told them, "I am not conferring an honor upon you. I am asking you to consider a special responsibility. There exists here an opportunity for a rare *kiddush hashem* [sanctification of His Name]. You and your family have been in the forefront of the effort to revitalize Orthodox Judaism in Scranton.... The stereotypical picture of the impoverished, ghetto-dwelling Jew, left behind by progress to weave nostalgic dreams of a romanticized shtetl is all too common even today."[90] By calling the *Life* story an opportunity to honor God... Geller reminded the Finks that public relations were vital to Orthodox Judaism. If Jews like David and Tobi Fink wanted a future for brand of Judaism, Geller exhorted, they had to help create a better narrative about Orthodoxy.

"One of the great tasks which challenges leaders of Torah-true Jewry today is that of presenting orthodox Judaism in a manner intelligible to the American Jew," Simon Dolgin, a Los Angeles Orthodox rabbi wrote in the pages of *Jewish Life*, in 1953.[91] It was not helpful, he explained, for Orthodox rabbis to simply tell Jews what they should and should not be doing. Rather, the Orthodox should adopt a "basic" and positive approach of explaining Orthodox Judaism, "so that it can be understood by all." Dolgin wanted Orthodox Jews to think along the lines of Introductions to Judaism, for "Were Jews at large to be made aware of the basic differences between Judaism proper and the movements which have lost faith"—by which Dolgin meant Reform and Conservative Judaism—those Jews would understand the superiority of Orthodoxy. If the Orthodox took the steps to figure out their principles and articulate them clearly, the movement could win over adherents. "Once we set up a clear list of basic principles which distinguish true Judaism, all else may logically follow in the struggle for Torah in America."[92]

Dolgin was not exaggerating in describing the situation as a struggle for Torah in America. In the postwar suburbs, that is what the movements experienced as they competed for suburban Jewish adherents. Reform, Conservative, and Orthodox representatives made the case for their own movement, and bid for affiliation, often from Jews who had grown up in Orthodox households, but were now considering the other Jewish movements.[93] As Jeffrey Gurock observes, the Conservative movement was mostly winning on the suburban front in the 1950s.[94] But Conservative

Judaism's presumed victory likely inspired competitiveness. That Orthodox Judaism might experience wins on the suburban front was not obvious, considering the culture clash between postwar suburban lifestyle options and the restrictiveness of Orthodox Judaism.[95] And yet, as social historian Etan Diamond notes, postwar suburbia and Orthodox Judaism shared emphases on family and children.[96] Orthodox families like the Finks were getting the message—from communal leaders such as Geller—that they could help bring about Orthodoxy's resurgence. By 1957, "Orthodox Jews Build in the Suburbs" was a *New York Times* headline that described Orthodoxy as "in the midst of a revival" in the suburbs where "new synagogues are springing up almost over night."[97]

Unlike these news articles which portrayed Judaism as a Biblical religion, the *Life* issue represented an opportunity to tell the story of Orthodox Judaism in America as it had never been told. "Think of the many stories that we have seen full of errors, distortions and outright violations of the Torah point of view," Geller told the Finks.[98] Here was an opportunity to get the story right, and to tell it to the largest audience. If they declined, Geller warned, the next family that was selected might not offer as positive a representation of Orthodoxy. The Finks were persuaded. They became the Orthodox family that *Life* profiled.

But Geller envisioned something more from the *Life* coverage of Orthodoxy. At Yeshiva University, where Geller worked, Rabbi Joseph Soloveitchik, known as the Rav, had succeeded his father as Rosh Yeshiva, in 1941, and was considered the leader of mainstream Orthodoxy. For the reporters to truly understand American Orthodoxy, Geller felt, they needed exposure to Soloveitchik. After receiving his doctorate in philosophy from the University of Berlin, Soloveitchik emigrated to the United States. In Brookline, Massachusetts, he founded the Maimonides school, one of the first institutions in which girls studied Talmud, and thus Rabbi Soloveitchik had unusual credentials as a head of yeshiva and a mentor to hundreds of Orthodox rabbis.[99] If *Life* were to cover Judaism, Geller wanted their reporters to experience Yeshiva University's head rabbi and the culture of learning he instilled. Jozefa Stuart and Cornell Capa agreed. Arrangements were made so that the reporter and photographer would meet with Soloveitchik for two hours. Afterward, Stuart felt she needed more time with the rabbi. Soloveitchik then issued an unusual invitation: he allowed the two *Life* staffers to sit in on his Talmud shiur (lesson) with rabbinical students. It was likely the first time a woman had sat in the rabbi's class. "It was so unprecedented," Geller wrote of Soloveitchik's class with the *Life* staff, "that no one commented on his gallantly rising to greet his special guest as she entered. He instructed the young men in the back row to provide a place for her. Jozefa, fully sensitive to the circumstance, was very modestly dressed and wore a dark kerchief on her head." While Capa took photos, moving "around the room silently on crepe soled shoes," Stuart took notes. As Geller remembered it: "The only one who was conscious of the two was Rav. He repeatedly made side comments designed to help his guests comprehend the particular concept of Jewish law under discussion. Being a master teacher, Rav Soloveitchik had a powerful effect on the Life team. Their visit extended to the following day when they again sat through the entire shiur."[100] Those positive experiences with Soloveitchik and his class no doubt colored the *Life* reporters' story about Judaism.

Like "an essay on Protestantism featuring the Amish"

The cover of *Life*'s June 13, 1955, issue showed a photograph of Mrs. Tobi Fink, of Scranton, Pennsylvania, with her hands above Sabbath candles (Figure 7.1). The caption read, "Scranton Mother Blesses Sabbath Lights." Her dark hair pulled back in a kerchief, Fink wore a long-sleeved, embroidered peasant blouse and skirt. It was a very different look from that of the suburban mothers depicted in popular 1950s television shows such as *The Adventures of Ozzie and Harriet*, *Father Knows Best*, and *I Love Lucy*, and an even farther cry from that of a woman just three years younger than Tobi Fink—Marilyn Monroe. Monroe's film *The Seven Year Itch* had just premiered in early June 1955. With its famous shot of Monroe standing on a subway grate as her white dress blew upward, it had turned what once would have seemed an immodest moment into one that viewers instantly recognized as sexy and fun. Norms were changing. And images of women in a range of middlebrow media including television, movies, and photojournalism played a powerful role in influencing ideas about sex and gender.

Marilyn Monroe's image showed the postwar shift in attitudes toward sex, while Tobi Fink's *Life* photograph showed how Jewish mothers were desexualized in the postwar era—not assumed to be lust-worthy bodies.[101] Tobi Fink's *Life* image suggested a backward glance, and a vision of a plainer America, with religion at its core. That the 1950s contained both cultural impulses, an openness toward sexual fun *and* old-fashioned religion, is a

Figure 7.1 Tobi Fink blesses Sabbath candles. Photo by Cornell Capa © International Center of Photography/Magnum Photos

reminder of the complexity of all eras, as well as the specifically contradictory 1950s images of female gender norms. In previous months, *Life*'s cover women had included Princess Margaret; actress Shelley Winters, her wrists dripping with diamonds, but otherwise naked in a bubble bath; and the cool, elegant beauty of Grace Kelly, winner of the 1955 Academy Award for Best Actress. To some readers, accustomed to these other kinds of *Life* images, the Tobi Fink cover was the first sign that in this issue, the magazine had chosen to render Jews quaint and exotic.

"Why is Henry so anxious to make people think that a Jewish woman looks like something in a Turkish harem?" a television network official asked a rabbi-friend, upon seeing the June 13 issue.[102] The rabbi, Samuel Silver, who served as director of public relations at the Reform movement's Union of American Hebrew Congregations, then wrote to Jozefa Stuart, who authored most of the article. Rabbi Silver went beyond simply critiquing the cover image, explaining to Stuart in his letter that although the "writing is excellent . . . especially the description of the function of the prophets, the role of the Talmud, the Jewish belief in the free will, etc.," the problem was in how *Life* chose to depict Jews in its photographs. *Life* was primarily a picture magazine, and "the illustrations and some of the captions, are, as I feared, in the Luce tradition of picturing the Jew as quaint." Silver elaborated on the specifics of how *Life* offended American Jewry by selecting images from outside the mainstream: "The truth of the matter is that in real life only a very small minority of Jews look like Life's Jews. Beardlessness is true not only of Reform rabbis and laymen, but of Conservative laymen and rabbis, and of the vast majority of Orthodox laymen and a majority of Orthodox rabbis. You would never know that if you received your impressions from Life's spread."[103]

As Silver's letter suggested, a mainstream middlebrow publication like *Life* had the potential to reassure members of a minority religious group—when it reflected back a vision of those readers as accepted in American society. But the magazine could also disrupt a group's positive self-image. Silver's letter revealed his frustration with his own emotional response to *Life*'s photos, as he launched into a defensive sermon on Jews and beards: "I hope you do not construe these remarks as indicating a personal dislike for beards. I cherish Jews who wear them; my grandfather did. Nor do I feel that a magazine should not publish photos of bearded Jews. Nor do I feel troubled when I see such a photo for I admire Jews who wear them as a badge, as it were, of their traditionalism."[104]

Notwithstanding Silver's protestations of affection for "Jews with beards," the images clearly touched a nerve. The photos likely caused Silver additional distress for what felt like shame at the depiction of traditional Jews—the kind of Jews associated with those who perished in the Holocaust. The article had in fact referenced the European Jewish tragedy only briefly: once, in an image of an Israeli Torah scribe captioned "Repairing the Torah, a scribe in Jerusalem mends a scroll of the Law. Behind him are some 80,000 Torah fragments saved from European synagogues ruined by Nazis." And in a section on Hassidic Jews, the article explained that the Williamsburg community, "most of them survivors of Nazi concentration camps, used to live in the town of Satmar, Romania. After World War II they followed their rabbi to the U.S."[105] The destruction of European Jewry by the Nazis was essential background, but not the focus of the *Life* article.

In his letter to *Life*, Silver rationalized his response to the images of "old-fashioned" Jews, explaining that the magazine's portrayal of such religious Jews was poor journalism, a distortion of the American Jewish scene. It was like "an essay on Protestantism featuring the Amish."[106] To Silver, it seemed that *Life* had deliberately sought an exotic, colorful version of Judaism for its photographic treatment. But many Jewish readers looked to the pages of *Life* hoping to find confirmation of their perceived normalcy and acceptance. In the case of the June 13 special issue, some of these Jews were disappointed, and perhaps a bit discombobulated, as Silver was, by their own reactions.

The *Life* article followed the Fink family through a range of Jewish rituals and customs that would not have been typical of most suburban, middle-class Jewish families. A photo showed the father, David Fink, teaching his son "How to put on *t'fillin* (phylacteries)," with the black leather straps wound around their arms, and the small black box of the *t'fillin* atop Mr. Fink's forehead (Figure 7.3). It was an image of Jewish religious practice that would have appeared unfamiliar and strange to non-Jewish readers, and as Silver's letter suggested, it was a daily religious practice atypical of non-Orthodox Jews. Another photo, captioned "In Kosher Kitchen," showed Mrs. Fink and her daughter Shirley, stacking dishes, "making sure—as dietary law requires—that none used for meat touch any used for dairy foods" (Figure 7.4).

Dishpans in the photo were labeled "meat" and "milk," for the "non-Jewish help employed by family"—a clue that the family was indeed upper-middle class. The article also included photographs from Mr. Fink's brother's Orthodox wedding. An image of the groom lifting his bride's veil—a custom that was "supposed to assure him that the bride is the girl who was promised him"—lent the image a biblical appearance (Figure 7.2).[107]

The photos included a surfeit of bearded Jews (Figures 7.5 and 7.6).

168 POSTWAR STORIES

AT ORTHODOX WEDDING Moishe Fink, 29, the brother of David Fink (*preceding page*), lifts veil of his bride, Sonya Klein, before ceremony. Custom is supposed to assure him that the bride is the girl who was promised him.

Figure 7.2 "At an Orthodox Fink family Wedding." Photo by Cornell Capa © International Center of Photography/Magnum Photos

LIFE'S "OLD-FASHIONED JEWS" 169

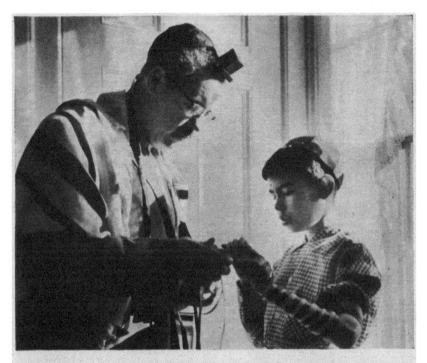

FATHER TEACHES SON how to put on *t'fillin* (phylacteries), worn at weekday morning prayer. They are leather strips with boxes containing scriptural verses. One is placed around arm near the heart, other around the head.

Figure 7.3 "David Fink teaches his son how to wear t'fillin." Photo by Cornell Capa © International Center of Photography/Magnum Photos

In his letter to Jozefa Stuart, Silver essentially accused *Life* of having intentionally chosen a Jewish family that was exotic, rather than typical: "You yourself know, Jo, how atypical even your Scranton family is," Silver wrote, detailing what was so unusual about the Fink family: "The family with the grandfather who pulls his shawl over his head, with the children eating with hats, with the veil-lifting to make sure the right bride is below, with the boy learning to put on tfillin, with the bearded rabbi and contract signers. You know how atypical the family is, because you had such a hard time finding it. Did not the rarity of this type of family actuate you to report to your editors that there would be something unrepresentative about devoting so much space to them?"[108] Although Silver was angered by the exoticization of Judaism in *Life*, his letter suggested that he knew that *Life* knew that American Jews were more "normal" than the magazine had portrayed them,

Figure 7.4 "Tobi Fink and her daughter stack dishes in their kosher kitchen." Photo by Cornell Capa © International Center of Photography/Magnum Photos

and that the magazine had gone out of its way to find Jews outside the Reform and Conservative mainstream. Silver's letter inadvertently revealed that Jews had indeed become more like other Americans—so much so that *Life* had to rely on extreme examples to create a colorful display.

Rabbi William Rosenblum, of Manhattan's Reform Temple Israel, also wrote to *Life's* editors in response to the special issue. Rosenblum was a leader in ecumenical efforts who had met with Pope Pius XII in 1946 and 1948, and would soon play a large role in midcentury middlebrow Jewish culture through his forays into television-writing.[109] Rosenblum began his letter to *Life* on a friendly note: "Now that the June 13th issue of Life has appeared, I am especially happy that at our recent conference you expressed a readiness, on future occasions when you consider publishing articles on Judaism, to be in consultation with us of the Synagogue Council. You will always find us prepared to be of every possible help."[110] Rosenblum went on to explain his reservations: "Just as I anticipated, while the article in general has been well done, some errors, misconceptions and greatly distorted portrayals of the Jew have crept in which authentic editing would have kept out." It was particularly distressing, Rosenblum wrote, that the *Life* article asserted "that Reform does not consider the Torah binding. This is just not true. Reform

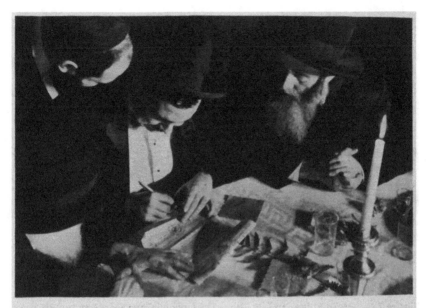

MARRIAGE CONTRACT is signed before ceremony. It stipulates husband's obligations, including support of wife in case of divorce. Practice was begun to protect wife who in old Jewish law could be divorced without her consent.

Figure 7.5 "Bearded Jews in Life." Photo by Cornell Capa © International Center of Photography/Magnum Photos

does not accept all the literalness of the Scriptures but looks upon the Bible as its basic document and source of its spiritual integration. I do hope that this and some other inaccuracies about Reform Judaism might be corrected in some future issue."[111]

If *Life* would only avoid stereotypes and distortions of Jews and Judaism in the future, Rosenblum urged, the magazine might achieve something truly extraordinary in its reporting on Judaism. He wrote: "So much of the article is so well written that it is a pity that you fell, once again, for those stereotypes and caricatures of the Jew which may appear 'interesting' because they are bizarre but, certainly, do not represent the Jew of today, especially the American Jew, as he is." Like Silver, Rosenblum implored *Life* not to exoticize Jews and Judaism in the future, lest *Life* offend more Jewish readers:

> There is the impression in many Jewish circles that LIFE is more apt to "caricature" the Jew than to characterize Judaism and the Jew accurately. I said

BRIDE DANCES WITH RABBI, Joel Fink, a cousin of the bridegroom. Both hold handkerchief because, by ancient custom, rabbi should not touch a strange woman. Seven rabbis officiated, one to say each of seven blessings.

Figure 7.6 "Bearded Jews in Life." Photo by Cornell Capa © International Center of Photography/Magnum Photos

then that this was the danger to be averted in what was then "the forthcoming article" on Judaism.... I am sure that you wanted to do a good job on Judaism, and in the main, did. But the job you did on "The American Jew" has served to perpetuate in your vast army of readers a stereotype that is no longer representative, that of the Jew whose chief concern is with his kosher diet rather than his eternal ethics, who still dresses in large measure in bizarre attire, a fact true now only of less than 1% of our people in this country.[112]

At least to some Reform Jews, the *Life* special issue had been deeply offensive.

Did Orthodox Jews share those feelings about *Life*'s treatment of Judaism? There is some evidence that more religious Jews viewed the magazine's portrayal from a very different angle. In their minds, there was a need for positive portrayals of religious Jews in popular media such as *Life* magazine. That was the feeling of the Fink family.

As the story was transmitted down through the generations, *Life* was delighted to find a three-generation Jewish farming family. "They were ecstatic," Moishe Fink, one of David's sons, recalled of *Life*'s reaction at hearing about his father's work on the family's poultry farm. As of the writing of this book, Moishe and his brothers continue to run the family poultry farm.[113]

At the time of the special issue, Moishe's oldest brother was almost thirteen years old, about to have a bar mitzvah, and David's brother was soon to be married. Both celebrations would become part of the article. But the family member who became most famous as a result of the *Life* treatment was Moishe's mother, Tobi Fink. Reciting the Sabbath blessings over the lighted Sabbath candles and wearing an Israeli blouse embroidered by a Yemenite woman, Tobi Fink's was the first image that readers saw when they received the magazine.

A dissertation could be written about that embroidered Yemenite blouse, gifted to an Ashkenazi American woman, that became the image of Orthodox Judaism to millions of *Life* readers. Through the magazine, Mizrachi Jewish culture (that of Jews of Middle Eastern ancestry) inadvertently became part of the aesthetic portrayal of American Judaism, even as Mizrachi Judaism remained marginal to Eastern European, or Ashkenazic, Jewish culture and religion. At the beginning of the twentieth century, Yemenite Jews were photographed by Hermann Burchardt, an affluent, young German Jew. Burchardt set out to understand and document the lives of what seemed to him like the more exotic Jews of the Middle East.[114] His images of Yemenite Jews came to represent what many German Jews would see, within an Orientalist framework, as the most "authentic Jews" of the world, seemingly untouched by surrounding cultures.[115] To Tobi Fink, too, the Yemenite blouse from Israel represented a kind of authentic Judaism. Her son, Moishe, remembers that it was her custom to wear the blouse every year for Passover. It has been saved by her children.

Some thirty years after the *Life* article, Moishe Fink unexpectedly came face to face with the *Life* image of his mother. He was picking up his wife from a Brooklyn shop that styled Orthodox women's wigs. Moishe's wife, Etty, had telephoned him to pick her up, and asked him to come inside the shop. The woman who was styling her wig wanted to meet Moishe. She had heard the family name and immediately asked Etty if it was the same Fink family from the 1955 *Life* issue. When David met her that day in the shop, she still had her copy of the magazine. The woman had saved it, she told David Fink, because that June 13, 1955, issue of *Life* had saved her.

The woman had survived the concentration camps in Europe, only to return to her hometown in Poland to find herself unwelcome. Stones were thrown at her. In postwar Poland, she felt that dogs were shown more sympathy and affection than Jews. Convinced that the life of a Jew was worthless in Poland, she immigrated to New York. Having shaved heads in the camps, she declared herself a hairdresser. But her life was without meaning. "I existed," she told Moishe, years later. She put food in her mouth, went to work, came home. But it wasn't a real life. Like the other hairdressers, she read *Life* to stay current on hairstyles. And then one day, she saw the June 13, 1955, issue. It changed everything, she told Moishe. To see a Jewish lady lighting candles on the cover! It meant that a Jewish life was worth something in America. Even more stunning, it meant that the life of a Jewish woman mattered. It is not difficult to imagine how empowering it felt for countless Jewish women to see that image of someone like themselves on the cover of such a popular magazine. The woman in the wig shop had saved her copy of the magazine for years. It would always sound corny in the retelling, but *Life* had given her life again.

It was an example of what middlebrow could accomplish. The magazine had brought Orthodox Jews, a group that seemed perpetually on the margins of American life, into the very center (how else to describe the America of *Life* magazine?). For some Orthodox Jews in America, the June 13 issue marked a turning point.[116]

Although the 1950s would be remembered as a decade of conformity, hints of non-conformity and growing pluralism were becoming evident. Indeed, a year before Tobi Fink's photograph landed on newsstands, the first Black woman, actress Dorothy Dandridge, appeared on the cover of *Life*.[117] The magazine's combination of photographs and text were a powerful platform for bringing difference into the living rooms of millions of readers. At times, the effect of this middlebrow literature was to make *Life* readers more comfortable with people different from themselves. The more specific these images and presentations were—for example, in conveying particular forms of Judaism—the more powerfully did they teach readers about the distinctiveness of Judaism. As readers of *Life* looked at photographs of a father and son tying leather straps onto their arms and foreheads, and a mother and daughter separating dairy and meat dishes, they saw some of the ways that Jewish domestic life differed from that of Christians. For some readers, that glimpse into the private lives of Jewish families was enough to confirm suspicions that Jews really were different. Who knew what else went on in a Jewish home? For others, the Finks' reassuringly familiar appearance as a middle-class family made their distinctive rituals less threatening. All readers were reminded that it was possible to learn about this religious tradition.

In the 1950s, Judaism—even Orthodox Judaism—became knowable to Americans, because *Life* showed it to them through words and photographs. For some Orthodox Jews, *Life*'s portrayal was a heady experience of being seen in their distinctiveness. For other Jews, such as the Reform rabbis who wrote to *Life* in frustration, it was discomfiting, and rather like having the most embarrassing parts of one's background exposed in public. The postwar era had seemed to offer the possibility of hiding Jewish difference under the protective umbrella of Judeo-Christianity. But as early as the mid-1950s, middlebrow culture came looking for what was interesting and colorful in Judaism to present to Americans, to educate and to titillate them. In 1955, *Life* found that interestingness in Orthodoxy and in the story of a Scranton family. In seeing the particular lives of the Finks in the pages of *Life*, Jews discovered that their personal stories could find an American audience.

8
"Why I Choose to Be a Jew"

By the end of the 1950s, it was becoming clear that there were two kinds of Introductions to Judaism flourishing in the United States: those with a how-to approach and those with a why-to approach.[1] The former explained the basics of Judaism, as Milton Steinberg had done. The latter began with the assumption that readers struggled with the choice of whether and how to live Jewishly, amid many options. This subgenre suggested that postwar American Jews were choosing Jewish religious paths as a result of what they learned and read in adulthood, and not necessarily because of what they imbibed during childhood. To some, this development seemed like a reversal of the natural order of things: what once was transmitted in the home by parents and family members was now acquired in adulthood through books and articles. To others, it seemed as though the Jewish universe was finally opening. Anyone who could read English now had access to Judaism.

Among the prominent midcentury writers who gave voice to their experience of finding Jewish paths as adults were two writers who published their Introduction to Judaism texts in 1959. For both men, the journey to writing about Judaism had begun years earlier.

In the fall of 1945, seventeen-year-old Arthur Cohen, then an undergraduate at the University of Chicago, had just recovered from a crisis of faith. Confronted with the attractions of Western culture, which he associated with Christianity, Arthur even considered conversion to Christianity. "When an American Jew studies at an American university," Cohen later wrote, "it is difficult for him not to be overwhelmed . . . by the recognition that Western values are rooted in the Greek and Christian tradition."[2]

With the support of his family and rabbi, Cohen found his way back into the Jewish fold, becoming more committed to Judaism than ever. As he wrote of his parents' response to his spiritual floundering: "I was rushed, not to a psychoanalyst, but to a Rabbi—the late Milton Steinberg, one of the most gifted and profound Jewish thinkers of recent years. Leading me gently, he retraced the path backwards through Christianity to Judaism, revealing the groundwork of Jewish thought and experience which supported what I have come to regard as the scaffolding of Christian 'unreason.'"[3]

Arthur Cohen (1928–1986) would soon move beyond his teenage angst, blossoming in multiple spheres. After a privileged Manhattan upbringing, Cohen continued in the lifestyle to which he had become accustomed. Four years after his 1959 Introduction to Judaism was published, *Time* magazine called Cohen "the current *enfant terrible* in the field" of modern Jewish thought, who, at age thirty-four, was editor of the intellectual quarterly *Judaism*, "but just as often writes for the *Christian Century*."[4] Married in 1956, Cohen and his wife, the graphic artist Elaine Lustig Cohen, lived in a five-story, Upper East Side Italianate townhouse valued at almost $11 million after Elaine's death in 2016.[5] On the garden floor, Arthur immersed himself in one of his many passions. It was there that he and Elaine opened Ex Libris, a rare-book store, in the 1970s.

As with other individuals profiled in *Postwar Stories*, Cohen was not a typical Jew. His talents and accomplishments were impressive, as were his advantages. Cohen's choice to turn to Judaism as an adult spoke to midcentury changes in the American Jewish experience. With its mainstreamed, "third faith" status, Judaism had shifted from a burdensome inheritance, to which one must resign oneself à la Harry Wolfson, to something much closer to the glorious treasure that Rabbi Milton Steinberg hoped more Jews would discover through Introduction to Judaism literature.

Understanding Cohen's socioeconomic status alongside his intellectual and Jewish interests is important, for it suggests that Jewish religion and thought had become legitimate interests for someone who moved in rarefied circles and could afford to do pretty much whatever he wanted. For Cohen, Jewish thought was a chosen pursuit alongside many others. Although he died relatively young, Cohen's many contributions to the worlds of art, literature, and religion emerged from his roles as art critic, theologian, publisher, novelist, and Jewish Studies scholar. Literary scholar Julian Levinson writes: "There were perhaps five different Arthur A. Cohens, and nearly all had cult followings. In order of appearance (roughly speaking), they are: Cohen the neo-Orthodox Jewish theologian; Cohen the astonishingly successful book publisher, herald of the 'paperback revolution'; Cohen the magnanimous organizer of salon gatherings and anthologies; Cohen the aggadic novelist; and Cohen the challenging and occasionally cryptic post-Holocaust theorist."[6] Levinson notes that at the time of Cohen's death, he had no lack of admirers, and "his inclusion in Dan Cohn-Sherbrook's *Fifty Key*

Jewish Thinkers (of all time) is testimony to the seriousness with which he has been taken." Those who knew him would have categorized Cohen as highbrow, but as this chapter shows, in the late 1950s, Cohen's was a case of Jewish highbrow abetting the cause of Jewish middlebrow.

In this context, Cohen is worth considering alongside another Jewish writer with a remarkable career—Herman Wouk (1915–2019). Both men published important middlebrow Introduction to Judaism texts in 1959. And unlike previous examples of the genre, which were in the form of primers to the religion, these men employed a different approach. Each brought his personal story of turning to Judaism as an adult into his writing. Cohen's contribution to the genre was his essay "Why I Choose to Be a Jew," published in *Harper's* magazine. For Wouk it was his book *This Is My God*, a touchstone in postwar expositions of Orthodox Judaism. Like most of Wouk's books, *This Is My God* was a bestseller, with newspapers reporting, in early 1960, that the book had "won such wide acceptance during the pre-holiday buying that it is safe to assume both Christians and Jews welcomed it."[7] Unlike Wouk's, Cohen's writings were not generally middlebrow. His "Why I Choose to Be a Jew" essay was the anomaly in his overwhelmingly highbrow oeuvre. Although the cultural capital represented by *Harper's* was of a higher "brow" than *Life* magazine, Cohen's *Harper's* essay fits the middlebrow category in this book because of its readable content, the intentions of the editor and the author to make Judaism accessible, and the relationship that it represented between author and readers seeking self-improvement.[8]

Cohen and Wouk offered their autobiographies as models for how and why individuals might choose Judaism when they had many life options available to them. Like the 1955 *Life* special issue on Judaism discussed in the previous chapter, the texts by these two men showcased observant Jewish lives. In his essay, Cohen made clear that his turn to Judaism was not about the Holocaust, nostalgia, grandparents, or ethnicity—the last a category that midcentury sociologists found meaningful for Jewishness.[9] By highlighting the voluntary nature of Judaism, it went without saying that Judaism was not a matter of race. Judaism was a choice that Cohen made *not* "out of loyalty to the Jewish people or to the Jewish state. My choice was religious. I chose to believe in the God of Abraham, Isaac, and Jacob; to acknowledge the law of Moses as the Word of God; to accept the people of Israel as the holy instrument of divine fulfillment; to await the coming of the Messiah and the redemption of history."[10] Where choice had belonged to the gentile majority in the early 1940s, when Laura Z. Hobson wrote "Choice—for Gentiles," by the late 1950s and for the rest of the twentieth century, Jewish writers focused on the choices that American Jews were—and were not—making about their Jewishness.[11]

This Is My God offered different possibilities than did Cohen's essay, because it was a full-length book, and because Wouk, by this point, was a celebrity writer. In *This Is My God*, readers caught glimpses of Wouk pivoting seamlessly from his routine as a Manhattan novelist and Broadway playwright to his Orthodox Jewish home life. Wouk described, for instance, leaving a Broadway theater on a Friday afternoon before the Sabbath, while one of his plays was in production. "I have sometimes felt guilty of treason, holding to the Sabbath in such a desperate situation." But then, Broadway plays-in-progress always appeared in danger of falling apart, Wouk reasoned. "Leaving the gloomy theatre, the littered coffee cups, the jumbled scarred-up scripts, the haggard actors, the shouting stagehands, the bedeviled director . . . and the dense tobacco smoke and backstage dust, I have come home. It has been a startling change, very like a brief return from the wars. My wife and my boys, whose existence I have almost forgotten in the anxious shoring up of the tottering ruin, are waiting for me, gay, dressed in holiday clothes, and looking to me marvelously attractive."[12] Through this family portrait Wouk upheld his version of traditional gender roles. Indeed, forgetting his wife and children while at work was just the kind of detail that showed Wouk was a family man—*and* an important figure in the secular world.

If readers came to *This Is My God* thinking that only old-fashioned, immigrant Jews strictly observed the Sabbath, Wouk showed them otherwise. Unlike the 1955 *Life* special issue about Judaism, discussed in the previous chapter, in which an Orthodox family was portrayed as largely enmeshed in their own religious subculture, and at a remove from secular life, *This Is My God* presented a successful intermingling of Judaism and American culture. For some midcentury readers, it was their first glimpse of the possibility that a religiously Jewish life could be glamorous.

Where once the middlebrow genre seemed to exclude the more religious from its small circle of tolerated Jews, by the late 1950s, space was made for the Orthodox, and eventually, the European and even the bearded Jews. During the 1950s, "Orthodox" remained a vague, large-tent affiliation.[13] In the context of postwar Jewish culture, I use it to designate Jews who self-identified as Orthodox or were identified by others as Orthodox by virtue of their religious community or their level of religious observance and faith. Cohen and Wouk both identified as Orthodox, although for Cohen that identity would

180 POSTWAR STORIES

change in the coming decades. Through middlebrow publications, both men expressed what it meant to choose a life of Jewish faith and observance.

Forging Jewish Paths

A new Jewish life began to take shape for Arthur Cohen when he returned to college after his crisis of faith. Arthur's concerns at the time were those typical of an ambitious undergraduate. What should he do with his life? Become a rabbi? A teacher? "Your darling, secure son is at this moment lost in a web of confusion," seventeen-year-old Arthur wrote to his parents at their Park Avenue address.[14] Like other well-educated and idealistic young people, Arthur wondered how he could make a significant contribution to the world, and whether his current preoccupation with what he vaguely termed "social action" was in fact the best use of his abilities.

Arthur was fortunate to have parents who took his concerns seriously. The Cohens shared many of their son's interests in liberal causes and in Jewish life, and they were financially able to help him realize his dreams. Isidore Cohen, Arthur's father, and soon-to-be the president of Joseph H. Cohen & Sons Clothing Manufacturer, was a successful businessman, philanthropist, and art collector whose Picassos and Matisses would become part of the collections of leading art museums.[15] As his long letters with their affectionate sign-offs and encouraging words demonstrate, Isidore was proud of his precocious and academically high-achieving son, even as he felt his own intellect no match to Arthur's. After graduating from Townsend Harris High School in Queens, Isidore never made it to college. Instead, he joined the family clothing business and the navy.[16] But when Arthur wrote home in the fall of 1945, Isidore was determined to guide his son through career choices that he had never faced. "You see," Isidore wrote to Arthur, "basically I am not an intellect, and when I get out of my class, I am not very comfortable. However, since I can remember other times in my life when I wasn't particularly comfortable with you, I figure that such experience does not make much difference, and say, 'Here goes!'"[17]

Isidore did not hold back. "I read your recent letter with keen interest," he wrote, "and to me, it was just another stanza to the song, 'June is bustin out all over.'" The elder Cohen was a fan of Broadway's theatrical offerings, including the most recent Rodgers & Hammerstein musical *Carousel*, in which the character Nettie Fowler sings "June is bustin' out all over!" Isidore continued his letter, "You're an unusual kid, in that you possess a dynamic personality, an unusually good brain, a heart that is as big as a house, a great deal of sentimentality together with a fine power of reasoning. You are a materialist as well as an aesthete. With all this you have a yearning for learning. (That last line could be put to music, but that's another story.)"[18]

As to Arthur's struggle over what to do with his future, it was Isidore's belief that becoming a rabbi—one of Arthur's ideas—would *not* suit his son. Arthur lacked the required "godliness," Isidore felt. "Furthermore, there's the responsibility of a staid, conventional congregation that would give you a pain in your A--, which to my way of thinking, doesn't go well with a rabbi; it just isn't high-class." Neither would becoming a teacher satisfy his son's ambitions or vanities, Isidore wrote with his usual candor. Instead, Isidore advised Arthur to "continue being just as you are without worrying where the cards will fall. . . . If you are sufficiently idealistic, you can devote yourself to the avenues that will open up for you when the moment arrives, and God knows what that endeavor will be at the moment you are ready for it. It may be as a leader among Jews. It may even be as leader for the colored race. It may be as a labor leader. Or, it may be as commentator."[19] To contemporary ears, the elder Cohen's remarks about Arthur becoming a leader among African Americans sound like white privilege, but at the time, Isidore's comments showed his engagement with civil rights and labor issues.

Isidore saw unusual potential in his son. Rather than push Arthur into the family business, he encouraged him to pursue his interests, hoping that Arthur would find contentment along the way. "Remember," Isidore wrote, "it isn't necessary that you save the whole world. If in your particular spot, you can do the job that pleases you, that should be all you need to bring you happiness. . . . I know you understand, when I say 'happiness' I don't mean the material things in life. I mean true and genuine happiness, which I know only too well you can readily understand."[20] Financial security was something that Isidore could give his son. "Fortunately for you," Isidore reminded his son, "You have no financial troubles ahead of you. . . . You can always be happy from a practical viewpoint because I shall always have an income insured for you."[21] Not many young people enjoyed this kind of support from their parents. It was a significant factor in making Arthur's life so extraordinary.

"Extraordinary" might also describe Herman Wouk's life. He was one of the first openly Orthodox American Jewish celebrities. A September 1955 *Time* magazine cover story about Wouk included discussion of his religious observance. His day began, *Time* reported, "in prayer, for which he dons the traditional black-and-white prayer shawl and straps phylacteries (small leather cases containing texts from the Pentateuch) to his left arm and his forehead. He prays twice more each day."[22] While *Time* did not include a photo of the novelist in his prayer shawl and phylacteries, there was a photograph showing the writer's family on the beach of Fire Island, a summer retreat in New York State, where they vacationed. Wouk may have been a poster child for Modern Orthodoxy as early as the mid-1950s, but he was also an example of the power of celebrity when it came to introducing Americans to a formerly alien tradition: when any celebrity was religious, the religion (Orthodoxy) became more acceptable.[23] But there were still limits to the peculiarities of Judaism that could be portrayed in middlebrow culture.

By the 1950s, Wouk was aware of how alien his way of life appeared to many Jews, including the children of his sister, whose father was not a religiously observant Jew.[24] A younger generation, Wouk realized, might benefit from the kind of reading material he could produce—a book about Orthodoxy. Having won a Pulitzer Prize for his 1951 war novel *The Caine Mutiny*, and countless fans from his bestselling novels, Wouk believed his readers would follow him, even to this seemingly less popular subject of Orthodox Judaism.[25]

Judaism in an American Idiom

Wouk had not personally needed Introduction to Judaism literature. And it was because he understood the Jewish advantages of his upbringing that he dedicated *This Is My God* to his grandfather, who was a rabbi in Minsk before immigrating to the United States. Wouk wrote in his dedication that "His lifetime of ninety-four years stretched from the last days of Abraham Lincoln to the first years of the nuclear era. He served as a Jewish jurist and minister under czarism and communism, in the freedom of America, and in the reborn land of Israel, where his bones lie."[26] His grandfather's presence during Wouk's childhood and young adulthood influenced the young man's awareness of the varieties of religious observance, even within his own family, cultivating in Wouk a feeling of closeness to what many Jews deemed foreign.

Wouk's grandfather also provided an opportunity to observe the arc of an Eastern European Jewish life. "My grandfather maintained pretty well unaltered in his own life the life of the east European pale," Wouk wrote.[27] Like so many Jews of his generation, Wouk had moved rapidly down a path of Americanization. His growing distance from his grandfather's way of life affected his perspective, as he came to see his grandfather through the eyes of an American: "His black coat reached to his black shoe tops. His black round hat never was violated with a Western crease. His beard did not know the touch of the barber. He was, in short, to the best of his ability, a walking replica of the east European Jew of the past two hundred years."[28]

Wouk grasped how the aesthetics of his grandfather's Jewishness would strike other Americans, who would not understand what lay beneath the foreign-looking black hat and coat. They would see only the strangeness of his grandfather's exterior, and that would be enough to brand his grandfather as alien and obsolete. "He had no clear program for the future," Wouk observed of his grandfather's Jewishness. "Integrity for him was all. For him it lay in the law, and he held to the manners, dress, and language in which he had first studied."[29]

As much as he admired his grandfather's commitment to Judaism, Wouk understood its cost. "The price he paid at last was an evaporation of his congregation in the Bronx, as the younger members looked around for a rabbi who spoke English. He did not mind that. But he could not hold the attention of the young people in his own family after a while. That cut deep."[30] Even as Wouk's life had taken him far from his grandfather's, the relationship allowed Wouk to feel his grandfather's pain at being deemed irrelevant, and not just irrelevant to American life, which would not have bothered him, but to Jewish life.

That the English language had become so central to Judaism was a rude awakening to those who felt, often viscerally, that Jewishness was altered when translated into an American idiom. When Wouk was a young man, he rode in a New York City taxicab with his grandfather to the ship that would take the older man to Israel. During that trip, Wouk's grandfather expressed his sense of defeat by the modern world and its language. The rabbi said to his grandson, "I should have learned English. But the sound of it was so harsh to me!"[31] Wouk thus wrote his book about Judaism with the knowledge that to say it in English was already to make Jewishness different from what it had been as recently as during his grandfather's lifetime. But how else to say it in a way that spoke to postwar Americans? The compromise of rendering Judaism as middlebrow, as someone like Will Herberg saw it, was that Judaism came across as too reassuring, too simple, and too accommodating to American culture. But Wouk seemed willing to accept this—along with the financial gains that came with a writing style that regularly made the bestseller list. As he learned from his grandfather's life, there was also a high cost to *not* compromising.

In Herberg's view, writing a middlebrow book about Judaism came with serious pitfalls. "Herman Wouk has written the 'intelligent woman's guide to orthodox Judaism,'" Herberg opined in the *New York Times*, adding generously, "and it will do for intelligent men as well."[32] Despite having seen women's capabilities while serving as educational director of the International Ladies Garment Workers Union from 1933 to 1954, Herberg fell easily into 1950s gender stereotypes.[33] His gendered ascription of a middlebrow book was not atypical (reviewers of anti-antisemitism fiction during the 1940s articulated similar views about the target audience of middlebrow novels).[34] Given the homosocial nature of the milieu of Introduction to Judaism writers, in which the majority of authors, editors, and publishers were male, it was telling that Herberg imagined Wouk's readers as women. *Explainers* of Judaism were still assumed to be men. But the hypothetical reader was female.[35]

Like other social networks, as Charles Kadushin observed, the ones that Wouk and Cohen belonged to were "exclusionary and unfair," and primarily constituted of people like themselves, in this case, educated, white, Jewish men.[36] In spite of Cohen's perception that he had been denied the benefits of a religious upbringing, his social network was undoubtedly helpful to his career as a Jewish writer. Even as a twenty-year-old in Israel, Cohen was tapping into these contacts. He wrote to his parents: "I should like to write a small article on my impressions of religious life, which I am perhaps competent to do. . . . Would you ask Milton whether he believes such an article could be placed, as such a minor squib could not be officially described as the beginning of my publishing career. It would be not even an article, but a note."[37] That Cohen had the idea to write about his impressions of Israeli religious life, that he felt there was a chance of publication, and that he was comfortable sharing this idea with his parents and soliciting Milton Steinberg's advice all evidence the professional and emotional support his social network provided.

It was precisely those who did not have access to such social networks for whom Introduction to Judaism books had particular value, as Herberg recognized in his review of *This Is My God*. "Even those who do not agree with Mr. Wouk's presentation and emphasis at all points will be grateful for what he has done to make orthodox Judaism intelligible to large numbers of Americans, Jewish and non-Jewish alike, whose cultural presuppositions are so remote from those of the ancient Jewish faith."[38] Herberg recognized that "a work of popular theology by one of the best known of American novelists" had unique benefits. It was unlikely, for instance, that the *Los Angeles Times* would have published excerpts of *This Is My God* throughout the fall of 1959, were it not written by such a famous author. Herberg conceded that Mr. Wouk "makes no concession on essentials for the sake of popularity, and it is poles apart from all the familiar 'peace of mind' literature of the day," referring to Joshua Loth Liebman's *Peace of Mind* (1946) and Norman Vincent Peale's *The Power of Positive Thinking* (1952). And yet, "to this reader," Herberg wrote, "Mr. Wouk's presentation of Judaism seems to me to be too relaxed, too externalistic and too partisan to be fully satisfactory."[39]

Herberg went on to explain what middlebrow could not deliver: "Authentic religion, as I understand it, is a profound, often agonizing venture of the spirit, not a pleasant relaxing activity that fits in well with the pattern of gracious living in modern suburbia. Whether he intends to or not, Mr. Wouk gives the impression that being a Jew is lots of fun; the true pathos of Jewish existence is better given, I suggest, in the age-old Jewish plaint, which Mr. Wouk must surely have heard from his grandfather, the rabbi, to whom the book is dedicated: 'It's hard to be a Jew!'" Less than fifteen years after the Holocaust, Wouk may not have felt he needed to remind anyone that it was hard to be a Jew. As when he criticized Reform Rabbi Philip Bernstein's 1950 *Life* depiction of Judaism, Herberg showed his desire for a Judaism modeled after Niebuhr's neo-Orthodox Protestantism that unapologetically made demands of adherents.

The 1950s were in fact years of debating the merits of easy-versus-difficult religion. In the women's middlebrow magazine *Redbook*, "Both sides of the stormiest controversy about religion today" were laid out in a 1955 article titled "The Case Against 'Easy' Religion."[40] The article called Norman Vincent Peale, the bestselling author of the *Power of Positive Thinking*, the "high priest of this cult of reassurance."[41] But it also pointed out that the origin of this postwar religion of reassurance was Reform Rabbi Joshua L. Liebman's *Peace of Mind*—referred to by publishers as a "blue skies" book, because of its religious optimism.[42] Jewish writers such as Herberg felt the need to distance themselves from the likes of Liebman and Wouk (authors of so-called easy religion)—and to make readers aware that there were alternative narratives about postwar Judaism. Herberg was also making clear what he counted as true religion.

Middlebrow literature transformed Judaism, or at least how Jewish and non-Jewish readers comprehended it. When Judaism—including Orthodox Judaism—was something interesting to read about in the colorful pages of *Life* magazine, or when it was explained as central to the life of a celebrity writer, readers were likely to experience positive emotional responses, replacing the ubiquitous swirl of antisemitic tropes. Those uplifting ideas might also hold true for the Jewish reader accustomed to feeling shame and defensiveness about Jewishness. For those who understood the significance of explaining Judaism to a wider audience (Herberg was, after all, writing for the *New York Times*), Wouk's primer had clear value. In the end, Herberg granted that Wouk had managed to do what others had not. He had provided a clear explanation of "what orthodox Judaism means to an informed and intelligent orthodox Jew, who is at the same time thoroughly American in outlook and culture."[43]

Wouk had been able to write about Judaism in an accessible manner, because his path to Judaism had marked a return to religion—and a return in which books were essential. After a religious upbringing, Wouk's postcollege, Manhattan life included years of secular living, while he worked as a writer for the radio comic Fred Allen. In *This Is My God*, Wouk described his journey back to Judaism; after achieving "Quite young what many people consider the dream life of America: success by my own efforts, a stream of dollars to spend, a penthouse in New York, forays to Hollywood, the companionship of pretty women, all before I was twenty-four. . . . I dreamed of higher success as a playwright or novelist—like my Noel Airman in *Marjorie Morningstar* all I wanted was a succession of hits—but even as I lived this conventional smart existence of inner show business, and dreamed the conventional dreams, it all seemed thin. . . . I began to read again, following an interlude after college which had been all chase and no thought. Without reaching any conclusions, I moved into a freely chosen observant life."[44] Even for Wouk, brought up in an Orthodox home, books would prove central to his return to a religious life. Indeed, for those intellectually inclined, reading often seemed like the only respectable route to religion.[45]

Finding Teachers and Friends

While Wouk imbibed the Jewish education that came with an Orthodox upbringing, and then made a conscious decision to return to Jewish learning as an adult, Cohen found teachers for himself along the way. Among them was Milton Steinberg, the rabbi at Park Avenue Synagogue, who had assisted the Cohens during Arthur's teenage spiritual floundering. Both Steinberg and Cohen came to cherish their relationship more than either could have predicted. In a letter to a nineteen-year-old Cohen, Steinberg remembered, to his surprise, that had he missed Arthur's bar mitzvah because of travel. "At that time, you were just another youngster to me," Steinberg wrote to Cohen. "Curious, isn't it, that I should have failed to be present at the Bar Mitzvah of one of the boys who has meant most in my career as a Rabbi? Believe me, a transcontinental trip or no transcontinental trip, if I could have predicted and foreread the future, I would have been at that ritual ceremony."[46]

To Cohen, Steinberg was an intellectual and spiritual father figure. The older man encouraged the younger in his studies and in forging intellectually nourishing connections. In addition to suggesting books and looking over Cohen's college course selection, Steinberg suggested people. By nature, Steinberg was a collector and connector of people, as his archived collection of papers reveals. When Steinberg heard of someone interesting—a writer, rabbi, or academic—in the Chicago area, he relayed the information to Cohen. In a 1947 letter, after listing a few names, including the sociologist Daniel Bell, Steinberg asked, "Do you know these people? If not, may I urge upon you that you come to know them. Virtue, as Plato recognized long ago, is as easily caught as taught, and that applies to Jewish virtue as to any other. It's none of my business, but I'd like to see you exposed to the stimulation and inspiration of people like that. Besides, I hate to think of you missing that sort of opportunity."[47]

Steinberg was also tough on Cohen, making it clear that the younger man would have to earn his Judaism through study. When Cohen told the rabbi that he had not yet read a recommended book about rabbinic literature, Steinberg roared back, "What do you mean you've been 'thinking and reading religious experience' when you haven't completed the most basic text of all, and when the books you read are all studiously 'Goy'? What kind of religion do you expect you will have some day, if you achieve any? Gentile or Jewish I'm not parochial. But don't give me that line so common among Jews about having time for everything but not for their own Jewish heritage."[48] As usual, Steinberg concluded the letter by sending his "love" to Cohen. In an atmosphere of affection and respect, Cohen learned from Steinberg, but Steinberg, who was writing *Basic Judaism* at the time, was also learning how young people approached Judaism.

The relationship was helped by Cohen's understanding that Steinberg, like him, chose Judaism as an adult.[49] As a young man beginning to adopt religious practices such as daily prayer, Cohen took comfort in this shared path with his mentor, writing to Steinberg, "Often I imagine your entrance into religious activity must have paralleled in many ways my own evolution, though

I do not suppose you underwent the same perilous temptation of conversion."[50] Cohen may have been fishing for a confession from Steinberg that he, too, had felt tempted by Christianity, but even without such an offering, Cohen expressed gratitude: "I am deeply indebted to you for your wisdom, your equanimity, and your kindness. Every religious form which I now indulge I feel somehow has taken its origin in the exemplary human form to which your life is witness." With few role models who were as Jewishly knowledgeable and as well-read in secular fields as Steinberg, Cohen leaned heavily on him for reassurance that there was, in fact, a path forward for an intellectually satisfying life in both Jewish and secular spheres. The wealthy young man from the Upper East Side and the rabbi who came from modest means had more in common than might have been apparent to outsiders. As Cohen would later write about his teacher and friend, Steinberg "came to Judaism out of the secular culture of America. He did not return to the ancestral faith; he had not strayed only to come home."[51] Religious Judaism was a choice for both men, a turn toward a new future. But while Steinberg had not included his turn to Judaism after a secular upbringing in his 1947 Introduction to Judaism book, Cohen would make his own life story central to his text. For Cohen and Wouk, these personal encounters with Judaism were not a bug, but an appealing feature of an Introduction to Judaism, reassuring readers that there were many kinds of Jewish journeys.

That Steinberg never ceased to take Cohen seriously was crucial to the success of their relationship. Steinberg did not relinquish his support, even when Cohen's confidence got the better of him, veering dangerously close to arrogance, as when the twenty-one-year-old wrote to Steinberg, "It seems however more and more certain that I shall lead the theological future of Judaism. This is not said with pride, but with the immediate consciousness that my intellectual equipment is exceedingly vigorous, that my thought is essentially clear and unambiguous, that I know precisely the sense in which the challenge to Jews and Christians alike must be phrased. It is my hope in the years to come that you will join this insistent demand for courageous theological encounter."[52] To his credit, Steinberg responded warmly, acknowledging the young man's vision for himself: "Given the philosophical background which you have built up and will continue to build, given the Jewish knowledge which you are in the process of acquiring, it may well be that you shall have a unique place in the evolution of Judaism in the future." Steinberg affirmed Cohen's contributions, writing, "We have need, desperate need, for persons of your native endowments and acquired equipment, persons who know the religious problem and who love religious values in general and in Jewish values in particular."[53] At that point, Steinberg's health had taken a downturn. He would live only a few months more. Steinberg may have doubted he would be around to participate in the future that Cohen imagined. But there was no bitterness in his reply. He never stopped encouraging the young man who still needed his encouragement. As Steinberg acknowledged, he needed Cohen, too: "Needless to say, there could be nothing more deeply rewarding to me as a rabbi and a human being than your expression of indebtedness to my influence. As the rabbis used to put it, more than the calf wishes to suckle, the cow desires to be suckled."[54] Steinberg remained a mentor to Cohen up until Steinberg's early death, in 1950, and Cohen would edit a volume of Steinberg's essays, titled *Anatomy of Faith*, published in 1960.[55]

Writing about a Freely Chosen Religious Life

When *Harper's* editor Robert Silvers—soon to become a coeditor of the *New York Review of Books*—invited Cohen's submission, it was part of a Protestant-Catholic-Jew series that the magazine published in 1959—another sign of the tri-faith religious schema's ascendancy.[56] Interestingly, *Harper's* initially proposed an essay by a nonbeliever, the German-born Princeton philosopher Walter Kaufmann (although he did not identify as Jews, Kaufmann's grandparents were all Jews). *Harper's* suggested the title, "The Faith of an Agnostic." Kaufmann was uncertain about whether he wanted to contribute, but having been pleasantly surprised by the magazine's decision to include a nonbeliever's perspective, he felt that "one could hardly say: congratulations, gentleman, on your decision to present this point of view along with more popular attitudes, but if you don't mind, ask someone else."[57] He thus relented, but preferred "The Faith off an Infidel," to which the editors responded: "That would not do: it would look as if, along with two Christians and a Jew, a Muslim had been included. The editors proposed 'The Faith of a Pagan.' I did not think I was a pagan and, after some further thought, hit on 'The Faith of a Heretic.'"[58] If one did not fit neatly into the Judeo-Christian paradigm, one's categorization was open to negotiation.

To Cohen, Silvers suggested that he make his essay personal, writing that "we would want to encourage you to show something of the process by which you arrived at your beliefs," urging Cohen not to hold back.[59] "In the course of doing this you could perhaps make your critique of other positions by giving an account of your own contact with them and your recognition of their shortcomings for you. We would also like to encourage you to pull no punches in your critiques throughout, either in dealing with the views held by other Jewish thinkers or in indicating why you believe that Christianity is less than adequate. The commentary on Christianity will be especially interesting to readers." It was a long way from the days when *Life* asked Reform Rabbi Bernstein to explain Judaism in ways that would be agreeable to Christian readers. Silver elaborated, "It is important that you be as graphic and concrete as possible in describing the position of such leaders as Hertzberg, to whom you are opposed.[60] When I talked to him he emphasized to me that he felt that theological considerations were secondary for Jews: that one could not ask a Jew 'what he believes' in the same way that one could ask this of a Protestant or a Catholic. For him the central considerations were a) that Jews were born into a peculiar community which has always been, and probably always will be, marked off from the Gentile community around it and b) that emphasis on theological questions of individual faith and piety could well threaten the vitality and solidarity of this community's group life."[61] Unlike Hertzberg, a Polish-born, American rabbi, scholar, and Jewish communal leader, Cohen made it clear that in his view, individual faith and piety were central to Judaism.

Creating Jewish Literacy

In the late 1950s, as Cohen's and Wouk's Introduction to Judaism texts were published, institutions ordaining clergy recognized the need for more introductory reading material about Judaism. Rabbinical schools noted the change in the kinds of young men choosing the rabbinate. The 1957–1958 *American Jewish Year Book* observed that, "In 1957–58 more JTS [the Conservative movement's Jewish Theological Seminary] students were graduates of Harvard than of Yeshiva University, from which a plurality of JTS students had come in earlier years. One reason to emphasize Talmud in the curriculum was to compensate for the sparse traditional knowledge of its new kind of student."[62] The rabbinate was receiving more young men who, like Cohen, had the combination of an elite secular education and a paltry Jewish education. Relying on active recruitment of undergraduates "at Brandeis, Cornell, Harvard, and Yale," the JTS advisor met with undergraduates referred to him by Hillel directors and local Conservative rabbis. He found Brandeis and Harvard to be the most promising sources of recruitment. While less intensive backgrounds in Talmud were required for the Conservative and Reform rabbinate, "Most of the Orthodox rabbinical students come ready-made, as it were, from Yeshiva's high-school system" and its higher education and other orthodox schooling.[63] But for non-Orthodox Jews, the path to the rabbinate might be eased by enjoyable reading material about Judaism. For young Jewish men who had not been reared in the world of traditional Jewish text study, opening an English-language book about Judaism by a well-known American author, or a reading an article in *Harper's*, was immeasurably more accessible. By the twenty-first century, that calculation changed even more, as translations made Hebrew and Aramaic texts available.

Judaism as Choice

When *Cosmopolitan* magazine published a "Who Goes into the Religious Life?" article about up-and-coming young clergymen (and one woman who served as a Salvation Army cadet) in 1958, the magazine profiled Jack Bloom. A twenty-six-year-old rabbinical student about to complete his last year at the Jewish Theological Seminary, Bloom explained his religious interests: eighteen years earlier, his father had met a group of Jewish refugees from Europe who had remained religiously observant. The experience impressed Jack's father who, in turn, became more religious. He decided to send his son to a Jewish high school instead of public school. By the time he was an undergraduate at Columbia, Bloom realized that "a great many modern Jews were unaware of the contributions their people has [*sic*] made, and I wanted to help make them aware of our traditions." Invoking the Holocaust, Bloom spoke of his religious duties as a post-Holocaust Jew: "I have always had a strong feeling about the six million Jews who were destroyed by the Nazis. I would like to help see to it that the destruction wrought by the Nazis was only physical, and that what those people represented will be carried on."[64] Choosing lives with greater religious content became one way that a younger generation of American Jews responded to the Holocaust.

Becoming more (or less) religious was also a way for younger generations to declare their independence from their families, in cases where upward social mobility had already been achieved, and to make up for what was missing in childhood. In 1949, a decade before his *Harper's* essay, a twenty-one-year-old Cohen made such a move when he traveled to Israel. "I have through Israel and the contemplative possibilities it has offered me rediscovered my people, my tradition, and my God," Cohen wrote proudly to his parents five weeks into his visit.[65] In his fashion, Cohen asserted his autonomy from his parents, who nonetheless financed his adventures. "Henceforth," Cohen wrote in his characteristically formal style, "the day of rest shall be a day of contemplation, for on that day shall the Book be my delight." In Israel, Cohen began spending "exultant hours reading Torah, memorizing the Hebrew, and reciting it to myself with passion and commitment."[66] These were not the customs of Cohen's parents. Although he did not admit his insecurities about these new religious practices to his parents, in a letter to Milton Steinberg from Israel, Cohen wrote, "I am sure I lay tefillin badly and pray with complete embarrassment."[67]

His time in Israel broadened Cohen's perspective on Orthodox Judaism. Observing Orthodox Jews on the streets of Jerusalem, Cohen wrote to his parents about the appearance of the Orthodox: "Where is the beauty of the Orthodox Jew? His paiot, his furred hat, his long coat, his poverty, his sombre [sic] face that comes alive on Sabbath, his beard curried and loved."[68] These marks of ultra-Orthodoxy were often the cause of embarrassment and resentment for assimilated Jews in the United States. There was even a fear of being identified with these walking symbols of the ghetto. Cohen observed of American Jews, "We turn away when one passes, for in him we feel ourselves, the Jewish self to be shunted, to be covered with the veil of culture and sophistication. We turn from him as well to avoid the thrusting acknowledgement of the Christian bystander—who either wonders, or laughs, or mimics his existence."

Herman Wouk noted the same dynamic between Orthodox and assimilated Jews in *This Is My God*. In his book, Wouk described a fictional scenario in which a modern American Jew walking down Fifth Avenue passes two Orthodox men who look as though they hail from another world. "As they pass our man, these two unmistakable Jews, he is filled with resentment. He cries out in his heart—it will not do to shout it in the street—'I am not one of you! If you are Jews, I am not a Jew!' His misery is double because he knows that he could actually shout this through a bull horn to all the world, and it would make no difference. He is one of them."[69] Wouk explained, "these men who pass him on Fifth Avenue offend him not only because they tar him with the brush of the alien; they offend him by being alive in 1959, by keeping up that dead culture and confronting him with it, by insisting with their mere presence in the street that he is burying a part of his background that cannot be buried. They are skeletons out of his closet."[70] In that same year, the novelist Philip Roth also memorialized the postwar encounter with bearded,

Orthodox Jews from Eastern Europe in his short story "Eli, the Fanatic." For midcentury Jews, this experience of encountering *haredi* (strictly religious) Jews—often refugees or survivors from Europe—on the streets of a modern American city could be a destabilizing experience, unleashing a mix of emotions.

As twenty-one-year-old Cohen saw it, American Jews struggled with the ultra-Orthodox Jews in their midst: "We present him as our courage to the world. We who are not pious use him as the agent of our pride. He stands to announce our consciousness to the goyim. In either case we do not take him for the immensely rich fact which he is. He is either our scourge or our advertisement, but never a fact."[71] For midcentury Jews, *haredi* Jews represented an extreme case—an example of the kind of Jew who did not fit in to modern society. Cohen marveled that in Israel, the *haredi* Jew (it was always a man in these writers' examples) was unremarkable. "His presence here is an unaccountable presence. He is passed unheralded. He is but another Jew, differentiated merely by his position in the Law, which all acknowledge and share."[72] Cohen understood that "It is in the West that the Orthodox Jew is an object of contumely. His presence causes our apology, for through him we are thrust into the past we had struggled to escape."

In Israel, Cohen caught a glimpse of what it meant *not* to feel embarrassed and defensive about Orthodox Jews. "Here the Orthodox Jew is a fact. He is accounted with as a human being, not an anomaly or a contradiction, or a shameful dog of the ghetto. He is thirty percent of the national existence. I take pride in this fact, for through his unannounced presence I feel the liberation that is brought by the return from Exile. The physical exile has passed and with it has passed the psychological exile, the exile of our minds in an anti-Jewish world. The gentile standard by which all our lives has been measured these long centuries is over."[73] In Israel in 1949, Cohen could see that normalization of Orthodox Judaism was not only possible, but had already been achieved.

Acceptance of Orthodox Judaism had not been evident during Cohen's upbringing, when the "gentile standard" was still extant and religious Judaism was considered alien. In his *Harper's* essay, Cohen clarified this background: "I come from a fundamentally unobservant Jewish home."[74] He explained that his parents were second-generation American Jews who attended synagogue on the major holidays, "but worship at home, knowledge of the liturgy, familiarity with Hebrew, concern with religious thought and problems, did not occupy them." Their real concern, Cohen wrote, "was adjusting to American life, achieving security, and passing to their children and those less fortunate the rewards of their struggle."[75] Cohen expressed gratitude for what his parents had provided, "but although the flesh was nourished, the spirit was left unattended." It was a postwar trope for an American Jew to look beyond his parents' dreams of an upper-middle-class existence and toward the goal of a more religiously Jewish home.

By the end of his Israel visit, Cohen was looking forward to his return to university life, where he intended "to struggle for religious knowledge, to challenge Christian assertion, to in effect cease all attempt at compromise. I hope never again to use such naïve, compromising statements as 'Judeo-Christian tradition.' There is no such concept. To admit it, is to admit a deceit, a falsehood, a compromise."[76] These were ideas that Cohen developed over time, leading to his "Myth of the Judeo-Christian Tradition" essay published in *Commentary* magazine in 1969, and then as a book by the same title, in which he lamented that so much of Judeo-Christianity seemed to be a matter of Jews being asked "to sit in the audience, watch the show, and keep silent" as Christians commenced their purportedly Judeo-Christian discourse. Rather than be faithful to some Judeo-Christian concept of religion in general, Cohen was moving toward a deeper understanding of the particular practices of Judaism. In the coming years, he would further articulate this rejection of Judeo-Christianity, which he understood as a "dishonest compact of love and admiration."[77] In his letter to his parents, Cohen listed his new observances, which included laying tefillin regularly, attending Friday night services, lighting Shabbat candles, reciting the end of Sabbath ceremony, Havdalah, on Saturday night, and praying before bed. As he would write, a decade later, in his "Why I Choose to Be a Jew" essay, he considered this turn to a more religiously observant Judaism a conversion.[78]

Cohen was being intentionally provocative by using terms that would have been less familiar to Jews in the context of Judaism. He was pushing those accustomed to thinking of Jewishness as an unfortunate fact of their birth, to instead recognize Judaism as a religion they could choose to embrace. "Many Jews will find my beliefs unfamiliar or unacceptable—perhaps outrageous," he wrote in *Harper's*.[79] Cohen's language, redolent of Christianity, with its references to theology, beckoned Christian readers. Cohen bemoaned the lack of theology at Jewish seminaries (he spent some time studying at the Jewish Theological Seminary after college) but suspected that Jewish distrust of theology arose from a feeling that "it is a Christian pastime—that it may by insinuation and subtle influence, Christianize Judaism. In this view,

Christianity is a religion of faith, dogma and theology, and Judaism is a religion which emphasizes observance of God's Law, not speculation about it." Cohen found this an oversimplification and an error. Judaism has a theology, he countered. "It is merely a question of making what is now a minor chord in Jewish tradition sound a more commanding note."[80]

Cohen's discussion of theology inspired encomiums from the Catholic theologian Gustave Weigel, a prominent Catholic voice in ecumenical dialogue. Weigel wrote to Cohen that it "was high time that a Jewish voice spoke in resonance with the trimillenial [sic] tradition of Israel."[81] It was disturbing, Weigel explained, to read so many exponents of the Jewish religion "describe Judaism as if it were a deistic moral system, unconcerned with the nature of the Name and disdainful of the question whether man will survive his own death." Weigel felt those Jewish writers "are falsifying their own tradition and weakening faith in the general community in which we all live." Going on to criticize Martin Buber's writing, Weigel wrote, "The difference between you and Buber is that he is a philosopher and you are a theologian. In your position you must be lonely. Whatever be the reason, modern Jews in contrast to their forefathers shrink away from theology."[82] Cohen found support among Christian thinkers, even as he became a critic of the Judeo-Christian tradition.

Cohen may have been a critic, but his 1959 essay was, inadvertently, an act of Judeo-Christianity; it employed a Christian lexicon, foregrounding words such as faith, conversion, theology, belief, mission, and messiah, that were not exclusive to Christians. But such words resonated differently with Christians than with Jews. The *Harper's* essay thus served as a bridge for readers to help them move from their own, Christian-influenced ideas about religion to an understanding of Judaism as a religion. As Cohen wrote in *Harper's*, he had come to Judaism through "the medium of Christianity... after having first received the impress of Western education and Christian thought."[83] For Cohen, there was a unique significance to choosing Judaism at this moment in history: "In the United States today, it is at last possible to choose not to remain a Jew," he observed, referring to increased social acceptance of Jews. Harry Wolfson's understanding of Jewishness as an unfortunate fact of birth held less sway by the late 1950s.[84] Cohen may have overstated the degree to which 1950s Jews actually felt their Jewishness was their individual choice. But his essay made clear that he was writing from his personal experience.[85] "Since it would have been possible to become a Christian—to accept the Christian version of Judaism as the grounds of my own repudiation of

Judaism, to believe that a Messiah had redeemed me—I could only conclude that Judaism was not an unavoidable fate, but a destiny to be chosen freely."[86] In the pages of *Harper's*, Cohen described a new postwar orientation toward Judaism.

A view of Judaism as a religion and choice worked its way into postwar middlebrow culture. The year before Cohen's essay, the *Ladies' Home Journal* published a letter from a convert to Judaism named Elsa Doran, who took "strong exception" to an article in which Judaism was referred to as a racial religion. "No American magazine should print such a statement without refuting it as patent untruth," Doran protested, illustrating her point: "Though I was born of a German family of loosely Protestant affiliation (thus neither racially nor ethnically Semitic or Jewish), I became a Jew a few years ago in a ceremony which involved declaring myself willing to enter into 'the Covenant of Israel' and to fulfill all the commandments incumbent upon a 'daughter of the Covenant.' I have been a full-fledged Jew ever since, fully accepted as such in the Jewish community."[87] Doran continued her lesson on race and religion: "Haven't you ever heard of the Negro Jewish community in Harlem?—of the Falasha Jews in Abyssinia?—or seen pictures of people walking the streets in modern Tel Aviv, Israel—verily a United Nations as far as races are concerned. And all of them Jews."[88] Doran may have sounded like a voice from the future, with her comfort in her Jew-by-choice identity and her awareness of Jewish diversity.[89] But she was also in tune with the midcentury moment in middlebrow Jewish literature. The culture of anti-antisemitism and an interest in learning about Judaism informed Doran's outlook, as did her preference for categorizing Jewishness as religion rather than race. The themes of midcentury Jewish middlebrow literature had become part of her own postwar Jewish story.

While a select group of writers authored the anti-antisemitism and Introduction to Judaism genres, their stories spoke to an ever-wider circle of readers. Jewish middlebrow book culture would be integral to the flourishing of Judaism in the coming decades, the content of these books and articles informing what average Americans understood about Judaism far more than traditional Jewish texts. Future generations would continue to find new iterations of accessibly written explanations of Judaism in the form of books and websites such as My Jewish Learning.com, Chabad.org, and Sefaria.org.

For authors, an Introduction to Judaism might be something to write because one had been born into an intensely Jewish family. Or because one had not. Herman Wouk, whose grandfather was an Orthodox rabbi, had comfortably claimed the mantle of authority when it came to writing about Judaism. But so had Arthur Cohen, who turned his lack of Jewish upbringing into his motivation. What some Jews had instilled in them by their families, Cohen had to seek out on his own. And yet, even as a young thirty-something, he knew that he was not alone in his path to Judaism and that others might benefit from reading about his experience. Cohen explained that he decided to write his Introduction to Judaism essay because he realized his experiences "were fairly common: I come from a fundamentally unobservant Jewish home and my first religious inclination was to become a Christian."[90] In effect, Cohen, like other authors of the genre, let readers with tenuous connections to Jewishness know that they had company, and that there were resources available to them if they were interested in engaging with Judaism.

For readers, Introductions to Judaism were guides to learning about Jewish religion and to learning about oneself. In the twenty-first century, with more stories of celebrities converting to Judaism or tapping into its spiritual resources, it became clear that one did not need to be born Jewish to learn about Judaism and to learn about oneself through the resources of Judaism. Introductions to Judaism could illuminate the paths of all manner of seekers. What did Judaism offer a modern American life? Just as Joshua Loth Liebman found that question to be a winning formula for his 1946 bestselling *Peace of Mind*, so would future generations of writers, including Rabbi Harold Kushner, who wrote *When Bad Things Happen to Good People* (1981), and Sarah Hurwitz, author of *Here All Along* (2019).

At midcentury, Judaism became one of the "big three" American religions by virtue of fitting well enough into the religion category. Long after the "tri-faith" moment in American religious history had receded in the late 1960s, Judaism remained central in American culture because of what midcentury Jewish middlebrow genres achieved in normalizing Judaism and Jewishness, and because Jewishness continued to offer paths for exploring and developing personal identity. The midcentury Jewish middlebrow moment faded out during the last third of the twentieth century, as newer (and older) kinds of Jewish stories were embraced by American readers. Nonetheless, the next stage of Jewish stories bore the imprint of what the postwar era had accomplished. Having helped to make Judaism an American religion in the minds of Americans, the legacy of Jewish middlebrow culture would show up again and again in the stories of American Jews.

Conclusion

After the Middlebrow Moment

On a Sunday evening in early May 1976, a crowd gathered in the book-lined Manhattan apartment of Bel Kaufman.[1] The granddaughter of Sholem Aleichem, the Russian-Jewish creator of the *Tevye the Dairyman* stories that became *Fiddler on the Roof*, Kaufman hosted the time-honored tradition stipulated in her grandfather's will. The famous writer requested that his stories be read every year on the anniversary of his 1916 death to his friends and descendants. Readings in any language were acceptable. In 1976, in Kaufman's Park Avenue apartment, only one Sholem Aleichem story was read in English. Otherwise, "the night still belonged to Yiddish."[2] Among the guests who read in Yiddish that evening was Herman Wouk.

"I read it with love, so I don't want to apologize for it. But I was a little concerned whether I could do well," Wouk remarked of his Yiddish.[3] As it happened, Kaufman was delighted with his performance. "I think the fact that Herman Wouk read a Yiddish story is an important statement," she told the *New York Times*.[4]

And it was symbolic that Wouk should read in Yiddish because he was so representative of the midcentury middlebrow moment. Almost twenty years after he wrote *This Is My God*, and after the midcentury heyday of the anti-antisemitism and Introduction to Judaism genres, Americans valued different kinds of Jewish books and stories. Instead of the middlebrow presentations of Judaism as a modern American religion, the Jewish stories popular in the 1970s often looked backward in time, toward Eastern European Jewishness.

Judaism as a religion had become a nearly taken-for-granted fact, an idea that faded into the background as Jews, like other Americans, gravitated toward stories about their ethnic roots. By 1976, as Americans celebrated the country's bicentennial, they were more than a decade into an ethnic revival that invited those of ancestries including Jewish, Italian, Polish, Greek, and African to celebrate their cultural heritage.[5] After the dawning of this age of ethnicity, anti-antisemitism and the presentation of Judaism as an American religion were no longer so vital to American Jewish popular culture as they were during the immediate postwar years.

As if taking cues from the phenomenal success of *Fiddler on the Roof*, American Jewish narratives increasingly provided readers with a view into the world of European-born grandparents.[6] As *Fiddler* opened its Broadway run in 1964, the show "gave Gentile post-McCarthy America—and the world—the Jews it could, and wanted to love," Alisa Solomon observes. "It gave Jews nothing less than a publicly touted touchstone for authenticity."[7] Midcentury Jewish middlebrow culture had prepared American audiences for the old-country Judaism of *Fiddler*, and for the more ethnic Jewish literary explorations that followed. One prominent example of the latter was Irving Howe's National Book Award–winning *World of Our Fathers: The Journey of the East European Jews to America and the Life They Found and Made* (1976). Like *Fiddler*, *World of Our Fathers* reminded Americans that the Eastern European Jewish backgrounds that so many Jews of the first half of the twentieth century had tried to hide contained a rich ethnic heritage. This "Yiddish flavor," as a reviewer observed, was one that all Americans, newly awakened to the value of ethnicity, could finally appreciate.[8]

Some of the authors of midcentury Jewish middlebrow shifted to writing in these ethnic modalities in the last third of the twentieth century. When the *New York Times* checked in with seventy-nine-year-old Laura Z. Hobson in the summer of 1979, she explained that her new novel *Above and Beyond* "explores the complexities of being Jewish in America," among three generations of an American family.[9] It was a definite shift from her *Gentleman's Agreement* days when, according to reviewers, Hobson's focus on gentile characters evidenced too little concern with the complexities of the Jewish experience. But even earlier, in 1964, the same year as *Fiddler*'s Broadway premiere, Hobson's novel *First Papers* portrayed characters clearly based on her Russian-born parents. In their glowing review, *Life* magazine could not resist introducing the novelist with her full Russian-Jewish identity: "Michael Zametkin's daughter Laura has written her most autobiographical and therefore best novel."[10] Margaret Halsey was also looking more closely at her roots. Her 1977 book *No Laughing Matter: The Autobiography of a WASP* opened with these lines: "We have heard a great deal from Jewish writers about what it means to come from a Jewish background, but so far not much has been written about growing up WASP."[11] The Jewish literary trend of exploring ethno-religious-cultural roots was making an impact on other kinds of writers. Wouk, too, turned inward, writing more autobiographically than ever in his 1985 novel *Inside, Outside* about a Russian-Jewish family's efforts to get ahead in America. After the midcentury middlebrow moment had done its work in making *anti*-antisemitism central to good Americanism and promoting the idea that Judaism was an American religion, the American Jewish literary focus moved on.

The legacies of the anti-antisemitism and Introduction to Judaism genres are evident in the choices of late twentieth-century American Jews. When Wouk joined the group of Yiddish storytellers in Kaufman's apartment, he, like other Jews who opted for ethnic modalities, was enacting a relatively new kind of privilege. Accepted as a mainstream white American—in part because of the success of midcentury anti-antisemitism and Introduction to Judaism texts—a Jew and celebrity like Wouk could embody ethnic Jewishness in the 1970s without fear of tainting his Americanness. Indeed, by the last decades of the twentieth century, ethnicity seemed to prove Americanness.[12] It was an era when presidential candidates from Kennedy and Nixon to Reagan and Dukakis leveraged ethnicity to make their pitch to Americans, as Matthew Jacobson has shown.[13] Advocates of the country's ethnic revival of the 1960s and 1970s made the case for diversity as an essential ingredient of American society. Ethnic trends were also felt in literary culture. Railing against the melting-pot model of assimilation, literary critic Alfred Kazin, with Irish-American novelist James Farrell at his side, argued that ethnic identity had "contributed more creative power to American life and literature than any dream of a melting pot."[14] Kazin told City College students at a 1972 conference on "The Heritage and Identity of Ethnic Groups in New York" that he had grown up among people "with an exaggerated respect for American—meaning Anglo-Saxon—culture." But by the 1970s, Kazin recognized that "the melting pot was essentially an Anglo-Saxon effort to rub out the past of others." Kazin did not reflect on whether lessons of the Holocaust had affected his view of Anglo-Saxon culture. But it is hard to ignore the racist harm that Kazin described as endemic to the melting-pot ideal, and its parallel to Hitler's goals of obliterating races of people.

By the last third of the twentieth century, the idea that Judaism was an American religion felt less relevant as more Americans looked to both Israel and Europe for what some referred to as authentic Judaism. Susannah Heschel observes that "America was no longer a place where Judaism could be nurtured and experience a renaissance; instead, America was enticing Jews to assimilate and intermarry. . . . In a reversal of the earlier American

CONCLUSION: AFTER THE MIDDLEBROW MOMENT

Jewish attitude, Europe was no longer viewed as a place of confinement, but as a source of inspiration that would rescue American Judaism from what was felt to be its moribund state."[15] Mining their European roots was one way American Jewish writers attempted to inject authenticity into their books and essays.

Many observers felt that Jews and Judaism had become accepted, and as a result, so assimilated, watered down, and bland, that the immediate postwar years in suburbia and away from the thickly religious urban enclaves of first settlement were often regarded with disdain and regret, by Jews. If only 1950s Jews had not opted for paths of assimilation and suburban comfort, the argument went, they might have retained their edge, allowing them to be stronger allies to other marginalized groups.[16] The 1950s civil rights movement spurred such criticism, as Jews charged each other with fleeing from urban problems.[17] Jews were "running from the cities to the suburbs and carrying their temples with them because of a purported invasion of white neighborhoods by nonwhites," a Jewish lawyer and member of the National Commission on Social Action for Reform Judaism told the *New York Times* in 1959.[18] The cultural work that midcentury Jewish middlebrow had done to position Jews as respectable, white, middle-class Americans took on a more problematic cast in light of shifting national ideas about race.

Postwar comfort also raised spiritual anxieties. Toward the end of *This Is My God*, Wouk expressed concern for what would become of American Jews on the suburban frontier: "There will be no death camps in the United States that we live in," he wrote. But there was a different kind of threat of Jewish oblivion in America. "It is the threat of pleasantly vanishing down a broad highway at the wheel of a high-powered station wagon, with the golf clubs piled in the back."[19] The comfort of American Jewish life now seemed to pose the greatest danger to continued Jewish existence. A famous 1964 *Look* magazine article, "The Vanishing American Jew," pointed to increasing rates of intermarriage as a reason for Jews' eventual disappearance.[20] In its way, midcentury middlebrow culture had helped to create that comfort through its reassuring portrayals of American Jews.

What midcentury Jewish middlebrow left in its wake was thus a mixed bag. Fortitude could be found in watching Gregory Peck and Frank Sinatra stand up for Jews and condemn antisemitism. And when popular culture portrayed Jewish religious life positively, Americans could more easily embrace Judaism as part of their religious landscape.

But the further in time one stood from these books and magazine articles, the more difficult it became to recognize their cultural significance. They became relics of the past, and a past that is still being judged harshly for its assimilationist tendencies.[21]

Few of the middlebrow texts at the heart of this book would meet a kind reception from later critics and scholars, if they were given attention at all. Instead, they became part of personal canons, touchstones in the lives of individuals who lived through the mid-twentieth century. They helped to usher Jews out of formerly defeatist attitudes and toward more secure and positive Jewish identities. As the reviews and letters from readers in *Postwar Stories* demonstrate, magazine articles and books about Judaism, novels and films tackling antisemitism and prejudice—all offered lifelines to individuals who were heartened upon discovering an assemblage of popular culture that reflected an image of Jews and Judaism as accepted, mainstream, and flourishing.

In addition to this affirming role, Jewish middlebrow culture provided inspiration for the imaginations of writers, artists, and photographers who discovered, in their own experiences and memories of this era, material to rebel against, argue with, criticize, satirize, and supersede. The glories of postwar American Jewish literature—acclaimed fiction by Saul Bellow, Grace Paley, Philip Roth, Cynthia Ozick, Bernard Malamud, and others—are not counted among the middlebrow titles. The celebration of this cohort of American Jewish writers largely occurred in a generation overlapping with and following midcentury Jewish middlebrow.[22] Whereas Jewish middlebrow worked to create an early midcentury stage, widely introducing Jews and Judaism as middle class and American, by the last third of the twentieth century, Roth, Bellow, and other writers bore witness to an era that saw even greater Jewish acceptance.

At times, many of the names and titles from this middlebrow past were reduced to punchlines in jokes about postwar Jewish life. But in their day, they were much more, widening the horizons of readers and viewers. In the wake of destruction, and at the dawn of creating new phases of Jewish life, these middlebrow texts allowed Jews to see themselves and their religion as reassuringly familiar, worthy of respect, normal, and most important, American. This culture also enabled Americans to understand and feel connected to people and traditions that had once seemed exotic and alien, if not subhuman. The work of midcentury middlebrow genres was very much tied to its historical moment—a time when Jews were becoming middle-class consumers, and when Americans sought to claim their moral distance from Nazis. It was an era when Americans were beginning to look more sympathetically at a group which had been hunted like animals. In the coming decades, Jews and Judaism would not need to be introduced to Americans in quite the same way as they had at midcentury. So it would be difficult, in retrospect, to understand just what it meant to celebrate bestselling novels exposing American antisemitism, or to see a Jewish woman on the cover of *Life* magazine blessing Sabbath candles. Looking back, it would become tempting to dismiss all of this as "just middlebrow." But to those who lived through the midcentury, these texts were powerful, as they helped to usher in a time when Americans began to understand the importance of integrating without obscuring the religious particularities of those outside the white, Christian power structure.

The genres at the center of this book illuminate midcentury Jewish desires and imaginations. What once seemed impossible—non-Jews seeking to understand the marginalization of Jews, or a Jew explaining his religion with self-respect in the pages of a national magazine—had become reality. Midcentury middlebrow Jewish culture shows us how much has changed over time. And for those who feel inspired by it, it reveals how much still needs to change.

Notes

Introduction

1. Laura Z. Hobson, *Gentleman's Agreement* (New York: Simon & Schuster, 1947), 63.
2. The high temperature on Sunday, February 1, 1948, was 24 degrees. Boston area was at https://www.weather.gov/wrh/Climate?wfo=box.
3. Andrew Heinze, "Peace of Mind (1946): Judaism and the Therapeutic Polemics of Postwar America," *Religion and American Culture: A Journal of Interpretation* 12, no. 1 (Winter 2002): 31–58.
4. Joshua Loth Liebman, "Gentleman's Agreement," Addresses Broadcast by Stations WBZ and WBZA Sunday Morning, February 1 and February 15, 1948, from Temple Israel, Boston. Published and distributed by the Brotherhood of Temple Israel. Harvard University Widener Library, Judaica Collection.
5. Joshua Liebman, *Peace of Mind* (New York: Simon & Schuster, 1946), 9.
6. On how religions become "American Religions," see Catherine Albanese, "Exchanging Selves, Exchanging Souls: Contact, Combination, and American Religious History," in *Retelling U.S. Religious History*, ed. Thomas Tweed (Berkeley: University of California Press, 1997), 203. On Judaism becoming an American religion, see Tisa Wenger, *Religious Freedom: The Contested History of an American Ideal* (Chapel Hill: University of North Carolina Press, 2017), 171.
7. On America as a "tri-faith" nation, see Kevin Schultz, *Tri-Faith America: How Catholics and Jews Held Postwar America to Its Protestant Promise* (New York: Oxford University Press, 2011). Ronit Stahl, "A Jewish America and a Protestant Civil Religion: Will Herberg, Robert Bellah, and Mid-Twentieth Century American Religion," *Religions* 6, no. 2 (2015): 434–450. On the greater popularity of "tri-faith," rather than Judeo-Christian, discourse among New York rabbis after Pearl Harbor, see K. Healan Gaston, *Imagining Judeo-Christian America* (Chicago: Chicago University Press, 2019), 101, 119.
8. Sally Bedell Smith, *In All His Glory: The Life and Times of William S. Paley and the Birth of Modern Broadcasting* (New York: Simon & Schuster, 1947), 281.
9. "At Home & Abroad," *Time*, January 5, 1948, 40. On Americans' television-owning habits, see the 1949 Gallup poll #441, question QN14a. When asked, "Do you happen to have a television set in your own home?" 95 percent said no.
10. On Americans' moviegoing habits, see Joel Finler, *The Hollywood Story* (New York: WallFlower Press, 2003), 378; James T. Patterson, *Grand Expectations: The United States, 1945–1974* (New York: Oxford University Press, 1997), 12; Michelle Pautz, "The Decline in Average Weekly Cinema Attendance, 1930–2000," *Political Science Faculty Publications* 25 (Summer 2002), https://ecommons.udayton.edu/

cgi/viewcontent.cgi?article=1023&context=pol_fac_pub. According to Gallup Brain, which compiles Gallup polling data from the 1930s forward, over 12 percent of Americans answered that they went to the movies four or five times a month in 1944. On the Production code's guidelines for twin beds for married couples: Thomas Doherty, *Hollywood's Censor: Joseph I. Breen and the Production Code Administration* (New York: Columbia University Press), 273.
11. James A. Jerauld, "'Gentleman's Agreement' An Exceptional Picture," *Boxoffice*, November 15, 1947, 28-A.
12. Stephen J. Whitfield, *The Culture of the Cold War* (Baltimore: Johns Hopkins University Press, 1996).
13. William Zinsser, *A Family of Readers: An Informal Portrait of the Book-of-the Month Club and Its Members on the Occasion of Its 60th Anniversary* (New York: Book of the Month Club, 1986), 54.
14. "National Affairs," *Time*, January 5, 1948, 20.
15. Frederick Lewis Allen, *The Big Change: America Transforms Itself* (New York: Harper & Brothers, 1952), 200–202.
16. Allen, *The Big Change*, 201.
17. Elaine Tyler May, *Homeward Bound: American Families in the Cold War Era*, 4th ed. (New York: Basic Books, 2017), 1–2. Wini Breines, *Young, White, and Miserable: Growing Up Female in the Fifties* (Chicago: University of Chicago Press, 1992), 4–6.
18. Patterson, *Grand Expectations*, 65, 70.
19. U.S. Bureau of the Census, *Statistical Abstract of the United States: 1980* (Washington, DC: Government Printing Office, 1980), 60. Cited in Robert Wuthnow, *After Heaven*, 36.
20. "National Affairs," *Time*, January 5, 1948, 20.
21. "National Affairs," 20.
22. Patterson, *Grand Expectations*, 20–21.
23. "G.L.K. Smith Nominated: Christian Nationalist Party Asks," *New York Times*, August 22, 1948, 46; Elizabeth Dias, "The Far-Right Christian Quest for Power: 'We are Seeing Them Emboldened,'" *New York Times*, July 8, 2022, A1.
24. "Religion," *Time*, March 15, 1948, 56.
25. "The Cushing Sisters," *Life*, August 11, 1947, 41.
26. "Mrs. William Paley Wears Polished Black Broadcloth," *Vogue* 110, no. 5 (September 1, 1947): 181.
27. Smith, *In All His Glory*, 332–334.
28. On the history of this social antisemitism, see Britt Tevis, "'Jews Not Admitted': Anti-Semitism, Civil Rights, and Public Accommodation Laws," *Journal of American History* 107, no. 4 (March 2021): 847–870.
29. Donald Young, *American Minority Peoples* (New York: Harper & Brothers, 1932), 296. On Jews' whiteness during the 1930s and 1940s, see Eric Goldstein, *The Price of Whiteness: Jews, Race, and American Identity* (Princeton, NJ: Princeton University Press, 2006).

30. Betty Smith, *A Tree Grows in Brooklyn* (1943), 19. On the popularity of *A Tree Grows in Brooklyn* among the Armed Services, see Molly Guptill Manning, *When Books Went to War: The Stories That Helped Us Win World War II* (New York: Mariner Books, 2015).
31. Jeffrey Alexander, "On the Social Construction of Moral Universals: The 'Holocaust' from War Crime to Trauma Drama," *European Journal of Social Theory* 5, no. 11 (2002): 13–16.
32. On Jews as problem during the first decades of the twentieth century, see Goldstein, *Price of Whiteness*, 119.
33. On nineteenth-century remaking of Judaism into an American religion: Zev Eleff, *Who Rules the Synagogue? Religious Authority and the Formation of American Judaism* (New York: Oxford, 2016); Shari Rabin, *Jews on the Frontier: Religion and Mobility in Nineteenth-Century America* (New York: NYU Press, 2017); Jonathan Sarna, *American Judaism* (New Haven, CT: Yale University Press, 2004); Steven Weisman, *The Chosen Wars: How Judaism Became an American Religion* (New York: Simon & Schuster, 2018); Laura Yares, *Jewish Sunday Schools: Teaching Religion in Nineteenth Century America* (New York: NYU Press, 2023).
34. Wendy Wall, *Inventing the American Way: The Politics of Consensus from the New Deal to the Civil Rights Movement* (New York: Oxford University Press, 2008); Kevin Kruse, *One Nation under God: How Corporate America Invented Christian America* (New York: Basic Books, 2015); Schultz, *Tri-Faith America*.
35. On nineteenth-century Reformers' motivations, see Hasia Diner, *A Time for Gathering: The Second Migration, 1820–1880* (Baltimore: Johns Hopkins University Press, 1995), 117. On limited religious pluralism as a hallmark of postwar America, see Schultz, *Tri-Faith America*, 74.
36. Charles Bezalel Sherman, *The Jew within American Society: A Study in Ethnic Individuality* (Detroit: Wayne State University Press, 1961), 73, 132.
37. Howard Sachar, *A History of the Jews in America* (New York: Knopf, 1992), 125.
38. Michael Meyer, *Response to Modernity: A History of the Reform Movement in Judaism* (Detroit: Wayne State University Press, 1988), 319–324.
39. Sherman, *The Jew within American Society*, 211–212; Nathan Glazer, *American Judaism* (Chicago: University of Chicago Press, 1957), 128, 130–131. Relatedly, the 1956 *American Jewish Year Book* reported on a 1955 "nation-wide attack on 'adult Jewish illiteracy'" planned by the National Women's League of the United Synagogue of America. Jacob Sloan, "Communal Affairs: Religion," *American Jewish Year Book*, vol. 57 (Philadelphia: Jewish Publication Society, 1956), 198–200.
40. Paul Cowan, *An Orphan in History: One Man's Triumphant Search for His Jewish Roots* (New York: Doubleday, 1982).
41. Richard Shepard, "Books: A Writer's Homecoming," *New York Times*, January 6, 1983, C18.
42. Ann Birstein, *The Rabbi on 47th Street* (New York: Dial Press, 1982).
43. Josh Lambert, *Jewish Literary Mafia: Jews, Publishing, and Postwar American Literature* (New Haven, CT: Yale University Press, 2022), 27.

44. David D. Kirkpatrick, "The Book of the Month Club Tries to Be More of the Moment," *New York Times*, June 28, 2001, 59. Janice Radway, *A Feeling for Books: The Book-of-the-Month Club, Literary Taste, and Middle-Class Desire* (Chapel Hill: University of North Carolina Press, 1999).
45. "How to Get Rid of an Inferiority Complex," *Life*, October 25, 1937, 5. See also Adam Kirsch, "The 'Five-foot Shelf' Reconsidered," *Harvard Magazine*, November–December 2001, https://www.harvardmagazine.com/2001/11/the-five-foot-shelf-reco.html.
46. Al Silverman, "A Fragile Pleasure," *Daedalus* 112, no. 1 (Winter 1983): 39.
47. Edward Larocque-Tinker, "New Editions, Fine & Otherwise," *New York Times*, May 29, 1938.
48. Ray Walters, "1945: The First 'Instant' Paperback," *New York Times*, April 30, 1989, 96. On the paperback revolution: Jeremy Lewis, *Penguin Special: The Story of Allen Lane, the Founder of Penguin Books and the Man Who Changed Publishing Forever* (New York: Penguin, 2005); Manning, *When Books Went to War*; Kenneth Davis, *Two-Bit Culture: The Paperbacking of America* (Boston: Houghton Mifflin, 1984).
49. Clive Thompson, "The Revolutionary Effect of the Paperback Book," *Smithsonian Magazine*, May 2013, https://www.smithsonianmag.com/arts-culture/the-revolutionary-effect-of-the-paperback-book-36209689/.
50. Matthew Hedstrom, *The Rise of Liberal Religion: Book Culture and American Spirituality in the Twentieth Century* (New York: Oxford University Press, 2012), 5.
51. Amy Hungerford, *Postmodern Belief: American Literature and Religion since 1960* (Princeton, NJ: Princeton University Press, 2010), 1.
52. Whitfield, *The Culture of the Cold War*, 86.
53. Wall, *Inventing the American Way*, 79–80. Andrew Preston, *Sword of Spirit, Shield of Faith: Religion in American War and Diplomacy* (New York: Anchor, 2012), 412.
54. Gallup Poll #602, Field date: 07/30/1958–08/04/1958.
55. Douglas Miller and Marion Nowak, *The Fifties: The Way We Really Were* (Garden City: Doubleday, 1977), 90. Elinor Goulding Smith's 1956 *Harper's* essay about being afraid to declare her atheist identity evidences this thinking that good Americans needed to be religious Americans. Elinor Goulding Smith, "Why Won't Somebody Tolerate Me?" *Harper's* (August 1956), 36–38.
56. Hungerford, *Postmodern Belief*, 2.
57. Hobson, *Agreement*, 155.
58. Judith E. Smith, *Visions of Belonging: Family Stories, Popular Culture, and Postwar Democracy, 1960–1960* (New York: Columbia University Press, 2004), 140.
59. On American religion as *white* religion, see Emily Clark, "Nineteenth-Century New Orleans Voudou: An American Religion," *American Religion* 2, no. 1 (Fall 2020): 154.
60. On the post–World War II era as a period when religion was accentuated in American public life: Sydney E. Ahlstrom, *A Religious History of the American People*, 2nd ed. (New Haven, CT: Yale University Press, 2004), 950–963. Kruse, *One Nation under God*, xiv. Paul Harvey and Philip Goff, *The Columbia Documentary History of Religion in America since 1945* (New York: Columbia University Press, 2005), 6. Schultz, *Tri-Faith America*, 73–80. Will Herberg, *Protestant-Catholic-Jew: An Essay in American Religious Sociology* (New York: Doubleday, 1955), 1.

61. K. Healan Gaston, "The Cold War Romance of Religious Authority: Will Herberg, William F. Buckley Jr. and the Rise of the New Right," *Journal of American History* 99, no. 4 (March 2013): 1136. Tomoko Masuzawa, *The Invention of World Religions, or How European Universalism Was Preserved in the Language of Pluralism* (Chicago: University of Chicago Press, 2005), 28. Mark Silk, "Notes on the Judeo-Christian Tradition in America," *American Quarterly* 36, no. 1 (Spring 1984): 65–85, esp. 67–68. See also Mark Silk, *Spiritual Politics: Religion and America since World War II* (New York: Simon & Schuster, 1988), 40.

62. On the 1920s and 1930s as years of religious depression: Ahlstrom, *A Religious History of the American People*, 950. Beth Wenger, *New York Jews and the Great Depression: Uncertain Promise* (New Haven, CT: Yale University Press, 1996), chapter 7. Meyer, *Response to Modernity*, 296. Robert T. Handy, "The American Religious Depression, 1925–1935," *Church History* 29, no. 1 (March 1960): 3–16. On church membership rates changing during after the Depression, see Whitfield, *The Culture of the Cold War*, 83. For a different perspective on the way the Depression reinvigorated religion in the South, see Alison Greene, *No Depression in Heaven: The Great Depression, the New Deal, and the Transformation of Religion in the Delta* (Oxford: Oxford University Press, 2015).

63. For scholarly investigations of the changed postwar status of American Jews and Judaism, see Deborah Dash Moore, "Jewish GIs and the Creation of the Judeo-Christian Tradition," *Religion and American Culture: A Journal of Appreciation* 8, no. 1 (Winter 1998): 31–53; Silk, *Spiritual Politics*; Gaston, *Imagining Judeo-Christian America*; Schultz, *Tri-Faith America*; Joseph Blau, *Judaism in America: From Curiosity to Third Faith* (Chicago: Chicago History of American Religion, 1976).

64. Deborah Dash Moore and Kevin Schultz's scholarship does not discuss the postwar shift from an emphasis on Jews as racial group to Jews as religious group. Rather, their studies focus on the wartime and postwar process of Jews being recognized as part of Judeo-Christianity. Goldstein, *The Price of Whiteness*, is one of the few studies that examines Jews' midcentury transition from race.

65. Nathan Glazer, *American Judaism* (Chicago: University of Chicago Press, 1957), 1.

66. Glazer was not alone in making this observation about the change in status of American Judaism. See also Marshall Sklare and Ted Solotaroff, "Introduction," in *Jews in the Mind of America*, ed. Charles Stember (New York: Basic Books, 1966), 16. See also Alan Mintz, *Popular Culture and the Shaping of Holocaust Memory in America* (Seattle: University of Washington Press, 2012), 6.

67. Scholarship on Jews' changing midcentury racial status includes Goldstein, *The Price of Whiteness*, and Karen Brodkin, *How Jews Became White and What That Says about Race in America* (New Brunswick, NJ: Rutgers University Press, 1998).

68. The mid-twentieth century is not the only religion moment in the American Jewish experience. The nineteenth century also witnessed a religion moment for American Jews. See Shari Rabin, *Jews on the Frontier: Religion and Mobility in Nineteenth-Century America* (New York: New York University Press, 2017); Sarna, *American Judaism*, chapter 4; Jessica Cooperman, *Making Judaism Safe for America: World War I and the Origins of Religious Pluralism* (New York: New York University Press,

2018); Schultz, *Tri-Faith America*; Kraut, "A Wary Collaboration: Jews, Catholics, and the Protestant Goodwill Movement," in *Between the Times: The Travail of the Protestant Establishment in America, 1900-1960*, ed. William Hutchison (Cambridge: Cambridge University Press, 1989), 193-230.

69. Other recent studies that have analyzed similar engine-mirror dynamics between books and culture: June Cummins, *From Sarah to Sydney: The Woman Behind All-of-a-Kind Family* (New Haven, CT: Yale University Press, 2021); and Leah Garrett, *Young Lions: How Jewish Authors Reinvented the American War Novel* (Evanston, IL: Northwestern University Press, 2015).

70. On phrenology and middlebrow, see Christina Klein, *Cold War Orientalism: Asia in the Middlebrow Imagination, 1945-1961* (Berkeley: University of California Press, 2003), 64, Lawrence Levine, *Highbrow/Lowbrow: The Emergence of Cultural Hierarchy in America* (Cambridge, MA: Harvard University Press, 1988), 221-222.

71. Klein, *Cold War Orientalism*, 64.

72. Beth Driscoll, "The Middlebrow Family Resemblance: Features of the Historical and Contemporary Middlebrow," *Post45*, July 1, 2016.

73. Nicola Humble, *The Feminine Middlebrow Novel, 1920s to 1950s* (New York: Oxford University Press, 2001), 1.

74. Driscoll, "The Middlebrow Family Resemblance."

75. On the feminine as Jewish, see Daniel Boyarin, *Unheroic Conduct: The Rise of Heterosexuality and the Invention of the Jewish Man* (Berkeley: University of California Press, 1997); and Sander Gilman, *The Jew's Body* (New York: Routledge, 1991). On the emotional as Jewish, see Peter Novick, *That Noble Dream: The "Objectivity Question" and the American Historical Profession* (New York: Cambridge University Press, 1988), 172-174; and David Hollinger, *Science, Jews, and Secular Culture* (Princeton, NJ: Princeton University Press, 1996).

76. On the American roots of this Protestant disdain for displays of commercialism see Noam Maggor, *Brahmin Capitalism: Frontiers of Wealth and Populism in America's First Gilded Age* (Cambridge: Harvard University Press, 2017).

77. Russell Lynes, "Highbrow, Lowbrow, Middlebrow," *Harper's* (February 1949), 19-28; Russell Lynes, "Everyday Tastes from High-Brow to Low-Brow are Classified on Chart," *Life*, April 11, 1949, 99-101.

78. Russell Lynes, "Highbrow, Lowbrow, Middlebrow" (reprint of the 1949 essay), *Wilson Quarterly* 1, no. 1 (Autumn 1976): 147.

79. Reviews of these books as popular/middlebrow by highbrow writers/publications: on Milton Steinberg's *Basic Judaism*: "Books in Brief," *Jewish Spectator* (November 1947), 31; Irving Kristol, "How Basic Is 'Basic Judaism'?" *Commentary* (January 1, 1948), 27-34. On Liebman's *Peace of Mind*: "The Year in Books," *Time*, December 16, 1946, 108. On *Gentleman's Agreement*: Diana Trilling, "America without Distinction," review of Laura Hobson's *Gentleman's Agreement*, *Commentary* (March 1947), 290-292.

80. Rebecca Davis, *Public Confessions: The Religious Conversions That Changed American Politics* (Chapel Hill: University of North Carolina Press, 2021), 94. Riv-Ellen Prell, *Fighting to Be Americans: Assimilation and the Trouble between Jewish Women and Jewish Men* (Boston: Beacon Press, 2000), 127.

81. For examples of how popular culture figures into histories of post–World War II American Jews and Judaism, see Sarna, *American Judaism*; Garrett, *Young Lions*; Matthew Silver, *Our Exodus: Leon Uris and the Americanization of Israel's Founding Story* (Detroit: Wayne State University Press, 2010); Jeffrey Shandler, *Entertaining America: Jews, Movies, and Broadcasting* (Princeton, NJ: Princeton University Press, 2003); Shandler, *Jews, God, and Videotape: Religion and Media in America* (New York: New York University Press, 2012).
82. On the dismissal of middlebrow as generic and conventional, see Lauren Berlant, *The Female Complaint: The Unfinished Business of Sentimentality in American Culture* (Durham, NC: Duke University Press, 2008), chapter six.
83. Virginia Woolf, "Middlebrow," in *The Death of the Moth* (London: Hogarth Press, 1942), 113–119.
84. Louis Finkelstein, "Foreword," in *The Jews: Their History, Culture, and Religion* (New York: JPS, 1949), xxii.
85. Richard Breitman and Alan Lichtman, *FDR and the Jews* (Cambridge, MA: Harvard University Press, 2013), 173–174, 181, 186, 189. Peter Novick, *The Holocaust in American Life* (Boston: Houghton Mifflin, 2000), 27–28, 51.
86. Deborah Lipstadt, *Beyond Belief: The American Press and the Coming of the Holocaust, 1933–1945* (New York: Touchstone, 1986), 257, 262.
87. Jaime Harker, *America, the Middlebrow: Women's Novels, Progressivism, and Middlebrow Authorship between the Wars* (Amherst: University of Massachusetts Press, 2007), 19.
88. On what sentimental education involved: Christina Klein, *Cold War Orientalism: Asia in the Middlebrow Imagination, 1945–1961* (Berkeley: University of California Press, 2003), 14.
89. Lila Corwin Berman, *Speaking of Jews: Rabbis, Intellectuals, and the Creation of an American Public Identity* (Berkeley: University of California Press, 2009), 1.
90. Not until the last third of the twentieth century did ethnic Jewishness, as constructed by midcentury Jewish social scientists such as Nathan Glazer and Oscar Handlin, gain wider currency as part of a nationwide ethnic revival, and manifest in American popular culture. Matthew Jacobson, *Roots Too: White Ethnic Revival in Post–Civil Rights America* (Cambridge, MA: Harvard University Press, 2004), 4.
91. On fiction providing greater access to interior lives than nonfiction, see Rita Felski, *The Uses of Literature* (New York: Wiley-Blackwell, 2008), 89–93.
92. On Western definitions of religion that rely on Protestantism as a standard, see Jason Nongbri, *Before Religion, A History of a Modern Concept* (New Haven, CT: Yale University Press, 2013); Talal Asad, *Genealogies of Religion: Discipline and Reasons of Power in Christianity and Islam* (Baltimore: Johns Hopkins University Press, 1993), 27–54; Bruce Lincoln, *Holy Terrors: Thinking about Religion after September 11*, 2nd ed. (Chicago: University of Chicago Press, 2006).
93. Maura Farrelly, "Protestant-Catholic Ecumenism and the Meanings of American Freedom," in *The Cambridge Companion to American Protestantism*, ed. Jason E. Vickers and Jennifer Woodruff Tait (New York: Cambridge University Press, 2022), 277–296; Maura Farrelly, *Anti-Catholicism in America, 1620–1860*

(New York: Cambridge University Press, 2018); Stringfellow Bar, *American Catholics; A Protestant-Jewish View* (New York: Sheed & Ward, 1959), 79–80; Preston, *Sword of Spirit, Shield of Faith*, 413.

94. Walter Russell Mead, *The Arc of a Covenant: The United States, Israel, and the Fate of the Jewish People* (New York: Knopf, 2022), 162.

95. Many thanks to Josh Lambert for helping me fill out the archive of 1940s anti-antisemitism novels. As Lambert writes of antisemitism during the 1940s, "Many novels treated the phenomenon centrally, including Gwethalyn Graham's *Earth and High Heaven* (1944), Arthur Miller's *Focus* (1945), Jo Sinclair's *Wasteland* (1946), Abraham Bernstein's *Home Is the Hunted* (1947), Laura Z. Hobson's *Gentleman's Agreement* (1947), and Saul Bellow's *The Victim* (1947). So did many notable plays and films of the period, including Ernst Lubitsch's *To Be or Not to Be* (1942), Arthur Laurents's *Home of the Brave* (1945), Edward Dmytryk's *Crossfire* (1947), Darryl Zanuck's film adaptation of *Gentleman's Agreement* (1948), and Mark Robson's 1949 film adaptation of Laurents's play." Josh Lambert, "Fictions of Anti-Semitism and the Beginning of Holocaust Literature," in *American Literature in Transition, 1940–1950*, ed. Christopher Vials (Cambridge: Cambridge University Press, 2017), 44–45. The 1950 *American Jewish Year Book* listed the following novels with antisemitism themes: George Abbe, *Mr. Quill's Crusade* (1948); Sylvia Chatfield Bates, *The Weather Breeder* (1948); Jean Beressy, *Walk in Darkness* (1948); Kay Boyle, *His Human Majesty* (1949); Bianca Bradbury, *The Curious Wine* (1948); John Burns, *Lucifer with a Book* (1949); Allen Chase, *Shadow of a Hero* (1949); Haakon Chevalier, *For Us the Living* (1949); Alex Comfort, *On This Side Nothing* (1949); Burke Davis, *Whisper My Name* (1949); Ralph Freedman, *Divided, a Novel* (1948); Martha Gellhorn, *The Wine of Astonishment* (1948); Ludwig Lewisohn, *The Vehement Flame: The Story of Stephen Escott* (1948); Jean-Paul Sartre, *The Wall and Other Stories* (1948); Joel Sayre, *The House without a Roof* (1948); Daniel Taylor, *The Move with the Sun* (1948). Lambert, *Literary Mafia*, 39.

96. A 1963 article in *Time* listed Introductions to Judaism books including Basic Judaism and Morris Kertzer's *What Is a Jew?* As part of Elizabeth Taylor's conversion study. "Religion: Convert," *Time*, April 6, 1959, 81. The Goodreads.com profile for Steinberg's *Basic Judaism* evidences the book's usage in religion courses and for those considering conversion; https://www.goodreads.com/book/show/1077452.Basic_Judaism. Similarly, the posts for Wouk's Introduction to Judaism, *This Is My God*, show the book used in religion courses and by converts: https://www.goodreads.com/book/show/106316.This_is_My_God. A decade after the publication of his Introduction to Judaism essay, "What the Jews Believe," in *Life* magazine, Rabbi Philip Bernstein wrote to *Life*: "It has been used for religious instruction for converts like Elizabeth Taylor, Marilyn Monroe, and Sammy Davis. It is a reference book on Judaism in the colleges and universities where Comparative Religion is taught. Etc. etc." Philip Bernstein to Edward Thompson, April 14, 1960, Bernstein papers, Box 6 Publications What the Jews the Jews Believe, Folder 5: Correspondence, University of Rochester. On *Basic Judaism* as a standard text for converts, see Ruth Hanna Sachs, *Life with Ruth: A Collection of Personal Essays* (Las Vegas: Exclamation Publishers, 2002), 3.

97. Trude Weis-Rosmarin, activist, editor, and sole author of an early midcentury Introduction to Judaism book, *Judaism and Christianity: the Differences* (1943), is one of the exceptions, as are Tamar de Sola Pool, who coauthored midcentury books about Judaism with her husband David, and Bertie Schwartz, who coauthored *Faith through Reason: A Modern Interpretation of Judaism* (1946) with her husband, Charles.
98. Edith A. Steinberg, "Midwife to a Novel," undated, Box 10, folder 4: Writings-Other-short stories of the Steinberg Family, undated, 1938, Milton Steinberg P-369 Collection of American Jewish Historical Society, New York, NY.
99. On male domination in midcentury American religion, see Matthew Hedstrom, "Psychology and Mysticism in 1940s Religion," in *Religion and the Culture of Print in Modern America*, ed. Charles L. Cohen and Paul S. Boyer (Madison: University of Wisconsin Press, 2008), 258.
100. On the Cold War masculinity of *This Is My God*, see Rachel Gordan, "Alfred Kinsey and the Remaking of Jewish Sexuality in the Wake of the Holocaust," *Jewish Social Studies* 20, no. 3 (Spring/Summer 2014): 72–99.
101. Herman Wouk, *Marjorie Morningstar* (New York: Doubleday, 1955), 69.
102. On the history of the sentimental novel and its association with white, women writers beginning in the nineteenth century, see Shirley Samuels, "Sentimentalism and Domestic Fiction," *Oxford Bibliographies Online* (2012). On how nineteenth-century origins of sentimental literature initiated a pattern of giving women moral authority, see Jane Tompkins, *Sensational Designs: The Cultural Work of American Fiction, 1790–1860* (New York: Oxford University Press, 1985), chapter 5. Gregory Jay, *White Writers, Race Matters: Fictions of Racial Liberalism from Stowe to Stockett* (New York: Oxford University Press, 2018), 74–75.
103. This book complements the work of historians examining the efforts of Jewish organizations such as the American Jewish Committee, the Anti-Defamation League, and the American Jewish Congress, in combating antisemitism at midcentury, including: Marc Dollinger, *Quest for Inclusion: Jews and Liberalism in Modern America* (Princeton, NJ: Princeton University Press, 2000); and Stuart Svonkin, *Jews against Prejudice* (New York: Columbia University Press, 1999). While both Dollinger and Svonkin showed how Jewish communal leaders made their liberalism central to American politics, *Postwar Stories* shows how middlebrow literature helped open a midcentury national conversation about antisemitism and Judaism as an America religion.
104. David Michaelis, *Eleanor* (New York: Simon & Schuster, 2020), 137.
105. See the index of the Eleanor Roosevelt Papers, Digital Edition, at the GWU website https://erpapers.columbian.gwu.edu/my-day for ER's column's addressing racism and antisemitism.
106. Raymond Clapper, "Mrs. Roosevelt Sees No Evil," *Liberty*, April 4, 1942, 11.
107. Eleanor Roosevelt, "My Day, December 16, 1941," The Eleanor Roosevelt Papers Digital Edition (2017).
108. Eleanor Roosevelt, "My Day," December 9, 1947, The Eleanor Roosevelt Papers, Digital Edition, GWU, https://www2.gwu.edu/~erpapers/myday/displaydoc.cfm?_y=1947&_f=md000831.

214 NOTES

109. On Yezierska reimagining "the Jewish immigrant for the American middlebrow readers of the early twentieth century," see Lisa Botshon, "Anzia Yezierska and the Marketing of the Jewish Immigrant in 1920s Hollywood," in *Middlebrow Moderns: Popular American Women Writers of the 1920s*, ed. Lisa Botshon and Meredith Goldsmith (Boston: Northeastern University Press, 2003), 203–224.
110. Orville Prescott, "Books of the Time," *New York Times*, September 11, 1950, 21.
111. I am grateful to Professor Wendy Zierler of Hebrew Union College for calling my attention to earlier instances of American Jewish middlebrow culture. Edna Ferber, Anzia Yezierska, Mary Antin, and Sidney Nyberg are Jewish writers, during the first half of the twentieth century, who achieved bestseller status, or close to it. Similar to Hobson, a generation later, Ferber is already using anthropology in her fiction, to push the conversation away from Jewishness as race to Jewishness as religion. Lawrence R. Rodgers, "Introduction," in *Fanny Herself* (Urbana: University of Illinois Press, 2001), xi.
112. On Emma Wolf, see Lori Harrison-Kahan, *Heirs of Yesterday* (Detroit: Wayne State University Press, 2020).
113. On the heightened postwar popularity of the Judeo-Christian tradition, see Gaston, *Imagining Judeo-Christian America*, part 2; Schultz, *Tri-Faith America*.
114. A prominent example of Jews sensing this possibility is found in Louis Marshall and Henry Ford's exchange over the latter's apology for his public antisemitism. See Victoria Saker Woeste, *Henry Ford's War on Jews and the Legal Battle against Hate Speech* (Stanford, CA: Stanford University Press, 2012).
115. Mead, *Arc of a Covenant*, 160.
116. Television producer Norman Lear's TV show *The Jeffersons*, which ran from 1975 to 1985, was an earlier show that featured an upper-middle-class Black family. Unlike the Cosbys, the Jeffersons were not of the educated professional class.
117. Felski, *The Uses of Literature*, 9.
118. Charles Taylor, *Multiculturalism: Examining the Politics of Recognition* (Princeton, NJ: Princeton University Press, 1994), 64, 25.
119. Melani McAlister, *Epic Encounters: Culture, Media, and U.S. Interests in the Middle East since 1945* (Berkeley: University of California Press, 2005). This effect of popular culture on public awareness is also central to Jeffrey Shandler, *While American Watches: Televising the Holocaust* (Oxford, 2000).
120. *The American Jewish Year Book* registered the new prominence of Jewish popular culture as early as 1950, as Jonathan Sarna and Jonathan Golden observed, as *AJYB* subject headings such as "Films," and "Radio and Television" "reflected a growing appreciation for the significance of popular culture." Jonathan Sarna and Jonathan Golden, "The Twentieth Century through American Jewish Eyes: A History of the American Jewish Year Book, 1899–1999," *American Jewish Year Book 2000*, 51.
121. Sklare and Solotaroff, "Introduction," in *Jews in the Mind of America*, 4.
122. By the late 1960s, academics and intellectuals, especially, noted the problems of the Judeo-Christian tradition. Sklare and Solotaroff, *Jews in the Mind of America*, 24. Also, Arthur A. Cohen's *The Myth of the Judeo-Christian Tradition and Other Dissenting Essays* (New York: Schocken Books, 1971); Eugene Borowitz, *The*

Mask Jews Wear: The Self-Deceptions of American Jewry (New York: Simon & Schuster, 1973).
123. Arthur A. Cohen, "The Myth of the Judeo-Christian Tradition," *Commentary*, November 1969.
124. Marc Dollinger, *Black Power, Jewish Politics: Reinventing the Alliance in the 1960s* (Waltham: Brandeis University Press, 2018); Dollinger, "American Jewish Liberalism Revisited: Two perspectives: Exceptionalism and Jewish Liberalism," *Journal of American Jewish History* 90, no. 2 (June 2002): 161.
125. "Letters to the Editors," *Life*, July 4, 1955, 6.
126. "Letters to the Editors," *Life*, July 4, 1955, 6.

Chapter 1

1. Oscar Handlin, *Al Smith and His America* (Boston: Little Brown & Co., 1958), 118.
2. Handlin, *Al Smith*, 118.
3. Mead, *Arc of a Covenant*, 169.
4. Lee Levinger, *Anti-Semitism in the U.S.: Its History and Causes* (New York: Bloch Publishing Co., 1925), 73.
5. Linda Gordon, *The Second Coming of the KKK: The Ku Klux Klan of the 1920s and the American Political Tradition* (New York: Liveright, 2017); Michael Dobkowski, *That Tarnished Dream: The Basis of American Antisemitism* (New York: Greenwood Press, 1979), 229.
6. Wall, *Inventing the American Way*, 22–23. Daniel Okrent, *The Guarded Gate: Bigotry, Eugenics, and the Law That Kept Two Generations of Jews, Italians, and other European Immigrants Out of America* (New York: Scribner, 2019), 255.
7. Cited in Dobkowski, *That Tarnished Dream*, 6.
8. Oscar Handlin, *Race and Nationality in American Life* (New York: Doubleday Anchor Books, 1957), 173–174; Daniel Platt, "The Natures of Capital: Jewish Difference and the Decline of American Usury Law, 1910–1925," *Journal of American History* 104, no. 4 (March 2018): 863.
9. On the history of antisemites connecting Jews and Jewishness with money and property, see David Nirenberg, *Anti-Judaism: The Western Tradition* (New York: W. W. Norton, 2014).
10. Kenneth L. Roberts, "The Existence of an Emergency," *Saturday Evening Post*, April 30, 1921, 93.
11. Platt, "The Natures of Capital," 872.
12. "Congress to Tighten Immigration Curb," *New York Times*, January 27, 1924, 59.
13. Mead, *The Arc of a Covenant*, 155, 166.
14. "Dr. Wise Attacks New Quota Bill," *New York Times*, January 7, 1924, 3.
15. Wisconsin Historical Society, Keep America American poster, 96582. Viewed online at https://www.wisconsinhistory.org/Records/Image/IM96582

16. Thomas C. Leonard, *Illiberal Reformers: Race, Eugenics, and American Economics in the Progressive Era* (Princeton, NJ: Princeton University Press, 2016), 142.
17. "America of the Melting Pot Comes to End," *New York Times*, April 27, 1924, 181.
18. Sachar, *A History of Jews in America*, 455. Leonard Dinnerstein, "Jews and the New Deal," *American Jewish History* 72, no. 4 (June 1983): 461.
19. Stember, *Jews in the Mind*, 56–57.
20. Dobkowski, *That Tarnished*, 235.
21. Levinger, *Anti-Semitism in the United States*, 94.
22. Dinnerstein, *Antisemitism in America*, 107, 126–127.
23. Edith Wharton, *The House of Mirth* (New York: Dover Thrift Editions, 2002), 12.
24. F. Scott Fitzgerald, *The Beautiful and the Damned* (New York: Vintage, 2010), 664.
25. Meyer Wolfsheim in *The Great Gatsby*.
26. William Faulkner, *The Sound and the Fury* (New York: Vintage, 1990), 191.
27. Oz Almog, *The Sabra: The Creation of the New Jew* (Berkeley: University of California Press, 2000); Arye Naor, "Jabotinsky's New Jew: Concepts and Models," *Journal of Israeli History* 30, no. 2 (September 2011): 141–159.
28. Milton Hindus, "F. Scott Fitzgerald and Literary Anti-Semitism: A Footnote on the Minds of the '20s," *Commentary*, January 1, 1947, 510.
29. Hindus, "F. Scott Fitzgerald," 510.
30. Hindus, "F. Scott Fitzgerald," 510.
31. Hindus, "F. Scott Fitzgerald," 510.
32. Arthur L. Scott, "In Defense of Robert Cohn," *College English* 18, no. 6 (March 1957): 309. A similar modification was made in 1948, when the Manhattan publisher Grosset & Dunlap "disclosed that they had withdrawn an edition of the Arabian Nights and revised it. The American Jewish Congress objected to one of the illustrations, and to references in the text to 'a cunning Jew.'" As reported in "Prejudice Is Where You Find It," *Time*, January 12, 1948, 36.
33. Charles Bezalel Sherman, *The Jew within American Society: A Study in Ethnic Individuality* (Detroit: Wayne State University Press, 1961), 212.
34. Sherman, *The Jew Within*, 214.
35. Morris Kertzer, *What Is a Jew?* (New York: World Publishing Co., 1953), 7–8.
36. Leonard, *Illiberal Reformers*, 119.
37. Robert Wald Sussman, *The Myth of Race: The Troubling Persistence of an Unscientific Idea* (Cambridge, MA: Harvard University Press, 2016).
38. Charles King, *Gods of the Upper Air: How a Circle of Renegade Anthropologists Reinvented Race, Sex, and Gender in the Twentieth Century* (New York: Doubleday, 2019), 81.
39. Stember, *Jews in the Mind*, 52.
40. Goldstein, *Price of Whiteness*, 169.
41. "Roosevelt Stresses Religious Freedom, Hits Axis Efforts to Stir Discord," Jewish Telegraphic Agency, January 7, 1941, https://www.jta.org/archive/roosevelt-stresses-religious-freedom-hits-axis-efforts-to-stir-discord.
42. Deborah Dash Moore, *GI Jews: How World War II Changed a Generation* (Cambridge, MA: Harvard University Press, 2004), 118–155. Kevin Schultz, *Tri-Faith*

America: How Catholics and Jews Held Postwar America to Its Protestant Promise (New York: Oxford University Press, 2011), 3.
43. Tisa Wenger, *Religious Freedom: The Contested History of an American Ideal* (Chapel Hill: University of North Carolina Press, 2017), 146. Matthew Jacobson dates Jews' whiteness as beginning after World War II. Matthew Frye Jacobson, *Whiteness of a Different Color: European Immigrants and the Alchemy of Race* (Cambridge, MA: Harvard University Press, 1999), 176.
44. Judah Isseroff, "American Judaism between Religion and Race: Reflections on Mordecai Kaplan and Jewish Whiteness," *Religion and American Culture: A Journal of Interpretation* 32, no. 1 (Summer 2022): 12.
45. Wenger, *Religious Freedom*, 145; Glazer, *American Judaism*, 116.
46. Wenger, *Religious Freedom*, 145.
47. Isseroff, "American Judaism between Religion and Race," 18.
48. Sherman, *The Jew Within*, 218.
49. Meyer, *Response to Modernity*, 226.
50. Schultz, *Tri-Faith*, 29–31.
51. Schultz, *Tri-Faith*, 36–37. Proselytizing Jews: Schultz, *Tri-Faith*, 30–33.
52. Michaelis, *Eleanor*, 414–415.
53. Roger Merriman, "An Historian Looks at the Young Entry," *Atlantic Monthly*, October 1945, https://www.theatlantic.com/magazine/archive/1945/10/an-historian-looks-at-the-young-entry/656665/.
54. "What You Should Know about Eugenics," *New York Times*, March 30, 1941, 84.
55. The irony of Wise's situation was that his Reform predecessors helped create this problem by successfully emphasizing race over religion as a category for Jews. See Goldstein, *Price of Whiteness*, 11.
56. "Persecution and the Jew," *New York Times*, December 18, 1933, 16.
57. Frantz Fanon's *Black Skin, White Masks* (1952) is a midcentury example of a writer analyzing the experience of racism and its effects.
58. Leonard Dinnerstein, "Antisemitism Exposed and Attacked, 1945–1950," *American Jewish History* 71, no. 1 (September 1981): 134–149.
59. Milton Steinberg, "The Jew Faces Anti-Semitism," *The Reconstructionist* 2, no. 2 (March 6, 1936): 7.
60. Steinberg, "The Jew Faces," 7.
61. Steinberg, "The Jew Faces," 8.
62. Steinberg, "The Jew Faces," 8.
63. Steinberg, "The Jew Faces," 9.
64. Steinberg, "The Jew Faces," 13.
65. Charles Thomas Hallinan, "The Liberal and the Jew," *The Nation*, January 23, 1924, 81.
66. Hallinan, "The Liberal and the Jew," 81.
67. Steinberg, "The Jew Faces," 9.
68. John Cournos, "An Epistle to the Jews," *Atlantic Monthly*, December 1937, https://www.theatlantic.com/magazine/archive/1937/12/an-epistle-to-the-jews/652150/. A few years before Steinberg, Maurice Samuel made a similar point in his 1932 book: Maurice Samuel, *Jews on Approval* (New York: Liveright, 1932), 10.

69. Joshua Trachtenberg, *The Devils of the Jews: The Medieval Conception of the Jew and Its Relation to Modern Antisemitism* (New Haven, CT: Yale University Press, 1943), xii.
70. Trachtenberg, *The Devils of the Jews*, xii.
71. Stember, *Jews in the Mind*, 81.
72. Stember, *Jews in the Mind*, 82.
73. Stember, *Jews in the Mind*, 84.
74. Stember, *Jews in the Mind*, 83.
75. Leonard, *Illiberal Reformers*, 110.
76. Leonard, *Illiberal Reformers*, 110–111.
77. Daniel Tichenor, *Dividing Lines: The Politics of Immigration Control in America* (Princeton, NJ: Princeton University Press, 2002), 160.
78. Ibram X. Kendi, *Stamped from the Beginning: The Definitive History of Racist Ideas in America* (New York: Bold Type Books, 2016), 5.
79. Milton Steinberg, *A Partisan Guide to the Jewish Problem* (New York: Bobbs-Merrill, 1945), 60–61.
80. Kendi, *Stamped*, 302.
81. Gordon, *The Second Coming of the KKK*, 27.
82. Steinberg, *A Partisan Guide to the Jewish Problem*, 66. Only when power tipped in favor of the victim, through race, class, or gender identity, did sympathy more easily lie with the victim, as in the case of middle-class, white victims of Black assault. Edwin J. Juh, "The Social Disability of the Jew," *Atlantic Monthly*, April 1908, https://www.theatlantic.com/magazine/archive/1908/04/the-social-disability-of-the-jew/306261/. Historian Michelle Mart describes a tendency among the American press, in the 1930s, to blame Jews for the antisemitism they faced: Michelle Mart, *Eye on Israel: How America Came to View Israel as an Ally* (Albany: State University of New York Press, 2006), 2. On segregationists blaming Blacks for racial discrimination, Kendi, *Stamped*, 2. On this blame-the-victim mentality and rape law, see Michelle J. Anderson, "From Chastity Requirement to Sexuality License: Sexual Consent and a New Rape Shield Law," *George Washington Law Review* (February 2002), 3, 5.
83. Ludwig Lewisohn, "Jews in Trouble," *Atlantic Monthly*, January 1936, https://www.theatlantic.com/magazine/archive/1936/01/jews-in-trouble/308964/.

    Charles Stember also found, based on public opinion surveys from 1938 and 1939, an American assumption that German Jews were at least partly responsible for their own persecution. Stember, *Jews in the Mind*, 208.
84. 1938 Gallup Poll #121, QN6A: Do you think the persecution of the Jews in Europe has been their own fault? 64 percent answered either "entirely" or "partly," while 35 percent answered "not at all."
85. S. Andhil Fineberg, "Memorandum on 'Crossfire,'" Moving Pictures/AJC, October 22, 1942, American Jewish Committee Archives.
86. Steinberg, *A Partisan Guide*, 66.
87. "Two Mothers Look at America," *Parents' Magazine*, September 1944, 131, 132.
88. "Two Mothers Look," 131, 132.
89. Harry Wolfson, "Escaping Judaism," *Menorah Journal* 7 (1921): 167. Wolfson was not the only prominent Jew of this era writing about Jews accepting their fate as Jews in this way. In a similar vein: Ludwig Lewisohn, "The Jew Meditates," *The Nation*, February 20, 1924, 200–201.

90. Paul Mendes-Flohr, "Jewish Scholarship as a Vocation," in *Perspectives on Jewish Thought and Mysticism: Proceedings of the International Conference Held by the Institute of Jewish Studies*, ed. Alfred L. Ivry, Elliot R. Wolfson, and Allan Arkush (London: Routledge, 1998), 38; Isadore Twersky, "Harry Austryn Wolfson, 1887–1974," *Journal of the American Oriental Society* 95, no. 2 (April–June 1975): 182.
91. Eli E. Cohen, "Economic Status and Occupational Structure," *American Jewish Year Book* 1950, 67–68.
92. Wolfson's experiences evidence similarities with that of another successful Jewish academic of the same generation, the sociologist Louis Wirth, whose experiences are recounted in Berman, *Speaking of Jews*, chapter 2.
93. Harry Wolfson, "Escaping Judaism" (New York: Intercollegiate Menorah Association, 1923), 51.
94. Charles Silberman, *A Certain People: American Jews and Their Lives* (New York: Summit Books, 1985), 31. Similarly, in his 1963 study *Stigma*, sociologist Erving Goffman described the perception of an attribute as a sickness as the experience of stigma. Erving Goffman, *Stigma: Notes on the Management of Spoiled Identity* (New York: Simon & Schuster, 1963).
95. Wolfson, "Escaping Judaism," 51.
96. Wolfson, "Escaping Judaism," 29.
97. Wolfson, "Escaping Judaism," 47.
98. On Jewishness as handicap discourse in the realm of Jews seeking name changes, see Kristen Fermaglich, *A Rosenberg by Any Other Name: A History of Name Changing in America* (New York: New York University Press, 2018), chapter 1.
99. Bethamie Horowitz, "Old Casks in New Times: the Reshaping of American Jewish Identity in the 21st Century," in *Ethnicity and Beyond: Theories and Dilemmas of Jewish Group Demarcation*, ed. Eli Lederhendler (New York: Oxford University Press, 2011), 79; Shaul Magid, *American Post-Judaism Identity and Renewal in a Postethnic Society* (Bloomington: Indiana University Press, 2013), 21.
100. Barbara Cantalupo and Lori Harrison-Kahan, eds., *Heirs of Yesterday* by Emma Wolf (Detroit: Wayne State University Press, 2020), 114. In Wolf's novel, when a Jewish woman reveals that she is Jewish, a non-Jewish man assures her with the remarkable line that highlights the gendered nature of antisemitism: "You are a woman. Your sex unsects you," 114.
101. Edwin J. Kuh, "The Social Disability of the Jew," *Atlantic Monthly*, April 1908, https://www.theatlantic.com/magazine/archive/1908/04/the-social-disability-of-the-jew/306261/.
102. Mordecai Kaplan, *Judaism as a Civilization: Toward a Reconstruction of American-Jewish Life* (Philadelphia: Jewish Publication Society, 2010), 4.
103. Kaplan, *Judaism as a Civilization*, 4.
104. Freda B. Joel, "Co-Author of 'Christians Only' Says Search for Discrimination against Jews Met with Evasion," *Jewish Advocate*, June 17, 1930, 2.
105. Edna Ferber, *Fanny, Herself* (Urbana: University of Illinois Press, 1917), 121.
106. Horace Kallen, "The Education of Jews in Our Time," *Journal of Jewish Education* 11, no. 2 (1939): 85.

107. Herman Wouk, *This Is My God* (New York: Doubleday, 1959), 29–30.
108. "Rabbi Mortimer Cohen on 'Christians Only,'" *The Jewish Exponent*, February 10, 1933, 7.
109. Steinberg, *A Partisan Guide*, 115
110. Susan A. Glenn, "The Vogue of Jewish Self-Hatred in Post–World War II America," *Jewish Social Studies* (Spring/Summer 2006): 95–136.
111. *The Jewish Foundation Reconstructionist Platform* (New York: Jewish Reconstructionist Foundation, 1942), 4.
112. Michael Beschloss, *The Conquerors: Roosevelt, Truman, and the Destruction of Hitler's Germany* (New York: Simon & Schuster, 2003), 46.
113. Isadore Twersky, "Harry Austryn Wolfson, in Appreciation," *American Jewish Year Book 76* (1976): 99–111. Lewis S. Feuer, "Recollections of Harry Austryn Wolfson," describes Wolfson as having "an abiding loyalty to Harvard University" that guided Wolfson's behavior. Lewis S. Feuer, "Recollections of Harry Austryn Wolfson," *American Jewish Archives* 28, no. 1 (April 1976): 33. Abraham Leon Sachar, *Brandeis University: A Host at Last* (Boston: Little, Brown and Co., 1976), 81–82. Leo Schwarz, *Wolfson at Harvard: Portrait of a Scholar* (Philadelphia: Jewish Publication Society, 1978).
114. Jerome Karabel, *The Chosen: The Hidden History of Admissions and Exclusion at Harvard, Yale, and Princeton* (New York: Mariner Books, 2005).
115. Feuer, "Recollections of Harry Austryn Wolfson," 33.
116. Feuer, "Recollections of Harry Austryn Wolfson," 34.
117. Twersky, "Harry Austryn Wolfson, in Appreciation," 106; Feuer, "Recollections of Harry Austryn Wolfson," 33; Sachar, *Brandeis University*, 85; Schwarz, *Wolfson at Harvard*, 5; Feuer, "Recollections of Harry Austryn Wolfson," 41.
118. Feuer, "Recollections of Harry Austryn Wolfson," 43.
119. Wolfson, "Escaping Judaism," 28.
120. Wolfson, "Escaping Judaism," 29.
121. Wolfson, "Escaping Judaism," 30.
122. Wolfson, "Escaping Judaism," 31.
123. Horace Kallen, "Can Judaism Survive in the United States?" *Menorah Journal* 11, no. 2 (April 1925): 102–103.
124. As Healan Gaston shows in her masterly study, Judeo-Christianity had many meanings between the late 1930s and the 1970s. Healan Gaston, *Imagining Judeo-Christian America* (Chicago: University of Chicago Press, 2019).
125. Wolfson, "Escaping Judaism," 47.
126. Wolfson, "Escaping Judaism," 48.
127. Wolfson, "Escaping Judaism," 165, 166.
128. Wolfson, "Escaping Judaism," 166.
129. Elliot Dorff, *Conservative Judaism: Our Ancestors to Our Descendants* (New York: United Synagogue of America, 1977), 162, 191; Marc Lee Raphael, *Judaism in America* (New York: Columbia University Press, 2005), 85.
130. John Hood, "In Defense of 'Happy Holidays,'" *National Review*, December 18, 2007, https://www.nationalreview.com/corner/defense-happy-holidays-john-hood/.

NOTES 221

131. Cynthia Baker, *Jew* (New Brunswick, NJ: Rutgers University Press, 2017), 49.
132. Deborah Dash Moore, "Jewish GIs and the Creation of the Judeo-Christian Tradition," *Religion and American Culture: A Journal of Interpretation* 8, no. 1 (1998): 31–53; Mark Silk, *Spiritual Politics: Religion and America since World War II* (New York: Simon & Schuster, 1988); K. Healan Gaston, "Interpreting Judeo-Christianity in America," *Relegere: Studies in Religion and Reception* 2, no. 2 (2012): 291–304; Mark Silk, "Notes on the Judeo-Christian Tradition in America," *American Quarterly* 36, no. 1 (Spring 1984): 54–85.
133. Wolfson, "Escaping Judaism," 50. Jonathan Krasner, "On the Origins and Persistence of the Jewish Identity Industry in Jewish Education," *Journal of Jewish Education* 82, no. 2 (2016): 132–158.
134. Andrew Solomon, *Far from the Tree: Parents, Children and the Search for Identity* (New York: Simon & Schuster, 2012), 5.
135. Milton Steinberg, "To Be or Not to Be a Jew," *Common Ground* 1, no. 3 (Spring 1941): 44.
136. Jonathan Krasner, "On the Origins and Persistence of the Jewish Identity Industry in Jewish Education," *Journal of Jewish Education* 82, no. 2 (2016): 132–158.
137. Solomon, *Far From*, 10.
138. Solomon, *Far From*, 10.

Chapter 2

1. Henry S. Canby, "A Plaster on a Wound?" *Saturday Review*, December 13, 1947, 20.
2. Canby, "A Plaster," 20.
3. Antisemitism was also a theme in several 1940s novels that are more accurately categorized as war novels, including Merle Miller's *That Winter* (1948), Irwin Shaw's *The Young Lions* (1948), and Norman Mailer's *The Naked and the Dead* (1948). These and other Jewish war novels are examined in Leah Garrett, *Young Lions: How Jewish Authors Reinvented the American War Novel* (Evanston, IL: Northwestern University Press, 2015).
4. Sociologist Jeffrey Alexander sees roots of anti-antisemitism as early as the 1930s but also finds that anti-antisemitism "became particularly intense after the US declared war on Nazi Germany." Jeffrey Alexander, "On the Social Construction of Moral Universals: The 'Holocaust' from War Crime to Trauma Drama," *European Journal of Social Theory* 5, no. 1 (2002): 15.
5. Randy W. Roberts and David Welky, eds. *Charles A. Lindbergh: The Power and Peril of Celebrity, 1927–1941* (New York: Wiley Blackwell, 2003); Sarah Churchwell, *Behold, America: The Entangled History of "American First" and "the American Dream"* (New York: Basic Books, 2018).
6. Lynne Olson, *Those Angry Days: Roosevelt, Lindbergh, and America's Fight over World War II, 1939–1941* (New York: Random House, 2013), 168, http://www.charleslindbergh.com/americanfirst/speech.asp.

7. Charles Gallagher, *Nazis of Copley Square: The Forgotten Story of the Christian Front* (Cambridge, MA: Harvard University Press, 2021), 36, 44, 102. Donald Warren, *Radio Priest Charles Coughlin, the Father of Hate Radio* (New York: Free Press, 1996).
8. Churchwell, *Behold, America*, 280.
9. On American condemnation of Lindbergh after the Des Moines speech, see Leonard Dinnerstein, *Anti-Semitism in America*, 129–130.
10. "Assail Lindbergh for Iowa Speech: White House Aide Links It to Berlin," *New York Times*, September 13, 1941, 1.
11. Olson, *Those Angry Days*, 103.
12. Churchwell, *Behold*, 280–281.
13. Churchwell, *Behold*, 281
14. Laura Z. Hobson, *Laura Z: A Life* (New York: Arbor House, 1983), 280.
15. Stember, *Jews in the Mind*, 114.
16. Stember, *Jews in the Mind*, 114.
17. On the significance of Pearl Harbor for a developing culture of anti-antisemitism, see Marc Dollinger, *Quest for Inclusion*, 78, 82.
18. "Is Lindbergh a Nazi?" CharlesLindbergh.com, http://www.charleslindbergh.com/pdf/Lindbergh.pdf.
19. "Stay Out of Texas, House Roars Out to Lindbergh," *Austin Statesman*, September 18, 1941, 1.
20. "Asks Lindbergh Debate," *New York Times*, September 15, 1941, 2.
21. The reckoning with antisemitism that took place in the wake of Lindbergh's Des Moines speech differed from the public uproar after Kristallnacht, in 1938, because it focused on American antisemitism. On the coding of Nazis as evil, after Kristallnacht, see Alexander, "The Social Construction of Moral Universals," 14–15.
22. On America First's response to Lindbergh's speech: Herman Klurfeld, *Winchell, His Life and Times* (New York: Praeger, 1976), 90. "The Un-American Way," *New York Times*, September 26, 1941, 22.
23. "The Un-American Way," 22.
24. Breitman and Lichtman, *FDR and the Jews*, 188.
25. "Here and There," *The Jewish Exponent*, September 26, 1941, 4.
26. "Here and There," 4.
27. "Here and There," 4
28. "Dewey Assails Lindbergh for Des Moines Talk," *Chicago Daily Tribune*, September 15, 1941, 9; "Assail Lindbergh for Iowa Speech," 1.
29. "Willkie Terms Lindbergh's Des Moines Talk Un-American," *The Sun*, September 14, 1941, 1.
30. Olson, *Those Angry Days*, 387.
31. In the 1940s. they actually used "anti-anti-Semitism." I follow the scholarly convention of not capitalizing "semitism." See David Engel, "Away from a Definition of Antisemitism: An Essay in the Semantics of Historical Description," in *Rethinking European Jewish History*, ed. Jeremy Cohen and Moshe Rosman (London: Littman Library of Jewish Civilization, 2009), 30–53.
32. Alexander, "The Social Construction of Moral Universals," 115.

NOTES   223

33. On the merging of Jewish and American fates: Henry L. Feingold, *The Jewish People in America: A Time for Healing* (Baltimore: Johns Hopkins University Press, 1992), 16.
34. Dinnerstein, *Anti-Semitism in America* (New York: Oxford University Press, 1994), 153.
35. Gordon Hutner, *What America Read: Taste, Class, and the Novel, 1920–1950* (Chapel Hill: University of North Carolina Press, 2011), 249.
36. *Crossfire* was a 1947 film noir drama, directed by Edward Dmytrick, based on the 1945 novel *The Brick Foxhole* by Richard Brooks (Reuben Sax). It received five Oscar nominations.
37. For an example of anti-antisemitism on the governmental level, see Tichenor, *Dividing Lines*, 167.
38. On antisemitism increasing during World War II: Dollinger, *Quest for Inclusion*, 78; Stephen Norwood, "Marauding Youth and the Christian Front: Antisemitic Violence in Boston and New York during World War II," *American Jewish History* 91, no. 2 (June 2003): 233–267. On antisemitism eventually decreasing in the late 1940s, see Salo Baron, "The Year in Retrospect," *American Jewish Year Book 1947–1948*, 108; Dinnerstein, *Anti-Semitism in America*, chapter 8, "The Tide Ebbs, 1945–1969."
39. Leonard Dinnerstein, "Anti-Semitism Exposed and Attacked, 1945–1950," *American Jewish History* 71, no. 1 (September 1981): 134–135.
40. Dinnerstein, *Anti-Semitism in America*, 150, 165; Stember, *Jews in the Mind of America*, 291.
41. "Brief Reviews," *College English* 8, no. 8 (May 1947): 445.
42. Fermaglich, *A Rosenberg*, 3.
43. Mark Oppenheimer, *Squirrel Hill: The Tree of Life Synagogue Shooting and the Soul of a Neighborhood* (New York: Alfred A. Knopf, 2021).
44. On antisemitism of the 1940s, see Naomi Cohen, *Jews in Christian America: The Pursuit of Religious Equality* (New York: Oxford University Press, 1992), 123–130.
45. David Hollinger, *Science, Jews, and Secular Culture: Studies in Mid-Twentieth Century American Intellectual History* (Princeton: Princeton University Press, 1996), 9.
46. John Cournos, "Jews in a Gentile World," *Atlantic Monthly*, March 1942, https://www.theatlantic.com/magazine/archive/1942/03/jews-in-a-gentile-world/653588/.
47. "The Atlantic Bookshelf: Under Cover," *Atlantic Monthly*, September 1943, 130–131.
48. "The Atlantic Bookshelf: Judah P. Benjamin: Confederate Statesman," *Atlantic Monthly*, September 1943, 130.
49. Philip Wylie, "Memorandum on Anti-Semitism," *American Mercury*, January 1945, 66–73; Struthers Burt, "The Poison in Our Body Politic," *Saturday Review of Literature*, March 1, 1947, 14.
50. "Under Forty: A Symposium," *Contemporary Jewish Record*, February 1, 1944, 3–36.
51. "Under Forty," 36.
52. "Under Forty," 36.
53. Edna Ferber, *A Peculiar Treasure* (New York: Doubleday, 1939), 8, 11. The *New York Times* review noted Ferber's constant invocation of her Jewishness in her autobiography: Katherine Woods, "Edna Ferber and Her America," *New York Times*, February 5, 1939, BR1.

54. Ferber, *A Peculiar*, 43, 9.
55. Emma Lazarus wrote most self-consciously and proudly as a Jew, beginning in the 1880s, with her *Songs of a Semite: The Dance to Death and Other Poems* (1882). Emma Wolfe's first novel, *Other Things Being Equal* (1892), portrays proud Jewish identity through the character of Jean Willard.
56. Ferber, *A Peculiar*, 11–12.
57. Ibram X. Kendi, *How to Be an Antiracist* (New York: Vintage, 2019), 61.
58. Breitman and Lichtman, *FDR and the Jews*, 135–138.
59. Erin Blakemore, "A Ship of Jewish Refugees Was Refused US Landing in 1939. This Was Their Fate," History, June 4, 2019. https://www.history.com/news/wwii-jewish-refugee-ship-st-louis-1939.
60. Breitman and Lichtman, *FDR and the Jews*, 138.
61. Lazarus penned "The New Colossus" in 1883, and the poem was affixed to the statue's pedestal in 1903.
62. Sarah Churchwell, in *Behold, America*, 264, discusses this article as circulating widely.
63. "We Are Lost If We Accept This Crime," *The Courier-Journal*, Louisville, June 17, 1940.
64. Michael Anft, "How a Jewish Charity's Long Game Readied It for Today's Turbulence," *The Chronicle of Philanthropy*, November 1, 2018, https://www.philanthropy.com/article/how-a-jewish-charitys-long-game-readied-it-for-todays-turbulence/?cid=gen_sign_in. For example, Matthew Delmont's study *Half American: The Epic Story of African Americans Fighting World War II at Home and Abroad* (2022) illuminates one example of how the war experience incubated new ideas about equality at home. Deborah Dash Moore's *GI Jews* illuminates how service in World War II accelerated Jewish visions of greater equality in the United States.
65. John F. Kennedy, *A Nation of Immigrants* (New York: Anti-Defamation League, 1958), 33–34.
66. James Whitman, *Hitler's American Model: The United States and the Making of Nazi Race Law* (Princeton, NJ: Princeton University Press, 2017).
67. Koppel S. Pinson, "Antisemitism in the Postwar World," *Jewish Social Studies* 7, no. 2 (April 1945): 99. William Zukerman, "The Silver Lining," *Ladies' Home Journal*, June 1947, 68.
68. Pinson, "Antisemitism in the Postwar World," 100.
69. Alexander, "On the Social Construction of Moral Universals."
70. Awareness of danger of antisemitism and the new equation about Nazis and antisemites: Pinson, 99, 100. On not recognizing the trauma of the Holocaust: Alexander, "On the Social Construction of Moral Universals," 10–11. On discrediting of antisemitism as a result of the Nazis: Oscar and Mary Handlin, "The Acquisition of Political and Social Rights by the Jews in the United States," *American Jewish Year Book* 1955, 86.
71. Hobson, *Laura Z*, 280.
72. Hobson, *Laura Z*, 280–282.
73. Hobson, *Laura Z*, 96.
74. Hobson, *Laura Z*, 282.

Chapter 3

1. Hobson to Richard Simon, October 18, 1944, "Scrapbook," box 21, Laura Keane Zametkin Hobson Papers, Columbia University Library (hereafter cited as Hobson Papers).
2. Margaret Halsey, *Some of My Best Friends Are Soldiers* (New York: Simon & Schuster, 1944).
3. Jo Sinclair–*Wasteland NYT* mentions in the mid-1940s: "Brooklyn Woman's Novel on Immigrants Wins $10,000 Prize in Harper Context," *New York Times*, January 3, 1946, 17; John Hutchens, "People Who Read and Write," *New York Times*, January 6, 1946, 18; Orville Prescott, "Books of the Times," *New York Times*, February 15, 1946, 23; W. McNeil Lowry, "Of Being and Belonging," *New York Times Book Review*, February 17, 1946, 5; John K. Hutchens, "People Who Read and Write," *New York Times*, March 10, 1946, 27.
4. A March 1947 *New York Herald Tribune* article about Hobson discusses her awareness of other anti-antisemitism novelists. Dorothy Dunbar Bromley, "Mrs. Hobson Deluged with Mail in Her Novel on Anti-Semitism," *New York Herald Tribune*, March 9, 1947, 8.
5. Hobson to Richard Simon, October 18, 1944, "Scrapbook," box 21, Hobson Papers, Columbia University Library.
6. Josh Lambert, "Fictions of anti-Semitism and the Beginning of Holocaust Literature," in *American Literature in Transition, 1940–1950*, ed. Christopher Vials (Cambridge: Cambridge University Press, 2017), 44–59.
7. Hobson, *Agreement*, 51.
8. Hobson, *Agreement*, 51. On *Agreement* in the category of undercover fiction, see Mark Pittenger, *Class Unknown: Undercover Investigations of American Work and Poverty from the Progressive Era to the Present* (New York: New York University Press, 2012).
9. Hobson, *Agreement*, 192.
10. Hobson, *Agreement*, 192.
11. Hobson, *Agreement*, 192.
12. This change in thinking about antisemitism as not a Jewish problem, but rather an American problem, mirrored a transformation in thinking about racism: Gunnar Myrdal, *An American Dilemma: The Negro Problem and American Democracy* (New York: McGraw-Hill, 1964), lxxi.
13. Jean-Paul Sartre, *Anti-Semite and Jew* (New York: Schocken Books, 1948), 13, 17.
14. Hobson, *Agreement*, 268.
15. Hobson, *Laura Z: The Early Years and Years of Fulfillment* (New York: Donald L. Fine, 1986), 396.
16. Hobson, *Laura Z: The Early Years and Years of Fulfillment*, 218–222.
17. Hobson's previous novel, *The Trespassers* (1943), had studiously avoided Jews, even though it was about refugees from Europe.
18. Hobson, *Agreement*, 133.
19. On post-WWII universalism, see Werner Sollors, "Holocaust and Hiroshima: American Ethnic Prose Writers Face the Extreme," *PMLA* 118 (1): 56–61.

20. Hobson, *Laura Z*, 9.
21. Hobson, *Laura Z*, 10.
22. Hobson, *Laura Z*, 23.
23. Smith, *Visions of Belonging*, 156.
24. Hobson, *Laura Z: The Early Years and Years of Fulfillment*, 525-530. Hobson, *Laura Z*, 189-190.
25. Ralph G. Martin, *Henry and Clare: An Intimate Portrait of the Luces* (New York: Perigee Books, 1992), 188.
26. Hobson, *Laura Z*, 41, 70, 82.
27. Hobson, *Agreement*, 13.
28. On Phil changing his name, see Hobson, *Agreement*, 13.
29. Anonymous, "I Changed My Name," *Atlantic Monthly*, February 1948, 72–74; David Cohn, "I've Kept My Name," *Atlantic Monthly*, April 1948, 42–44, https://www.theatlantic.com/magazine/archive/1948/04/ive-kept-my-name/306256/.
30. Cohn, "I've Kept My Name."
31. Hobson, *Laura Z: A Life*, 7.
32. Hobson, *Laura Z: The Early Years and Years of Fulfillment*, 16.
33. Hobson, *Laura Z*, 57.
34. Hobson, *Laura Z*, 57.
35. Hobson, *Laura Z*, 57.
36. On this cohort of highbrow, mostly male American Jewish writers, see Julian Levinson, *Exiles on Main Street: Jewish American Writers and American Literary Culture* (Bloomington: Indiana University Press, 2008), 143–146.
37. Marjorie Farber, "Refugees' Dilemma," *New York Times Book Review*, September 19, 1943, 5.
38. Masha Leon, "An Interview: Laura Z(ametkin) Hobson," *Jewish Forward* (English insert), September 14, 1984, 5.
39. The editor's reasoning was not without basis in fact. In a 1952 article in the Jewish publication, *Congress Weekly*, for instance, Abraham Rothberg reflected on the pressures faced by Jewish writers: "There are always the things from agents, editors, and publishers, that it might be wise, well, you know, to change one's name to something well, you know not quite so Semitic. . . . Or there is the half ashamed, half regretful rejection that says this is beautiful but we cannot use it because we used one Jewish theme story six months ago and we don't want to be typed a 'Jewish house' or a 'Jewish magazine.'" Abraham Rothberg, "The Dilemma of the Jewish Writer," *Congress Weekly*, March 24, 1952, in Harold Ribalow, *These Your Children* (New York: The Beechhurst Press, 1952), 14.
40. Hobson, *Agreement*, 254.
41. Hobson, *Agreement*, 250.
42. Hobson, *Agreement*, 138, 139.
43. Hobson, *Agreement*, 106.
44. Hobson, *Agreement*, 254.
45. On the novel depicting self-introspection and encouraging it in readers, see Felski, *The Uses of Literature*, 25–26.

46. Felski, *The Uses of Literature*, 26.
47. Hobson, *Agreement*, 27.
48. Hobson, *Agreement*, 6.
49. Hobson, *Agreement*, 1.
50. Hobson, *Agreement*, 12, 14.
51. Howard W. Cosell to Hobson, March 4, 1947, "Gentleman's Agreement: Correspondence, Fan Mail, 1947," box 20, Hobson Papers. Cosell would become one of the best-known sports commentators.
52. Howard W. Cosell to Hobson, March 4, 1947.
53. Mrs. Irma M. Gasser to Hobson, March 27, 1947, "Gentleman's Agreement: Correspondence, Fan Mail 1947," box 20, Hobson Papers.
54. Hobson to Mrs. Irma M. Gasser, April 10, 1947, "Gentleman's Agreement: Correspondence, Fan Mail 1947," box 20, Hobson Papers.
55. Hobson to Miss May Lewis, April 12, 1947, "Gentleman's Agreement: Cosmopolitan Correspondence," box 20, Hobson Papers.
56. Rodger J. Moran, "Gwethalyn Graham," *The Canadian Encyclopedia*, September 28, 2011, https://www.thecanadianencyclopedia.ca/en/article/gwethalyn-graham.
57. Moran, "Gwethalyn Graham."
58. Allen Marple to Betty Smith, October 11, 1944. Box 5, folder 85. Betty Smith Papers.
59. Hobson to Richard Simon, September 10, 1944, "Scrapbook," box 21, Hobson Papers.
60. On the emergence of 1940s anti-antisemitism literature as a genre, see Leslie Fiedler, *To the Gentiles* (New York: Stein and Day, 1972), 103-104.
61. Arthur Miller, *Focus* (New York: Penguin, 1984), vi.
62. Miller's speech excerpted in Harold Ribalow, *This Land, These People* (New York: The Beechhurst Press, 1950), 4. On Jewish self-consciousness and shame about experiencing antisemitism, see Fermaglich, *A Rosenberg by Any Other Name*, 30.
63. Hobson, *Agreement*, 139–140.
64. Hobson to Richard Simon, September 10, 1944, "Scrapbook," box 21, Hobson Papers.
65. Dinitia Smith, "Margaret Halsey, 86, a Writer Who Lampooned the English," *New York Times*, February 7, 1997, D18.
66. Jane Cobb, "Riffraff?" *New York Times*, October 1, 1944, 56.
67. Margaret Halsey, *The Folks at Home* (New York: Simon & Schuster, 1952), 37,
68. Halsey, *The Folks*, 38.
69. Halsey, *The Folks*, 38.
70. Halsey, *The Folks*, 37–38.
71. Margaret Halsey, *Color Blind: A White Woman Looks at the Negro* (New York: Simon & Schuster, 1946), 4.
72. Halsey, *Color Blind*, 159.
73. Halsey, *Color Blind*, 159.
74. Orville Prescott, "Books of the Times," *New York Times*, October 2, 1946, 27.
75. Lester B. Granger, "New Books on Our Bookshelf," *Opportunity: Journal of Negro Life* 20, no. 3 (1942): 46.
76. Hobson to Richard Simon, September 24, 1944, "Scrapbook," box 21, Hobson Papers.

77. Halsey, *No Laughing Matter: The Autobiography of a WASP* (New York: Lippincott, 1977), 113.
78. Halsey, *Some of My Best Friends Are Soldiers*, 67.
79. William Du Bois, "Searing Novel of the South," *New York Times*, March 5, 1944, B1.
80. "Hub Head Cop Blackens City in Book Ban," *The Billboard* 56, no. 14 (April 1, 1944): 3. Judith Louise Stephens, *Strange Fruit: Plays on Lynching by American Women* (Bloomington: Indiana University Press, 1998), 222. Elizabeth Diefendorf, *The New York Public Library's Books of the Century* (New York: Oxford University Press, 1996), 58.
81. *Strange Fruit* and *Gentleman's Agreement* are worth consideration together because they are considered the two exemplary social problem novels of the 1940s. Tom Perrin, *The Aesthetics of Middlebrow Fiction: Popular US Novels, Modernism, and Form, 1945–75* (New York: Palgrave, 2015), 38.
82. Richard Simon to Hobson, September 26, 1944, "Scrapbook," box 21, Hobson Papers.
83. Richard Simon to Hobson, September 26, 1944.
84. Kevin Schultz, *Tri-Faith America: How Catholics and Jews Held Postwar America to Its Protestant Promise* (New York: Oxford University Press, 2011), 8.
85. Hobson, *Agreement*, 253.
86. Hobson to Richard Simon, October 18, 1944, "Scrapbook," box 21, Hobson Papers.
87. On the experience of a Jew in New York, as compared with elsewhere, see Jeffrey Gurock, *Jews in Gotham: New York Jews in a Changing City* (New York: New York University Press, 2015), xii.
88. Hobson to Richard Simon, October 18, 1944, "Scrapbook," box 21, Hobson Papers.
89. Richard Simon to Hobson, August 29, 1944, "Scrapbook," box 21, Hobson Papers.
90. On Sinatra's *The House That I Live In*, see James Kaplan, *The Voice* (New York: Anchor Books, 2010), 252.
91. Hobson, *Agreement*, 121–122.
92. On religion as internal faith, see Wilfred Cantwell Smith, *The Meaning and End of Religion* (Minneapolis: Fortress Press, 1991), 42, 114,141, Talal Asad, *Genealogies of Religion: Discipline and Reasons of Power in Christianity and Islam* (Baltimore: Johns Hopkins University Press, 1993), 28,
93. On the ways that American Jews, during the 1930s and 1940s, understood their Jewishness, see Stember, *Jews in the Mind of America* (New York: Basic Books, 1967), 49–52; Nathan Glazer, *American Judaism*, 130, 132. Albert Gordon, *Jews in Suburbia* (New York: Greenwood Press, 1959), 152.
94. Will Herberg, *Protestant-Catholic-Jew: An Essay in American Religious Sociology* (New York: Doubleday, 1955), 274.
95. Hobson, *Agreement*, 34.
96. Hobson, *Agreement*, 35.
97. On the prevalence of categorizing Jews as race: Mitchell Hart, *Jews and Race: Writings on Identity and Difference, 1880–1940* (Waltham, MA: Brandeis University Press, 2011), xxxiii.
98. Elisabeth Sandberg, "Jo Sinclair: A Gardener of Souls," *Studies in American Jewish Literature* 12 (1993): 74.

NOTES 229

99. Jo Sinclair, *Wasteland* (New York: Jewish Publication Society, 1946, 1987), 146.
100. None of the several 1946 *New York Times* reviews and mentions of *Wasteland* noted its lesbian/homophobia theme. Nor did reviews of *Wasteland* in the *Washington Post*, *Boston Globe*, *The Globe and Mail*, or the *Philadelphia Inquirer*.
101. Sinclair, *Wasteland*, 146.
102. Hobson, *Agreement*, 26.
103. Aswell's letter: Edward Aswell to Jo Sinclair, January 4, 1946, "Business Correspondence, 1945–1961," box 36, folder 13, Jo Sinclair [Ruth Seid] Collection, Contemporary Collections 530, Howard Gotlieb Archival Research Center, Boston University (hereafter cited as Sinclair Collection).
104. John K. Hutchens, "People Who Read and Write," *New York Times*, January 6, 1946, 52.
105. Jo Sinclair, *The Seasons: Death and Transfiguration: A Memoir by Jo Sinclair* (New York: The Feminist Press, 1993), 5.
106. Nolan Miller to Ed Aswell, March 7, 1946, "Wasteland: Fan Mail, 1945–1946," box 36, folder 14, Sinclair Collection.
107. Nolan Miller to Ed Aswell, March 7, 1946.
108. A translation of this *Jewish World* review is in the Sinclair Collection 530, Box 36, folder 14. On *The Jewish World*, see Lucy S. Dawidowicz, "Louis Marshall's Yiddish Newspaper, 'The Jewish World': A Study in Contrasts," *Jewish Social Studies* 25, no. 2 (April 1963): 102–163.
109. A translation of this *Jewish World* review is in the Sinclair Collection 530, Box 36, folder 14.
110. See Margaret Metcalf to Jo Sinclair, May 12, 1946; Juliette Reagan to Miss Sinclair, July 10, 1946; Mrs. Prescott H. Brown to Jo Sinclair, undated; Kirk Glenn to Miss Sinclair, September 5, 1946, all from "Wasteland: Fan Mail, 1945–1946," box 36, folder 14, Sinclair Collection.
111. Betty E. Breaux to Miss Sinclair, May 29, 1946, "Wasteland: Fan Mail, 1945–1946," box 36, folder 14, Sinclair Collection.
112. Frances Cohen to Sinclair, February 15, 1946, "Wasteland: Fan Mail, 1947–1951," Box 36, folder 15, Sinclair Collection.
113. Edward Aswell to Sinclair, January 4, 1946, box 36, folder 13, Sinclair Collection.
114. Arnold Rampersad, Introduction to Richard Wright, *Native Son* (New York: Harper Perennial, 2005), xxi.
115. Ed Aswell to Sinclair, December 19, 1945, "Wasteland," box 36, folder 13, Sinclair Collection.
116. Richard Wright to Sinclair, December 29, 1945, "Personal," box 35, folder 7, Sinclair Collection.
117. Michel Fabre, *The Unfinished Quest of Richard Wright* (Chicago: University of Illinois Press, 1994), 290–291.
118. J. L. Teller, "Everybody's 'Wasteland,'" *Jewish Exponent*, February 22, 1946, 5.
119. Jessie R. Wendell to Sinclair, February 28, 1946, "Wasteland: Fan Mail, 1945–1946," box 36, folder 14, Sinclair Collection.

230 NOTES

120. Harold Schwartz to Sinclair, February 22, 1946, "Business Correspondence, 1945–1961," box 36, folder 13, Sinclair Collection.
121. Edna Pegregon to Sinclair, May 19, 1951, "Wasteland: Fan Mail, 1947–1951," box 36, folder 15, Sinclair Collection. On "Bohunk" as a derogatory term for immigrants from Central Europe, see Earnest Elmo Calkins, "My Country, Right or Wrong?" *Atlantic Monthly*, December 1931, https://www.theatlantic.com/magazine/archive/1931/12/my-country-right-or-wrong/650396/.
122. Pegregon to Sinclair, May 19, 1951, "Wasteland: Fan Mail, 1947–1951," box 36, folder 15, Sinclair Collection.
123. Pegregon to Sinclair, May 19, 1951.
124. Hobson, *Agreement*, 206.

Chapter 4

1. Dorothy Fletcher to Hobson, March 7, 1947, "Gentleman's Agreement: Fan Mail," box 20, folder 5, Hobson Papers.
2. Donald Pease, *The New American Exceptionalism* (Minneapolis: University of Minnesota Press, 2009).
3. Cecilia Ager, "A Great Deal More than a Great Movie," *PM*, November 12, 1947, 19. Bettina Berch, *From Hester Street to Hollywood: The Life and Work of Anzia Yezierska* (New York: Sefer International, 2009), 178.
4. On post–World War II American exceptionalism and what Geoffrey Hodson refers to as the "calm assumption of the ethical superiority not only of the American condition but also of American ideals," see Geoffrey Hodgson, *The Myth of American Exceptionalism* (New Haven, CT: Yale University Press, 2010), 92, 94; Pease, *The New American Exceptionalism*; Seymour Martin Lipset, *American Exceptionalism: A Double-Edged Sword* (New York: W. W. Norton, 1997); and on American Jewish exceptionalism, see Rachel Gordan, "The Sin of American Jewish Exceptionalism," *AJS Review* 45, no. 2 (2021): 282–301; Tony Michels, "Is America 'Different?' A Critique of American Jewish Exceptionalism," *American Jewish History* 96, no. 3 (2010): 201–224.
5. Zoe Trodd, "The Civil Rights Movement and Literature of Social Protest," in *The Cambridge Companion to American Civil Rights Literature*, ed. Julie Buckner Armstrong (Cambridge: Cambridge University Press, 2015), 18.
6. Arthur Miller, *Focus* (New York: Penguin), 182.
7. Charles Poore, "Books of the Times," *New York Times*, November 24, 1945, 17.
8. Miller, *Focus*, 217.
9. James Baldwin, "Everybody's Protest Novel," in *Notes of a Native Son* (Boston: Beacon Press, 1955), 19. On Baldwin's critique of reading as a substitute for change, see Joseph Darda, "The Race Novel: An Education," *MELUS* 45, no. 3 (2020): 1–24.
10. Wendy Wall, *Inventing the American Way: The Politics of Consensus from the New Deal to the Civil Rights Movement* (New York: Oxford University Press, 2008), 5–6.

11. On the shortcomings of white liberalism in midcentury social message literature, see Gregory Jay, *White Writers, Race Matters: Fictions of Race Liberalism from Stowe to Stockett* (New York: Oxford University Press, 2017).
12. Jay, *White Writers*, 4.
13. Joe R. Feagin, *The White Racial Frame: Centuries of Racial Framing and Counter-Framing* (New York: Routledge, 2020); Karen Brodkin, *How Jews Became White Folks and What That Says about Race in America* (New Brunswick, NJ: Rutgers University Press, 1998); Eric Goldstein, *The Price of Whiteness: Jews, Race, and American Identity* (Princeton, NJ: Princeton University Press, 2006).
14. Sinclair, *Wasteland*, 46.
15. Sinclair, *Wasteland*, 59.
16. Sinclair, *Wasteland*, 313.
17. On Jewish and Christian blood shaping family, race, and nation, see Gil Anidjar, *Blood: A Critique of Christianity* (New York: Columbia University Press, 2016).
18. "Red Cross to Use Blood of Negroes," *New York Times*, January 29, 1942, 13.
19. Sinclair, *Wasteland*, 282.
20. On Sinclair's incorporation of Blacks into her discussion of otherness in Wasteland, see Warren Hoffman, *The Passing Game: Queering Jewish American Culture* (Syracuse University Press, 2009), 104–105.
21. Sinclair, *Wasteland*, 289–290.
22. "Opposition to Segregation of Bloods from White and Negro Donors in Blood Banks," *Journal of the American Medical Association*, July 4, 1942, 801.
23. Feagin, *The White Racial Frame*.
24. On these postwar traditional gender roles and the structure of American manhood, see Laura Belmonte, *Selling the American Way: US Propaganda and the Cold War* (Philadelphia: University of Pennsylvania Press, 2010), 136–137. May, *Homeward Bound*, 85–86.
25. Sinclair, *Wasteland*, 290.
26. On bachelor status in midcentury America: John Donald Gustav-Wrathall, *Take the Young Stranger by the Hand: Same Sex Relations and the YMCA* (Chicago: University of Chicago Press, 1998); Howard P. Chudacoff, *The Age of the Bachelor: Creating an American Subculture* (Princeton, NJ: Princeton University Press, 2000).
27. Sinclair, *Wasteland*, 136.
28. Sinclair, *Wasteland*, 193.
29. Hobson, *Agreement*, 122.
30. Matthew Jacobson, "Becoming Caucasian: Vicissitudes of Whiteness in American Politics and Culture," *Identities* 8: no. 1 (2001): 93.
31. On the persistence of racial understandings of Jewishness, see Goldstein, *The Price of Whiteness*, 4, chapter 8.
32. Gwethalyn Graham, *Earth and High Heaven* (New York: Sun Dial Press, 1944), 289.
33. Miller, *Focus*, 9, 26, 32, 33.
34. Miller, *Focus*, 33.
35. Miller, *Focus*, 178.
36. Bellow, *The Victim*, 56.

37. "Meet the Panel of Americans," *Seventeen*, August 1947, 74.
38. "Meet the Panel of Americans," 207.
39. Graham, *Earth and High Heaven*, 256.
40. Graham, *Earth and High Heaven*, 256.
41. Hobson, *Agreement*, 212.
42. Hobson, *Agreement*, 196.
43. See boxes 25 and 26, Hobson Papers. "The Races of Mankind and The Brotherhood of Man," retrieved from Social Welfare History Project, http://socialwelfare.library.vcu.edu/eras/wwii-1950s/influence-controversy-races-mankind-brotherhood-man/. Ruth Benedict and Gene Weltfish, *The Races of Mankind* (New York: Public Affairs Committee, 1943), 11.
44. On *The Races of Mankind* as "a first shot in a war on racism," see Joseph Darda, *The Strange Career of Racial Liberalism* (Stanford: Stanford University Press, 2022), 23–26.
45. Benedict and Weltfish, "The Races of Mankind," 11.
46. As she was finishing *Agreement*, Hobson might have read about Albert Einstein's reaction to racism: in 1946, Einstein told a university group that "the separation of the races is not a disease of the colored people, but a disease of white people." Fred Jerome and Rodger Taylor, *Einstein on Race and Racism* (New Brunswick, NJ: Rutgers University Press, 2005), 88. Gwethalyn Graham's use of science in her anti-antisemitism novel bears some similarities: Graham, *Earth and High Heaven*, 308.
47. Hobson, *Agreement*, 122.
48. On Hobson and communism: Hobson, *Laura Z: The Early Years and Years of Fulfillment*, 465–471. On Hobson and Zionism, see Hobson, *Laura Z: The Early Years and Years of Fulfillment*, 447.
49. Hobson, *Laura Z: The Early Years and Years of Fulfillment*, 447.
50. Benedict and Weltfish, "The Races of Mankind," 31.
51. Ethel Alpenfels, "Sense and Nonsense about Race" (New York: Friendship Press, 1946), 17.
52. Melvin Tumin, "The Idea of 'Race' Dies Hard," *Commentary* 8 (July 1949): 80.
53. Tumin, "The Idea," 81.
54. Tumin, "The Idea," 80. On Jewish attachment to race as a category of self-definition that allowed Jews to "assert a minority consciousness in American society, something that was extremely central to many Jews' self-conception," see Goldstein, *Price of Whiteness*, 6.
55. Chris Asch and George Musgrove, *Chocolate City: A History of Race and Democracy in the Nation's Capital* (Chapel Hill: University of North Carolina Press, 2017), 342.
56. Lolita Brown to Margaret Halsey, December 13, 1946, "Hobson—Misc.—Authors and Books," box 2, Hobson Papers.
57. Lolita Brown to Margaret Halsey, December 13, 1946.
58. Lolita Brown to Margaret Halsey, December 13, 1946.
59. Margaret Halsey to Time Magazine, December 18, 1946, "Hobson—Misc.—Authors and Books," box 2, Hobson Papers.
60. Hobson to Miss Amy S. Lifton, April 16, 1947, "Gentleman's Agreement: Correspondence," box 20, Hobson Papers.
61. Hobson to Mr. Starr, February 12, 1947, "Gentleman's Agreement Correspondence," box 20, Hobson Papers.

62. "Elinor Rice Hays, 92, Biographer of Women" (obituary), *New York Times*, March 23, 1994, B20.
63. Elinor Rice, "What Am I?" *Woman's Day*, April 1949, 91.
64. Canby, "A Plaster on a Wound?" 20.
65. Tom Perrin, *The Aesthetics of Middlebrow Fiction: Popular US Novels, Modernism, and Form, 1945–75* (New York: Palgrave, 2015), 38.
66. William Du Bois, "Schuyler Green's Metamorphosis," *New York Times Book Review*, March 2, 1947, 5, 36.
67. Rosemary Carr Benet, "Drawing Room 'Abie's Irish Rose,'" *Saturday Review*, October 7, 1944, 9.
68. Hobson to Richard Simon, September 24, 1944, "Scrapbook," box 21, Hobson Papers.
69. L. M. Birkhead to Hobson, February 21, 1947, "Gentleman's Agreement: Correspondence, Fan Mail, 1947," Box 2, Hobson Papers.
70. James Reid Parker, "Gentleman's Agreement," *Survey Graphic*, May 1947, 313. The reviewer's remarks bring to mind W. E. B. Du Bois's 1926 declaration, "I do not care a damn for any art that is not used for propaganda." Du Bois, "Criteria of Negro Art," *The Crisis*, October 1926, 296.
71. James Reid Parker, "Gentleman's Agreement," *Survey Graphic*, May 1947, 313.
72. On this gendered dynamic of middlebrow fiction reading, see Janice Radway, *A Feeling for Books: The Book-of-the-Month Club, Literary Taste, and Middle-Class Desire* (Chapel Hill: University of North Carolina Press, 1997).
73. Dorothy Dunbar Bromley, "Mrs. Hobson Deluged with Mail on Her Novel on Anti-Semitism," *New York Herald Tribune*, March 9, 1947, 6.
74. Ruth Follman to Hobson, March 9, 1946, box 20, Hobson Papers.
75. Mrs. Dana Kopper to Hobson, March 15, 1947, box 20, Hobson Papers.
76. Mrs. Liebeskind to Hobson, March 31, 1947, box 20, Hobson Papers.
77. James Baldwin, "Everybody's Protest Novel," in *Notes of a Native Son* (Boston: Beacon Press, 1955), 19
78. Sacvan Bercovitch, *The Puritan Origins of the American Self* (New Haven, CT: Yale University Press, 1977).
79. Diana Trilling, "Americans without Distinction," *Commentary*, March 1947, 290.
80. Hobson's liberal vision of religious pluralism fits into what Tracy Fessenden, Catherine Albanese, and Laura Levitt describe as a dominant if tacit religious system in which secular space was permeated by Protestantism, and religious others such as Jews felt pressured to fit the Protestant mold of religious identity. Tracy Fessenden, *Culture and Redemption: Religion, the Secular, and American Literature* (Princeton, NJ: Princeton University Press, 2007), 4–5; Catherine Albanese, *America: Religions and Religion*, 5th edition (Belmont, California: Wadsworth, 2012), 395–398; Laura Levitt, "Impossible Assimilations, American Liberalism, and Jewish Difference: Revisiting Jewish Secularism," *American Quarterly* 59, no. 3 (September 2007): 825, 827.
81. Hobson, *Agreement*, 52.
82. Hobson, *Agreement*, 52.
83. On heterosexuality securing Cold War American identity, see Carolyn Lewis, *Prescription for Heterosexuality: Sexual Citizenship in the Cold War Era* (Chapel Hill: University of North Carolina Press, 2010).
84. Hobson, *Agreement*, 51.

85. Hobson, *Agreement*, 52.
86. Hobson to Mr. Lenderovsky, April 7, 1947, "Gentleman's Agreement: The Movie," box 21, Hobson papers.
87. Hobson, *Agreement*, 101.
88. Trilling, "Americans without Distinction," 291–292.
89. "Good Jews" and "Good Judaism" bear a strong resemblance to Robert Orsi's conception of "good religion." Robert Orsi, *Between Heaven and Earth: The Religious Worlds People Make and the Scholars Who Study Them* (Princeton, NJ: Princeton University Press, 2006), 186, 188.
90. Graham, *Earth and High Heaven*, 32.
91. Hobson, *Agreement*, 209.
92. Myriam Kubowitzki, "Letter to an Author," *Jewish Frontier*, July 1947, 27.
93. On Hobson's background, see Hobson, *Laura Z: A Life* (1983); and Rachel Gordan, "Laura Z. Hobson and the Making of Gentleman's Agreement," *Studies in American Jewish Literature* 34, no. 2 (2015): 231–256. On assimilation as achievement for Jewish immigrants, see Michael Kramer, "The Art of Assimilation: Ironies, Ambiguities, Aesthetics," in *Modern Jewish Literatures*, ed. Sheila Jelen, Michael Kramer, and Scott Lerner (Philadelphia: University of Pennsylvania Press, 2011), 303–326.
94. Hobson, *Agreement*, 242.
95. On the middlebrow as a space for feminine preoccupation with middle-classness: Nicola Humble, *The Feminine Middlebrow Novel, 1920s to 1950s: Class, Domesticity, and Bohemianism* (New York: Oxford University Press, 2001), 59–60.
96. Hobson, *Agreement*, 154.
97. Kubowitzki, "Letter to an Author," 27.
98. Kubowitzki, "Letter to an Author," 27.
99. On this melting-pot era of American Jewish history and Jewish assimilation, see Michael Kramer, "Assimilation in the Promised Land: Mary Antin and the Jewish Origins of the American Self," *Prooftexts* 18, no. 2 (May 1998): 121–148.
100. "Anti-Semitism—Is Hollywood's Praiseworthy Effort to Combat It Obscuring the Central Point?" *Life*, December 1, 1947, 44.
101. Frances Grossman to Jo Sinclair, February 25, 1946, "Wasteland: Fan Mail, 1945–1946," box 36, folder 14, Sinclair Collection.
102. Hobson, *Agreement*, 34.
103. Fermaglich, *A Rosenberg*, 47.
104. Wendy Brown, *Regulating Aversion: Tolerance in the Age of Identity and Empire* (Princeton, NJ: Princeton University Press, 2006), 53. On the pressures of twentieth-century Jews to comply with expectations to fit into American conceptions of religion, see Laura Levitt, "Impossible Assimilations, American Liberalism and Jewish Difference: Revisiting Jewish Secularism," *American Quarterly* 59, no. 3 (2007): 807–832.
105. Judith Weisenfeld, *Hollywood Be Thy Name: African American Religion in American Film, 1929–1945* (Princeton, NJ: Princeton University Press, 2007), 206–208.
106. John H. Johnson to Hobson, November 21, 1947; Laura Z. Hobson to Mr. Johnson, November 25, 1947, both from "Gentleman's Agreement: Correspondence, Fan Mail, 1947," box 20, Hobson Papers.

107. Hobson to Mr. Johnson, November 25, 1947, "Correspondence: Fan Mail, 1947," box 20, Hobson Papers.
108. June Gilliam to Hobson, September 29, 1947, "Correspondence: Fan Mail, 1947," box 20, Hobson Papers.
109. Gilliam to Hobson, September 29, 1947.
110. Mark Tushnet, *Making Civil Rights Law: Thurgood Marshall and the Supreme Court, 1936–1961* (New York: Oxford University Press, 1994), 142.
111. Asch and Musgrove, *Chocolate City*, 279
112. "Killing of Negroes Is Protested Here," *New York Times*, March 2, 1946, 26.
113. "Killing of Negroes is Protested Here," 26.
114. On the American roots of Nazism's racism, see James Whitman, *Hitler's American Model: The United States and the Making Nazi Race Law* (Princeton, NJ: Princeton University Press, 2017).
115. This question was posed in the Myrdals' previous work, Alva and Gunnar Myrdal, *Kontakt med Amerika* (Stockholm: A. Bonnier, 1941), 52. Cited in Walter A. Jackson, *Gunnar Myrdal and America's Conscience: Social Engineering and Racial Liberalism, 1938–1987* (Chapel Hill: University of North Carolina Press, 1990), 149.
116. James T. Patterson, *Brown v. Board of Education: A Civil Rights Milestone and Its Troubled Legacy* (New York: Oxford University Press, 2001), 54; Mark Tushnet and Katya Lezin, "What Really Happened in Brown v. Board of Education," *Columbia Law Review* 91, no. 8 (December 1991): 1888; Shari Cohen, "The Lasting Legacy of an American Dilemma," *Carnegie Results*, Fall 2004, https://www.carnegie.org/media/filer_public/98/65/9865c794-39d9-4659-862e-aae1583278a8/ccny_cresults_2004_americandilemma.pdf. See also Jackson, *Gunnar Myrdal and America's Conscience*, 149–150.
117. Gunnar Myrdal, *The American Dilemma: The Negro Problem and Modern Democracy* (New York: Harper & Row, 1964), lxix.
118. Myrdal, *The American Dilemma*, 29. A similar observation about the relationship between the situations of Jew and Blacks in America was made twenty years later by E. Digby Baltzell, *The Protestant Establishment: Aristocracy and Caste in America* (New York: Random House, 1964), x.
119. Dinnerstein, *Anti-Semitism in America*, 150, 165.

Chapter 5

1. March 31, 1947, Park Avenue Synagogue Bulletin, "Rabbinic Career—Park Avenue Synagogue—Bulletins—1941–1960," box 11, folder 8, Milton Steinberg Collection, P-369, American Jewish Historical Society, Collection of the American Jewish Historical Society, New York, NY (hereafter cited as Steinberg Collection).
2. John Mason Brown, "If You Prick Us," *Saturday Review*, December 6, 1947, 71.
3. Philip T. Hartung, "Not for Escapists," *The Commonweal*, November 21, 1947, 145.
4. Diana Trilling, "Americans without Distinction," *Commentary*, March 1947, 290.
5. Herman Wouk, *This Is My God* (New York: Doubleday, 1959).

6. Midcentury Introduction to Judaism books, broadly defined, include: Philip Bernstein, *What the Jews Believe* (New York: Farrar, Straus & Young 1950); Beryl David Cohon, *Judaism in Theory and Practice* (New York: Bloch Publishing, 1948); Samuel S. Cohon, *Judaism—A Way of Life* (Cincinnati: Union of American Hebrew Congregations, 1948); Abraham Cronbach, *Judaism for Today: Jewish Thoughts for Contemporary Jewish Youth* (New York: Bookman Associates, 1954); Daniel Davis, *Understanding Judaism* (New York: Philosophical Library, 1958); Samuel Dresner, *Three Paths of God and Man* (New York: Harper, 1960); Ira Eisenstein, *What We Mean by Religion* (New York: Behrman House, 1946); Louis Finkelstein, *The Beliefs and Practices of Judaism* (New York: Devin-Adair, 1952); Theodore Friedman, *Jewish Life in America* (New York: Horizon Press, 1955); Arthur Gilbert and Oscar Tarcov, *Your Neighbor Celebrates* (New York: Friendly House Publishers, 1957); Eli Ginzberg, *Agenda for American Jews* (New York: King's Crown Press, 1950); Morris Goldstein, *Jesus in Jewish Tradition* (New York: Macmillan, 1950); Robert Gordis, *Judaism for the Modern Man* (New York: Farrar, Straus & Cudahy, 1955); Robert Gordis, *A Faith for Moderns* (New York: Bloch Publishing, 1960); G. George Fox, *An American Jew Speaks* (Chicago: Falcon Press, 1946); Oscar Handlin, *Adventure in Freedom: 300 Years of Jewish Life in America* (New York: McGraw-Hill, 1954); Ben Hecht, *A Guide for the Bedeviled* (New York: Charles Scribner's Sons, 1943); Bernard Heller, *Epistle to an Apostate* (New York: Bookman's Press, 1951); Abraham Joshua Heschel, *The Earth Is the Lord's* (New York: Farrar, Straus & Giroux, 1949), Abraham Joshua Heschel, *The Sabbath: Its Meaning for Modern Man* (New York: Farrar, Straus & Young, 1951); Abraham Joshua Heschel, *God in Search of Man: A Philosophy of Judaism* (New York: Farrar, Straus & Cudahy, 1955); Ferdinand Isserman, *This Is Judaism* (Chicago: Willett, Clark & Co., 1944); Mordecai Kaplan, *Know How to Answer: A Guide to Reconstructionism* (New York: The Reconstructionist Foundation, 1951); Morris Kertzer, *What Is a Jew?* (Cleveland: World Publishing, 1953); Ludwig Lewisohn, *The American Jew, Character and Destiny* (New York: Farrar, Straus, 1950); Ludwig Lewisohn, *What Is This Jewish Heritage?* (New York: Schocken Books, 1954); Joshua Loth Liebman, *Peace of Mind* (New York: Simon & Schuster, 1946); Samuel H. Markowitz, *Leading a Jewish Life in the Modern World* (Cincinnati: Union of American Hebrew Congregations, 1958); Julian Morgenstern, *As a Mighty Stream* (Philadelphia: Jewish Publication Society of America, 1949); David de Sola Pool, *Why I Am a Jew* (New York: T. Nelson, 1957); Samuel Price, *Outlines of Judaism* (New York: Bloch Publishing, 1946); Harold Ribalow, *What's Your Jewish I.Q.?* (New York: Twayne, 1954); Maurice Samuel, *Gentleman and the Jew* (New York: Knopf, 1950); Charles and Gertie G. Schwartz, *Faith through Reason* (New York: Macmillan, 1946); Maxwell Silver, *The Way to God* (New York: Philosophical Library, 1950); Abba Hillel Silver, *Where Judaism Differed: An Inquiry into the Distinctiveness of Judaism* (New York: Macmillan 1956); Milton Steinberg, *Basic Judaism* (New York: Harcourt Brace, 1947); Meyer Waxman, *Handbook of Judaism: As Professed and Practiced through the Ages* (New York: Bloch Publishing, 1947); Trude Weiss-Rosmarin, *Judaism and Christianity: The Differences* (New York: Jewish Book Club, 1943); Herman Wouk, *This Is My God* (New York: Dell, 1959); Louis Finkelstein, *Thirteen

Americans: Their Spiritual Biographies (New York: Harper, 1953). Wallace Stegner and the editors of *Look* also published *One Nation* about America's minority groups, including Jews (Houghton Mifflin, 1945).
7. On religion books reinscribing tri-faith America, see "The Year's Best Religion Books," *The Saturday Review*, March 5, 1955, 30; Harold Ribalow, "Jewish Tercentenary: People of the Book," *Saturday Review*, September 18, 1954, 20.
8. Rachel Gordan, "Nathan Glazer's American Judaism: Evaluating Post-World War II American Jewish Religion," *Jewish Quarterly Review* 105, no. 4 (Fall 2015): 482–506. Leonard Dinnerstein and Gene Koppel, *Nathan Glazer, a Different Kind of Liberal* (Tucson: University of Arizona Press, 1973), v.
9. Salo Baron to Alexander J. Morin, May 28, 1956, University of Chicago Press, Records, box 194, folder 4, Hanna Holborn Gray Special Collections Research Center, University of Chicago Library.
10. On the criticism of the *Saturday Review* as a middlebrow publication, see Christina Klein, *Cold War Orientalism: Asia in the Middlebrow Imagination, 1945–1961* (Berkeley: University of California Press, 2003), 67.
11. Boris Kachka, *Hothouse: The Art of Survival and the Survival of Art at America's Most Celebrated Publishing House, Farrar, Straus & Giroux* (New York: Simon & Schuster, 2013), 114.
12. Harold Ribalow, "Answers to Man's Ultimate Questions," *Saturday Review*, March 3, 1956, 38.
13. Reinhold Niebuhr, "The Mysteries of Faith," review of *God in Search of Man* by Abraham Joshua Heschel, *Saturday Review*, April 21, 1956, 18.
14. On the postwar era as a golden era in religious books publication, see Steven Prothero, *God the Bestseller: How One Editor Transformed American Religion a Book at a Time* (New York: HarperCollins, 2022), 130–134.
15. Rebecca Alpert, "From Jewish Science to Rabbinical Counseling: The Evolution of the Relationship between Religion and Health by the American Reform Rabbinate, 1916–1954" (PhD diss., Temple University, 2008); Matthew Hedstrom, "Psychology and Mysticism in 1940s Religion: Reading across the Divide of Faith, Liberal Book Culture and Interfaith Encounters in Print, 1921–1948," in *American Religious Liberalism*, ed. Leigh Schmidt and Sally Promey (Bloomington: Indiana University Press, 2012), 207–226; Andrew Heinze, *Jews and the American Soul: Human Nature in the Twentieth Century* (Princeton, NJ: Princeton University Press, 2004), chapters 9 and 10.
16. Arthur Cohen, "Introduction," in *Anatomy of Faith*, ed. Arthur Cohen (New York: Harcourt Brace, 1960), 49. Steinberg's second novel would be published posthumously. On the readership and influence of *As a Driven Leaf*, see Jonathan Steinberg, "Milton Steinberg: American Rabbi—Thoughts on His Centenary," *Jewish Quarterly Review* 95, no. 3 (Summer 2005): 579–600.
17. Steinberg's second novel, *The Prophet's Wife*, was published posthumously. Milton Steinberg, *The Prophet's Wife* (New York: Behrman House, 2010).
18. Cohen, "Introduction," in *Anatomy of Faith*, 49.

19. Steinberg's writing about Elisha Ben Abuyah in *As a Driven Leaf* shows some connection to Martin Buber's writing about Elisha Ben Abuya in a poem cycle that also used this ancient figure to discuss contemporary concerns. See Yaniv Feller, "From Aher to Maricon: Martin Buber's Understanding of Gnosis," *Jewish Studies Quarterly* 20, no. 4 (2013): 374–397.
20. March 31, 1947, Park Avenue Synagogue Bulletin, box 11, folder 8, Steinberg Collection.
21. Marshall Sklare, *Conservative Judaism: An American Religious Movement* (Glencoe, IL: Free Press, 1955), 38.
22. Sklare, *Conservative Judaism*, 38.
23. Nathan Glazer, *American Judaism* (Chicago: University of Chicago Press, 1957), 132.
24. Herberg, *Protestant-Catholic-Jew*, 274.
25. For example: of the 1930s and 1940s novels listed in the *American Jewish Fiction: A JPS Guide*, none of them features positive portrayals of religious Jews. Josh Lambert, *American Jewish Fiction: A JPS Guide* (New York: JPS, 2009).
26. The Editor, "Review of the Year 5701: Introduction," in *American Jewish Year Book 1941–1942*, 28.
27. Andrew Heinze, *Jews and the American Soul: Human Nature in the Twentieth Century* (Princeton, NJ: Princeton University Press, 2004), 195.
28. Milton Steinberg, "Between Religion and Psychiatry," *The Reconstructionist* 12, no. 10 (1946): 29.
29. Milton Steinberg to Lambert Davis, December 27, 1945, box 9, folder 7, Steinberg Collection.
30. Robert T. Handy, "The American Religious Depression," *Church History*, March 1960, 3–16. On the 1930s as a time of spiritual depression, see Beth Wenger, *New York Jews and the Great Depression: Uncertain Promise* (New Haven, CT: Yale University Press, 1996), chapter 7.
31. James W. Wise and Lee Levinger, *Mr. Smith, Meet Mr. Cohen* (New York: Reynal & Hitchcock, 1940), 2.
32. Wise and Levinger, *Mr. Smith, Meet Mr. Cohen*, 1.
33. See Louis Finkelstein's anecdotes about non-Jewish colleagues' impressions of Judaism: Finkelstein, "Foreword," *The Jews*, xxiii.
34. Louis Finkelstein, *The Jews*, "Foreword," xxii–xxiii.
35. See Jeffrey Shandler and Elihu Katz, "Broadcasting American Judaism: The Radio and Television Department of JTS," in *Tradition Renewed: A History of the Jewish Theological Seminary of America*, ed. Jack Wertheimer (New York: Jewish Theological Seminary of America, 1997), 363–401. Markus Krah, "Role Models or Foils for American Jews? 'The Eternal Light', Displaced Persons, and the Construction of Jewishness in Mid-Twentieth-Century America," *American Jewish History* 96, no. 4 (December 2010), 265–286.
36. When the Southern Jewish camp named Camp Blue Star was established in the early 1950s, it included a "Living Judaism" program. See Jennie Jones Giles, "Building Their Own Southern Tradition," Blue Ridge Now, June 29, 2003, https://www.blueridgenow.com/news/20030629/building-their-own-southern-tradition.

In 1950, the Reform movement named its new Fifth Avenue headquarters the "House of Living Judaism."

Americans: Their Spiritual Biographies (New York: Harper, 1953). Wallace Stegner and the editors of *Look* also published *One Nation* about America's minority groups, including Jews (Houghton Mifflin, 1945).

7. On religion books reinscribing tri-faith America, see "The Year's Best Religion Books," *The Saturday Review*, March 5, 1955, 30; Harold Ribalow, "Jewish Tercentenary: People of the Book," *Saturday Review*, September 18, 1954, 20.
8. Rachel Gordan, "Nathan Glazer's American Judaism: Evaluating Post-World War II American Jewish Religion," *Jewish Quarterly Review* 105, no. 4 (Fall 2015): 482–506. Leonard Dinnerstein and Gene Koppel, *Nathan Glazer, a Different Kind of Liberal* (Tucson: University of Arizona Press, 1973), v.
9. Salo Baron to Alexander J. Morin, May 28, 1956, University of Chicago Press, Records, box 194, folder 4, Hanna Holborn Gray Special Collections Research Center, University of Chicago Library.
10. On the criticism of the *Saturday Review* as a middlebrow publication, see Christina Klein, *Cold War Orientalism: Asia in the Middlebrow Imagination, 1945–1961* (Berkeley: University of California Press, 2003), 67.
11. Boris Kachka, *Hothouse: The Art of Survival and the Survival of Art at America's Most Celebrated Publishing House, Farrar, Straus & Giroux* (New York: Simon & Schuster, 2013), 114.
12. Harold Ribalow, "Answers to Man's Ultimate Questions," *Saturday Review*, March 3, 1956, 38.
13. Reinhold Niebuhr, "The Mysteries of Faith," review of *God in Search of Man* by Abraham Joshua Heschel, *Saturday Review*, April 21, 1956, 18.
14. On the postwar era as a golden era in religious books publication, see Steven Prothero, *God the Bestseller: How One Editor Transformed American Religion a Book at a Time* (New York: HarperCollins, 2022), 130–134.
15. Rebecca Alpert, "From Jewish Science to Rabbinical Counseling: The Evolution of the Relationship between Religion and Health by the American Reform Rabbinate, 1916–1954" (PhD diss., Temple University, 2008); Matthew Hedstrom, "Psychology and Mysticism in 1940s Religion: Reading across the Divide of Faith, Liberal Book Culture and Interfaith Encounters in Print, 1921–1948," in *American Religious Liberalism*, ed. Leigh Schmidt and Sally Promey (Bloomington: Indiana University Press, 2012), 207–226; Andrew Heinze, *Jews and the American Soul: Human Nature in the Twentieth Century* (Princeton, NJ: Princeton University Press, 2004), chapters 9 and 10.
16. Arthur Cohen, "Introduction," in *Anatomy of Faith*, ed. Arthur Cohen (New York: Harcourt Brace, 1960), 49. Steinberg's second novel would be published posthumously. On the readership and influence of *As a Driven Leaf*, see Jonathan Steinberg, "Milton Steinberg: American Rabbi—Thoughts on His Centenary," *Jewish Quarterly Review* 95, no. 3 (Summer 2005): 579–600.
17. Steinberg's second novel, *The Prophet's Wife*, was published posthumously. Milton Steinberg, *The Prophet's Wife* (New York: Behrman House, 2010).
18. Cohen, "Introduction," in *Anatomy of Faith*, 49.

19. Steinberg's writing about Elisha Ben Abuyah in *As a Driven Leaf* shows some connection to Martin Buber's writing about Elisha Ben Abuya in a poem cycle that also used this ancient figure to discuss contemporary concerns. See Yaniv Feller, "From Aher to Maricon: Martin Buber's Understanding of Gnosis," *Jewish Studies Quarterly* 20, no. 4 (2013): 374–397.
20. March 31, 1947, Park Avenue Synagogue Bulletin, box 11, folder 8, Steinberg Collection.
21. Marshall Sklare, *Conservative Judaism: An American Religious Movement* (Glencoe, IL: Free Press, 1955), 38.
22. Sklare, *Conservative Judaism*, 38.
23. Nathan Glazer, *American Judaism* (Chicago: University of Chicago Press, 1957), 132.
24. Herberg, *Protestant-Catholic-Jew*, 274.
25. For example: of the 1930s and 1940s novels listed in the *American Jewish Fiction: A JPS Guide*, none of them features positive portrayals of religious Jews. Josh Lambert, *American Jewish Fiction: A JPS Guide* (New York: JPS, 2009).
26. The Editor, "Review of the Year 5701: Introduction," in *American Jewish Year Book 1941–1942*, 28.
27. Andrew Heinze, *Jews and the American Soul: Human Nature in the Twentieth Century* (Princeton, NJ: Princeton University Press, 2004), 195.
28. Milton Steinberg, "Between Religion and Psychiatry," *The Reconstructionist* 12, no. 10 (1946): 29.
29. Milton Steinberg to Lambert Davis, December 27, 1945, box 9, folder 7, Steinberg Collection.
30. Robert T. Handy, "The American Religious Depression," *Church History*, March 1960, 3–16. On the 1930s as a time of spiritual depression, see Beth Wenger, *New York Jews and the Great Depression: Uncertain Promise* (New Haven, CT: Yale University Press, 1996), chapter 7.
31. James W. Wise and Lee Levinger, *Mr. Smith, Meet Mr. Cohen* (New York: Reynal & Hitchcock, 1940), 2.
32. Wise and Levinger, *Mr. Smith, Meet Mr. Cohen*, 1.
33. See Louis Finkelstein's anecdotes about non-Jewish colleagues' impressions of Judaism: Finkelstein, "Foreword," *The Jews*, xxiii.
34. Louis Finkelstein, *The Jews*, "Foreword," xxii–xxiii.
35. See Jeffrey Shandler and Elihu Katz, "Broadcasting American Judaism: The Radio and Television Department of JTS," in *Tradition Renewed: A History of the Jewish Theological Seminary of America*, ed. Jack Wertheimer (New York: Jewish Theological Seminary of America, 1997), 363–401. Markus Krah, "Role Models or Foils for American Jews? 'The Eternal Light', Displaced Persons, and the Construction of Jewishness in Mid-Twentieth-Century America," *American Jewish History* 96, no. 4 (December 2010), 265–286.
36. When the Southern Jewish camp named Camp Blue Star was established in the early 1950s, it included a "Living Judaism" program. See Jennie Jones Giles, "Building Their Own Southern Tradition," Blue Ridge Now, June 29, 2003, https://www.blueridgenow.com/news/20030629/building-their-own-southern-tradition.

In 1950, the Reform movement named its new Fifth Avenue headquarters the "House of Living Judaism."

NOTES 239

37. Jonathan Sarna, *American Judaism: A History* (New Haven, CT: Yale University Press, 2004), 245–249.
38. Arthur Cohen, "Introduction," in Milton Steinberg, *Anatomy of Faith* (New York: Harcourt Brace, 1960), 37.
39. "Lambert Davis, 88, Editor and Publisher" (obituary), *New York Times*, November 13, 1993, 31.
40. Lambert Davis to Milton Steinberg, April 25, 1945, box 6, folder 1, Steinberg Collection.
41. In 1939, Steinberg submitted papers to the Department of Taxation and Finance in Albany, New York, explaining his financial situation: "Because of my profession," Steinberg wrote that he was "compelled to live in a high-bracket rental neighborhood near the institution which I serve." in addition to his wife and children, Steinberg was the sole financial supporter of his parents, who lived in Brooklyn, near Milton's sisters, who were unable to contribute to the financial support of their parents, Samuel and Fanny Steinberg. Steinberg explained that since 1937, his financial responsibility to his parents "is growing increasingly heavier with time." Milton Steinberg to Mr. Roy Palmer, Department of Taxation and Finance, March 24, 1939, box 3, folder: "Personal—Correspondence "with others"—Miscellaneous—1939-1949," Steinberg Collection.
42. Lambert Davis to Milton Steinberg, April 25, 1945, box 6, folder 1; Milton Steinberg to Lambert Davis, July 8, 1945, box 9, folder 7, both from Steinberg Collection.
43. "Helen Fox Dead; a Garden Expert" (obituary), *New York Times*, January 14, 1974, 30.
44. Helen Fox to Milton Steinberg, undated, box 7, folder 9: "Writings—Books: The Making of the Modern Jew—Correspondence—1933-1948," Steinberg Collection.
45. Merle Miller, "The Book Club Controversy," *Harper's*, June 1948, 519.
46. Miller, "Book Club Controversy," 519.
47. Milton Steinberg to "Henry" at Volkenning, June 17, 1948, box 7, folder 9, Steinberg Collection.
48. Box 3, folder 8, Steinberg Collection.
49. Edith A. Steinberg, "Midwife to a Novel," undated, box 10, folder 4: "Writings—Other—Short Stories of the Steinberg Family, undated, 1938," Steinberg Collection.
50. Glazer, *American Judaism*, 114.
51. On Baeck and *The Essence of Judaism*, see Michael Meyer, *Rabbi Leo Baeck: Living a Religious Imperative in Troubled Times* (Philadelphia: University of Pennsylvania Press, 2020). Yaniv Feller, *The Jewish Imperial Imagination: Leo Baeck and German-Jewish Thought* (Cambridge: Cambridge University Press, 2023).
52. Leo Jung, *The Essence of Judaism* (Philadelphia: Haldeman-Julius Co., 1924). Leo Baeck's 1905 *The Essence of Judaism*.
53. Anita Diamant's Introduction to Judaism books include *Living a Jewish Life: Jewish Traditions, Customs, and Values* (New York: Harper's, 1991); *Choosing a Jewish Life: A Handbook for People Converting to Judaism and for Their Families and Friends* (New York: Schocken, 1998); *Saying Kaddish: How to Comfort the Dying, Bury the Dead, and Mourn as a Jew* (New York: Schocken, 2007); Irving Greenberg, *The Jewish Way: Living the Holidays* (New York: Touchstone, 1993).

240 NOTES

54. Milton Steinberg, "How the Jew Does It," *Atlantic Monthly*, July 1933, 26.
55. Milton Steinberg, *The Making of the Modern Jew* (Indianapolis: Bobbs-Merrill, 1934), 293.
56. Even in 1955, social scientists observed the scarcity of Jews in America, and the absence of "contact opportunities" between Jews and non-Jews: see John P. Dean, "Patterns of Socialization and Association between Jews and Non-Jews," *Jewish Social Studies* 17, no. 3 (July 1955): 256.
57. Steinberg, "How the Jew Does It," 27.
58. Steinberg, "How the Jew Does It," 29.
59. Steinberg, "How the Jew Did It," *Atlantic Monthly*, May 1933, 659.
60. Milton Steinberg, *A Partisan Guide to the Jewish Problem* (New York: Bobbs-Merrill, 1945), 11.
61. Milton Steinberg, *The Making of the Modern Jew* (New York: Behrman's, 1943), 230.
62. Jonathan Steinberg, "Milton Steinberg, American Rabbi—Thoughts on His Centenary," *Jewish Quarterly Review* 95, no. 3 (Summer 2005): 583. As Arthur Cohen writes, Steinberg "came to Judaism out of the secular culture of America." Cohen, "Introduction," in *Anatomy of Faith*, 32. For Steinberg's secular Jewish memory: Steinberg, *The Making of the Modern Jew*, 230; Simon Noveck, "Milton Steinberg," in *The Other New York Jewish Intellectuals*, ed. Carole Kessner (New York: New York University Press, 1994), 331–314.
63. Cohen, "Introduction," in *Anatomy of Faith*, 24.
64. Simon Noveck, "Milton Steinberg," in *The Other New York Jewish Intellectuals*, 322.
65. Ben Halpern, book review of *Anatomy of Faith*, *Commentary* 30 (January 1, 1960): 550.
66. Milton Steinberg to Arthur Cohen, March 8, 1948, box 11, folder 9, Steinberg Collection.
67. Arthur Cohen, "Introduction," in *Anatomy of Faith*, 46.
68. Milton Steinberg to Mrs. Judah Goldin, March 1, 1948, box 3, folder 8, Steinberg Collection.
69. Cohen, "Introduction," in *Anatomy of Faith*, 46–47, 39.
70. Milton Steinberg, "American Jewry's Coming of Age," in *A Believing Jew* (New York: Harcourt Brace, 1951), 108.
71. Steinberg, "First Principles for American Jews," *Contemporary Jewish Record*, December 1, 1941, 594.
72. Steinberg, "First Principles," 595.
73. "Rabbi Steinberg Speaks on 'Indignation,'" Park Avenue Synagogue Bulletin, February 1945, box 11, folder 8: "Rabbinic Career—Park Avenue Synagogue—Bulletins—1941–1960," Steinberg Collection. See also Kurt Lewin, "Self-Hatred among Jews," in *Resolving Social Conflict*, ed. Gertrude Weiss-Lewin (New York: Harper & Brothers, 1948), 186–200.
74. "Rabbi Steinberg Speaks on 'Indignation.'"
75. Mrs. Ogden Reid, "Address by Mrs. Ogden Reid Delivered at Dedication of Milton Steinberg House," September 19, 1954, box 5, folder 1, Steinberg Collection.

76. "Message from the Rabbi," January 6, 1947, Park Avenue Synagogue Bulletin, box 11, folder 8: "Rabbinic Career—Park Avenue Synagogue—Bulletins—1941–1960," Steinberg Collection.
77. January 6, 1947, Park Avenue Synagogue bulletin, box 11, folder 7, Steinberg Collection.
78. Steinberg to Israel Goldstein, July 22, 1942, box 11, folder 7, Steinberg Collection.
79. Steinberg, *Basic Judaism*, viii.
80. On "empty vessels," see Milton Steinberg, "The Future of Judaism in America," in *A Believing Jew*, 77–78.
81. Stephen S. Wise to Cantor Glass of Beth-el Zedek, May 23, 1933, box 11, folder 1: "Rabbinic Career—Indianapolis Rabbinate and Continuing Correspondence, 1929, 1933, 1949"; Box 11, folder 8 "Rabbinic Career—Park Avenue Synagogue—Bulletins—1941–1960," both from Steinberg Collection.
82. Stephen S. Wise to Cantor Glass of Beth-el Zedek, May 23, 1933.
83. Milton Steinberg to Philip Bernstein, May 10, 1933, box 3, folder 5, Steinberg Collection.
84. Steinberg to Arthur Cohen March 8, 1948, box 11, folder 9, Steinberg Collection.
85. Irving Kristol, "How Basic Is 'Basic Judaism'?" *Commentary*, January 1, 1948, 27.
86. Steinberg, *Basic Judaism*, viii.
87. Robert Orsi describes good religion as the "rational, word-centered, non-ritualistic, middle-class, unemotional, compatible with democracy and the liberal state" that has been taught and endorsed in academic institutions. Orsi, "On Not Talking to the Press," *Religious Studies News* 19, no. 3 (2004): 15. Part of what Fessenden adds in her discussion of Orsi's framework is that good religion is associated with freedom and enlightenment and is part of the progressive narrative of democracy. Fessenden, *Culture and Redemption* (Princeton, NJ: Princeton University Press, 2007), 2–3.
88. Kristol, "How Basic Is 'Basic Judaism'?" 30.
89. Robert Wuthnow, *After Heaven: Spirituality in America since the 1950s* (Berkeley: University of California Press, 1998), 23–24. See Daniel Walden's recollections of growing up near a Catholic neighborhood in the 1930s and 1940s: Daniel Walden, *On Being Jewish: American Jewish Writers from Cahan to Bellow* (Greenwich: Fawcett, 1974), 22.
90. Milton Steinberg, "What Religion Is Not," *The Reconstructionist* 3, no. 14 (1937): 15.
91. Steinberg, "What Religion Is Not," 15.
92. Steinberg, "Between Religion and Psychiatry," 28, 29.
93. "Basic Judaism," *New Yorker*, September 13, 1947, 123.
94. Steinberg to Judah Goldin, February 7, 1947, Box 3, Folder 8. Milton Steinberg P-369 AJHS.
95. Steinberg, *Basic Judaism*, 111.
96. Steinberg, *Basic Judaism*, 71.
97. Steinberg, *Basic Judaism*, 89.
98. Steinberg, *Basic Judaism*, 89.
99. Steinberg, *Basic Judaism*, 89.
100. Steinberg, *Basic Judaism*, 34.

101. Steinberg, *Basic Judaism*, 91.
102. Steinberg, *Basic Judaism*, 96.
103. Steinberg, *Basic Judaism*, 98.
104. Steinberg, *Basic Judaism*, 99.
105. Robert Goldy, *The Emergence of Jewish Theology in America* (Bloomington: Indiana University Press, 1990), 13.
106. Steinberg, *Basic Judaism*, 99.
107. Steinberg, *Basic Judaism*, 99.
108. Steinberg, *Basic Judaism*, 100.
109. Steinberg's distance from the New York Jewish intellectuals is captured by his inclusion in Carole S. Kessner's book *The Other New York Jewish Intellectuals* (New York: New York U Press, 1994).
110. Nancy Sinkoff, *From Left to Right: Lucy S. Dawidowicz, the New York Intellectuals, and the Politics of Jewish History* (Detroit: Wayne State University Press, 2020).
111. Steinberg's distance from Jewish intellectuals is also apparent in his famous 1949 lecture at Park Avenue Synagogue, "Commentary Magazine—Benefit or Detriment to American Judaism?" See Markus Krah, *American Jewry and the Re-Invention of the East European Jewish Past* (Boston: De Gruyter, 2017), 96.
112. Kristol, "How Basic," 28.
113. Kristol, "How Basic," 32.
114. Kristol, "How Basic," 32.
115. Theologian Eugene Borowitz would later criticize *Basic Judaism* in similar terms: Eugene Borowitz, "Jewish Theology: Milton Steinberg and After," *The Reconstructionist* 31, no. 7 (May 14, 1965): 9.
116. Arthur Cohen, "Introduction," in *Anatomy of Faith*, 32. Milton Steinberg to Arthur Cohen, January 24, 1947, subseries 2: "Correspondence with Others, 1928–1950," Steinberg Collection.
117. Steinberg, "The Outlook of Reinhold Niebuhr: A Description and Appraisal," *The Reconstructionist* 11 (December 14, 1945): 15.
118. Milton Steinberg, "A Specimen Jew," in *A Believing Jew* (New York: Harcourt Brace, 1951), 98–99.
119. Steinberg, "A Specimen Jew," 99.
120. Jonathan Sarna captures this idea of harmony between Judaism and Americanism in "The Cult of Synthesis in American Jewish Culture," *Jewish Social Studies* 5 (Fall 1998–Winter 1999): 52–79. Steinberg, "To Be or Not to Be a Jew" *Common Ground* 1, no. 3 (Spring 1941): 49, 50.
121. Gabriel Schonfeld, "From the Talmud: A Dynamic Tradition of Self-Study," *Saturday Review*, February 21, 1959, 43.
122. Schonfeld, "From the Talmud," 43.
123. The majority of 1940s and 1950s Introduction to Judaism books did not include substantial discussion of Talmud and Jewish law. Exceptions include: *Basic Judaism*, *Where Judaism Differed: An Inquiry into the Distinctiveness of Judaism* by Abba Hillel Silver, *The Way to God* by Maxwell Silver, and *Why I Am a Jew* by David de Sola Pool.

Chapter 6

1. Alan Brinkley, *The Publisher: Henry Luce and His American Century* (New York: Vintage: 2010), 213.
2. "Movies: An American Queen," *Life*, September 11, 1950, 80.
3. Miller and Nowak, *The Fifties*, 84; Herberg, *Protestant-Catholic-Jew*, 56.
4. Miller and Nowak, *The Fifties*, 85–86.
5. Ari Kelman, "Hear Israel," Tablet, January 7, 2011, https://www.tabletmag.com/sections/arts-letters/articles/hear-israel.
6. D. Schocher, "Tzena, Tzena—On Hit Parade—Is Israel's Biggest Export," *The Jewish Advocate*, September 28, 1950, 1. The song's popularity in the United States made it a global phenomenon. A headline in November in the *Irish Times* asked, "Who Wrote 'Tzena'? And What Is It?," reflecting the global confusion over its meaning and origins. "Who Wrote 'Tzena'? And What Is It?" *Irish Times*, November 18, 1950, 9.
7. John McCarten, "The Current Cinema," *New Yorker*, January 14, 1950, 75.
8. James Selwyn, "Rosh Hashanah and Yom Kippur," *Redbook*, September 1950, 34–37, 80–81.
9. Stephen Whitfield, *Culture of the Cold War*, 83.
10. Reinhold Niebuhr, "Is There a Revival of Religion?" *New York Times*, November 19, 1950, SM7.
11. Chambers, *Faith for a Lenten Age*, 70.
12. *Time*, March 8, 1948.
13. Miller and Nowak, *The Fifties*, 91.
14. "Sees Revival of Judaism," 4.
15. "The Fatal Cushion," *Time*, January 5, 1948, 40.
16. "The Fatal Cushion," 40.
17. "The Fatal Cushion," 42. A 1948 Gallup poll revealed Americans to be the fourth most God-fearing nation (94%), after Brazilians, Australians, and Canadians, and with the French as the least at 66%. *Time*, January 19, 1948, 66.
18. As Robert Ellwood observes, Gallup polls revealed that "the highest historical level of church attendance, about 47 percent of the US population on an average Sunday, was reached in 1955 and 1958." Ellwood, *The Fifties Spiritual Marketplace: American Religion in a Decade of Conflict* (New Brunswick, NJ: Rutgers University Press, 1997), 1.
19. Walter Ruch, "Religious Revival Urged by Truman," *New York Times*, July 23, 1950, 37.
20. J. Edgar Hoover, "God or Chaos," *Redbook*, February 1949, 61, 62, 63.
21. Hoover, "God or Chaos," 63.
22. Solomon J. Sharfman, "Foreword," *Tradition* 1, no. 1 (Fall 1958): 5.
23. Sharfman, "Foreword," 5.
24. Norman Lamm, "The Need for Tradition: The Editor's Introduction to a New Journal," *Tradition* 1, no. 1 (Fall 1958): 10.
25. David Hollinger, *Protestants Abroad: How Missionaries Tried to Change the World but Changed America* (Princeton, NJ: Princeton University Press, 2017), 24.

26. Joseph Epstein, "Henry Luce," in *Joseph Epstein: Essays in Biography* (Virginia: Axios Press, 2012), 94–95.
27. Henry Luce, "The American Century," *Life*, February 17, 1941, 65.
28. Pete Hamill, "More Irrelevant than Irreverent," *Village Voice*, January 16, 1969.
29. Brinkley, *The Publisher*, 208.
30. Deborah Solomon, American Mirror: The Life and Art of Norman Rockwell (New York: Farrar, Straus, and Giroux, 2013), 176.
31. Brinkley, *The Publisher*, 234–239. On *Life* as embodying the American Way of Life, see Wendy Kozol, *Life's America: Family and Nation in Postwar Photojournalism* (Philadelphia: Temple University Press, 1994).
32. Philip Bernstein, "What Jews Believe," *Life*, September 11, 1950, 151; "Life Goes to a Bar Mitzvah," *Life*, October 13, 1952, 170.
33. Real estate covenants were not legally enforceable after the 1948 Supreme Court ruling in *Shelley v. Kraemer* struck down racially restrictive housing covenants, but towns and neighborhoods continued to be known as "restricted" into the 1960s.
34. William Attwood, "The Position of the Jews in America Today," *Look*, November 29, 1955, 27.
35. John Dean, "Patterns of Socialization and Association between Jews and Non-Jews," *Jewish Social Studies* 17, no. 3 (July 1955): 251.
36. *The World's Great Religions by Life* (New York: Time Life, 1957). Life worked within the standard framework of world religions of the time, which Tomoko Masuzawa has explained is de facto Protestant. Tomoko Masuzawa, *The Invention of World Religions* (Chicago: University of Chicago Press, 2005).
37. Letter from Henry Luce to Phil Wootten, April 25, 1955, box 435, folder 20, Time Inc. Records, MS 3009, New-York Historical Society (hereafter cited as Time Inc. Records). "The Editors of Life Present a New Series on the World's Great Religions," *Life*, February 7, 1955, 57.
38. Henry R. Luce, "The Rise and Decline of Opportunities," January 1958, RG 1, box 436, folder 7, Time Inc. Records.
39. Luce, "The Rise and Decline of Opportunities."
40. Henry Luce to Phil Wooten, April 25, 1955, box 435, folder 20, Time Inc. Records.
41. Three *Life* articles on Judaism in the 1950s: Philip Bernstein, "What the Jews Believe," *Life*, September 11, 1950; "Life Goes to a Bar Mitzvah," *Life*, October 13, 1952, 170–175; "Part V: The World's Great Religions Judaism," *Life*, June 13, 1955, 88–111.
42. Peter Eisenstadt, *Affirming the Faith: A History of Temple B'rith Kodesh, 1848–1998* (Syracuse: Syracuse University Press, 1999), 127.
43. Shirley Idelson, *We Shall Build Anew: Stephen S. Wise, the Jewish Institute of Religion and the Reinvention of American Liberal Judaism* (Tuscaloosa: University of Alabama Press, 2022), 96.
44. Eisenstadt, *Affirming the Faith*, 129.
45. Ben Samuel, "Rabbi Philip Bernstein, The Chaplain's Friend," *Jewish Advocate*, January 18, 1945, 7.
46. Samuel, "Rabbi Philip Bernstein," 7.

47. John Shaw Billings to Philip Bernstein, January 12, 1950, Philip S. Bernstein Papers, D.269, Rare Books, Special Collections, and Preservation, River Campus Libraries, University of Rochester (hereafter cited as Bernstein Papers).
48. Billings to Bernstein, January 12, 1950.
49. Billings to Bernstein, January 12, 1950.
50. Daniel Poling, "A Protestant's Faith," *Life*, November 7, 1949, 113–121.
51. John Shaw Billings to Bernstein, September 15, 1950. Daniel Poling, "A Protestant's Faith," 113.
52. Philip S. Bernstein to Mr. John Shaw Billings, February 17, 1950, D269 49.11, Bernstein Papers; Bernstein, "What the Jews Believe," 161.
53. Bernstein, "What the Jews Believe," 161.
54. The Ngram of "democratic faith" shows a peak in the early 1940s: https://books.google.com/ngrams/graph?content=democratic+faith&year_start=1800&year_end=2000&corpus=15&smoothing=3&share=&direct_url=t1%3B%2Cdemocratic%20faith%3B%2Cc0#t1%3B%2Cdemocratic%20faith%3B%2Cc0. Bernstein, "What the Jews Believe," 161.
55. This presentation of Judaism, in which rabbis appeared unnecessary, met with criticism from rabbis: Baruch Haba, "Correct but Not Adequate," *Jewish Exponent*, September 22, 1950, 9.
56. Bernstein, "What the Jews Believe," 162
57. Steinberg on Jesus: Milton Steinberg, *Basic Judaism*, 109. Bernstein on no mediator: Bernstein, "What the Jews Believe," 167.
58. Bernstein, "What the Jews Believe," 171.
59. Bernstein, "What the Jews Believe," 161.
60. Bernstein, "What the Jews Believe," 161.
61. Bernstein, "What the Jews Believe," 161.
62. Bernstein, "What the Jews Believe," 161.
63. Bernstein, "What the Jews Believe," 167.
64. Bernstein, "What the Jews Believe," 167.
65. Bernstein, "What the Jews Believe," 167.
66. Herbert Feibelman, "Letters to the Editors," *Life*, October 2, 1950, 8.
67. Melvin Gladstone, "Letters to the Editors," *Life*, October 2, 1950, 8.
68. Helen Strauss to Bernstein, October 8, 1950, Bernstein Papers.
69. Israel G. Jacobson to Bernstein, October 2, 1950, box 1: "Publications: What the Jews Believe (Correspondence from and to readers of article and book)," folder 1, Bernstein Papers.
70. Israel G. Jacobson to Bernstein, October 2, 1950, Bernstein Papers.
71. Rabbi Eugene Blackshleger to Bernstein, October 2, 1950, box 1: "Publications: What the Jews Believe (Correspondence from and to readers of article and book)," folder 1, Bernstein Papers.
72. ADL director letter: Benjamin Epstein to Bernstein, October 5, 1950, box 6, folder 1, Bernstein Papers.
73. "Letters to the Editors," *Life*, October 2, 1950, 8.

74. Olive M. Duntley to Bernstein, October 1, 1950, box 1: "Publications: What the Jews Believe (Correspondence from and to readers of article and book)," folder 1, Bernstein Papers.
75. Mrs. Violet Darman to Bernstein, undated 1950, box 1: "Publications" What the Jews Believe (Correspondence from and to readers of article and book)," folder 1, Bernstein Papers.
76. Will Herberg, "What Is Jewish Religion? Reflections on Rabbi Philip Bernstein's Article in Life," *Jewish Frontier*, October 1950, 8.
77. K. Healan Gaston, "The Cold War Romance of Religious Authority: Will Herberg, William F. Buckley Jr. and the Rise of the New Right," *Journal of American History* 99, no. 4 (March 2013): 1138, 1157.
78. Herberg, "What Is Jewish Religion?" 8.
79. Herberg, "What Is Jewish Religion?" 8.
80. Herberg, "What Is Jewish Religion?" 9.
81. "Religion: What Jews Believe," *Time*, May 14, 1951. This *Time* review was of Bernstein's 1951 book *What the Jews Believe*, which was an expanded version of his 1950 *Life* article.
82. Bernstein to Rabbi Herbert J. Wilner, November 10, 1950, Bernstein Papers.
83. Irving Kristol, "How Basic Is 'Basic Judaism?'" *Commentary*, January 1, 1946, 32–33.
84. Kristol, "How Basic," 33.
85. Herberg, "What Is Jewish Religion?" 9.
86. Rita Felski, *The Limits of Critique* (Chicago: University of Chicago Press, 2022), 6, 7.
87. Albert S. Goldstein to Bernstein, October 27, 1950, Bernstein Papers.
88. Goldstein to Bernstein, October 27, 1950.
89. Reinhold Niebuhr, "America's Three Melting Pots," *New York Times*, September 26, 1955, BR6; Kevin Schultz, "Protestant-Catholic-Jew, Then and Now," First Things, January 2006. https://www.firstthings.com/article/2006/01/protestant-catholic-jewthen-and-now.

Chapter 7

1. 1950s predictions of Orthodoxy's demise include Howard Polsky, "A Study of Orthodoxy in Milwaukee: Social Characteristics, Beliefs, and Observances," in *The Jews: Social Patterns of an American Group*, ed. Marshall Sklare (Glencoe, IL: Free Press, 1958), 335. Marshall Sklare, *Conservative Judaism* ((Glencoe, IL: Free Press, 1955), 43. George Dugan, "Orthodox Jews Seen in Minority," *New York Times*, June 28, 1958, 20.
2. For pronouncements of Orthodoxy's resurgence during the last third of the twentieth century, see Charles Liebman, "Orthodoxy in American Jewish Life," in *American Jewish Year Book 1965*, 21–22; "Judaism: Orthodoxy's New Look," *Time*, January 19, 1968, 58; Eleanor Blau, "Dynamic Rabbi Is Leading a Renascence of Orthodox Judaism in Elizabeth," *New York Times*, November 4, 1972, 57; Kenneth

A. Briggs, "Orthodox Judaism Is Buoyed by a Resurgence in New York," *New York Times*, March 29, 1983; Tibor Weiss, "Judaism's Alive and Well and Living in America; Orthodox Revival," *New York Times*, June 20, 1990, A24. Even in the late 1950s, there were pronouncements of Orthodoxy's resurgence: "Orthodox Jews Build in Suburbs," *New York Times*, April 28, 1957, 71; Riv-Ellen Prell, "Assimilation and Authenticity: Some Thoughts on a Jewish Response," *Muslim World* 104, no. 4 (2014): 394.

3. Jeffrey Gurock, *Orthodox Jews in America* (Bloomington: Indiana University Press, 2009), 17. Liebman, "Orthodoxy in American Jewish Life," 21–22. Kenneth Briggs, "Orthodox Judaism's Rise Affects Conservative and Reform Branches," *New York Times*, September 12, 1977, 14; Briggs, "Orthodox Judaism Is Buoyed By a Resurgence in New York"; Weiss, "Judaism's Alive and Well and Living in America," A24.

4. During the 1950s, individual Orthodox leaders spoke out against predictions of their movement's decline, providing inspiration for the movement's laity: Irving Spiegel, "Rabbi Sees Gains for Orthodoxy," *New York Times*, July 5, 1958, 25; George Dugan, "Leader of Nation's Orthodox Jews," *New York Times*, May 28, 1976, 15; Menachem Keren-Kartz, "The Contemporary Study of Orthodoxy: Challenging the One-Dimensional Paradigm," *Tradition: A Journal of Orthodox Jewish Thought* 49, no. 4 (Winter 2016): 24–52

5. Irving Spiegel, "Orthodox Jews Plan Expansion," *New York Times*, November 16, 1958, 62.

6. The Ramaz school in Manhattan and the Maimonides school in Brookline, Massachusetts, were both founded in 1937, and Miami's Hebrew Academy was established in 1947.

7. Adam Ferziger, "From Lubavitch to Lakewood: The Chabadization of American Orthodoxy," *Modern Judaism* 33, no. 2 (May 2013): 101.

8. Joseph Telushkin, *Rebbe: The Life and Teachings of Menachem M. Schneerson, the Most Influential Rabbi in Modern History* (New York: HarperCollins, 2014); Samuel Heilman, *The Rebbe: The Life and Afterlife of Menachem Mendel Schneerson* (Princeton, NJ: Princeton University Press, 2012); Sue Fishkoff, *The Rebbe's Army: Inside the World of Chabad-Lubavitch* (New York: Schocken, 2005).

9. Timothy Lytton, *Kosher Private Regulation in the Age of Industrial Food* (Cambridge, MA: Harvard University Press, 2013), 46–49.

10. Adi Mahalel, "We Will Not Be Silent: I. L. Peretz's 'Bontshe the Silent' vs. 1950s McCarthyism in America and the Story of the Staging of *The World of Sholom Aleichem*," *Studies in American Jewish Literature* 34 (2015): 204–230.

11. Alisa Solomon, *Wonder of Wonders: A Cultural History of "Fiddler on the Roof"* (New York: Metropolitan Books, 2013).

12. "Religion: What Judaism Has to Offer," *Time*, October 24, 1955, 45.

13. Despite my phrasing, I am not drawing on Isaac Deutscher's concept of the "Non-Jewish Jew" here, which Deutscher first published around this time, in a 1958 essay. Deutscher's idea of a secular, universalistic Jew is at the opposite pole from what of what most of these middlebrow essays and books show, which is a religious Judaism.

248   NOTES

14. James Loeffler, "Hava Nagila's Long. Strange Trip: The Unlikely Story of a Hasidic Melody," MyJewishLearning.com; Joshua Walden, *The Cambridge Companion to Jewish Music* (Cambridge: Cambridge University Press, 2015), 64. In 1953, the popular singer Perry Como recorded an album of traditional religious hymns. The album was called "I Believe," and it was subtitled "Songs of All Faiths Sung by Perry Como."
15. Henry Luce to Ed Thompson, "Re: Possible continuation of religion series to include Judaism and Christianity," folder: "Life, 1954, Edit. Misc. Jan–June," Time Inc. Collection.
16. Luce to Thompson, "Re: Possible continuation of religion series to include Judaism and Christianity."
17. Luce to Thompson, "Re: Possible continuation of religion series to include Judaism and Christianity."
18. "'Jews Revive Old Sabbatical Rite of Scroll-Reading in Holy Land," *New York Times*, October 7, 1952, 31.
19. "Jews Revive," 31.
20. "Jews Urge Orthodox Life," *New York Times*, March 7, 1950, 21.
21. "Jews Here Observe Shabuoth Festival," *New York Times*, June 4, 1949, 14; "Jews Will Mark Succoth," *New York Times*, October 8, 1957, 38.
22. Michael Berkowitz, *Western Jewry and the Zionist Project, 1914–1933* (Cambridge: Cambridge University Press, 2003), 97. Paula Hyman, *Gender and Assimilation in Modern Jewish History: The Roles and Representation of Women* (Seattle: University of Washington Press, 1995), 142.
23. On Conservative and Reform flourishing in 1950s suburbia, see Sarna, *American Judaism*, 284.
24. On this post–World War II relationship between American Judaism and Eastern European Judaism, see Susannah Heschel, "Imagining Judaism in America," in *The Cambridge Companion to Jewish American Literature*, ed. Hana Wirth-Nesher and Michael P. Kramer (New York: Cambridge University Press, 2003), 31–49.
25. International Organizations and Movements (Washington, DC: US Government Printing Office, 1956), 800. James L. Baughman, "Who Read Life?" in *Looking at Life Magazine*, ed. Erika Doss (Washington, DC: Smithsonian Institution Press, 2001), 44, 45.
26. Philip Roth, *Goodbye, Columbus* (1959, 1976), 201.
27. Roth, *Goodbye, Columbus*, 189.
28. M. M. Silver, *Our Exodus: Leon Uris and the Americanization of Israel's Founding Store* (Detroit: Wayne State University Press, 2010), 40.
29. Amy Kaplan, "Zionism as Anticolonialism: The Case of *Exodus*," *American Literary History* 25, no. 4 (Winter 2013): 880.
30. Silver, *Our Exodus*, 2.
31. Silver, *Our Exodus*, 39.
32. Peter Grose, *Israel in the Mind of America* (New York: Knopf, 1983), 303.
33. "The New Israel," *Life*, July 18, 1949, 71.
34. "The New Israel," 71.
35. "The New Israel," 71.

36. "The New Israel," 76.
37. Geoffrey G. Field, "Nordic Racism," *Journal of the History of Ideas* 38, no. 3 (1977): 523–540.
38. My conversations with Sarah Imhoff about this *Life* essay were very helpful to my analysis.
39. Maoz Azaryahu and Arnon Golan, "Photography, Memory, and Ethnic Cleansing: The Fate of the Jewish Quarter of Jerusalem, 1948—John Phillips' Pictorial Record," *Israel Studies* 17, no. 2 (Summer 2012): 62–76.
40. On the role of images of masculinity in American Zionism, see Sarah Imhoff, *Masculinity and the Making of American Judaism* (Bloomington: Indiana University Press, 2017), chapter 6.
41. The 1953 *American Jewish Year Book* reported on continued interest in Israel among American synagogues, with all three movements establishing links with the new state. Morris Kertzer, "The Impact of Israel," *American Jewish Year Book* 54 (1953): 105.
42. Ed Thompson to Henry Luce, April 20, 1954, "Life, 1954: Edit. Misc. Jan–June," Time Inc. Records. For Orthodoxy as authentic Judaism as a 1960s concern, see Zev Eleff, *Authentically Orthodox: A Tradition-Bound Faith in American Life* (Detroit: Wayne State University Press, 2020).
43. The 1954 *American Jewish Year Book* noted this embrace of traditional practice: Morris Kertzer, "Religion," in *American Jewish Year Book* 1954, 83.
44. Werner Sollors, "Holocaust and Hiroshima: American Ethnic Prose Writers Face the Extreme," *PMLA* 118, no. 1 (January 2003): 59.
45. John Hersey, "The Mechanics of a Novel," *Yale University Library Gazette* 27, no. 1 (July 1952): 3.
46. David Hollinger, *Protestants Abroad: How Missionaries Tried to Change the World but Changed America* (Princeton, NJ: Princeton University Press, 2017), 24.
47. Hollinger, *Protestants Abroad*, 54.
48. For a Black, non-Jewish perspective on the Warsaw Ghetto, see W. E. B. Du Bois, "The Negro and the Warsaw Ghetto," *Jewish Life*, May 1952, and Michael Rothberg's discussion of it in *The Implicated Subject: Beyond Victims and Perpetrators* (Stanford, CA: Stanford University Press, 2019), chapter 4.
49. Alfred Kazin, "Books," *New Yorker*, March 4, 1950, 96.
50. Proving the significance of "non-Jewish Jewish culture" to the Jewish community was the awards they gave him: "John Hersey Gets Degree," *New York Times*, June 2, 1950, 21.
51. Kazin, "Books," *New Yorker*, March 4, 1950, 96.
52. Julian Levinson, *Exiles on Main Street: Jewish American Writers and American Literary Culture* (Bloomington: Indiana University Press, 2008), 156–166.
53. Hersey, "The Mechanics of a Novel," 6.
54. Nancy Sinkoff, "Fiction's Archive: Authenticity, Ethnography, and Philosemitism in John Hersey's *The Wall*," *Jewish Social Studies* 17, no. 2 (Winter 2011): 48–79.
55. Marshall Sklare, Marc Vosk, and Mark Zborowski, "Forms and Expressions of Jewish Identification," *Jewish Social Studies* 17, no. 3 (July 1955): 215. This mirrors Jeffrey

Shandler's findings about the post-Holocaust Yiddish culture in America: Jeffrey Shandler, *Adventures in Yiddishland* (Berkeley: University of California Press, 2020).
56. Shandler, *Adventures*, 4.
57. Sklare, Vosk, and Zborowski, "Forms and Expressions," 215.
58. Levinson, *Exiles*, 144.
59. John Updike, "Introduction," *The Best American Short Stories of the Century* (New York: Houghton Mifflin, 2000), xx.
60. Levinson, *Exiles*, 144–145.
61. Howard Devree, "Exhibition Tide Rises to a Flood," *New York Times*, February 10, 1946, 50.
62. Edward Alden Jewell, "Modern Art Exhibits Works of Chagall," *New York Times*, April 10, 1946, 23.
63. George Biddle, "The Artist on the Horns of a Dilemma," *New York Times*, May 19, 1946, 44.
64. "Books," *Seventeen* 5, no. 12 (December 1946): 224; Emily Genauer, "Does Modern Art Annoy You?" *Cosmopolitan* 124, no. 5 (May 1948): 28–31; "How Come Modern Art?" *Seventeen* 11, no. 6 (June 1952): 74.
65. Phil Wootton to Bob Elson, "Office Memorandum," April 21, 1955, Time Inc. Records.
66. Rachel Gordan, "The Sin of American Jewish Exceptionalism," *AJS Review* 45, no. 2 (November 2021): 282–301.
67. "Jews in America," ed. *Fortune Magazine* (February 1936), 79.
68. "Jews in America," ed. *Fortune Magazine* (February 1936), 128.
69. Werner Cahnman, "Socio-Economic Causes of Antisemitism," *Social Problems* 5, no. 1 (July 1957): 27.
70. Thompson to Luce, April 20, 1954.
71. Henry Luce, "A Speculation About A.D. 1980," in *The Fabulous Future: America in 1980*, ed. David Sarnoff (New York: E.P. Dutton, 1955), 196.
72. "Judaism," *Life*, June 13, 1955, 89.
73. "Judaism," 89.
74. Irving Spiegel, "Challenge Posed to Orthodox Jews," *New York Times*, January 29, 1958, 16. The article reveals Orthodoxy's new confidence that it could uniquely meet the challenges of the atomic age.
75. Samuel Hartstein, "A Public Relations Program for Orthodox Jewry," *Jewish Life*, April 1949, 63.
76. Victor Geller, *Orthodoxy Awakens: The Belkin Era and Yeshiva University* (New York: Urim Publications, 2003), 196.
77. Jonathan Porath, "A Passover Seder to Remember with Patton's Army in Occupied Germany '45," *Jerusalem Post*, April 18, 2019.
78. Deborah Dash Moore, *GI Jews: How World War II Changed a Generation* (Cambridge, MA: Harvard University Press, 2004), 125–126.
79. Geller, *Orthodoxy Awakens*, 198.
80. Geller, *Orthodoxy Awakens*, 193.
81. Geller, *Orthodoxy Awakens*, 196.
82. Geller, *Orthodoxy Awakens*, 196.

83. "Jozefa Stuart: Robert Capa in Love and War," American Masters Digital Archive (WNET), January 7, 2002, https://www.pbs.org/wnet/americanmasters/archive/interview/jozefa-stuart/.
84. I. F. Stone, *This Is Israel* (New York: Boni & Gaer, 1948); Irwin Shaw and Robert Capa, *Report on Israel* (New York: Simon & Schuster, 1950).
85. Geller, *Orthodoxy Awakens*, 99–100.
86. John Wicklein, "Judaism on Rise in the Suburbs," *New York Times*, April 5, 1959, 80.
87. Glazer, *American Judaism*, 84.
88. Sociologist Herbert Gans made similar observations about urban versus suburban 1950s Jewish life in Chicago: Herbert Gans, "Progress of a Suburban Jewish Community," *Commentary*, February 1957, 120–125.
89. John Wicklein, "Judaism on Rise," 80.
90. Geller, *Orthodoxy Awakens*, 200.
91. Simon A. Dolgin, "Let's Strike at the Roots," *Jewish Life*, July–August 1953, 11.
92. Dolgin, "Let's Strike," 13.
93. Jeffrey Gurock, *Orthodox Jews in America* (Bloomington: Indiana University Press, 2009), 202–204.
94. Gurock, *Orthodox Jews*, 204.
95. Etan Diamond, *And I Will Dwell in Their Midst: Orthodox Jews in Suburbia* (Chapel Hill: University of North Carolina Press, 2000), 5–7, 9.
96. Diamond, *And I Will Dwell*, 9–10.
97. "Orthodox Jews Build in Suburbs," *New York Times*, April 28, 1957, 71.
98. Geller, *Orthodoxy Awakens*, 200.
99. Maimonides was not the first Orthodox coeducation Jewish day school in America. The Yeshiva of Flatbush was founded in 1927 and the Ramaz school was founded in 1937. Seth Farber, *An American Orthodox Dreamer: Rabbi Joseph B. Soloveitchik and Boston's Maimonides School* (Hanover, NH: University Press of New England, 2004), chapter 4. On Soloveitchik's background, see Aaron Rakeffet-Rothkoff, "Rabbi Joseph B. Soloveitchik: The Early Years," *Tradition: A Journal of Orthodox Jewish Thought* 30, no. 4 (Summer 1996): 193–209. On the innovativeness of Ramaz and Maimonides, see Gurock, *Orthodoxy in America*, 200–201.
100. Geller, *Orthodoxy Awakens*, 206.
101. Joseph Litvak chronicles how the postwar Americanization of the Jew has led to the "Jew's (rather equivocal) success story, has consisted largely in 'her' desexualization" Joseph Litvak, "Jew Envy," *Women's Studies Quarterly* (Fall–Winter, 2006), 84.
102. Rabbi Samuel Silver to Mrs. Jozefa Stuart, January 13, 1955, box 435, folder 20, Time Inc. Records.
103. Silver to Stuart, January 13, 1955.
104. Silver to Stuart, January 13, 1955.
105. "Judaism," *Life*, June 13, 1955, 97, 101.
106. Silver to Stuart, January 13, 1955.
107. "Judaism," *Life*, June 13, 1955, 92.
108. Silver to Stuart, June 13, 1955.

109. "Rabbi William Rosenblum Dies" (obituary), *New York Times*, February 10, 1968, 33.
110. William Rosenblum to Robert Elson, June 30, 1955, RG 1, box 435, folder 20, Time Inc. Records.
111. Rosenblum to Elson, June 30, 1955.
112. William F. Rosenblum to Life Magazine Deputy Managing Editor Robert T. Elson, June 17, 1955, RG 1, box 435, folder 20, Time Inc. Records; Rosenblum to Elson, June 30, 1955.
113. Author conversation with Moishe Fink, May 21, 2020.
114. Sue-Ann Harding, *An Archival Journey through the Qatar Peninsula: Elusive and Precarious* (Cham, Switzerland: Springer International Publishing, 2022), 125–140.
115. In 1949, Israel airlifted more than 40,000 Yemenite Jews to Israel as part of Operation Magic Carpet. On the marginalization of Mizrahi Jews by Ashkenazi Jews in Israel, see Lital Levy, Poetic Trespass—Writing between Hebrew and Arabic in Israel/Palestine (Princeton, NJ: Princeton University Press, 2014), 36–37.
116. On the mid-to-late 1950s as a turning point for Orthodox Judaism, see Zev Eleff, *A Century at the Center: Orthodox Judaism and the Jewish Center* (New York: Toby Press, 2018), 279–299; Riv-Ellen Prell, "Triumph, Accommodation, and Resistance: American Jewish Life from the End of World War II to the Six Day War," in *The Columbia History of Jews and Judaism*, ed. Marc Lee Raphael (New York: Columbia University Press, 2008), 125–126.
117. *Life*, November 1, 1954.

Chapter 8

1. Matthew Hedstrom, "Psychology and Mysticism in 1940s Religion: Reading the Readers of Fosdick, Liebman, and Merton," in *Religion and the Culture of Print in Modern America*, ed. Charles L. Cohen and Paul S. Boyer (Madison: University of Wisconsin Press, 2008), 259.
2. Arthur A. Cohen, "Why I Choose to Be a Jew," *Harper's*, April 1959, 62.
3. Cohen, "Why I Choose," 62.
4. "Judaism: A Choice for the Chosen," *Time*, February 15, 1963, 98.
5. The property was listed at almost $11 million shortly after Mrs. Cohen's death. Candace Taylor, "New York Brownstone of Artist Elaine Lustig Cohen Asks $11 Million," *Wall Street Journal*, January 12, 2017.
6. "Historic UES Townhouse Owned by Famed Graphic Designer Elaine Lustig Cohen Hits the Market," *The Real Deal: Real Estate News*, January 13, 2017; Julian Levinson, "Arthur A. Cohen's Resplendent Vision," *Prooftexts*, May 1, 2003, 259.
7. Harry Hansen, "Publishing House Finds Huge Sales of Its Books," *Chicago Daily Tribune*, January 3, 1960, G6.

8. Matthew Hedstrom, *The Rise of Liberal Religion: Book Culture and American Spirituality in the Twentieth Century* (New York: Oxford University Press, 2013), 9; Erin A. Smith, "The Religious Book Club: Print Culture, Consumerism, and the Spiritual Life of Protestants between the Wars," in *Religion and the Culture of Print in Modern America*, ed. Charles L. Cohen and Paul S. Boyer (Madison: University of Wisconsin Press, 2008), 217–242.
9. On postwar Jews and ethnicity, see Lila Corwin Berman, *Speaking of Jews: Rabbis, Intellectuals, and the Creation of an American Public Identity* (Berkeley: University of California Press, 2009), chapter 5. On the limited postwar embrace of ethnicity discourse about Jews, see Eric Goldstein, *Price of Whiteness: Jews, Race, and American Identity* (Princeton, NJ: Princeton University Press, 2006), 190.
10. Cohen, "Why I Choose," 61–62.
11. On American religion as a matter individual choice, see Peter Berger, *The Sacred Canopy: Elements of a Sociological Theory of Religion* (New York: Anchor Books, 1967), 199; Robert Bellah, *Habits of the Heart: Individualism and Commitment in American Life* (Berkeley: University of California Press, 1985); Robert D. Putnam, David Campbell, and Shaylyn Garrett, *American Grace: How Religion Divides and Unites Us* (New York: Simon & Schuster, 2010); Richard Madsen, "The Archipelago of Faith: Religious Individualism and Faith Community in America Today," *American Journal of Sociology* 114, no. 5 (March 2009): 1263–1301.
12. Cohen, "Why I Choose," 61–62; Wouk, *This Is My God*, 59–60.
13. On "Modern Orthodoxy" becoming a more popular term during the 1960s, see Zev Eleff, *Modern Orthodox Judaism: A Documentary History* (Philadelphia: Jewish Publication Society, 2016), xxxvii–xxxviii.
14. Arthur A. Cohen to Mother and Dad, undated, YCAL_MSS_496_Box 42, folder: "AAC Correspondence, 1940s, Arthur A. Cohen Papers, Yale Collection of American Literature, Beinecke Rare Book and Manuscript Library (hereafter cited as Cohen Papers).
15. Examples of Isidore M. Cohen's collection: https://www.metmuseum.org/art/collect ion/search/370055; https://www.moma.org/collection/works/69724; https://www. moma.org/documents/moma_catalogue_2011_300299031.pdf.
16. "Isidore M. Cohen, 93, a Clothing Executive" (obituary), *New York Times*, July 15, 1991, D10.
17. Isidore M. Cohen to Arthur Cohen, November 2, 1945, Arthur A. Cohen Correspondence, 1938–1950, folder 2, Cohen Papers.
18. Isidore M. Cohen to Arthur Cohen, November 2, 1945.
19. Isidore M. Cohen to Arthur Cohen, November 2, 1945.
20. Isidore M. Cohen to Arthur Cohen, November 2, 1945.
21. Isidore M. Cohen to Arthur Cohen, November 2, 1945.
22. "The Wouk Mutiny," *Time*, September 5, 1955, 52.
23. Rebecca Davis, "'These Are a Swinging Bunch of People': Sammy Davis, Jr., Religious Conversion, and the Color of Jewish Ethnicity," *American Jewish History* 100, no. 1 (January 2016): 25–50, 168.
24. Author interview with Herman Wouk at his home in Palm Springs, February 11, 2011.

25. Author interview with Herman Wouk, February 11, 2011.
26. Wouk, *This Is My God*, dedication page.
27. Wouk, *This Is My God*, 234.
28. Wouk, *This Is My God*, 234.
29. Wouk, *This Is My God*, 234.
30. Wouk, *This Is My God*, 235.
31. Wouk, *This Is My God*, 235.
32. Will Herberg, "Confession of Faith," Review of *This Is My God*, by Herman Wouk, *New York Times*, September 27, 1959, BR50.
33. David G. Dalin, "Will Herberg in Retrospect," *Commentary*, July 1988. K. Healan Gaston, "The Cold War Romance of Religious Authenticity: Will Herberg, William F. Buckley Jr., and the Rise of the New Right," *Journal of American History* 99, no. 4 (March 2013): 1137.
34. Jewish men were never very far removed from the influence of women: Sarah Imhoff, *Masculinity and the Making of American Judaism* (Bloomington: Indiana University Press, 2017), 275–276.
35. Nicola Humble, *The Feminine Middlebrow Novel, 1920s to 1950s: Class, Domesticity, and Bohemianism* (New York: Oxford University Press, 2004).
36. Charles Kadushin, *Understanding Social Networks: Theories, Concepts, and Findings* (New York: Oxford University Press, 2012), 9, 172.
37. Arthur Cohen to Mom and Dad, November 15, 1949, AAC Correspondence 1940s (folder 1 of 2), Cohen Papers.
38. Herberg, "Confession of Faith," BR50.
39. Herberg, "Confession of Faith," BR50.
40. William Peters, "The Case against 'Easy' Religion," *Redbook* 105, no. 5 (September 1955): 22.
41. William Peters, "The Case against 'Easy' Religion" *Redbook* 105, no. 5 (September 1955): 22.
42. Peters, "The Case against 'Easy' Religion," 22; "Books: The Year in Books," *Time*, December 16, 1946.
43. Herberg, "Confession of Faith," BR50.
44. Wouk, *This Is My God*, 273.
45. On the challenge of approaching Judaism as a midcentury Jewish intellectual: Leslie Fiedler, "Plight of the Jewish Intellectual," *Congress Weekly: A Review of Jewish Interests*, April 9, 1951, 9.
46. Arthur Cohen to Milton Steinberg, March 25, 1947, Subseries 2: "Correspondence with Others, 1928–1950," Steinberg Collection.
47. Milton Steinberg to Arthur Cohen, November 24, 1947, Subseries 2: "Correspondence with Others, 1928–1950," Steinberg Collection.
48. Milton Steinberg to Arthur Cohen, June 30, 1946, Subseries 2: "Correspondence with Others, 1928–1950," Steinberg Collection.
49. Arthur A. Cohen to Milton Steinberg, October 24, 1949, YCAL MSS 496, box 43: "Steinberg, Milton Correspondence," Cohen Papers.
50. Cohen to Steinberg, October 24, 1949, box 3, folder 10, Steinberg Collection.

51. Arthur Cohen, "Introduction," in *Anatomy of Faith*, ed. Arthur Cohen (New York: Harcourt Brace, 1960), 32.
52. Cohen to Steinberg, October 24, 1949, box 3, folder 10, Steinberg Collection.
53. Steinberg to Cohen, November 7, 1949, box 3, folder 10, Steinberg Collection.
54. Steinberg to Cohen, November 7, 1949.
55. Milton Steinberg, *Anatomy of Faith*, ed. Arthur Cohen (New York: Harcourt Brace, 1960).
56. Peter Scharper, former editor of *Commonweal*, wrote "What a Modern Catholic Believes," *Harper's*, March 1959, 40–49. A young philosopher, William Warren Bartley III, wrote "I Call Myself a Protestant," *Harper's*, May 1, 1959, 49–56.
57. Walter Kaufmann, *The Faith of a Heretic* (Princeton, NJ: Princeton University Press, 2013), 8–9.
58. Kaufmann, *The Faith of a Heretic*, 8.
59. R. B. Silvers to Arthur A. Cohen, June 4, 1958, box 24, folder: "Why I Choose to Be a Jew, 1959," Cohen Papers.
60. Jonathan Sarna, "Recalling Arthur Hertzberg: Public Intellectual," *New York Jewish Week*, April 21, 2006, 22. Known for the frankness with which he expressed his views and his leadership in Jewish organizations, in addition to his scholarship, Hertzberg was more of a public figure than Cohen. Jeffrey Gurock, *A Jew in America: My Life and a People's Struggle for Identity* by Arthur Hertzberg (review), *Shofar* 24, no. 1 (2005): 148–149.
61. Silvers to Cohen, June 4, 1958.
62. Marc Tanenbaum, "Religion," in *American Jewish Year Book* 60 (1960): 54. Gurock, "Yeshiva Students at the Jewish Theological Seminary," in *Tradition Renewed*, ed. Jack Wertheimer (Hanover, NH: University Press of New England, 2007), 473–474.
63. Tanenbaum, "Religion," 55.
64. Boyd Adler, "Who Goes into Religious Life?" *Cosmopolitan*, December 1958, 51.
65. Arthur A. Cohen to Mother and Dad, October 7, 1949, box 42, folder 1 of 1940s Correspondence, Cohen Papers.
66. Cohen to Mother and Dad, October 7, 1949.
67. Arthur Cohen to Milton Steinberg, October 2, 1949, Steinberg Collection.
68. Cohen to Steinberg, October 2, 1949.
69. Wouk, *This Is My God*, 28.
70. Wouk, *This Is My God*, 28–29.
71. Arthur A. Cohen to Mother and Dad, September 20, 1949, folder 1: "Correspondence, 1940s," Cohen Papers.
72. Cohen to Mother and Dad, September 20, 1949.
73. Cohen to Mother and Dad, September 20, 1949.
74. Cohen, "Why I Choose," 62.
75. Cohen, "Why I Choose," 62.
76. Arthur Cohen to Mom and Dad, November 15, 1949, AAC Correspondence 1940s, folder 1 of 2, Cohen Papers; Trude Weiss-Rosmarin, *Judaism and Christianity: The Differences* (New York: Jonathan David, 1943), 7.

77. Arthur Cohen, *The Myth of the Judeo-Christian Tradition and Other Dissenting Essays* (New York: Harper & Row, 1969), vii.
78. Cohen to Mother and Dad, November 15, 1949; Cohen, *The Myth of the Judeo-Christian Tradition*, 126; Cohen, "Why I Choose," 62.
79. Cohen, "Why I Choose," 62.
80. Cohen, "Why I Choose," 63.
81. Gustave Weigel to Arthur Cohen, April 13, 1959, box 24, folder: "Why I Choose to Be a Jew, April 1959," Cohen Papers.
82. Weigel to Cohen, April 13, 1959.
83. Cohen, "Why I Choose," 62.
84. Cohen, "Why I Choose," 61.
85. On postwar Jewishness as choice: Arthur Goren, "A 'Golden Decade' for American Jews: 1945–1955," *Studies in American Jewry* 8 (1992): 3–20.
86. Cohen, "Why I Choose," 61, 62.
87. Elsa Doran, "Not a Racial Religion," letter to the editor, *Ladies' Home Journal*, May 1958, 36.
88. Doran, "Not a Racial," 36.
89. Doran's expression of Jewish identity reflects elements of Shaul Magid's analytic perspective of post-Judaism (inspired by David Hollinger's "postethnic" perspective), in which "allegiances are more voluntary than inherited, more the result of consent rather than descent." Shaul Magid, *American Post-Judaism: Identity and Renewal in a Postethnic Society* (Bloomington: Indiana University Press, 2013), 5.
90. Cohen, "Why I Choose," 62.

Conclusion

1. Richard F. Shepard, "For Sholom Aleichem, There's Will and a Way," *New York Times*, May 11, 1976, 36.
2. Shepard, "For Sholom," 36.
3. Shepard, "For Sholom," 36.
4. Shepard, "For Sholom," 36.
5. On Jewish ethnic identity during the 1970s and 1980s, see Calvin Goldscheider, *Jewish Continuity and Change: Emerging Patterns in America* (Bloomington: Indiana University Press, 1986).
6. On the success of *Fiddler*, see Alisa Solomon, *Wonder of Wonders: A Cultural History of Fiddler on the Roof* (New York: Metropolitan Books, 2013).
7. Solomon, *Wonder of Wonders*, 220.
8. Theodore Solotaroff, "World of Our Fathers," *New York Times*, February 1, 1976, BR1. On the late twentieth-century revived interest in ethnicity, see Matthew Jacobson, *Roots Too: White Ethnic Revival in Post–Civil Rights America* (Cambridge, MA: Harvard University Press, 2005).

9. Herbert Mitgang, "Publishing: New Laura Hobson Novel," *New York Times*, August 24, 1979, C22.
10. Brian O'Doherty, "Nostalgic Jab by an Angry Pen," *Life*, November 27, 1964, 16.
11. Margaret Halsey, *No Laughing Matter: The Autobiography of a WASP* (New York: J. B. Lippincott, 1977), 11.
12. The ethnic revival of the 1970s was not the first time that Americans made the case for the importance of ethnic roots to American culture. Lila Corwin Berman, *Speaking of Jews: Rabbis, Intellectuals, and the Creation of an American Public Identity* (Berkeley: University of California Press, 2009), 107.
13. On presidents employing ethnic pasts in their candidacy, see Jacobson, *Roots, Too*, 320–321.
14. Laurie Johnston, "Ethnic Awareness Praised as a Creative Force," *New York Times*, April 13, 1972, 45.
15. Susannah Heschel, "Imagining Judaism in America," 33.
16. On this regret of postwar American Jewish paths, see Rachel Gordan, "The Sin of American Jewish Exceptionalism," *AJS Review* 45, no. 2 (2021): 282–301.
17. On postwar Jewish flight and American cities, see Lila Corwin Berman, *Metropolitan Jews: Politics, Race, and Religion in Postwar Detroit* (Chicago: University of Chicago Press, 2015). On the postwar Jewish critique of suburban affluence, see Rachel Kranson, *Ambivalent Embrace: Jewish Upward Mobility in Postwar America* (Chapel Hill: University of North Carolina Press, 2017); Riv-Ellen Prell, "Community and the Discourse of Elegy: The Post War Suburban Debate," in *Imagining the American Jewish Community*, ed. Jack Wertheimer (Hanover, NH: University Press of New England, 2007), 67–90.
18. Irving Spiegel, "Jews Criticized on Suburb Trend," *New York Times*, November 18, 1959, 33.
19. Wouk, *This Is My God*, 281.
20. Morgan's thesis that intermarriage might lead to the end of American Jewry was immediately criticized by Jewish communal leaders: Irving Spiegel, "A Loss of Identity by Jews Disputed," *New York Times*, April 22, 1964, 44.
21. On readers' judgments of Jewish assimilationist texts, see Michael Kramer, "The Art of Assimilation: Ironies, Ambiguities, Aesthetics," in *Modern Jewish Literatures: Intersections and Boundaries*, ed. Sheila E. Jelen, Michael P. Kramer, and L. Scott Lerner (Philadelphia: University of Pennsylvania Press, 2011), 303–326.
22. Vivian Gornick, "Saul Bellow, Philip Roth, and the End of the Jew as Metaphor," in Vivian Gornick, *The Men In My Life* (Cambridge, MA: MIT Press, 2008), 100–145; Lori Harrison-Kahan and Josh Lambert, "Guest Editors Introduction: Finding Home: The Future of Jewish American Literary Studies," *MELUS* 37, no. 2 (Summer 2012): 5. Benjamin Schreier, *The Rise and Fall of American Jewish Literature: Ethnic Studies and Challenge of Identity* (Philadelphia: University of Pennsylvania Press, 2020).

References

Archives

American Jewish Archives, Cincinnati, OH
American Jewish Historical Society Archives, New York, NY
Beinecke Rare Book & Manuscript Library, New Haven, CT
Boston University Libraries, Howard Gotlieb Archival Research Center, Boston, MA
Columbia University Rare Book & Manuscript Library, New York, NY
Hanna Holborn Gray Special Collections Research Center, University of Chicago Library
New-York Historical Society Archives, New York, NY
University of Rochester Rare Books and Special Collection, Rochester, NY
University of North Carolina Wilson Special Collections Library Chapel Hill, NC

Secondary Sources

Adler, Boyd. "Who Goes into Religious Life?" *Cosmopolitan*, December 1958.
Ahlstrom, Sydney E. *A Religious History of the American People*. 2nd ed. New Haven, CT: Yale University Press, 2004.
Albanese, Catherine. *America: Religions and Religion* 5th ed. Belmont, CA: Wadsworth, 2012.
Albanese, Catherine. "Exchanging Selves, Exchanging Souls: Contact, Combination, and American Religious History." In *Retelling U.S. Religious History*, edited by Thomas Tweed, 200–226. Berkeley: University of California Press, 1997.
Alexander, Jeffrey. "The Social Construction of Moral Universals: The 'Holocaust' from War Crime to Trauma Drama." *European Journal of Social Theory* 5, no. 11 (2002): 13–16.
Allen, Frederick Lewis. *The Big Change: America Transforms Itself*. New York: Harper & Brothers, 1952.
Almog, Oz. *The Sabra: The Creation of the New Jew*. Berkeley: University of California Press, 2000.
Alpenfels, Ethel. "Sense and Nonsense about Race." New York: Friendship Press, 1946.
Alpert, Rebecca. "From Jewish Science to Rabbinical Counseling: The Evolution of the Relationship between Religion and Health by the American Reform Rabbinate, 1916–1954." Ph.D. diss., Temple University, 2008.
Anft, Michael. "How a Jewish Charity's Long Game Readied It for Today's Turbulence." *The Chronicle of Philanthropy*, November 1, 2018.
Anidjar, Gil. *Blood: A Critique of Christianity*. New York: Columbia University Press, 2016.
Anonymous. "I Changed My Name." *Atlantic Monthly*, February 1948, 72–74.
"Anti-Semitism—Is Hollywood's Praiseworthy Effort to Combat It Obscuring the Central Point?" *Life*, December 1, 1947, 44.

Asad, Talal. *Genealogies of Religion: Discipline and Reasons of Power in Christianity and Islam*. Baltimore: Johns Hopkins University Press, 1993.

Asch, Chris, and George Musgrove. *Chocolate City: A History of Race and Democracy in the Nation's Capital*. Chapel Hill: University of North Carolina Press, 2017.

"Asks Lindbergh Debate." *New York Times*, September 15, 1941, 2.

Attwood, William. "The Position of the Jews in America Today." *Look*, November 29, 1955, 27.

Azaryahu, Maoz, and Arnon Golan. "Photography, Memory, and Ethnic Cleansing: The Fate of the Jewish Quarter of Jerusalem, 1948—John Phillips' Pictorial Record." *Israel Studies* 17, no. 2 (Summer 2012): 62–76.

Baker, Cynthia. *Jew*. New Brunswick, NJ: Rutgers University Press, 2017.

Baldwin, James. "Everybody's Favorite Protest Novel." In *Notes of a Native Son*. Boston: Beacon Press, 1955.

Baron, Salo. "The Year in Retrospect." *American Jewish Year Book 1947–1948*, 108.

Barr, Stringfellow. *American Catholics; A Protestant-Jewish View*. New York: Sheed & Ward, 1959.

Bellow, Saul. *The Victim*. New York: Vanguard, 1947.

Belmonte, Laura. *Selling the American Way: US Propaganda and the Cold War*. Philadelphia: University of Pennsylvania Press, 2010.

Benedict, Ruth, and Gene Weltfish. "The Races of Mankind." New York: Public Affairs Committee, 1943.

Benet, Rosemary Carr. "Drawing Room 'Abie's Irish Rose.'" *Saturday Review*, October 7, 1944, 9.

Berch, Bettina. *From Hester Street to Hollywood: The Life and Work of Anzia Yezierska*. New York: Sefer International, 2009.

Bercovitch, Sacvan. *The Puritan Origins of the American Self*. New Haven, CT: Yale University Press, 1977.

Berkowitz, Michael. *Western Jewry and the Zionist Project, 1914–1933*. Cambridge: Cambridge University Press, 2003.

Berlant, Lauren. *The Female Complaint: The Unfinished Business of Sentimentality in American Culture*. Durham, NC: Duke University Press, 2008.

Berman, Lila Corwin. *Speaking of Jews: Rabbis, Intellectuals, and the Creation of an American Public Identity*. Berkeley: University of California Press, 2009.

Bernstein, Philip. "What the Jews Believe." *Life*, September 11, 1950, 151.

Beschloss, Michael. *The Conquerors: Roosevelt, Truman, and the Destruction of Hitler's Germany*. New York: Simon & Schuster, 2003.

Bezalel Sherman, Charles. *The Jew within American Society: A Study in Ethnic Individuality*. Detroit: Wayne State University Press, 1961.

Biddle, George. "The Artist on the Horns of a Dilemma." *New York Times*, May 19, 1946, 44.

Birstein, Ann. *The Rabbi on 47th Street*. New York: Dial Press, 1982.

Blau, Eleanor. "Dynamic Rabbi Is Leading a Renascence of Orthodox Judaism in Elizabeth." *New York Times*, November 4, 1972, 57.

Blau, Joseph. *Judaism in America: From Curiosity to Third Faith*. Chicago: Chicago History of American Religion, 1976.

Borowitz, Eugene. "Jewish Theology: Milton Steinberg and After." *The Reconstructionist* 31, no. 7 (May 14, 1965): 9.

Borowitz, Eugene. *The Mask Jews Wear: The Self-Deceptions of American Jewry*. New York: Simon & Schuster, 1973.

Botshon, Lisa. "Anzia Yezierska and the Marketing of the Jewish Immigrant in 1920s Hollywood." In *Middlebrow Moderns: Popular American Women Writers of the 1920s*, ed. Lisa Botshon and Meredith Goldsmith, 203–224. Boston: Northeastern University Press, 2003.

Boyarin, Daniel. *Unheroic Conduct: The Rise of Heterosexuality and the Invention of the Jewish Man*. Berkeley: University of California Press, 1997.

Breines, Wini. *Young, White, and Miserable: Growing Up Female in the Fifties*. Chicago: University of Chicago Press, 1992.

Breitman, Richard, and Alan Lichtman. *FDR and the Jews*. Cambridge, MA: Harvard University Press, 2013.

Briggs, Kenneth A. "Orthodox Judaism Is Buoyed by a Resurgence in New York." *New York Times*, March 29, 1983.

Brinkley, Alan. *The Publisher: Henry Luce and His American Century*. New York: Vintage: 2010.

Brodkin, Karen. *How Jews Became White and What That Says About Race in America*. New Brunswick, NJ: Rutgers University Press, 1998.

Bromley, Dorothy Dunbar. "Mrs. Hobson Deluged with Mail on Her Novel on Anti-Semitism." *New York Herald Tribune*, March 9, 1947, 6.

Brown, John Mason. "If You Prick Us." *Saturday Review*, December 6, 1947, 71.

Brown, Wendy. *Regulating Aversion: Tolerance in the Age of Identity and Empire*. Princeton, NJ: Princeton University Press, 2006.

Burt, Struthers. "The Poison in Our Body Politic." *Saturday Review of Literature*, March 1, 1947, 14.

Cahnman, Werner. "Socio-Economic Causes of Antisemitism." *Social Problems* 5, no. 1 (July 1957): 21–29.

Canby, Henry S. "A Plaster on a Wound?" *Saturday Review*, December 13, 1947, 20.

Chudacoff, Howard P. *The Age of the Bachelor: Creating an American Subculture*. Princeton, NJ: Princeton University Press, 2000.

Churchwell, Sarah. *Behold, America: The Entangled History of "American First" and "the American Dream."* New York: Basic Books, 2018.

Clapper, Raymond. "Mrs. Roosevelt Sees No Evil." *Liberty*, April 4, 1942, 11.

Clark, Emily. "Nineteenth-Century New Orleans Voudou: An American Religion." *American Religion* 2, no. 1 (Fall 2020): 131–155.

Cobb, Jane. "Riffraff?" *New York Times*, October 1, 1944, 56.

Cohen, Arthur. "Introduction." In *Anatomy of Faith*, by Milton Steinberg. Edited by Arthur Cohen, 11–60. New York: Harcourt Brace, 1960.

Cohen, Arthur A. *The Myth of the Judeo-Christian Tradition and Other Dissenting Essays*. New York: Schocken Books, 1971.

Cohen, Arthur. "Why I Choose to Be a Jew." *Harper's* 218, no. 1307 (April 1959): 63–66.

Cohen, David L. "I've Kept My Name." *Atlantic Monthly*, April 1948.

Cohen, Eli E. "Economic Status and Occupational Structure." *American Jewish Year Book 1950*, 67–68.

Cohen, Naomi. *Jews in Christian America: The Pursuit of Religious Equality*. New York: Oxford University Press, 1992.

Cohen, Shari. "The Lasting Legacy of an American Dilemma." *Carnegie Results*, Fall 2004. https://www.carnegie.org/media/filer_public/98/65/9865c794-39d9-4659-862eaae15 83278a8/ccny_cresults_2004_americandilemma.pdf.

Cooperman, Jessica. *Making Judaism Safe for America: World War I and the Origins of Religious Pluralism*. New York: New York University Press, 2018.

Cournos, John. "Jews in a Gentile World." *Atlantic Monthly*, March 1942.

Cowan, Paul. *An Orphan in History: One Man's Triumphant Search for His Jewish Roots*. New York: Doubleday, 1982.

Cummins, June. *From Sarah to Sydney: The Woman behind All-of-a-Kind Family*. New Haven, CT: Yale University Press, 2021.

"The Cushing Sisters." *Life*, August 11, 1947.

Dalin, David G. "Will Herberg in Retrospect." *Commentary*, July 1988.

Darda, Joseph. "The Race Novel: An Education." *MELUS* 45, no. 3 (2020): 1–24.

Darda, Joseph. *The Strange Career of Racial Liberalism*. Stanford, CA: Stanford University Press, 2022.

Davis, Kenneth. *Two-Bit Culture: The Paperbacking of America*. Boston: Houghton Mifflin, 1984.

Davis, Rebecca. *Public Confessions: The Religious Conversions That Changed American Politics*. Chapel Hill: University of North Carolina Press, 2021.

Davis, Rebecca. "'These Are a Swinging Bunch of People': Sammy Davis, Jr., Religious Conversion, and the Color of Jewish Ethnicity." *American Jewish History* 100, no. (January 2016): 25–50, 168.

Dean, John. "Patterns of Socialization and Association between Jews and Non-Jews." *Jewish Social Studies* 17, no. 3 (July 1955): 251.

Delmont, Matthew. *Half American: The Epic Story of African Americans Fighting World War II at Home and Abroad*. New York: Viking, 2022.

Diefendorf, Elizabeth. *The New York Public Library's Books of the Century*. New York: Oxford University Press, 1996.

Diner, Hasia. *A Time for Gathering: The Second Migration, 1820–1880*. Baltimore: Johns Hopkins University Press, 1995.

Dinnerstein, Leonard. "Antisemitism Exposed and Attacked, 1945–1950." *American Jewish History* 71, no. 1 (September 1981): 134–149.

Dinnerstein, Leonard. *Anti-Semitism in America*. New York: Oxford University Press, 1994.

Dinnerstein, Leonard, and Gene Koppel. *Nathan Glazer: A Different Kind of Liberal*. Tucson: University of Arizona Press, 1973.

Dobkowski, Michael. *That Tarnished Dream: The Basis of American Antisemitism*. New York: Greenwood Press, 1979.

Doherty, Thomas. *Hollywood's Censor: Joseph I. Breen and the Production Code Administration*. New York: Columbia University Press.

Dolgin, Simon A. "Let's Strike at the Roots." *Jewish Life*, July–August 1953, 11.

Dollinger, Marc. *Black Power, Jewish Politics: Reinventing the Alliance in the 1960s*. Waltham, MA: Brandeis University Press, 2018.

Dollinger, Marc. "American Jewish Liberalism Revisited: Two Perspectives: Exceptionalism and Jewish Liberalism." *Journal of American Jewish History* 90, no. 2 (June 2002): 161–164.

Dollinger, Marc. *Quest for Inclusion: Jews and Liberalism in Modern America*. Princeton, NJ: Princeton University Press, 2000.

Doran, Elsa. "Not a Racial Religion." Letter to the Editor. *Ladies' Home Journal*, May 1958.

Dorff, Elliot. *Conservative Judaism: Our Ancestors to Our Descendants*. N.p.: United Synagogue of America, 1977.

Du Bois, William. "Schuyler Green's Metamorphosis." *New York Times Book Review*, March 2, 1947, 5, 36.

Du Bois, William. "Searing Novel of the South." *New York Times*, March 5, 1944, B1.
Dugan, George. "Leader of Nation's Orthodox Jews." *New York Times*, May 28, 1976.
Eisenstadt, Peter. *Affirming the Faith: A History of Temple B'rith Kodesh, 1848–1998.* University of Syracuse, 1999.
Eleff, Zev. *A Century at the Center: Orthodox Judaism and the Jewish Center.* New York: Toby Press, 2018.
Eleff, Zev. *Modern Orthodox Judaism: A Documentary History.* Lincoln, NE: Jewish Publication Society, 2016.
Ellwood, Robert. *The Fifties Spiritual Marketplace: American Religion in a Decade of Conflict.* New Brunswick, NJ: Rutgers University Press, 1997.
Engel, David. "Away from a Definition of Antisemitism: An Essay in the Semantics of Historical Description." In *Rethinking European Jewish History*, edited by Jeremy Cohen and Moshe Rosman, 30–53. London: Littman Library of Jewish Civilization, 2009.
Epstein, Joseph. "Henry Luce." In *Joseph Epstein: Essays in Biography*, 93–127. Edinburg, Virginia: Axios, 2012.
Fabre, Michel. *The Unfinished Quest of Richard Wright.* Chicago: University of Illinois Press, 1994.
Farber, Seth. *An American Orthodox Dreamer: Rabbi Joseph B. Soloveitchik and Boston's Maimonides School.* Hanover, NY: University Press of New England, 2004.
Farrelly, Maura. *Anti-Catholicism in America, 1620–1860.* New York: Cambridge University Press, 2018.
Farrelly, Maura. "Protestant-Catholic Ecumenism and the Meanings of American Freedom." In *The Cambridge Companion to American Protestantism*, edited by Jason E. Vickers and Jennifer Woodruff Tait, 277–296. New York: Cambridge University Press, 2022.
Faulkner, William. *The Sound and the Fury.* New York: Vintage, 1990.
Feagin, Joe R. *The White Racial Frame: Centuries of Racial Framing and Counter-Framing.* New York: Routledge, 2020.
Feingold, Henry. *The Jewish People in America: A Time for Healing.* Baltimore: Johns Hopkins University Press, 1992.
Feller, Yaniv. *The Jewish Imperial Imagination: Leo Baeck and German-Jewish Thought.* Cambridge: Cambridge University Press, 2023.
Felski, Rita. *The Uses of Literature.* New York: Wiley-Blackwell, 2008.
Ferber, Edna. *A Peculiar Treasure.* New York: Doubleday, 1939.
Ferber, Edna. *Fanny, Herself.* Urbana: University of Illinois Press, 1917.
Fermaglich, Kirsten. *A Rosenberg by Any Other Name: A History of Name Changing in America* New York: New York University Press, 2018.
Ferziger, Adam. "From Lubavitch to Lakewood: The Chabadization of American Orthodoxy." *Modern Judaism* 33, no. 2 (May 2013): 101–124.
Fessenden, Tracy. *Culture and Redemption: Religion, the Secular, and American Literature.* Princeton, NJ: Princeton University Press, 2007.
Feuer, Lewis S. "Recollections of Harry Austryn Wolfson." *American Jewish Archives* 28, no. 1 (1976): 25–50.
Fiedler, Leslie. "Plight of the Jewish Intellectual." *Congress Weekly: A Review of Jewish Interests*, April 9, 1959.
Field, Geoffrey G. "Nordic Racism." *Journal of the History of Ideas* 38, no. 3 (1977): 523–540.
Finkelstein, Louis. *The Jews: Their History, Culture, and Religion.* New York: Jewish Publication Society, 1949.

Finler, Joel. *The Hollywood Story*. New York: WallFlower Press, 2003.
Fishkoff, Sue. *The Rebbe's Army: Inside the World of Chabad-Lubavitch*. New York: Schocken, 2005.
Fitzgerald, F. Scott. *The Beautiful and the Damned*. New York: Vintage, 2010.
Gallagher, Charles. *Nazis of Copley Square: The Forgotten Story of the Christian Front*. Cambridge, MA: Harvard University Press, 2021.
Gans, Herbert. "Progress of a Suburban Jewish Community." *Commentary*, February 1957, 120–125.
Garrett, Leah. *Young Lions: How Jewish Authors Reinvented the American War Novel*. Evanston, IL: Northwestern University Press, 2015.
Gaston, K. Healan. "The Cold War Romance of Religious Authority: Will Herberg, William F. Buckley Jr. and the Rise of the New Right." *Journal of American History* 99, no. 4 (March 2013): 1133–1158.
Gaston, K. Healan. *Imagining Judeo-Christian America*. Chicago: University of Chicago Press, 2019.
Gaston, K. Healan. "Interpreting Judeo-Christianity in America." *Relegere: Studies in Religion and Reception* 2, no. 2 (2012): 291–304.
Geller, Victor. *Orthodoxy Awakens: The Belkin Era and Yeshiva University*. New York: Urim Publications, 2003.
Genauer, Emily. "Does Modern Art Annoy You?" *Cosmopolitan* 124, no. 5 (May 1948): 28–31.
Giles, Jennie Jones. "Building Their Own Southern Tradition." Blue Ridge Now, June 29, 2003. https://www.blueridgenow.com/news/20030629/building-their-ownsouthern-Tradition.
Gilman, Sander. *Freud, Race and Gender*. Princeton, NJ: Princeton University Press, 1993.
Gilman, Sander. *The Jew's Body*. New York: Routledge, 1991.
Glazer, Nathan. *American Judaism*. Chicago: University of Chicago Press, 1957.
Glenn, Susan. "The Vogue of Jewish Self-Hatred in Post–World War II America." *Jewish Social Studies*, 12, no. 3 (Spring/Summer 2006): 95–136.
Goffman, Erving. *Stigma: Notes on the Management of Spoiled Identity*. New York: Simon & Schuster, 1963.
Goldscheider, Calvin. *Jewish Continuity and Change: Emerging Patterns in America*. Bloomington: Indiana University Press, 1986.
Goldstein, Eric. *The Price of Whiteness: Jews, Race, and American Identity*. Princeton, NJ: Princeton University Press, 2006.
Goldy, Robert. *The Emergence of Jewish Theology in America*. Bloomington: Indiana University Press, 1990.
Gordan, Rachel. "Alfred Kinsey and the Remaking of Jewish Sexuality in the Wake of the Holocaust." *Jewish Social Studies* 20, no. 3 (Spring/Summer 2014): 72–99.
Gordan, Rachel. "Laura Z. Hobson and the Making of *Gentleman's Agreement*." *Studies in American Jewish Literature* 34, no. 2 (2015): 231–256.
Gordan, Rachel. "The Sin of American Jewish Exceptionalism." *AJS Review* 45, no. 2 (2021): 282–301.
Gordon, Albert. *Jews in Suburbia*. New York: Greenwood Press, 1959.
Gordon, Linda. *The Second Coming of the KKK: The Ku Klux Klan of the 1920s and the American Political Tradition*. New York: Liveright, 2017.
Goren, Arthur. "A 'Golden Decade' for American Jews: 1945–1955." *Studies in Contemporary Jewry* 8 (1993): 3–20.

Gornick, Vivian. "Saul Bellow, Philip Roth, and the End of the Jew as Metaphor." In Vivian Gornick, *The Men in My Life*, 85–130. Cambridge, MA: MIT Press, 2008.
Graham, Gwethalyn. *Earth and High Heaven*. New York: Sun Dial Press, 1944.
Granger, Lester B. "New Books on Our Bookshelf." *Opportunity: Journal of Negro Life* 20, no. 3 (1942): 46.
Greene, Alison. *No Depression in Heaven: The Great Depression, the New Deal, and the Transformation of Religion in the Delta*. New York: Oxford University Press, 2015.
Grose, Peter. *Israel in the Mind of America*. New York: Knopf, 1983.
Guptill Manning, Molly. *When Books Went to War: The Stories That Helped Us Win World War II*. New York: Mariner Books, 2015.
Gurock, Jeffrey. *Jews in Gotham: New York Jews in a Changing City*. New York: New York University Press, 2015.
Gurock, Jeffrey. *Orthodox Jews in America*. Bloomington: Indiana University Press, 2009.
Gurock, Jeffrey. "Yeshiva Students at the Jewish Theological Seminary." In *Tradition Renewed: A History of the Jewish Theological Seminary of America*, edited by Jack Wertheimer, 473–513. Hanover, NH: University Press of New England, 2007.
Gustav-Wrathall, John Donald. *Take the Young Stranger by the Hand: Same-Sex Relations and the YMCA*. Chicago: University of Chicago Press, 1998.
Hallinan, Charles Thomas. "The Liberal and the Jew." *Nation*, January 23, 1924.
Halsey, Margaret. *Color Blind: A White Woman Looks at the Negro*. New York: Simon & Schuster, 1946.
Halsey, Margaret. *The Folks at Home*. New York: Simon & Schuster, 1952.
Halsey, Margaret. *No Laughing Matter: The Autobiography of a WASP*. New York: J. B. Lippincott, 1977.
Halsey, Margaret. *Some of My Best Friends Are Soldiers: A Kind of Novel*. New York: Simon & Schuster, 1944.
Hamill, Pete. "More Irrelevant than Irreverent." *Village Voice*, January 16, 1969.
Handlin, Oscar. *Al Smith and His America*. Boston: Little Brown, 1958.
Handlin, Oscar. *Race and Nationality in American Life*. New York: Doubleday Anchor Books, 1957.
Handy, Robert T. "The American Religious Depression, 1925–1935." *Church History* 29, no. 1 (March 1960): 3–16.
Harding, Sue-Ann. *An Archival Journey through the Qatar Peninsula: Elusive and Precarious*. Cham, Switzerland: Springer International Publishing, 2022.
Harker, Jaime. *America, the Middlebrow: Women's Novels, Progressivism, and Middlebrow Authorship between the Wars*. Amherst: University of Massachusetts Press, 2007.
Harrison-Kahan, Lori. "Introduction." In *Heirs of Yesterday*, by Emma Wolf. Detroit: Wayne State University Press, 2020.
Harrison-Kahan, Lori, and Josh Lambert. "Guest Editors Introduction: Finding Home: The Future of Jewish American Literary Studies." *MELUS* 37, no. 2 (Summer 2012): 5.
Hart, Mitchell. *The Healthy Jew: The Symbiosis of Judaism and Modern Judaism*. New York: Cambridge University Press, 2007.
Hart, Mitchell. *Jews and Race: Writings on Identity and Difference, 1880–1940*. Waltham, MA: Brandeis University Press, 2011.
Hartstein, Samuel. "A Public Relations Program for Orthodox Jewry." *Jewish Life*, April 1949, 63.
Hartung, Philip T. "Not for Escapists." *The Commonweal*, November 21, 1947.

Harvey, Paul, and Philip Goff. *The Columbia Documentary History of Religion in America since 1945*. New York: Columbia University Press, 2005.

Hedstrom, Matthew. "Psychology and Mysticism in 1940s Religion." In *Religion and the Culture of Print in Modern America*, edited by Charles L. Cohen and Paul S. Boyer, 343–367. Madison: University of Wisconsin Press, 2008.

Hedstrom, Matthew. *The Rise of Liberal Religion: Book Culture and American Spirituality in the Twentieth Century*. New York: Oxford University Press, 2012.

Heilman, Samuel. *The Rebbe: The Life and Afterlife of Menachem Mendel Schneerson*. Princeton, NJ: Princeton University Press, 2012.

Heinze, Andrew. *Jews and the American Soul: Human Nature in the Twentieth Century*. Princeton, NJ: Princeton University Press, 2004.

Heinze, Andrew. "Peace of Mind (1946): Judaism and the Therapeutic Polemics of Postwar America." *Religion and American Culture: A Journal of Interpretation* 12, no. 1 (Winter 2002): 31–58.

"Helen Fox Dead; a Garden Expert." *New York Times*, January 14, 1974, 30.

Herberg, Will. "Confession of Faith." Review of *This Is My God*, by Herman Wouk. *New York Times*, September 27, 1959, BR50.

Herberg, Will. *Protestant-Catholic-Jew: An Essay in American Religious Sociology*. New York: Doubleday, 1955)

Herberg, Will. "What Is Jewish Religion? Reflections on Rabbi Philip Bernstein's Article in Life." *Jewish Frontier*, October 1950, 8–13.

Hersey, John. "The Mechanics of a Novel." *Yale University Library Gazette* 27, no. 1 (July 1952): 6.

Heschel, Susannah. "Imagining Judaism in America." In *The Cambridge Companion to Jewish Literature*, edited by Hana Wirth-Nesher and Michael P. Kramer, 31–49. Cambridge: Cambridge University Press, 2004.

Hindus, Milton. "F. Scott Fitzgerald and Literary Anti-Semitism: A Footnote on the Minds of the '20s," *Commentary*, June 1947, 508–516.

"Historic UES Townhouse Owned by Famed Graphic Designer Elaine Lustig Cohen Hits the Market." *The Real Deal: Real Estate News*, January 13, 2017.

Hobson, Laura Z. *Gentleman's Agreement*. New York: Simon & Schuster, 1947.

Hobson, Laura. *Laura Z: A Life*. New York: Arbor House, 1983.

Hobson, Laura. *Laura Z: The Early Years and Years of Fulfillment*. New York: Donald L. Fine, 1986.

Hodgson, Geoffrey. *The Myth of American Exceptionalism*. New Haven, CT: Yale University Press, 2010.

Hoffman, Warren. *The Passing Game: Queering Jewish American Culture*. Syracuse, NY: Syracuse University Press, 2009.

Hollinger, David. *Protestants Abroad: How Missionaries Tried to Change the World but Changed America*. Princeton, NJ: Princeton University Press, 2017.

Hollinger, David. *Science, Jews, and Secular Culture*. Princeton, NJ: Princeton University Press, 1996.

Hood, John. "In Defense of 'Happy Holidays.'" *National Review*, December 18, 2007.

Hoover, J. Edgar. "God or Chaos." *Redbook*, February 1949, 61, 62, 63.

Horowitz, Bethamie. "Old Casks in New Times: The Reshaping of American Jewish Identity in the 21st Century." In *Ethnicity and Beyond: Theories and Dilemmas of Jewish Group Demarcation*, edited by Eli Lederhendler, 79–90. New York: Oxford University Press, 2011.

"How Come Modern Art?" *Seventeen* 11, no. 6 (Jun 1952): 74.
"Hub Head Cop Blackens City in Book Ban." *The Billboard* 56, no. 14 (April 1, 1944): 3.
Humble, Nicola. *The Feminine Middlebrow Novel, 1920s to 1950s*. New York: Oxford University Press, 2001.
Hungerford, Amy. *Postmodern Belief: American Literature and Religion since 1960*. Princeton, NJ: Princeton University Press, 2010.
Hutchens, John. "People Who Read and Write." *New York Times*, January 6, 1946, 52.
Hutner, Gordon. *What America Read: Taste, Class, and the Novel, 1920–1950*. Chapel Hill: University of North Carolina Press, 2011.
Hyman, Paula. *Gender and Assimilation in Modern Jewish History: The Roles and Representation of Women*. Seattle: University of Washington Press, 1995.
Idelson, Shirley. *We Shall Build Anew: Stephen S. Wise, the Jewish Institute of Religion and the Reinvention of American Liberal Judaism*. Tuscaloosa: University of Alabama Press, 2022.
Imhoff, Sarah. *Masculinity and the Making of American Judaism*. Bloomington: Indiana University Press, 2017.
Isseroff, Judah. "American Judaism between Religion and Race: Reflections on Mordecai Kaplan and Jewish Whiteness." *Religion and American Culture: A Journal of Interpretation* 32, no. 1 (Summer 2022): 1–29.
Jacobson, Matthew F. "Becoming Caucasian: Vicissitudes of Whiteness in American Politics and Culture." *Identities* 8, no. 1 (2001): 83–104.
Jackson, Walter. *A Gunnar Myrdal and America's Conscience: Social Engineering and Racial Liberalism, 1938–1987*. Chapel Hill: University of North Carolina Press, 1990.
Jacobson, Matthew F. *Roots Too: White Ethnic Revival in Post–Civil Rights America*. Cambridge, MA: Harvard University Press, 2004.
Jacobson, Matthew Frye. *Whiteness of a Different Color: European Immigrants and the Alchemy of Race*. Cambridge, MA: Harvard University Press, 1999.
Jay, Gregory. *White Writers, Race Matters: Fictions of Racial Liberalism from Stowe to Stockett*. New York: Oxford University Press, 2018.
Jerauld, James A. " 'Gentleman's Agreement' an Exceptional Picture." *Boxoffice*, November 15, 1947, 28-A.
Jerome, Fred, and Rodger Taylor. *Einstein on Race and Racism*. New Brunswick, NJ: Rutgers University Press, 2005.
Jewell, Edward Alden. "Modern Art Exhibits Works of Chagall." *New York Times*, April 10, 1946, 23.
"Jews Here Observe Shabuoth Festival," *New York Times*, June 4, 1949, 14.
Jews in America. New York: Random House, 1936.
"Jews Revive Old Sabbatical Rite of Scroll-Reading in Holy Land." *New York Times*, October 7, 1952, 31.
"Jews Urge Orthodox Life." *New York Times*, March 7, 1950, 21.
"Jews Will Mark Succoth." *New York Times*, October 8, 1957, 38.
"Jozefa Stuart: Robert Capa in Love and War." *American Masters Digital* Archive (WNET), January 7, 2002. https://www.pbs.org/wnet/americanmasters/archive/interview/jozefa-stuart/pbs.org/wnet/americanmasters/archive/interview/jozefa-sturt/.
"Judaism." *Life*, June 13, 1955, 97, 101.
Kachka, Boris. *Hothouse: The Art of Survival and the Survival of Art at America's Most Celebrated Publishing House, Farrar, Straus & Giroux*. New York: Simon & Schuster, 2013.

Kadushin, Charles. *Understanding Social Networks: Theories, Concepts, and Findings*. New York: Oxford University Press, 2012.

Kallen, Horace. "Can Judaism Survive in the United States?" *Menorah Journal* 11: no. 2 (April 1925): 102–103.

Kaplan, Amy. "Zionism as Anticolonialism: The Case of *Exodus*." *American Literary History* 25, no. 4 (Winter 2013): 870–895.

Kaplan, James. *The Voice*. New York: Anchor Books, 2010.

Kaplan, Mordecai. *Judaism as a Civilization: Toward a Reconstruction of American-Jewish Life*. Philadelphia: Jewish Publication Society, 2010.

Karabel, Jerome. *The Chosen: The Hidden History of Admissions and Exclusion at Harvard, Yale, and Princeton*. New York: Mariner Books, 2005.

Kaufmann, Walter. *The Faith of a Heretic*. Princeton, NJ: Princeton University Press, 2013.

Kazin, Alfred. "Books." *New Yorker*, March 4, 1950, 96.

Kelman, Ari. "Hear Israel." *Tablet*, January 7, 2011. https://www.tabletmag.com/sections/artsletters/articles/hear-israel.

Kendi, Ibram X. *How to Be an Antiracist*. New York: Vintage, 2019.

Kendi, Ibram X. *Stamped from the Beginning: The Definitive History of Racist Ideas in America*. New York: Bold Type Books, 2016.

Kennedy, John F. *A Nation of Immigrants*. New York: Anti-Defamation League, 1958.

Keren-Kratz, Menachem. "The Contemporary Study of Orthodoxy: Challenging the One-Dimensional Paradigm." *Tradition: A Journal of Orthodox Jewish Thought* 49, no. 4 (Winter 2016): 24–52.

Kertzer, Morris. "Religion." *American Jewish Year Book* 54 (1953): 98–108.

Kertzer, Morris. *What Is a Jew?* New York: World Publishing Company, 1953.

Kessner, Carole S. *The Other New York Jewish Intellectuals*. New York: New York University Press, 1994.

"Killing of Negroes Is Protested Here." *New York Times*, March 2, 1946, 26.

King, Charles. *Gods of the Upper Air: How a Circle of Renegade Anthropologists Reinvented Race, Sex, and Gender in the Twentieth Century*. New York: Doubleday, 2019.

Kirkpatrick, David. "The Book of the Month Club Tries to Be More of the Moment." *New York Times*, June 28, 2001, 59.

Kirsch, Adam. "The 'Five-foot Shelf' Reconsidered." *Harvard Magazine*, November–December 2001.

Klein, Christina. *Cold War Orientalism: Asia in the Middlebrow Imagination, 1945–1961*. Berkeley: University of California Press, 2003.

Klurfeld, Herman. *Winchell, His Life and Times*. New York: Praeger, 1976.

Kozol, Wendy. *Life's America: Family and Nation in Postwar Photojournalism*. Philadelphia: Temple University Press, 1994.

Krah, Markus. *American Jewry and the Re-Invention of the East European Jewish Past*. Boston: De Gruyter, 2017.

Krah, Markus. "Role Models or Foils for American Jews? 'The Eternal Light,' Displaced Persons, and the Construction of Jewishness in Mid-Twentieth-Century America." *American Jewish History* 96, no. 4 (December 2010): 265–286.

Kramer, Michael. "Assimilation in the Promised Land: Mary Antin and the Jewish Origins of the American Self." *Prooftexts* 18, no. 2 (May 1998): 121–148.

Kramer, Michael. "The Art of Assimilation: Ironies, Ambiguities, Aesthetics." In *Modern Jewish Literatures*, edited by Sheila E. Jelen, Michael P. Kramer, and L. Scott Lerner, 303–326. Philadelphia: University of Pennsylvania Press, 2011.

Kranson, Rachel. *Ambivalent Embrace: Jewish Upward Mobility in Postwar America*. Chapel Hill: University of North Carolina Press, 2017.

Krasner, Jonathan. "On the Origins and Persistence of the Jewish Identity Industry in Jewish Education." *Journal of Jewish Education* 82, no. 2 (2016): 132–158.

Kraut, Benny. "A Wary Collaboration: Jews, Catholics, and the Protestant Goodwill Movement." In *Between the Times: The Travail of the Protestant Establishment in America, 1900–1960*, edited by William Hutchison, 193–230. Cambridge: Cambridge University Press, 1989.

Kristol, Irving. "How Basic Is 'Basic Judaism'?" *Commentary*, January 1, 1948, 27–34.

Kruse, Kevin. *One Nation under God: How Corporate America Invented Christian America*. New York: Basic Books, 2015.

Kubowitzki, Myriam. "Letter to an Author." *Jewish Frontier*, July 1947, 27.

Kuh, Edwin. "The Social Disability of the Jew." *Atlantic Monthly*, April 1908.

Lambert, Josh. *American Jewish Fiction: A JPS Guide*. New York: Jewish Publication Society, 2009.

Lambert, Josh. "Fictions of anti-Semitism and the Beginning of Holocaust Literature." In *American Literature in Transition, 1940–1950*, edited by Christopher Vials, 44–59. Cambridge: Cambridge University Press, 2017.

Lambert, Josh. *Jewish Literary Mafia: Jews, Publishing, and Postwar American Literature*. New Haven: Yale University Press, 2022.

"Lambert Davis, 88, Editor and Publisher." *New York Times*, November 13, 1993, 31.

Lamm, Norman. "The Need for Tradition: The Editor's Introduction to a New Journal." *Tradition* 1, no. 1 (Fall 1958): 10.

Lederhendler, Eli. *New York Jews and the Decline of Urban Ethnicity, 1950–1970*. Syracuse, NY: Syracuse University Press, 2001.

Leonard, Thomas. *Illiberal Reformers: Race, Eugenics, and American Economics in the Progressive Era*. Princeton, NJ: Princeton University Press, 2016.

Levine, Lawrence. *Highbrow/Lowbrow: The Emergence of Cultural Hierarchy in America*. Cambridge, MA: Harvard University Press, 1988.

Levinger, Lee. *Anti-Semitism in the U.S: Its History and Causes*. New York: Bloch Publishing Co., 1925.

Levinson, Julian. "Arthur A. Cohen's Resplendent Vision." *Prooftexts*, May 1, 2003, 259.

Levinson, Julian. *Exiles on Main Street: Jewish American Writers and American Literary Culture*. Bloomington: Indiana University Press, 2008.

Levitt, Laura. "Impossible Assimilations, American Liberalism, and Jewish Difference: Revisiting Jewish Secularism." *American Quarterly* 59, no. 3 (September 2007): 807–832.

Levy, Lital. *Poetic Trespass-Writing between Hebrew and Arabic in Israel/Palestine*. Princeton, NJ: Princeton University Press, 2014.

Lewin, Kurt. "Self-Hatred Among Jews." In Resolving Social Conflict, edited by Gertrude Weiss-Lewin, 186–200. New York: Harper & Brothers, 1948.

Lewis, Carolyn. *Prescription for Heterosexuality: Sexual Citizenship in the Cold War Era*. Chapel Hill: University of North Carolina Press, 2010.

Lewis, Jeremy. *Penguin Special: The Story of Allen Lane, the Founder of Penguin Books and the Man Who Changed Publishing Forever*. New York: Penguin, 2005.

Liebman, Charles. "Orthodoxy in American Jewish Life." In *American Jewish Year Book 1965*, 21–22.

Liebman, Joshua Loth. *Peace of Mind*. New York: Simon & Schuster, 1946.

"Life Goes to a Bar Mitzvah." *Life*, October 13, 1952, 170–175.

Lincoln, Bruce. *Holy Terrors: Thinking about Religion after September 11*. 2nd ed. Chicago: University of Chicago Press, 2006.

Lipset, Seymour Martin. *American Exceptionalism: A Double-Edged Sword*. New York: W. W. Norton, 1997.

Lipstadt, Deborah. *Beyond Belief: The American Press and the Coming of the Holocaust, 1933–1945*. New York: Touchstone, 1986.

Luce, Henry. "The American Century." *Life*, February 17, 1941, 65.

Lynes, Russell. "Highbrow, Lowbrow, Middlebrow." *Harper's*, February 1949, 19–28.

Lytton, Timothy. *Kosher Private Regulation in the Age of Industrial Food*. Cambridge, MA: Harvard University Press, 2013.

Maggor, Noam. *Brahmin Capitalism: Frontiers of Wealth and Populism in America's First Gilded Age*. Cambridge, MA: Harvard University Press, 2017.

Magid, Shaul. *American Post-Judaism Identity and Renewal in a Postethnic Society*. Bloomington: Indiana University Press, 2013.

Mahalel, Adi. "We Will Not Be Silent: I. L. Peretz's 'Bontshe the Silent' vs. 1950s McCarthyism in America and the Story of the Staging of *The World of Sholom Aleichem*." *Studies in American Jewish Literature* 34 (2015): 204–230.

Mart, Michelle. *Eye on Israel: How America Came to View Israel as an Ally*. Albany: State University of New York Press, 2006.

Martin, Ralph G. *Henry and Clare: An Intimate Portrait of the Luces*. New York: Perigee Books, 1992.

Masuzawa, Tomoko. *The Invention of World Religions, or How European Universalism Was Preserved in the Language of Pluralism*. Chicago: University of Chicago Press, 2005.

May, Elaine Tyler. *Homeward Bound: American Families in the Cold War Era*. 4th ed. New York: Basic Books, 2017.

McAlister, Melani. *Epic Encounters: Culture, Media, and U.S. Interests in the Middle East since 1945*. Berkeley: University of California Press, 2005.

McCarten, John. "The Current Cinema." *New Yorker*, January 14, 1950, 75.

Mead, Walter Russell. *The Arc of a Covenant: The United States, Israel, and the Fate of the Jewish People*. New York: Knopf, 2022.

"Meet the Panel of Americans." *Seventeen*, August 1947, 74.

Mendes-Flohr, Paul. "Jewish Scholarship as a Vocation." In *Perspectives on Jewish Thought and Mysticism: Proceedings of the International Conference Held by the Institute of Jewish Studies*, edited by Alfred L. Ivry, Elliot R. Wolfson, and Allan Arkush, 33–48. London: Routledge, 1998.

Meyer, Michael. *Response to Modernity: A History of the Reform Movement in Judaism*. Detroit: Wayne State University Press, 1988.

Michaelis, David. *Eleanor*. New York: Simon & Schuster, 2020.

Michels, Tony. "Is America 'Different?' A Critique of American Jewish Exceptionalism." *American Jewish History* 96, no. 3 (2020): 201–224.

Miller, Arthur. *Focus*. New York: Penguin, 1984.

Miller, Douglas, and Marion Nowak. *The Fifties: The Way We Really Were*. Garden City, NY: Doubleday, 1960.

Miller, Merle. "The Book Club Controversy." *Harper's*, June 1948, 518–524.

Mintz, Alan. *Popular Culture and the Shaping of Holocaust Memory in America*. Seattle: University of Washington Press, 2001.

Moore, Deborah Dash. *GI Jews: How World War II Changed a Generation*. Cambridge, MA: Harvard University Press, 2004.

Moore, Deborah Dash. "Jewish GIs and the Creation of the Judeo-Christian Tradition." *Religion and American Culture: A Journal of Appreciation* 8, no. 1 (Winter 1998): 31–53.

Moran, Rodger J. "Gwethalyn Graham." In *The Canadian Encyclopedia*, September 28, 2011. thecanadianencyclopedia.ca.

"Movies: An American Queen." *Life*, September 11, 1950, 80.

Myrdal, Gunnar. *An American Dilemma: The Negro Problem and American Democracy*. New York: McGraw-Hill, 1964.

Nadell, Pamela. *America's Jewish Women, A History: From Colonial Times to Today*. New York: W.W. Norton, 2019.

Naor, Arye. "Jabotinsky's New Jew: Concepts and Models." *Journal of Israeli History* 30, no. 2 (September 2011): 141–159.

"The New Israel." *Life*, July 18, 1949, 71.

Niebuhr, Reinhold. "America's Three Melting Pots." *New York Times*, September 26, 1955, BR6.

Niebuhr, Reinhold. "Is There a Revival of Religion?" *New York Times*, November 19, 1950, SM7.

Niebuhr, Reinhold. "The Mysteries of Faith." Review of *God in Search of Man*, by Abraham Joshua Heschel. *Saturday Review*, April 21, 1956, 18.

Nirenberg, David. *Anti-Judaism: The Western Tradition*. New York: W. W. Norton, 2014.

Nongbri, Jason. *Before Religion: A History of a Modern Concept*. New Haven, CT: Yale University Press, 2013.

Norwood, Stephen. "Marauding Youth and the Christian Front: Antisemitic Violence in Boston and New York during World War II." *American Jewish History* 91, no. 2 (June 2003): 233–267.

Noveck, Simon. "Milton Steinberg." In *The Other New York Jewish Intellectuals*, edited by Carole S. Kessner, 313–52. New York: New York University Press, 1994.

Novick, Peter. *The Holocaust in American Life*. Boston: Houghton Mifflin, 2000.

Novick, Peter. *That Noble Dream: The "Objectivity Question" and the American Historical Profession*. New York: Cambridge University Press, 1988.

Okrent, Daniel. *The Guarded Gate: Bigotry, Eugenics, and the Law That Kept Two Generations of Jews, Italians, and Other European Immigrants Out of America*. New York: Scribner, 2019.

Oppenheimer, Mark. *Squirrel Hill: The Tree of Life Synagogue Shooting and the Soul of a Neighborhood*. New York: Alfred A. Knopf, 2021.

Orsi, Robert. *Between Heaven and Earth: The Religious Worlds People Make and the Scholars Who Study Them*. Princeton, NJ: Princeton University Press, 2006.

Orsi, Robert. "On Not Talking to the Press." *Religious Studies News* 19, no. 3 (2004): 15.

Parker, James Reid. "Gentleman's Agreement." *Survey Graphic*, May 1947.

Patterson, James T. *Brown v. Board of Education: A Civil Rights Milestone and Its Troubled Legacy*. New York: Oxford University Press, 2001.

Patterson, James T. *Grand Expectations: The United States, 1945–1974*. New York: Oxford University Press, 1997.

Pautz, Michelle. "The Decline in Average Weekly Cinema Attendance, 1930–2000." *Political Science Faculty Publications* 25 (Summer 2002). https://ecommons.udayton.edu/pol_fac_pub/25.

Pease, Donald. *The New American Exceptionalism*. Minneapolis: University of Minnesota Press, 2009.

Perrin, Tom. *The Aesthetics of Middlebrow Fiction: Popular US Novels, Modernism, and Form, 1945–75*. (New York: Palgrave, 2015.

Peters, William. "The Case against 'Easy' Religion." *Redbook* 105, no. 5 (September 1955): 22.

Pinson, Koppel, S. "Antisemitism in the Postwar World." *Jewish Social Studies* 7, no. 2 (April 1945): 99.

Pittenger, Mark. *Class Unknown: Undercover Investigations of American Work and Poverty from the Progressive Era to the Present*. New York: New York University Press, 2012.

Platt, Daniel. "The Natures of Capital: Jewish Difference and the Decline of American Usury Law, 1910–1925." *Journal of American History* 104, no. 4 (March 2018): 863–878.

Poling, Daniel. "A Protestant's Faith." *Life*, November 7, 1949, 113–121.

Polsky, Howard. "A Study of Orthodoxy in Milwaukee: Social Characteristics, Beliefs, and Observances." In *The Jews: Social Patterns of an American Group*, edited by Marshall Sklare, 325–335. Glencoe, IL: Free Press, 1958.

Poore, Charles. "Books of the Time." *New York Times*, November 24, 1945, 17.

Porath, Jonathan. "A Passover Seder to Remember with Patton's Army in Occupied Germany '45." *Jerusalem Post*, April 18, 2019.

Prell, Riv-Ellen. "Assimilation and Authenticity: Some Thoughts on a Jewish Response." *Muslim World* 104, no. 4 (2014): 392–396.

Prell, Riv-Ellen. "Community and the Discourse of Elegy: The Post War Suburban Debate." In *Imagining the American Jewish Community*, edited by Jack Wertheimer, 67–90. Hanover, NH: University Press of New England, 2007.

Prell, Riv-Ellen. *Fighting to Be Americans: Assimilation and the Trouble between Jewish Women and Jewish Men*. Boston: Beacon Press, 2000.

Prell, Riv-Ellen. "Triumph, Accommodation, and Resistance: American Jewish Life from the End of World War II to the Six Day War." In *The Columbia History of Jews and Judaism*, edited by Marc Lee Raphael, 125–126. New York: Columbia University Press, 2008.

Prescott, Orville. "Books of the Time." *New York Times*, September 11, 1950, 21.

Preston, Andrew. *Sword of Spirit, Shield of Faith: Religion in American War and Diplomacy*. New York: Anchor, 2012.

Prothero, Steven. *God the Bestseller: How One Editor Transformed American Religion a Book at a Time*. New York: HarperCollins, 2022.

Rabin, Shari. *Jews on the Frontier: Religion and Mobility in Nineteenth-Century America*. New York: New York University Press, 2017.

Radway, Janice. *A Feeling for Books: The Book-of-the-Month Club, Literary Taste, and Middle-Class Desire*. Chapel Hill: University of North Carolina Press, 1999.

Rakeffet-Rothkoff, Aaron. "Rabbi Joseph B. Soloveitchik: The Early Years." *Tradition: A Journal of Orthodox Jewish Thought* 30, no. 4 (Summer 1996): 193–209.

Rampersad, Arnold. Introduction to Richard Wright, *Native Son*. New York: HarperPerennial, 2005.

Raphael, Marc Lee. *Judaism in America*. New York: Columbia University Press, 2005.

"Religion: What Jews Believe." *Time*, May 14, 1951.

Ribalow, Harold. "Answers to Man's Ultimate Questions." *Saturday Review*, March 3, 1956, 38.

Ribalow, Harold. *This Land, These People*. New York: Beechhurst Press, 1950.

Rice, Elinor. "What Am I?" *Woman's Day*, April 1949, 91.

Roberts, Kenneth L. "The Existence of an Emergency." *Saturday Evening Post*, April 30, 1921, 93.

Roberts, Randy W., and David Welky, eds. Charles A. Lindbergh: The Power and Peril of Celebrity, 1927–1941. New York: Wiley Blackwell, 2003.

Rodgers, Lawrence R. "Introduction." In *Fanny Herself*, by Edna Feber, vii–xvii. Urbana: University of Illinois Press, 2001.

Roosevelt, Eleanor. "My Day." December 9, 1947, The Eleanor Roosevelt Papers, Digital Edition, GWU, https://www2.gwu.edu/~erpapers/myday/displaydoc.cfm?_y=1947&_f=md000831.

Roth, Phil. *Goodbye, Columbus*. New York: Houghton Mifflin, 1959.

Rothberg, Abraham. "The Dilemma of the Jewish Writer." *Congress Weekly*, March 24, 1952. In Harold Ribalow, *These Your Children*, 14. New York: Beechhurst Press, 1952.

Ruch, Walter. "Religious Revival Urged by Truman." *New York Times*, July 23 1950, 37.

Sachar, Howard. *A History of the Jews in America*. New York: Vintage, 1993.

Sandberg, Elisabeth. "Jo Sinclair: A Gardener of Souls." *Studies in American Jewish Literature* 12 (1993): 72–78.

Sarna, Jonathan. *American Judaism*. New Haven, CT: Yale University Press, 2004.

Sarna, Jonathan. "The Cult of Synthesis in American Jewish Culture." *Jewish Social Studies* 5 (Fall 1998–Winter 1999): 52–79.

Sarna, Jonathan. "Recalling Arthur Hertzberg: Public Intellectual." *New York Jewish Week*, April 21, 2006, 22.

Sarna, Jonathan, and Jonathan Golden. "The Twentieth Century through American Jewish Eyes: A History of the American Jewish Year Book, 1899–1999." In *American Jewish Year Book 100*, edited by David Singer and Lawrence Grossman, 3–103. New York: The American Jewish Committee, 2000.

Sartre, Jean-Paul. *Anti-Semite and Jew*. New York: Schocken Books, 1948.

Schocher, D. "Tzena, Tzena—On Hit Parade—Is Israel's Biggest Export." *The Jewish Advocate*, September 28, 1950, 1.

Schonfeld, Gabriel. "From the Talmud: A Dynamic Tradition of Self-Study." *Saturday Review*, February 21, 1959, 43.

Schreier, Benjamin. *The Rise and Fall of Jewish American Literature: Ethnic Studies and the Challenge of Identity*. Philadelphia: University of Pennsylvania Press, 2020.

Schultz, Kevin. "Protestant-Catholic-Jew, Then and Now." *First Things*, January 2006.

Schultz, Kevin. *Tri-Faith America: How Catholics and Jews Held Postwar America to Its Protestant Promise*. New York: Oxford University Press, 2011.

Schwarz, Leo Walzer. *Wolfson at Harvard: Portrait of a Scholar*. Philadelphia: Jewish Publication Society, 1978.

Scott, Arthur L. "In Defense of Robert Cohn." *College English* 18, no. 6 (March 1957): 309–314.

Selwyn, James. "Rosh Hashanah and Yom Kippur." *Redbook*, September 1950, 34–37, 80–81.

Shandler, Jeffrey. *Adventures in Yiddishland: Postvernacular Language and Culture*. Berkeley: University of California Press, 2020.

Shandler, Jeffrey. *Entertaining America: Jews, Movies, and Broadcasting*. Princeton, NJ: Princeton University Press, 2003.

Shandler, Jeffrey. *Jews, God, and Videotape: Religion and Media in America*. New York: New York University Press, 2012.

Shandler, Jeffrey. *While American Watches: Televising the Holocaust.* New York: Oxford University Press, 2000.

Shandler, Jeffrey, and Elihu Katz. "Broadcasting American Judaism: The Radio and Television Department of JTS." In *Tradition Renewed: A History of the Jewish Theological Seminary of America*, edited by Jack Wertheimer, 363-401. New York: Jewish Theological Seminary of America, 1997.

Sharfman, Solomon J. "Foreword." *Tradition* 1, no. 1 (Fall 1958): 5.

Silberman, Charles. *A Certain People: American Jews and Their Lives.* New York: Summit Books, 1985.

Silk, Mark. "Notes on the Judeo-Christian Tradition in America." *American Quarterly* 36, no. 1 (Spring 1984): 65-85.

Silk, Mark. *Spiritual Politics: Religion and America since World War II.* New York: Touchstone, 1988.

Silver, Matthew. *Our Exodus: Leon Uris and the Americanization of Israel's Founding Story.* Detroit: Wayne State University Press, 2010.

Silverman, Al. "A Fragile Pleasure." *Daedalus* 112, no. 1 (Winter 1983): 35-49.

Sinclair, Jo. *The Seasons: Death and Transfiguration: A Memoir by Jo Sinclair.* New York: Feminist Press, 1993.

Sinclair, Jo. *Wasteland.* New York: Jewish Publication Society, 1946, 1987.

Sinkoff, Nancy. "Fiction's Archive: Authenticity, Ethnography, and Philosemitism in John Hersey's *The Wall.*" *Jewish Social Studies* 17, no. 2 (Winter 2011): 48-79.

Sinkoff, Nancy. *From Left to Right: Lucy S. Dawidowicz, the New York Intellectuals, and the Politics of Jewish History.* Detroit: Wayne State University Press, 2020.

Sklare, Marshall. *Conservative Judaism: An American Religious Movement.* Glencoe, IL: Free Press, 1955.

Sklare, Marshall, and Ted Solotaroff. "Introduction." In *Jews in the Mind of America*, edited by Charles Stember, 3-28. New York: Basic Books, 1966.

Sklare, Marshall, Marc Vosk, and Mark Zborowski. "Forms and Expressions of Jewish Identification." *Jewish Social Studies* 17, no. 3 (July 1955): 215.

Smith, Betty. *A Tree Grows in Brooklyn.* New York: Harper & Brothers, 1943.

Smith, Dinitia. "Margaret Halsey, 86, a Writer Who Lampooned the English." *New York Times*, February 7, 1997, D18.

Smith, Elinor Goulding. "Why Won't Somebody Tolerate Me?" *Harper's*, August 1956, 36-38.

Smith, Erin A. "The Religious Book Club: Print Culture, Consumerism, and the Spiritual Life of Protestants Between the Wars." In *Religion and the Culture of Print in Modern America*, edited by Charles L. Cohen and Paul S. Boyer, 217-242. Seattle: University of Wisconsin Press, 2008.

Smith, Judith E. *Visions of Belonging: Family Stories, Popular Culture, and Postwar Democracy, 1960-1960.* New York: Columbia University Press, 2004.

Smith, Sally Bedell. *In All His Glory: The Life and Times of William S. Paley and the Birth of Modern Broadcasting.* New York: Simon & Schuster, 1947.

Smith, Wilfred Cantwell. *The Meaning and End of Religion.* Minneapolis: Fortress Press, 1991.

Sollors, Werner. "Holocaust and Hiroshima: American Ethnic Prose Writers Face the Extreme." *PMLA* 118, no. 1 (January 2003): 56-61.

Solomon, Alisa. *Wonder of Wonders: A Cultural History of Fiddler on the Roof.* New York: Metropolitan Books, 2013.

Solomon, Andrew. *Far from the Tree: Parents, Children and the Search for Identity.* New York: Simon & Schuster, 2012.
Solomon, Deborah. *American Mirror: The Life and Art of Norman Rockwell.* New York: Farrar, Straus & Giroux, 2013.
Spiegel, Irving. "Challenge Posed to Orthodox Jews." *New York Times*, January 29, 1958, 16.
Spiegel, Irving. "Orthodox Jews Plan Expansion." *New York Times*, November 16, 1958, 62.
Spiegel, Irving. "Rabbi Sees Gains for Orthodoxy." *New York Times*, July 5, 1958, 25.
Stahl, Ronit. "A Jewish America and a Protestant Civil Religion: Will Herberg, Robert Bellah, and Mid-Twentieth Century American Religion." *Religions* 6, no. 2 (2015): 434–450.
"Stay Out of Texas, House Roars Out to Lindbergh." *Austin Statesman*, September 18, 1941, 1.
Steinberg, Edith A. "Midwife to a Novel." Undated, Box 10, folder 4: "Writings—Other—Short Stories of the Steinberg Family, undated, 1938." Milton Steinberg P-369 Collection of American Jewish Historical Society, New York, NY.
Steinberg, Milton. *Basic Judaism.* New York: Harcourt Brace, 1947.
Steinberg, Milton. "Between Religion and Psychiatry." *The Reconstructionist* 12, no. 10 (1946): 28–30.
Steinberg, Milton. "First Principles for American Jews." *Contemporary Jewish Record*, December 1, 1941, 587–596.
Steinberg, Milton. "How the Jew Did It." *Atlantic Monthly*, May 1933, 659–658.
Steinberg, Milton. "How the Jew Does It." *Atlantic Monthly*, July 1933, 26–38.
Steinberg, Milton. "The Jew Faces Anti-Semitism." *The Reconstructionist* 2, no. 2 (March 6, 1936): 7–13.
Steinberg, Milton. *The Making of the Modern Jew.* New York: Behrman's, 1943.
Steinberg, Milton. "The Outlook of Reinhold Niebuhr: A Description and Appraisal." *The Reconstructionist* 11 (December 14, 1945): 10–15.
Steinberg, Milton. *A Partisan Guide to the Jewish Problem.* New York: Bobbs-Merrill, 1945.
Steinberg, Milton. "A Specimen Jew." In *A Believing Jew*, 98–99. New York: Harcourt Brace, 1951.
Steinberg, Milton. "To Be or Not to Be a Jew." *Common Ground* 1, no. 3 (Spring 1941): 43–50.
Steinberg, Milton. "What Religion Is Not." *The Reconstructionist* 3, no. 14 (1937): 15–16.
Stember, Charles. *Jews in the Mind of America.* New York: Basic Books, 1966.
Sussman, Robert Wald. *The Myth of Race: The Troubling Persistence of an Unscientific Idea.* Cambridge, MA: Harvard University Press, 2016.
Svonkin, Stuart. *Jews against Prejudice.* New York: Columbia University Press, 1999.
Tanenbaum, Marc. "Religion." *American Jewish Year Book* 60 (1959): 53–66.
Taylor, Charles. *Multiculturalism: Examining the Politics of Recognition.* Princeton, NJ: Princeton University Press, 1994.
Telushkin, Joseph. *Rebbe: The Life and Teachings of Menachem M. Schneerson, the Most Influential Rabbi in Modern History.* New York: HarperCollins, 2014.
Tevis, Britt. "'Jews Not Admitted': Anti-Semitism, Civil Rights, and Public Accommodation Laws." *Journal of American History* 107, no. 4 (March 2021): 847–870.
Thompson, Clive. "The Revolutionary Effect of the Paperback Book." *Smithsonian Magazine*, May 2013.

Tichenor, Daniel. *Dividing Lines: The Politics of Immigration Control in America*. Princeton, NJ: Princeton University Press, 2002.
Tompkins, Jane. *Sensational Designs: The Cultural Work of American Fiction, 1790–1860*. New York: Oxford University Press, 1985.
Trachtenberg, Joshua. *The Devils of the Jews: The Medieval Conception of the Jew and Its Relation to Modern Antisemitism*. New Haven, CT: Yale University Press, 1943.
Trilling, Diana. "Americans without Distinction." *Commentary*, March 1947, 290–292.
Trodd, Zoe. "The Civil Rights Movement and Literature of Social Protest." In *The Cambridge Companion to American Civil Rights Literature*, edited by Julie Buckner Armstrong, 17–34. Cambridge: Cambridge University Press, 2015.
Tumin, Melvin. "The Idea of 'Race' Dies Hard." *Commentary* 8 (July 1949): 80–85.
Tushnet, Mark, and Katya Lezin, "What Really Happened in *Brown v. Board of Education*." *Columbia Law Review* 91, no. 8 (December 1991): 1867–1930.
Twersky, Isadore. "Harry Austryn Wolfson, 1887–1974." *Journal of the American Oriental Society* 95, no. 2 (April–June 1975): 181–183.
"Two Mothers Look at America." *Parents' Magazine*, September 1944, 131, 132.
"The Un-American Way." *New York Times*, September 26, 1941, 22.
"Under Forty: A Symposium." *Contemporary Jewish Record*, February 1, 1944, 3–36.
Walden, Daniel. *On Being Jewish*. New York: Random House, 1975.
Wall, Wendy. *Inventing the American Way: The Politics of Consensus from the New Deal to the Civil Rights Movement*. New York: Oxford University Press, 2008.
Walters, Ray. "1945: The First 'Instant' Paperback." *New York Times*, April 30, 1989, 96.
Warren, Donald. *Radio Priest Charles Coughlin, the Father of Hate Radio*. New York: Free Press, 1996.
"We Are Lost If We Accept This Crime." *Courier-Journal* (Louisville, KY), June 17, 1940.
Weisenfeld, Judith. *Hollywood Be Thy Name: African American Religion in American Film, 1929–1945*. Princeton, NJ: Princeton University Press, 2007.
Weisman, Steven. *The Chosen Wars: How Judaism Became an American Religion*. New York: Simon & Schuster, 2018.
Weis-Rosmarin, Trude. *Judaism and Christianity: The Differences*. New York: Jewish Book Club, 1943.
Weiss, Tibor. "Judaism's Alive and Well and Living in America; Orthodox Revival." *New York Times*, June 20, 1990, A24.
Wenger, Beth. *New York Jews and the Great Depression: Uncertain Promise*. New Haven, CT: Yale University Press, 1996.
Wenger, Tisa. *Religious Freedom: The Contested History of an American Ideal*. Chapel Hill: University of North Carolina Press, 2017.
Wharton, Edith. *The House of Mirth*. New York: Dover Thrift Editions, 2002.
Whitfield, Stephen J. *The Culture of the Cold War*. Baltimore: Johns Hopkins University Press, 1996.
Whitman, James. *Hitler's American Model: The United States and the Making of Nazi Race Law*. Princeton, NJ: Princeton University Press, 2017.
Wicklein, John. "Judaism on Rise in the Suburbs." *New York Times*, April 5, 1959, 80.
"Willkie Terms Lindbergh's Des Moines Talk Un-American." *The Sun*, September 14, 1941, 1.
Wise, James W., and Lee Levinger. *Mr. Smith, Meet Mr. Cohen*. New York: Reynal & Hitchcock, 1940.

Woeste, Victoria Saker. *Henry Ford's War on Jews and the Legal Battle against Hate Speech*. Stanford, CA: Stanford University Press, 2012.

Wolfson, Harry. "Escaping Judaism." *Menorah Journal* 7 (1921): 167.

Woolf, Virginia. "Middlebrow." In *The Death of the Moth*, 176–186. London: Hogarth Press, 1942.

Wouk, Herman. *Marjorie Morningstar*. New York: Doubleday, 1955.

Wuthnow, Robert. *After Heaven: Spirituality in America since the 1950s*. Berkeley: University of California Press, 1998.

Wylie, Philip. "Memorandum on Anti-Semitism." *American Mercury*, January 1945, 66–73.

Yares, Laura. *Jewish Sunday Schools: Teaching Religion in Nineteenth Century America*. New York: New York University Press, 2023.

"The Year in Books." *Time*, December 16, 1946, 108.

Young, Donald. *American Minority Peoples*. New York: Harper & Brothers, 1932.

Zinsser, William. *A Family of Readers: An Informal Portrait of the Book-of-the-Month Club and Its Members on the Occasion of Its 60th Anniversary*. New York: Book of the Month Club, 1986.

Zukerman, William. "The Silver Lining," *Ladies' Home Journal*, June 1947, 68.

Index

Figures are indicated by *f* following the page number

Above and Beyond (Hobson), 199–200
Abrahamic religions, Judaism's position in, 158–59
acceptance of Jews. *See also* exclusion and marginalization; tri-faith of America
  choice to be an American Jew related to, 195–96
  as goal of anti-antisemitism, 8–9, 34
  as goal of Introduction to Judaism genre, 8–9, 17, 18, 22–23, 34, 127, 145
  Holocaust's effect on American acceptance, 6, 7, 16, 105
  impossible standard of acceptability for Jews, 35–36, 38–39, 99, 101–2, 134–35
  Jewish writers enjoying by last third of twentieth century, 202
  linked to whiteness of Jews, 31–32, 83
  normalization of Judaism in American culture, 12–13, 15–16, 99, 197
  Wolfson's view of impossibility of (*see* Wolfson, Harry)
Adler, Morris, 127–28
African Americans. *See* Blacks; racism
Ager, Ceclia, 81
Albanese, Catherine,
Aleichem, Sholom, 148–49, 198
Alexander, Jeffrey, 52, 221
alienation, 34, 54, 125. *See also* exclusion and marginalization; "others"
Alpenfels, Ethel, 89
America First, 48–49, 51, 53–54
"American Century" (Luce), 133–34
American culture. *See also* anti-antisemitism; antisemitism; popular culture
  divisiveness of, 23–24
  importance to have religion, 3–4, 7–8, 9, 10–11
  Jews' assimilation (*see* assimilation)
  Jews' presence in, 15, 155–56
  print media as primary vehicle of, 17
  resistance to altering racial discourse, 90
An American Dilemma: The Negro Problem and Modern Democracy (Myrdal), 104–5
American exceptionalism, 81–82, 157
Americanism, definition of, 27
American Israelite (magazine), 26–27
American Jewish Committee (AJC), 38, 51, 213
American Jewish Congress, 213
American Jewish self-perceptions
  ignorance of Judaism, 7–8, 193–94
  Jewish strategy of self-improvement, 35
  Jews' assimilation and, 200–1
  self-hating Jews, 42
  Steinberg on failure of Jews to appreciate Judaism, 119
  Wolfson advising to accept Jewishness and its burdens, 40–43, 92–93, 195–96 (*see also* Wolfson, Harry)
American Jewish Year Book, 39–40, 110, 190–91, 214
American Judaism (Glazer)
  as college text, 18, 107–8
  critical reception of, 107
American literature. *See also* anti-antisemitism literature; Introduction to Judaism genre
  antisemitism in, 28
  books, role of, 9–10
  ethnic trends in, 200
  revisions to texts to eliminate antisemitic references, 29–30
  role in changing views on Jews, 15
  Yiddish appearing in, 155–56
"Americans without Distinction" (Trilling), 96

Anatomy of Faith (Steinberg's essays edited by Arthur Cohen), 188–89
Andrews Sisters, 149
anti-antisemitism
  in Cold War, 132
  film depictions, 52 (see also *Gentleman's Agreement* (film))
  Holocaust's effect and, 6, 7, 16, 105
  literature (*see* anti-antisemitism literature)
  messaging for, 53
  of Eleanor Roosevelt, 20
  transformation of American thinking through, 8–9, 13, 17–18, 34, 105
  use of term, 52
anti-antisemitism literature, 2–3, *See also specific authors and titles*
  activist-writing of, 92
  audience increasing for, 196
  before-and-after views of characters undergoing transformation, 76
  community of readers forming around, 10
  compared to Introduction to Judaism genre, 19, 97
  connections between antisemitism and other kinds of bigotries, 11, 75–76, 78, 80
  democracy and freedom as critical elements, 80
  Holocaust and, 16, 67–68
  insight into Jewish characters, 17–18, 22–23, 30–31, 76
  legacy of, 200
  limits of, 81–105 (*see also* limits of anti-antisemitism literature)
  in middlebrow moment, 13, 196
  minimal information provided about Judaism, 97–98, 106–7, 108–10
  overlap with Introduction to Judaism genre, 129
  precursors of, 21, 48–58 (*see also* roots of anti-antisemitism fiction)
  religion, Jews as members of, 86, 101
  representative titles and authors, 21, 48
  teaching purpose of, 15, 17–18, 24, 73–74, 76, 80, 87–88, 93
  women as authors of (*see* women authors)
  women as readers of, 94–95, 184
Anti-Defamation League, 56, 142–43, 213
anti-immigration movement, 27, 37–38, 55–56
Antin, Mary, 214
Anti-Semite and the Jew (Sartre), 54, 61
antisemitism. *See also* Nazis; stereotypes of Jews
  in American novels, 28
  American writers describing experiencing, 34
  change in attitude toward Jews in WWII and after, 53, 61, 157–58
  civil rights movement and, 52–53
  in Cold War era, 10–11, 45
  as commonplace in American society of early twentieth century, 21–22, 28, 36, 53, 60–61
  contemporary resurgence of, 24
  contemporary willingness to discuss, 47
  emotional response of Jews to, 34–35, 119
  in Great Depression, 28
  Halsey's background and, 69–70
  in Hobson's *Gentleman's Agreement*, 1–2 (see also *Gentleman's Agreement*)
  humanity of Jews in question, 36
  illness and disability status accorded to being Jewish, 39
  Introduction to Judaism genre combating, 129, 185–86
  Jewish responsibility for, 38
  of Lindbergh and America First, 48–51, 56, 57, 58
  Miller and, 68–69
  Nazi atrocities compared to American religious bigotry, 81, 82–83
  persistence of, 105
  positive identity of Jews as response to, 46
  racial categorization of Jews contributing to, 36–37
  racism's linkage to, 2, 11, 31, 36–38, 73, 76, 80, 102
  Eleanor Roosevelt and, 20
  teaching Americans how to feel about (*see* middlebrow)
  terms for, 34
  as un-American, 13, 15, 21–22, 50, 51, 56, 57, 201

as vulgar behavior, 2
women's credibility in writing about, 19
Appiah, Kwame Anthony, 75
Arendt, Hannah, 125
As a Driven Leaf (Steinberg), 18–19, 108, 114
assimilation, 64–65, 100, 109, 150, 193–94, 200–1
Aswell, Edward, 76–77, 78–79
atheists, 10–11
Atlantic Monthly
  on Jews facing impossible standard of acceptability (1937), 36
  on *Jews in a Gentile World* (Graeber and Britt), 53–54
  on social disability of Jews (1908), 41–42
  Steinberg's essays in, 111–12, 115

Baeck, Rabbi Leo, 115
Baker, Cynthia, 45–46
Baldwin, James, 82, 95
Baron, Salo, 107
Basic Judaism (Steinberg), 121
  accused of accommodating "Main Street" America, 125–26
  advocating for harmony between American and Jewish traditions, 127
  collaboration of Edith Steinberg on, 114
  as college text, 18
  comparison with Christianity, 122, 123–25
  critical reception of, 121–22, 125–26, 144
  definition of Judaism, 30–31
  Jesus, discussion of, 122–23
  proposal for, 112–13
  purpose of, 110–11, 121, 187
  sales of, 112–13, 121
  tolerance of doctrinal differences in Judaism, 124
  Zionism and creation of Israel, 124
The Beautiful and the Damned (Fitzgerald), 28–29
Belkin, Samuel, 24
Bellafonte, Harry, 149
A Bell for Adano (Hersey), 154
Bellow, Saul, 48, 59–60, 75, 155–56, 202
Benedict, Ruth, 10, 88–90

Benjamin, Judah P., 53–54
Berg, Gertrude, 14–15
Berle, Milton, 14–15
Berlin, Irving, 45
Berman, Lila Corwin, 17
Bernstein, Rabbi Philip, 129–46, See also *What The Jews Believe*
  background of, 136–37
  chosen by *Life* to write on Judaism, 137–38
  as middlebrow author, 14
  as Steinberg's cousin, 107, 120, 136–37
  writing and publishing as areas of interest to, 137
Biddle, George, 156
Bilbo, Theodore, 4–5, 70
Billings, John Shaw, 137–38
Birstein, Ann, 8
Black, Hugo, 103–4
Blacks. See also racism; segregation
  first Black woman to appear on cover of *Life*, 174
  reaction to Hobson's *Gentleman's Agreement*, 82, 102–3
  television depiction of Black middle-class, 22, 214
Bloom, Jack, 191
Boas, Franz, 89–90
Book-of-the-Month Club, 9, 48
Brandeis, Louis, 37–38
Brandeis University, 120, 190–91
Britt, Steuart Henderson, 53–54
Brown, John Mason, 106
Brown v. Board of Education (1954), 104–5
Bruce, Lenny, 15
Buber, Martin, 195
Burchardt, Hermann, 173

Cahnman, Werner, 157–58
Canby, Henry Seidel, 48
Capa, Cornell, 151, 160–61, 163–64
Capa, Robert, 160–61
Caplan, Harry, 64
Catholicism
  added to Judeo-Christianity, 23–24
  antisemitism and, 121–22
  compared to Judaism, 18, 139
  prejudice against, 10–11, 18
  Steinberg using as foil for Judaism, 121–22, 123–24

Chagall, Marc, 156–57
Chambers, Whittaker, 130–31
"Choice—for Gentiles" (Hobson), 178–79
choice to be a Jew, 176–97,
  becoming a rabbi, 191
  becoming more religious, 191
  Arthur Cohen and, 176–79 (see also "Why I Choose to Be a Jew")
  dynamic between orthodox and assimilated Jews, 192–93
  as independence from families, 191–92, 193–94
  Introduction to Judaism genre and, 176
  later-in-life embrace of Judaism, 8
  post-Judaism and,
  rabbinical schools needing such material, 190–91
  Steinberg and, 116, 187–88 (see also *Basic Judaism*)
  Wouk and, 178–79, 186–87 (see also *This Is My God*)
Christian Century
  Arthur Cohen as author for, 177
  on reaction to Lindbergh's antisemitism, 50–51
Christian Front, 53–54, 81–82, 123–24
Christian nation, U.S. as
  Catholicism seen as threat to, 10–11, 18
  change to Judeo-Christian nation, 12, 16
  change to tri-religion nation (see tri-faith of America)
  Jews seen as threat to, 26
  safeguarding of white Christian America, 28
Christian Nationalist Party, 4–5
"Christians Only" The Story of Anti-Semitism in America, 41–42
Churchwell, Sarah, 48–49
City College conference on "The Heritage and Identity of Ethnic Groups in New York" (1972), 200
civil rights movement, 23–24, 103–4, 181, 201
Cohen, Arthur A., 126–27, See also *The Myth of the Judeo-Christian Tradition*
  background of, 176, 193–94
  diverse pursuits of, 177–78
  on dynamic between orthodox and assimilated Jews, 193–94
  finding Jewish path as adult, 176–79, 180–81, 186–87 (see also "Why I Choose to Be a Jew")
  interest in Christianity, 126–27, 176–77, 194–96
  Israel trip, effect of, 191–92, 194
  social network of, 177–78, 184
  Steinberg's relationship with, 10, 108, 118, 177, 186
Cohen, Elliot E., 100
Cohen, Isidore (Arthur's father), 180–81
Cohen, Morris Raphael, 117–18, 124–25
Cohen, Mortimer J., 42
Cold War
  America in leadership role in, 133–34
  religious affiliations and, 10
  religious affiliations' importance in, 3–4, 7–8, 9, 10–11, 130 (see also religiosity)
  Soviet rejection of religion, 10, 130
Collier's serializing Graham's *Earth and High Heaven*, 59, 68
Color Blind: A White Woman Looks at the Negro (Halsey), 70–71
Commentary (magazine)
  Arthur Cohen's "Myth of the Judeo-Christian Tradition" (1969), 194, 195–96
  "The Idea of 'Race' Dies Hard" (1949), 89
  Kristol's review of Steinberg's *Basic Judaism*, 125–27
  New York Jewish intelligentsia as contributors, 125
  symposium on "American Literature and the Younger Generation of American Jews" (1944), 54
Commonweal magazine on Hobson's *Gentleman's Agreement* (1947), 106
Communists. See also Cold War
  Hobson's twin and, 62
  Hoover on, 132
  Jews as, 26–27, 37–38, 132
  McCarthyism and, 3–4
Como, Perry, 149

Conservative Judaism
  popularity among suburban Jews,
    162–63
  Reconstructionist Judaism and, 111–12
  suburban life and, 45
Coolidge, Calvin, 27, 55
Cosmopolitan (magazine)
  on Chagall (1948), 156–57
  serialization of Hobson's *Gentleman's Agreement*, 95
Coughlin, Father Charles, 48–49, 123–24
country clubs, restricted, 46–47, 52–53, 134–35
Courier-Journal (Louisville) on acceptance of Nazi persecution of Jews, 56
Cowan, Paul, 8
Crossfire (film), 52

Dandridge, Dorothy, 174
Davis, Burke, 48
Davis, Lambert, 112
Davis, Rebecca, 15
Day, Dorothy, 139
Decter, Midge, 125
definition of Jew, 90–91
definition of Judaism, 7, 15, 30–31, 45–46
Derounian, Arthur, 53–54
A Design for General Education for Members of the Armed Forces (American Council on Education Studies), 33
Deutscher, Isaac,
Diamant, Anita, 115
Diamond, Etan, 162–63
The Diary of Anne Frank (play and film), 14–15
Dickens, Charles, 69–70
Dobkowski, Michael, 28
Dolgin, Simon, 162–63
Dollinger, Marc, 213
Donin, Rabbi Hayim, 24
SS *Dorchester* sinking (1942), 31–32, 138
Driscoll, Beth, 14
Du Bois, W. E. B., 115–16

Early, Stephen, 49
Earth and High Heaven (Graham), 59–60, 71, 76, 86
  categorization of Jewishness, 87
  critical reception of, 93
  as exemplar in anti-antisemitism literature, 212
  as exemplar of anti-antisemitism literature, 48
  Hobson's reaction to, 68
  separation of "good Jews" from undesirable ones, 97–98
Eastern Europe. *See also* Old World associations
  Jewish stories of 1970s looking to 198, 199
  nineteenth-century Jews distancing from, 7
  Orthodox Jews from, as authentic form of Judaism, 150–51
  post–Holocaust embrace of, 7
  Wouk's grandfather exemplifying Jewish life in, 182–83
Ebony, 102–3
Ed Sullivan Show, 5–6, 14–15
Eichenberg, Fritz, 139
Eisenhower, Dwight, 11, 153
Eisenstaedt, Alfred, 151, 160–61
Eisenstein, Ira, 111–12
"Eli, the Fanatic" (Roth), 151, 192–93
Eliot, Charles, 9
Elisha ben Abuyah, 108
empathy, 76
"Escaping Judaism" (Wolfson), 43, 44, 77, 99, 118
ethnicity
  Jewishness as ethnic identity, 7, 17, 200, 211
  as part of Americanness by end of twentieth century, 199–200
  religious freedom and, 32
  Yiddish in America's newly awakened value of ethnicity, 199
eugenics, 27, 33–34, 37–38
European Jews. *See also* Eastern Europe
  Jewish emancipation, 101–2
  mid-twentieth century interest in lives of, 154–55
"Everybody's Favorite Protest Novel" (Baldwin), 82

exclusion and marginalization. *See also* "others"
American Jewish experience of, 5, 31–32, 34, 53–54
impossible standard of acceptability for Jews, 35–36, 38–39, 99, 101–2, 134–35
Jewishness as illness and burden, 44 (*see also* Wolfson, Harry)
Jewish sensitivity to other forms of, 75–76
Jews excluding other Jews of certain ancestry, 97–98
of race from Judeo-Christianity, 11
restrictive housing covenants, college admission quotas, and hiring discrimination, 46–47, 52–53, 62, 101–2, 134–35
of women in Judaism, 8, 18–19
existentialism, 145–46
Exodus (Uris), 23, 151–52

"F. Scott Fitzgerald and Literary Anti-Semitism: A Footnote on the mind of the 20's" (Hindus), 29–30
Fanny, Herself (Ferber), 41–42, 60, 63
Farber, Marjorie, 64–65
Far from the Tree: Parents, Children, and the Search for Identity (Solomon), 46
Farrell, James, 200
Fast, Howard, 54
Faulkner, William, 29
Felski, Rita, 145
femininity
ascribed to Jews, 14
ascribed to middlebrow, 14, 70–71
Eleanor Roosevelt and, 19
Ferber, Edna, 21, 41–42, 54–55, 60, 214
Fessenden, Tracy,
Fiddler on the Roof (musical), 148–49, 199
Finkelstein, Rabbi Louis, 111, 130–31
Fink family in *Life* magazine (1955), 161–63, 164, 165, 168, 169, 170, 171, 172
First Papers (Hobson), 199–200
"First Principles for American Jews" (Steinberg), 119
Fitzgerald, F. Scott, 28–30

Focus (Miller), 48, 59–60, 68–69, 75, 77, 81–82, 86, 212
Ford, Henry, 26, 214
Fortune, "Jews in America" article (1936), 157–58
Fox, Helen Morgenthau, 113
Frank, Anne, 154–55
Frankfurter, Felix, 20, 37–38
freedom of religion. *See* religious freedom
Friends of Democracy, Inc., 94

Gaston, K. Healan,
Geller, Victor, 159–60, 161–64
gender. *See also* femininity; masculinity; women authors; women readers
Esquire publishing only male authors, 77
Herberg using gender stereotypes, 184
Jewish mothers' image in mid-1950s, 164–66
Judaism's traditional exclusion of women, 8
Life's cover photo of Orthodox Jewish woman, effect of, 165, 173–74
Talmud classes admitting girls, 163–64
women's changing image and attitudes toward sex in mid-1950s, 164–66
Wouk's family portrait of gender roles, 179
gentile expectations of Jews, 2–3, 35–36, 38–39, 99
Gentleman's Agreement (film), 3, 52, 60, 65, 81
Gentleman's Agreement (Hobson's novel), 1–2, 60
Americanness more important than Jewishness, 96–97
assumption of author as non-Jew, 65
Baldwin's criticism of, 82
as bestseller, 60, 202–3
Black reaction to, 82, 102–3
Christian girlfriend of Phil coming to terms with her latent antisemitism, 1, 98–99
compared to Miller's *Focus*, 81–82
compared to Sinclair's *Wasteland*, 80
compared to Smith's *Strange Fruit*, 73
Cosmopolitan serializing, 95

critical reception of, 64–65, 92, 93, 96, 97–98, 99–100, 106
as exemplar of anti-antisemitism genre, 2–3, 18, 20–21, 48, 75, 212
homogenized version of American Jews, 106–7, 134–35
interior monologues and confessions creating learning for readers, 76, 80, 87–88
Jewish character (Dave Goldman) and antisemitism, 65–66, 68–69, 85–86, 96
Liebman on, 106
masculinity of Jewish characters, 85–86
minimal information provided about Judaism, 97–98, 106–7, 108–10
mixed message on race, 86–88
name change of character, 63
non-Jewish protagonist (Phil), 1, 65–67, 106–7
pitching idea to Simon, 59, 72, 73–74, 94
plot, 1, 60–62, 63, 65–67, 73–74, 98–99, 101
public reaction to, 65, 67, 81, 94–95
reclaiming moral indignation, 64
religion, casting Jews as members of, 12, 86, 87–88
religion-blind ideal espoused in, 74–75, 87–88, 97
Eleanor Roosevelt's review of, 20
scientists' view of religion and race, 87–89
term "antisemitism" made part of manuscript, 61
women readers of, 94–95
Ginzburg, Louis, 127–28
Glazer, Nathan, 12, 18, 24, 109, 115, 125, 161, 211
Glenn, Susan, 42
God in Search of Man (Heschel), 107–8
Goffman, Erving,
The Goldbergs, 14–15
Golden, Harry, 14–15, 23
Goldin, Grace, 113–14
Goldstein, Rabbi Albert S., 145–46
Goldstein, Eric, 31–32
Goodman, Benny, 15
Goodwill Movement, 33

Graeber, Isacque, 53–54
Graham, Gwethalyn, 48, 59–60, 68, 71, 87
See also *Earth and High Heaven*
Great Depression, 28
The Great Gatsby (Fitzgerald), 28–30
Greenberg, Clement, 125
Greenberg, Rabbi Irving, 115
Gurock, Jeffrey, 162–63
Guys and Dolls (film), 155

Halpern, Ben, 117–18
Halsey, Margaret, 59–60, 69–72, See also *Some of My Best Friends Are Soldiers*
examining her WASP upbringing, 199–200
Hobson and, 67, 69, 71
on Nazis as absolute evil, 70
objecting to *Time*'s use of "Jew" in racial context, 90–91, 139
Hamill, Pete, 134
Handlin, Oscar, 211
"Happy Holidays" greeting, 45
Haredi Jews. *See* Hassidic Jews
Harper's (magazine)
Bernstein's articles published in, 137
Arthur Cohen's "Why I Choose to Be a Jew" published in, 178, 189–90
Introduction to Judaism titles published in, 18
on marriage views of postwar Americans, 4
on publishers' using advance copies to generate word-of-mouth buzz, 113
tri-faith series (1959), 189
Harper's Bazaar (magazine) on middlebrow, 14
Hart, Moss, 60
Hartstein, Samuel, 159
Harvard University, 190–91
Hassidic Jews, 156, 166–67, 192–93
Hebrew Benevolent Congregation (Atlanta bombing 1958), 52–53
Hedstrom, Matthew, 10
Heine, Heinrich, 40
Heirs of Yesterday (Wolfe), 41–42
Hemingway, Ernest, 29–30

Herberg, Will, 74, 109, 185–86,
  review of Bernstein's "What the Jews Believe," 143–44, 145–46, 185
  review of Wouk's *This Is My God*, 183–85
Here All Along (Hurwitz), 197
Hersey, John, 130, 154–55
Hertzberg, Arthur, 189–90
Heschel, Abraham Joshua, 107–8, 154–55
Heschel, Susannah, 200–1
highbrow
  in American Jewish culture, 14
  of anti-antisemitism genre, 75
  based on pseudoscience of phrenology, 13
  Arthur Cohen as, 177–78
  condescension for feminine middlebrow, 70–71
  criticism of Introduction to Judaism genre, 127, 145–46
  New York Jewish intelligentsia as, 125
Hindus, Milton, 29–30
hiring discrimination, 46–47, 52–53, 62, 134–35
Hobson, Laura Z., 60 See also *Gentleman's Agreement*
  anthropology's influence on, 10
  assimilation and secularism of, 64–65, 109
  autobiographical elements in writing of, 20–21, 58, 199–200
  background of, 62–65
  believing in America, 81–82
  on choice of religion by gentiles, 178–79
  in circle of anti-antisemitism authors, 48, 59–60
  essay on how Gentiles could end the Jewish problem, 57–58
  ethnicity as subject of later works, 199–200
  Halsey and, 67, 69, 71
  instructional writing about race and Jews, 92, 105
  John Harold Johnson and, 102–3
  Lindbergh's antisemitic speech, reaction to, 49, 57
  as middlebrow author, 14
  name change of, 63
  objecting to *Time*'s use of "Jew" in racial context, 88–89, 90–91, 139
  parents' view of United States as influence on, 62
  reclaiming moral indignation, 64
  religious pluralism and,
  science used to rebut Jewishness as racial category, 88–89
  Sinclair compared to, 77, 80
Hobson, Thayer, 58, 63, 64–65
Hodson, Geoffrey,
Hollinger, David, 154
Holocaust
  anti-antisemitism literature and, 16, 67–68
  effect on American acceptance of Judaism, 6, 7, 16, 105
  effect on American Jews' view of Eastern Europe, 7
  Hersey's *The Wall* as first American novel on, 154
  Jewish survivors as postwar reality, 16
  Life 1955 article referencing, 166–67
  survivor's experience after war, 173–74
  in Uris's *Exodus*, 151–52
Home of the Brave (film), 102
homosexuality and homophobia, 75–76, 77, 78
Hoover, J. Edgar, 132
The House of Mirth (Wharton), 28–29
The House That I Lived In (film), 73–74
housing covenants, restrictive, 52–53, 101–2, 134–35
Howe, Irving, 125, 155–56, 199
Hurwitz, Sarah, 197
Hutner, Gordon, 52

Ickes, Harold, 51
identity. *See* Jewishness; middle-class identity
Immigration Act (1965), 23–24
"In Defense of Robert Cohn" (Scott), 29–30
"In God We Trust" as national motto, 12
Inside, Outside (Wouk), 199–200
intermarriage, effect of, 201
Introduction to Judaism genre, 2–3, 109
  See also specific authors and titles

acceptance of Jews and Judaism as goal
of, 8–9, 17, 18, 22–23, 34, 127, 145
addressing American ignorance of
Judaism, 7–8, 138
all major Jewish sects participating
in, 107
audience increasing for, 196
choice of being a Jew and
(*see* choice to be a Jew)
as college and rabbinical school
texts, 18, 107–8, 190–91
community of readers forming
around, 10
compared to anti-antisemitism
novel, 19, 97
Cowan's memoir as, 8
criticism of, 127–28, 145
first published as essays in popular
magazines, 18
irony of, 121
in Jewish middlebrow moment, 13, 30–
31, 128, 145, 146, 178, 196
later-in-life embrace of Judaism in, 8
legacy of, 200
by men writers, 18, 19, 21, 184
overlap with anti-antisemitism
literature, 129
purpose of, 106–7, 110–11, 127, 130–
31, 197
readers' affirmation of, 22–23
representative titles and types, 107, 176
Sinclair's *Wasteland* foreshadowing,
83–84
tercentennial celebration of American
Jewish settlement (1954) as impetus
for, 107–8
women as readers of, 113, 184
women rarely as authors of, 21
isolationism, 48–49
Israel
American perception of, 23–24
establishment of (1948), 30
as home of authentic versions of
Judaism, 150–51, 200–1
Life (1949) on first anniversary of
founding, 152–53
Life (1955) on religious and Israeli
Jews, 149–52, 153, 157–58, 160–61

masculinity of Jewish men in, 152–53
"New Jew" of, 29, 150–51
Steinberg on, 124
Uris' *Exodus* on founding of, 151–52
It Can't Happen Here (Lewis), 56

Jacobson, Israel G., 142
Jacobson, Matthew F., 86
Jay, Gregory, 83
Jesus
in Bernstein's "What the Jews
Believe," 139–40
in Steinberg's *Basic Judaism*, 122–23
Jet, 102–3
"The Jew Faces Anti-Semitism"
(Steinberg), 34–35
Jewish Daily Forward, 62
Jewish emancipation, 101–2
Jewish Frontier
review of Bernstein's "What the
Jews Believe," 143–44
(*see also* Herberg, Will)
review of Hobson's *Gentleman's
Agreement*, 97–98, 99–100
Jewish Institute of Religion, 136
Jewish Labor Committee, 51
Jewishness
American Jews jettisoning
(*see* assimilation)
anti-antisemitism/Introduction to
Judaism genres providing way to
understand identity of, 12, 118–19
anti-antisemitism literature providing
way to understand identity of,
15, 16, 74
authenticity from *Fiddler on the Roof*
and Old Country roots, 199, 200–1
of celebrities, 15, 179, 181–82, 212
choice of (*see* choice to be a Jew)
as disability and burden, 39, 47, 73–74,
(*see also* Wolfson, Harry)
as economic identity, 14, 27, 28,
29, 37–38
English as American language of, 183
as ethnic identity, 17, 200
explaining to non-Jews, 17
identity of Jew, social connotation of,
90–91

Jewishness (*cont.*)
  lack of Jews' control over definition of, 92–93
  Nazis' racism determining who is Jewish, 92–93
  as positive identity, 16, 45–46
  pre-WWII American views on, 16
  as religion, 6, 7, 13, 17, 21–22, 31–32, 45–46, 109 (*see also* religion, Jews as members of)
  Steinberg on, 116, 124, 126–27
  stereotypes of (*see* stereotypes of Jews)
  trying to overcome through correcting behavior, 35–36, 38–39, 99, 134–35
Jewish problem
  Hobson's essay on how Gentiles could end, 57–58
  Steinberg acknowledging Jews as "strange," 116
"The Jewish Question," 45–46
Jewish Theological Seminary, 111–18, 190–91, 194–95
The Jews (Finkelstein), 111
Jews in a Gentile World (Graeber and Britt), 53–54
Jim Crow, 102–3, *See also* racism; segregation
Johnson, Albert, 27
Johnson, John Harold, 102–3
Johnson-Reed immigration law (1924), 27
Judaism. *See also* religion, Jews as members of; *specific sects*
  as Abrahamic religion, 158–59
  choice of (*see* choice to be a Jew)
  conversions to, 148–49, 194, 196, 197, 212
  diverse races as members of, 196
  diversity of practice in, 139 (*see also specific sects*)
  ignorance of American public about, 6, 7–8, 13, 111, 115–16, 138, 193–94, 199
  Israel and Europe as home of authentic versions of, 200–1
  liberalism of, 124–25
  as living faith, 111
  middlebrow teaching Americans how to feel about (*see* middlebrow)
  as modern faith, 116
  as monotheism, 158, 159
  popularity of, 130
  post-Judaism,
  pride in, 16, 30, 41–42, 51, 84, 106, 140
  theology and, 194–95
  transitioning into American religion (*see* religion, Jews as members of; tri-faith of America)
  writers explaining as religion, 6, 17, 111 (see also *Basic Judaism*; Introduction to Judaism genre; "What the Jews Believe")
Judaism (quarterly), 177
Judaism as a Civilization (Kaplan), 41–42
Judeo-Christianity. *See also* tri-faith of America
  American change from Christian to Judeo-Christian nation, 12, 16
  as antidote to totalitarian regimes, 11
  equality as tenet of, 11
  myth associated with, 23–24, 193–94, 195–96
  readerly interest in Jews as part of, 10, 172
Jung, Rabbi Leo, 115

Kadushin, Charles, 184
Kallen, Horace, 41–42, 43
Kaplan, Amy, 151–52
Kaplan, Rabbi Mordecai, as influence on Steinberg, 108–9, 111–18, 120
kashrut, Jewish laws of, 24–25, 44, 45, 147–48
Katkov, Norman, 48
Kaufman, Bel, 198, 200
Kaufmann, Walter, 189
Kaye, Danny, 130
Kazin, Alfred, 54, 125, 154, 155–56, 200
Kendi, Ibram X., 37–38
Kennedy, John F., 56
Kertzer, Morris, 30–31
King, Charles, 31
Klein, Christina, 13
Know Nothings party, 37–38
Kohn, Jacob, 118
kosher practices, 167, 170
Kotler, Rabbi Aharon, 147–48

Kristallnacht, 222
Kristol, Irving, 121–22, 125–27, 128, 144
Ku Klux Klan, 26, 37–38
Kushner, Rabbi Harold, 197

Ladies Home Journal referring to Judaism as "racial religion" (1958), 196
Lambert, Josh, 9, 212
Lawrence, Josephine, 48
Lazarus, Emma, 54–56
League of Nations, 26
Lee, Harper, 81
Leon, Masha, 65
Leonard, Thomas, 27, 37
Levinson, Julian, 155–56, 177–78
Levitt, Laura,
Lewis, Sinclair, 56, 58, 63
Lewisohn, Ludwig, 38
liberalism
　anti-antisemitism and, 83, 104
　"good Jews" resembling liberal Protestants, 97–98, 101–2
　ignorance of, 6
　of Judaism, 124–25
　race novels and, 83
Liebman, Rabbi Joshua Loth. See also *Peace of Mind*
　background of, 108, 110
　as middlebrow author, 14
　radio review of Hobson's *Gentleman's Agreement*, 2, 3, 106
　Steinberg on, 110
Life (magazine)
　capitalizing on the revival of religion in America, 135–36
　on Christianity (1949), 138
　on Hobson's *First Papers* (1964), 199–200
　on Hobson's *Gentleman's Agreement* (1947), 100
　influence of, 24, 129
　Introduction to Judaism titles published in, 18, 129
　on Judaism (see *Life* (magazine) 1955 article on Judaism; "What the Jews Believe")
　as middlebrow magazine, 128, 134, 166, 174
　photography as centerpiece of, 134
　on world religions, 10, 135, 158
Life (magazine) 1955 article on Judaism, 149–50, 151, 157–58, 202–3,
　as anti-antisemitism, 160
　exoticization of Judaism as criticism of, 166–70
　Holocaust and, 166–67, 173–74
　Israeli Jews and, 149–52, 153, 157–58, 160–61
　Jewish reaction to, 24–25, 166–72
　Orthodox Jewish family (the Finks) profile, 147–48, 159–63, 164
　photos used with article, 160–61, 163–64, 165, 166, 168, 169, 170, 171, 172, 173
　public reaction to, 24
　Reform Judaism's reaction to, 170–72, 175
　Stuart as author, 160–61, 163–64
limits of anti-antisemitism literature, 81–105,
　"acceptance, within reason," 95
　American exceptionalism and, 81–82
　"average American," 90
　connecting Jews and Blacks, 102
　false sense of reassurance of genre, 82–83
　gentleman's agreement of Jewish religion, 101
　Jewishness as race and scientific view of race, 87
　teaching purpose affecting critical assessment of genre, 93
　white racial order, 83
Lindbergh, Charles, 48–51, 56, 57, 58, 123–24
Literary Guild, 9
Litvak, Joseph,
Look (magazine)
　"The Position of the Jew in America Today" (1955), 134–35
　"The Vanishing American" (1964), 201
　on world religions, 10
Lost Boundaries (film), 102
lowbrow, 13, 14
Lowell, Robert, 23

Lubavitcher Rebbe. *See* Schneerson, Rabbi Menachem Mendel
Luce, Henry, 58, 62, 103, 133–34, 135–36, 149–50, 158–59

Magid, Shaul,
Maimonides school (Brookline, Massachusetts), 163–64
The Making of the Modern Jew (Steinberg), 113, 115
Malamud, Bernard, 202
Man Is Not Alone (Heschel), 107–8
marginalization. *See* exclusion and marginalization; "others"
Marjorie Morningstar (Wouk), 19, 23, 186
Marshall, Louis, 214
Marshall, Thurgood, 103–4
Mart, Michelle,
masculinity
   fragility of Jewish masculinity, 85–86
   Introduction to Judaism genre and, 19
   of Israeli men, 152–53
   in Wouk's *Marjorie Morningstar*, 19
A Mask of Privilege: Anti-Semitism in America (McWilliams), 54
McAlister, Melani, 22–23
McCarthyism, 3–4
McMahon, Francis, 50
McWilliams, Carey, 54
melting pot
   Coolidge ending with 1924 immigration restrictions, 200
   as effort to wipe out past of others, 200
   Hobson as assimilated Jew in generation of, 92
   Israel as, 152
Menorah Journal, Wolfson article on Jewish loneliness and despair in America, 39–40
Meyer, Michael, 32–33
middlebrow, 13
   accomplishments of, 15–16, 46–47, 105, 185–86, 199–200, 202–3
   in American Jewish culture, 14, 30–31
   anti-antisemitism literature and, 13, 196
   average Americans' vocabulary and, 90–91
   based on pseudoscience of phrenology, 13
   Arthur Cohen's "Why I Choose to Be a Jew" categorized as, 178
   contemporary assessment of, 202
   criticism of, 15, 144, 185
   distinguished from popular culture, 15–16
   of earlier eras, 21
   fading out in 1960s, 197
   femininity ascribed to, 14, 70–71
   interest in Jewish difference from Christianity, 148–49
   Introduction to Judaism genre and, 13, 30–31, 128, 145, 146, 178, 196
   Life (magazine) as part of culture of, 134, 166, 174
   Life's 1955 issue of interesting and colorful parts of Judaism and, 149–50, 153, 154–55, 167, 169–70, 175, 185–86
   limits of, 46–47
   middle-classness and, 14, 98–99, 134, 202–3
   Orthodox Judaism, treatment of, 147–48, 166, 179–80, 182
   power of midcentury Jewish middlebrow culture, 22, 109, 127, 128, 157, 185–86, 202–3
   social protest literature, tradition of, 81
   teaching Americans how to feel about Judaism and antisemitism, 15, 17, 24, 183, 196, 213 (*see also* anti-antisemitism literature)
   television coverage of Judaism and, 170–71
   women's changing image and, 164
   women's role as authors, 59–60
middle-class identity
   of American Jews, 21, 23–24, 101–2, 134–35, 145
   book clubs and, 9
   Life profile of Orthodox Jewish family in 1955 to show, 160
   middlebrow and, 14, 98–99, 134, 202–3
"Midwife to a Novel" (Edith Alpert Steinberg), 18–19, 114
Miller, Arthur, 48, 59–60, 64–65, 68–69, 75, 81–82, See also *Focus*
Miller, Nolan, 77

Mishnah, 143–44
Mizrachi Judaism, 173
Modernism, 13
Monroe, Marilyn, 164–66, 212
Morgenthau, Henry, 49
Morgenthau, Henry, III, 42–43
musical popularity of Jewish songs, 130, 149
"My Day" (Eleanor Roosevelt's column), 20
Myrdal, Gunnar, 104–5
The Myth of the Judeo-Christian Tradition (Cohen), 23–24, 194

NAACP, 103–4
name changes
　by Jews, 63, 77
　by women authors, 77
The Nation
　Bernstein's articles in, 137
　on Jewish strategy of self-improvement, 35
National Conference of Christians and Jews, 33
nationalism and patriotism, 26
　religiousness equated with, 3–4, 7–8, 10–11, 148–49
national motto of "In God We Trust," 12
A Nation of Immigrants (Kennedy), 56
Native Son (Wright), 72, 77, 78–79, 82
Nazis. *See also* Holocaust
　American bigotry compared to, 81, 82–83, 103–4
　anti-antisemitism as reaction to, 52, 57
　antisemitism equated with, 7, 33–34, 50–51, 55, 56, 57, 82–83
　Halsey seeing as absolute evil, 70
　Lindbergh as Nazi-sympathizer, 48–51
　as measure of absolute evil in postwar America, 103–4
　racial persecution of Jews by, 7, 11, 30, 33–34, 36–37, 73–74
Negro Digest, 102–3
neo-Orthodoxy, 126–27, 130–31, 185
New Deal, 28
"New Jew" of Zionism, 29, 150–51
The New Republic, Bernstein's articles in, 137

The New Yorker
　on Danny Kaye (1950), 130
　on Steinberg's *Basic Judaism* (1947), 122
New York Review of Books, New York Jewish intelligentsia as contributors, 125
New York Times
　on affordable books, 9–10
　on Chagall, 156
　comparing Southern racism to Nazism, 103–4
　on Cowan's memoir, 8
　on end of American melting pot, 28
　on eugenics, 33
　on Hobson's *Gentleman's Agreement*, 93
　on Lindbergh's antisemitism, 50
　on Miller's *Focus*, 81–82
　Niebuhr's review of Herberg's *Protestant-Catholic-Jew* in, 145–46
　on Orthodox Judaism's resurgence (1957), 147–48
　on Sinclair's *Wasteland* winning Harper Prize Novel contest, 76–77
　on Torah reading to commemorate ancient custom (1952), 150
Niebuhr, Reinhold, 107–8, 126–27, 130–31, 143, 145–46, 185
No Laughing Matter: The Autobiography of a WASP (Halsey), 199–200
non-Jews. *See also* gentile expectations of Jews
　limited contact with Jews in early twentieth century, 115–16
　writing about Jews, 13, 99, 154–55, 160–61
November Pogrom (1938), 55
Nyberg, Sidney, 214

Old Testament, 17, 111
Old World associations
　Chagall and, 156–57
　Jewish stories of 1970s looking to, 198, 199
　Orthodox Judaism considered as "old-time" religion, 150–51, 167
　Wouk's grandfather clinging to Eastern European Jewishness, 182–83
Olson, Lynne, 51–52

On Jewish Law and Lore (Ginzburg), 127–28
An Orphan in History: One Man's Triumphant Search for His Jewish Roots (Cowan), 8
Orsi, Robert,
Orthodox Judaism, 132–33,
  considered as "old-time" religion, 150–51, 167
  conversions to, 148–49
  dynamic between orthodox and assimilated Jews, 151, 166–67, 192–94
  Fink family as organizers of Orthodox congregations, 161, 162
  Life 1955 profile of Orthodox Jewish family (the Finks), 147–48, 159–63, 164, 165, 168, 169, 170, 171, 172
  Luce's view of, 149–50, 166
  middlebrow treatment of, 147–48, 166, 179–80, 182
  resurgence in late 1950s and 1960s, 147–48, 162–63
  Wouk's practice of, 179–80
Orthodoxy Awakens (Geller), 159–60
"others." *See also* exclusion and marginalization
  Jews' changing in 1950s from, 45–46, 202–3
  Jews' portrayal as, 21, 26, 37, 157–58, 174–75
  Steinberg understanding of his "alien other" status, 115–16
  Wouk's grandfather's foreignness, 182–83
Ozick, Cynthia, 202

Paley, Babe (Barbara Cushing Mortimer), 5
Paley, Grace, 202
Paley, William, 5
paperbacks, 9–10
Parents' magazine on Jewish responsibility for antisemitism (1944), 38–39
Park Avenue Synagogue, 108, 113, 119–20
A Partisan Guide to the Jewish Problem (Steinberg), 116

Paul (apostle), 124–25
Peace of Mind (Liebman)
  Herberg on, 184–85
  religion, casting Jews as members of, 12
  sales of, 110
  Steinberg on, 122
  in vanguard of Introduction to Judaism genre, 2–3, 197
Peale, Norman Vincent, 130–31, 184–85
Pearl Harbor, 50
Peck, Gregory, 3, 65, 201
A Peculiar Treasure (Ferber), 54–55
Petuchowski, Rabbi Jacob, 148–49
Phillips, John, 152–53
Pinky (film), 102
Pinson, Koppel, 57
Pledge of Allegiance, 12
pluralism, 23–24
Pocket Books, 9–10
Poling, Daniel, 138
Pontius Pilate, 140
popular culture
  antisemitism and, 28, 36, 53–54, 60–61
  changing attitudes during 1940s, 2
  importance of, 22–23
  Jewish songs and, 130, 149
  of Jews, 23, 214
  middlebrow distinguished from, 15–16
  non-Jews creating productions about Jews, 149
  religious revival of mid-century (*see* religiosity)
The Power of Positive Thinking (Peale), 130–31, 184–85
Prescott, Orville, 20–21, 70–71
Protestant-Catholic-Jew (Herberg), 74–75, 145–46
Protestantism. *See also* neo-Orthodoxy
  anti-Catholicism of, 10–11, 18
  compared to Judaism, 74
  marketing of middlebrow and, 14
  pressure for Jews to fit into mold of, 6–7, 97–98, 101–2
  Steinberg using as foil for Judaism, 121–22, 123–25
  as template for religion, 18

quota system. *See* hiring discrimination; restrictive housing covenants; university quotas

The Rabbi on 47th Street (Birstein), 8
race, Jews as members of, 2–3, 30
　in American literature, 29
　Chagall used as example, 156
　eugenics and, 27, 33–34
　exclusion based on, 5, 31–32, 53–54
　in Graham's *Earth and High Heaven*, 87
　in *Life*'s coverage of Israel at "age of one," 152–53
　meaning of race, 31
　Nazi persecution and, 7, 11, 30, 33–34, 36–37, 73–74
　persistence of notion of, 86–87, 90, 92–93
　psycho-social dynamic of, 34
　rejection of notion of, 13, 30–31, 196
　resistance to altering racial discourse, 90
　science used to rebut, 87–90
　in Sinclair's *Wasteland*, 87–88
　transitioning to members of religion, 7, 13, 21–22, 23, 31–32, 33, 83–84, 87–88, 101–2, 109, 128
　white race, Jews as members of (*see* whiteness of Jews)
"The Races of Mankind" (Benedict and Weltfish), 88–89
racism
　American difficulty in confronting, 105
　antiracism literature as inspiration for anti-antisemitism literature, 73
　antisemitism's linkage to, 2, 11, 31, 36–38, 73, 76, 80, 102
　blood donations of Jewish or Black blood, 84–85
　in Cold War era, 10–11, 104
　Coolidge and, 55
　Jews abandoning cities and, 201
　of Judeo-Christianity, 11
　liberal race novels intended to counter, 83
　Nazis' racial persecution (*see* Nazis)
　professional sports, desegregation of, 5–6
　race riots of World I era, 26
　Eleanor Roosevelt's anti-racism, 20
　Smith's *Strange Fruit* about, 72
　white racial order, 83
　whites, Jews as (*see* whiteness of Jews)
radicalism, 23–24, 26–27, 28, 37–38, 132
　Hobson's parents and, 62
radio
　Jewish middlebrow culture and, 14–15
　Liebman's review of Hobson's *Gentleman's Agreement* on, 2, 3, 106
Rahv, Philip, 125
Ramaz school (NYC),
Reconstructionist (magazine), 111–12
Reconstructionist Judaism, 42, 111–18
Redbook
　on easy-vs.-difficult religion, 185
　Hoover's "God or Chaos" essay, 132
　Jewish high holidays feature, 130
Red Ribbon on a White Horse (Yezierska), 20–21
Red Scare (1919–1920), 26
Reform Judaism
　Bernstein's "What the Jews Believe" and, 147, 149–50
　distancing from Eastern European roots, 7
　Life 1955 issue on Orthodox Jews and, 170–72, 175
　Living Judaism and,
　move toward center and reestablishment of traditions, 153
religion, Jews as members of, 2–3,
　in anti-antisemitism literature, 12, 86, 87–88, 101
　compared to Protestant sense of religion, 74–75
　middlebrow audience understanding (*see* middlebrow)
　preference for religion as classification, 32
　as taken-for-granted fact in 1970s America, 198–99
　transitioning from members of race to, 7, 13, 21–22, 23, 31–32, 33, 83–84, 87–88, 101–2, 109, 128
　twentieth-century efforts to establish, 6, 31–32
　writers explaining (*see* Introduction to Judaism genre)

religion-blind ideal, 73–74
religiosity
  broader definition of religion, 84
  choice of religion, 32–33
    (*see also* choice to be a Jew)
  equated with nationalism and
    patriotism, 10–11, 148–49
  "good religion," 121–22
  revival of religion in mid-twentieth
    century America, 12, 129–30,
    135–36, 153, 164–66
religious freedom
  ethnicity and, 32
  FDR on, 31–32
  immigrants seeking, 27
restrictive housing covenants, 52–53,
  101–2, 134–35
Ribalow, Harold, 107–8
Rice, Elinor, 92–93
righteous indignation, 64, 119
Robinson, Jackie, 5–6
Roosevelt, Eleanor, 19–20, 154–55
Roosevelt, Franklin D., 16, 28, 33, 48–49
Roosevelt, Sara Delano, 20
roots of anti-antisemitism fiction, 48–58,
  antisemitism as commonplace in
    America of 1920s and 1930s, 28, 36,
    53, 60–61
  antisemitism as un-American in WWII,
    50, 51, 56, 57
  antisemitism equated with Nazis, 7,
    50–51, 55, 56, 57, 82–83
  Hobson's essay on how Gentiles could
    end the Jewish problem, 57–58
  Lindbergh's antisemitic speech, reaction
    to, 48–51, 56, 57, 58
  mainstream media and popular culture
    discussing antisemitism, 53–54
Rosenblum, Rabbi William, 170–72
Rosenfeld, Isaac, 54
Rosh Yeshiva. *See* Soloveitchik,
  Rabbi Joseph
Roth, Philip, 151, 192–93, 202
Rothberg, Abraham, 65
Rukeyser, Muriel, 54

The Sabbath (Heschel), 107–8
Sarna, Jonathan, 214

Sartre, Jean-Paul, 54, 61
Saturday Evening Post
  on immigration as economic
    movement, 27
  as middlebrow magazine, 134
Saturday Review
  on futility of anti-antisemitism
    literature, 93
  on Graham's *Earth and High Heaven*, 93
  on Hobson's *Gentleman's Agreement*,
    106
  on Introduction to Judaism genre,
    127–28
  on tercentennial celebration of
    American Jewish settlement
    (1954), 107–8
Schneerson, Rabbi Menachem Mendel,
  147–48
Schoen, Isidore, 77–78
Schopenhauer, Arthur, 157–58
Scott, Arthur, 29–30
secularism, 30–31, 40, 47, 64–65, 86, 87–
  89, 96, 109, 116–17, 131–32
segregation, 84–85, 103–5. *See also* civil
  rights movement
"Sense and Nonsense about Race"
  (Alpenfels), 89
sentimentalists and sentimental fiction,
  19, 27, 60–61, 94, 145–46, 180–81
Servicemen's Readjustment Act
  (1944), 134
Seventeen magazine
  on Chagall (1946), 156–57
  on characterization of Jews as members
    of race or of religion (1947), 86–87
Shakespeare, William, 29–30
Shandler, Jeffrey, 155
Silberman, Charles, 40
Silver, Matthew, 151–52
Silver, Rabbi Samuel, 166–67
Silverman, Al, 9
Silvers, Robert, 189–90
Simon, Richard, 59, 68, 102
  on Hobson's *Gentleman's Agreement*,
    72, 73–74
  on Smith's *Strange Fruit*, 72–73
Sinatra, Frank, 73–74, 155, 201
Sinclair, Jo, 75–80. See also *Wasteland*

compared to Hobson, 77, 80
  as middlebrow author, 14
  name change of, 77
sinfulness, 121, 130–31, 140–41
Sklare, Marshall, 23, 109
Smith, Betty, 5
Smith, Elinor Goulding, 11
Smith, Gerald L. K., 4–5
Smith, Judith, 11
Smith, Lillian, 72
social problem films, 102
social protest literature, 19, 21, 81
Solomon, Alisa, 199
Solomon, Andrew, 46
Solomon, Deborah, 134
Solotaroff, Ted, 23
Soloveitchik, Rabbi Joseph, 163–64
Some of My Best Friends Are Soldiers (Halsey)
  confessional act offering learning experience to reader, 76
  critical reception of, 69, 71
  as exemplar of anti-antisemitism literature, 48
  Hobson's knowledge of, 59, 69
  plot, 71–72
The Sound and the Fury (Faulkner), 29
Soviet Union. *See* Cold War
"special pleading" of Jewish authors, 65, 77
SS *St. Louis* denied entry in U.S. and Cuba, 55
Statue of Liberty inscription (Lazarus), 55–56
Steinberg, Edith Alpert, 18–19, 114
Steinberg, Rabbi Milton, 34–35, 36, 38, 42, 46, 107, 108–23. *See also* *Basic Judaism*; *The Making of the Modern Jew*
  Atlantic Monthly essays by, 111–12, 115
  background of, 108–9, 116–20
  Bernstein as cousin of, 107, 120, 136–37
  choice of being a Jew and, 116, 187–88
  Arthur Cohen's relationship with, 10, 108, 118, 177, 186
  contemporary Jewish concerns of, 108–9, 111–19
  guidance about how to live a Jewish life from, 119–20, 176

  Kaplan's influence on, 108–9, 111–18, 120
  as middlebrow author, 14, 125
  modeling American Jewishness, 126–27, 177
  writing and publishing as areas of interest to, 113–14, 137
stereotypes of Jews
  in American literature, 28
  gender and, 184
  in Great Depression, 28
  international banker image, 26–27
  Jewish appearance and behavior, 31, 35, 38–39, 86, 89, 98–99, 134–35
  in *Life* magazine articles, 171–72
  love of learning, 140
  in mid-1940s, 36
  name-calling and, 71–72, 104–5
  of Orthodox Judaism, 162
  in World War I era, 26–27
Stern College (women's school), 147–48
stigmatization. *See* alienation; exclusion and marginalization; "others"; stereotypes of Jews
Stowe, Harriet Beecher, 19, 81
Strange Fruit (Smith), 72
  critical reception of, 72
  as liberal race novel, 83
  popularity of, 72
  Simon holding out as model for Hobson, 72
Straus, Oscar, 37–38
Stuart, Jozefa, author of *Life* 1955 article on religious Jews, 160–61, 163–64
  Silver's critical reception of, 166–67
Sullivan, Ed, 5–6
The Sun Also Rises (Hemingway), 29–30
Svonkin, Stuart, 213

Talmud, 127–28, 141, 163–64, 190–91, 242n.123
Taylor, Charles, 22–23
television
  changing American views on "others," 22
  introduced in 1940s, 3
  Jewish middlebrow culture and, 14–15
Teller, Judd, 79

theology and Judaism, 194-95
theology of crisis (Niebuhr), 126-27
third-faith status of Judaism. *See* tri-faith of America
This Is My God (Wouk), 182-83,
   audience of, 185-86
   critical reception of, 183-85
   dedicated to Wouk's grandfather, 182-83
   on dynamic between orthodox and assimilated Jews, 192-93
   as Introduction to Judaism showing religion's gendered side, 19
   Jewish pride noted in, 41-42
   as model for how and why individual may choose Judaism, 178-79
   Orthodox Judaism of Wouk described, 179-80
   popularity of, 107, 178
   reason to write, 196-97
   successful intermingling of Judaism and American culture, 179
   threat of Jewish oblivion in suburban life, 201
Thompson, Dorothy, 19, 58
Thompson, Edward, 158
Tiberius (Roman emperor), 140
Time (magazine)
   on Bernstein's "What the Jews Believe," 144
   influence of, 24
   Jew used in racial context by, 90-91
   on mid-1950s fears of Americans, 4
   on Niebuhr's neo-Orthodoxy, 130-31
   Petuchowski explaining Orthodox Judaism in, 148-49
   on postwar rich and powerful in US, 4
   on Eleanor Roosevelt, 20
   on television when introduced in 1940s, 3
   on Wouk (1955), 181-82
Time Inc. *See also Life; Time*
   middlebrow role of publications of, 128, 129
To Be a Jew: A Guide to Jewish Observance in Contemporary Life (Donin), 25
To Kill a Mockingbird (Lee), 81, 83

"Tolerance Trios," 33
To Pray as a Jew: A Guide to the Prayer Book and the Synagogue Service (Donin), 25
Torah, 139-40, 150, 158-59, 163, 170-71
Trachtenberg, Joshua, 36
Tradition (Orthodox Jewish journal), 132-33, 147-48
A Tree Grows in Brooklyn (Smith), 5
Trespassers (Hobson), 64-65, 72
tri-faith of America (Protestant-Catholic-Jewish), 2-3, 23-24, 31-32, 74, 107, 109, 197
   Harper's (magazine) series on (1959), 189
   people of color outside of, 11
Trilling, Diana, 96, 97, 106-7, 125
Trilling, Lionel, 54, 117, 125
Trodd, Zoe, 81-82
Truman, Harry, 132
Tumin, Melvin, 89-90

un-American policies
   antisemitism as, 13, 15, 21-22, 50, 51, 56, 57
   FDR's New Deal as, 28
Uncle Tom's Cabin (Stowe), 19, 81
   Baldwin's criticism of, 82
   as liberal race novel, 83
Under Cover: My Four Years in the Nazi Underworld of America (Derounian), 53-54, 72
Union of American Hebrew Congregations, 166
Union of Orthodox Jewish Congregations of America, 147-48
University of Chicago Press, 107
university quotas, 31-32, 34-35, 42-43, 52-54, 134-35
Uris, Leon, 23, 151-52

value of religion, 10
The Victim (Bellow), 48, 59-60, 68-69, 75, 86, 212
Vidler, Alec, 131-32
voluntary nature of Judaism. *See* choice to be a Jew

A Walker in the City (Kazin), 154
The Wall (Hersey), 130, 154–55
Ward, Mary Jo, 48
war novels, 221
Wasteland (Sinclair), 75–80,
   compared to Hobson's *Gentleman's Agreement*, 80
   confessional act offering learning experience to reader, 76
   critical reception of, 59, 75, 76–77, 78–79
   as exemplar of anti-antisemitism literature, 48, 212
   isolation imposed by racism to segregate people into "wastelands," 85–86
   Jewish lesbian character (Debby), 75–76, 78, 85–86
   Jewish reaction to, 77–78
   linkage of antisemitism and homophobia, 75–76, 78
   masculinity of Jewish characters, 85–86
   mixed message on Jews and race, 84–85, 86–87
   non-Jewish psychiatrist's respectful talk about Passover, 83–84
   readers' reaction to, 78, 79–80, 100–1
   transitioning from Jews as race to Jews as religion, 83–84, 87–88
Weavers (musical group), 130, 149
Weidman, Jerome, 64–65
Weigel, Gustave, 195
Weis-Rosmarin, Trude, 213
Weltfish, Gene, 10, 88–89
Wenger, Tisa, 32
Wharton, Edith, 28–29
What Is A Jew? (Kertzer), 30–31
"What the Jews Believe" (Philip Bernstein), 107, 129, 134, 136
   addressing questions from Christian clergy, 138–39
   broadening genre of Introduction to Judaism, 149
   capitalizing on anti-Catholic prejudice, 139
   critical reception of, 143–44, 153, 185
   direct communication with God, 139–40
   directions from *Life* on writing, 137–38, 189–90
   diversity of practice in Judaism, 139
   illustrated by Eichenberg, 139
   on Jesus and crucifixion, 139–40
   Jewish reaction to, 141–43, 145–46
   non-Jewish reaction to, 143, 149–50
   parallels between Christianity and Judaism, 140–41
   reasonableness of Judaism, 141
   religious Jews' rituals and practices, 140
   sinfulness, 140–41
   subsequent shift away from interest in Reform Judaism after, 153
When Bad Things Happen to Good People (Kushner), 197
whiteness of Jews, 5, 11, 13
   acceptance of Jews linked to, 31–32, 83
Whitfield, Stephen, 130
"Why I Choose to Be a Jew" (Arthur Cohen), 177
   on his family background, 193–94
   as middlebrow, 178
   as model for how and why individual may choose Judaism, 178–79
   personal approach to writing, 189–90, 195–96
   reason to write, 196–97
   terming choice to be a conversion, 194
   theology of Judaism, 194–95
Wilkie, Wendell, 51
Wirth, Louis,
Wise, Rabbi Isaac Mayer, 7, 26–27
Wise, Rabbi Stephen S., 27, 33–34, 120, 136
With Malice Toward Some (Halsey), 69
Wolfe, Emma, 41–42, 54–55
Wolfson, Harry, 39–41, 42–44, 46, 73–74, 77, 92–93, 99–100, 115, 118, 120, 142–43, 177, 195–96
Woman's Day on Jewishness and race, 92–93
women authors
   of anti-antisemitism literature, 18, 19, 20–21, 59–80 (*see also specific authors*)
   importance to Hobson, 64–65
   rare as authors of Introduction to Judaism genre, 21

women readers
- of anti-antisemitism literature, 94–95, 184
- Herberg using gender stereotype of, 184
- influence of, 20
- of Introduction to Judaism genre, 113
- of Steinberg's works, 119

Woolf, Virginia, 14
Wootton, Philip, 157
World of Our Fathers: The Journey of the East European Jews to America and the Life They Found and Made (Howe), 199
The World of Sholom Aleichem (play), 148–49
The World of the Talmud (Adler), 127–28
World War I and its aftermath, 26–27
World War II. *See also* Holocaust
- anti-antisemitism as response to, 52
- blood donations of Jewish or Black blood, 84–85
- Jews cast as warmongers, 48–50
- Lindbergh speech for isolationism and opposed to war, 48–51, 56, 57, 58, 123–24
- religious freedom as trope in, 31–32

Wouk, Herman, 10, 41–42, 107. See also *This Is My God*
- autobiographical novel by, 199–200
- choice of being a Jew and, 178–79, 186–87
- grandfather exemplifying Eastern European Jewish life, 182–83
- as middlebrow author, 14
- as Orthodox Jew, 179–80, 181–82
- reading as central to return to religious life, 186
- reading Sholem Aleichem story in Yiddish, 198, 200

Wright, Richard, 77, 78–79, 82
  See also *Native Son*
writers' communities, 10, 18
  See also highbrow; middlebrow

xenophobia, 27, 28–29, 55, 56
  See also anti-immigration movement

Yemenite Jews, 173
Yeshiva University, 147–48, 159–60, 163–64, 190–91
Yezierska, Anzia, 20–21, 81, 214
Yiddish
- America's newly awakened value of ethnicity and, 199
- in film *Guys and Dolls*, 155
- inclusion in works of fiction, 155–56
- nostalgic value of, 155
- postvernacular mode of, 155
- Wouk reading Sholem Aleichem story in, 198, 200

Zametkin, Adella Kean and Michael, 62
Zanuck, Darryl, 60
Zionism
- Bernstein writing on Judaism without mentioning, 138
- Steinberg on, 124

The manufacturer's authorised representative in the EU for product safety is
Oxford University Press España S.A. of el Parque Empresarial San Fernando
de Henares, Avenida de Castilla, 2 – 28830 Madrid (www.oup.es/en).

Printed in the USA/Agawam, MA
December 13, 2024

878851.013